Frommer's®

6th Edition

new york city
with kids

by Holly Hughes

MACMILLAN • USA

ABOUT THE AUTHORS

Holly Hughes is a freelance writer and editor who lives on the Upper West Side of Manhattan with her husband and three children. She has been the editor of Pocket Books' *Nancy Drew Mysteries,* a contributing editor to Scholastic's *Literary Cavalcade* magazine, and an executive editor of Fodor's Travel Guides. For Frommer's, she has been series editor for Frommer's Irreverent Guides and Frommer's By Night guides. New Zealander **Sonja Deely,** whose first child was born in June 1998, learned the ropes of raising a child in New York City by assisting Holly in fact-checking this edition.

Mercer Warriner is an editor and writer living in SoHo with her husband and two sons. She has been editor and writer on various Nancy Drew and Hardy Boys series; as a senior editor at Berkley Books, she acquired and edited romances and mysteries. She has also worked at William Morrow and Pocket Books.

Jennifer Lebin is a student in a joint degree program at Columbia University and the Jewish Theological Seminary. She has lived in New York since 1993.

MACMILLAN TRAVEL

A Simon & Schuster Macmillan Company
1633 Broadway
New York, NY 10019

Find us online at **www.frommers.com**

ISBN 0-02-862635-4
ISSN 1060-3719

Editor: Ron Boudreau
Production Editors: Kristi Hart and Lori Cates
Design by Michele Laseau
Digital Cartography by John Decamillis
Page Creation by Jerry Cole, Ellen Considine, and Natalie Evans

SPECIAL SALES

Bulk purchases (10+ copies) of Frommer's and selected Macmillan travel guides are available to corporations, organizations, mail-order catalogs, institutions, and charities at special discounts, and can be customized to suit individual needs. For more information write to Special Sales, Macmillan General Reference, 1633 Broadway, New York, NY 10019.

Manufactured in the United States of America

Contents

10 **Side Trips from New York City** **268**

by Mercer Warriner

Appendix: For Foreign Visitors **275**

Index **285**

List of Maps

AN INVITATION TO THE READER

In researching this book, we discovered many wonderful places—hotels, restaurants, shops, and more. We're sure you'll find others. Please tell us about them, so we can share the information with your fellow travelers in upcoming editions. If you were disappointed with a recommendation, we'd love to know that, too. Please write to:

Frommer's New York City with Kids, 6th Edition
Macmillan Travel
1633 Broadway
New York, NY 10019

AN ADDITIONAL NOTE

Please be advised that travel information is subject to change at any time—and this is especially true of prices. We therefore suggest that you write or call ahead for confirmation when making your travel plans. The authors, editors, and publisher cannot be held responsible for the experiences of readers while traveling. Your safety is important to us, however, so we encourage you to stay alert and be aware of your surroundings. Keep a close eye on cameras, purses, and wallets, all favorite targets of thieves and pickpockets.

WHAT THE SYMBOLS MEAN

✪ Frommer's Favorites

Our favorite places and experiences—outstanding for quality, value, or both.

The following abbreviations are used for credit cards:

AE	American Express	DISC	Discover
CB	Carte Blanche	MC	MasterCard
DC	Diners Club	V	Visa

FIND FROMMER'S ONLINE

Arthur Frommer's Budget Travel Online (www.frommers.com) offers more than 6,000 pages of up-to-the-minute travel information—including the latest bargains and candid, personal articles updated daily by Arthur Frommer himself. No other Web site offers such comprehensive and timely coverage of the world of travel.

How to Feel Like a New York Family

My first nine New York years BC—Before Children—I did all the things folks think Manhattanites do. I went to CBGBs to hear head-banging new bands; I did the standing-room thing at the Met and Carnegie Hall; I saw experimental theater pieces in dingy alternative spaces way downtown; I stood in line all day to get free tickets to Shakespeare in the Park. I checked out every art museum and shopped at Barneys and Bloomingdale's. I never made it to Times Square on New Year's Eve (somehow or other, there was always a party I had to go to instead), but on Thanksgiving eve I joined the throngs on the Upper West Side to watch the giant helium balloons being blown up for the Macy's parade. I ate at hole-in-the-wall ethnic restaurants and sought out atmospheric bars straight out of *The Lost Weekend*. I rode the subway everywhere and at all hours; I walked from one end of Manhattan to the other.

After my husband and I had our first baby, I felt initially as though my life as a Manhattanite was over. If ever we wanted to stay out late, we'd end up paying a fortune to a baby-sitter, and if we ordered tickets to anything in advance, most likely we'd have to give away our seats when the baby came down with an ear infection or roseola at the last minute. We made an effort to go out to eat as a family, but we stuck close to pizza, Chinese, and burger joints, where baby wails and spilled Cheerios would be tolerated. Drinking? Forget about it—if I wasn't either pregnant or nursing, I was so exhausted that one sip of alcohol would send me straight to sleep.

Well, we've got three kids now and I've come full circle. In fact, I feel as though I never really got to know Manhattan until I began exploring it with children. We actually talk to passersby now—there's no better way to strike up conversations with New Yorkers than by the simple virtue of having a baby strapped to your chest in a Snugli. (Alec Baldwin actually stopped *me* to have a chat when he spotted my week-old daughter, Grace.) Taxi drivers, most of them immigrants from far-flung foreign lands, teach us about their native countries and coach us to speak words in their own languages. Deli clerks slip us tidbits, greengrocers pop extra strawberries into our pint cartons. When we pass fire stations, we're allowed to go inside and climb all over the hook-and-ladder truck, not to mention pat the firehouse dog. Shopping with kids, you can really have a ball in this city—you're handed free popcorn and balloons with your shoes and lollipops with your haircuts.

I used to rush around the city underground, crammed into the subway cars at rush hour; now I take buses at off-peak hours, peering out the windows as the city rolls past, or we take the stroller across Central Park, stopping frequently to feed pigeons or watch the horses on the bridle trail. On weekends we do take the kids on subways—they love them, actually, so long as they can get a seat—because that's the best way to get out to the other boroughs, where there are some awesome attractions: the Bronx Zoo and the New York Botanical Garden, Brooklyn's Prospect Park sights, the zoo and museums in Queens's Flushing Meadows–Corona park.

I spend my weekends in the local playground now, getting to know neighborhood parents, instead of browsing beside strangers through stuffy museums. Of course, we still go to museums, but we go to the same ones over and over—I've been to the American Museum of Natural History no fewer than 85 times and I'm ready to go again today if the kids are willing. The Metropolitan Museum of Art, the Children's Museum of Manhattan, the New York Fire Museum, and the New York Transit Museum are all on our roster of favorite places to dawdle and hang out for an afternoon, making our ritual visits to certain nooks we know and love and dwelling on new displays until we *really see things.*

After much trial and error, our family has gradually discovered which restaurants are kid-friendly and still manage to have palatable food for adults. (Along the way, I've learned to accept the idea that a toddler will be just fine if he eats only bread or french fries for one night.) And with children's theater and puppet shows and dance concerts and classical concerts for kids, we're getting our children prepped for the time when we can take them with us to the Met or Carnegie Hall. They'll have to see the head-banging bands at CBGBs on their own—someday in the far, far future.

A lot of families we know ditch the city every weekend to flee out to a country house in the Hamptons or Connecticut, but so far we haven't felt the need. Weekends, when kids are out of school, are particularly rich times for pee-wee culture, and even if you don't have tickets to a show or concert, from spring to fall you can always find a street fair to wander through. Central Park alone is loaded with activities on weekends—from nature workshops up by Harlem Meer to folk dancing beside Turtle Pond to the never-failing carousel rides. With kids, a simple excursion like a bike ride to the park's Belvedere Castle can be an adventure—you'll always find plenty to see along the way. And there's always a cart selling ice cream or hot pretzels if your youngsters' energy starts to flag.

We're totally happy living here. More than that: We think it's the greatest city on earth and the greatest place to raise children.

The thing that really turned my perceptions around was realizing that Manhattan isn't one monolithic city but a strange amalgamation of different cities, all sharing the same space. And just as the Alternative Art New York is worlds apart from the Wall Street New York, so is New York with Kids a quite different place from Singles New York. It just takes time to scout out this new turf, that's all.

The chief requirements for enjoying life as a single Manhattanite are money, clothes sense, and an ability to stay up all night—but to make it as a New York parent you need time, patience, and a willingness to enjoy things on your child's level. So what if that SoHo art gallery has an installation of cutting-edge art? You'll learn more about the nature of art if you swing over to the nearby Children's Museum of the Arts afterward and help your youngster create his or her own wacked-out mask or mobile. So what if you protested against the Vietnam War when you were in college? Visiting the *Intrepid* Sea-Air-Space Museum, on its aircraft carrier anchored in the Hudson, doesn't automatically register as acquiescence in the military-industrial complex—it's just an opportunity for kids to explore their innate fascination with guns and vehicles. So what if your idea of classic TV is vintage *Playhouse 90* segments? Go to the Museum of Television and Radio or the American Museum of the Moving Image with your child and you may get more of a nostalgic rush from reruns of *Sesame Street*. So what if the jokes in that magic show are as old as the hills? Watching your child giggle hysterically makes it seem funny all over again.

1 Frommer's Favorite New York City Family Experiences

- **Watching Sea Lion Feeding Time at the Central Park Wildlife Center:** Check out the feeding schedule as you walk in the front entrance—the Sea Lion Pool is the centerpiece of this tidily landscaped little gem of a zoo, and an audience starts to gather well in advance. Claim a spot on the top steps where short people can most easily view the frisky sea lions, though chances are you'll need to hoist toddlers to your shoulders once the crowds close in. Have snacks and juice on hand so the wait won't seem so long. Don't expect fancy tricks, but there'll be enough barking and diving and splashing to satisfy everybody.
- **Spending a Sunday Afternoon at the American Museum of Natural History:** Weekends are definitely family time at this magnificent big museum on the Upper West Side, but the more the merrier—these dim, cool, high-ceilinged halls never seem too crowded. Kids 5 and older can get some hands-on experience in Discovery Room programs; the whole family can enjoy an awesome IMAX film; and on weekends, casual snack bars operate near the 77th Street entrance and in the Ocean Life Hall (known as "the whale room"), so it's easy to refuel.
- **Enjoying a Sunny Afternoon at a World-Famous Ball Park:** You've got two choices in New York: Yankee Stadium up in the Bronx, where the Bronx Bombers play, and Shea Stadium in Flushing, Queens, where the Mets play. Both are handy to the subway, and unless there's a full-blown pennant race in swing, you can usually buy tickets that day, at least for bleacher seats. Nobody minds if your kids make noise or if you get tired and leave early; and there's plenty of fast-food available—especially the hot dogs that are so much a part of the experience.
- **Taking the Ferry Ride to the Statue of Liberty and Ellis Island:** In many ways, the boat ride over is the best thing about this de rigueur sightseeing excursion—out on the sparkling waters of New York Harbor, with the wind in your hair and the seagulls shrieking overhead, you'll see the Manhattan skyline in all its glory. Even if there's a bit of a wait for the ferry at Battery Park, there are usually street musicians on hand to entertain you. Ride on the upper deck if you really want a dose of salt air and sun.
- **Heading to a Playground on a Weekday Afternoon:** Choose a neighborhood playground (see chapter 5), pack a picnic lunch, and head for the sandpits, swings, and slides where New York kids hang out. Mornings are when parents with infants and toddlers congregate, preschoolers start to arrive right after lunch, and the big kids hit the ground at 3 or 4pm, when their schools let out. In summer, many playgrounds have sprinklers that are a perfect way for youngsters to cool off without getting all wet.
- **Checking Out the Front-Car Views in the Subway:** For some reason, kids tend to love making any ride as scary as possible, which on a New York subway means standing in the front car and looking out the window as the train hurtles down the dark track into the tunnel. Signal lights blink on and off, sparks flash from

New York City Dateline

1524—Sailing under the French flag, Italian Giovanni da Verrazano is the first European to enter what's now New York Harbor.

1609—Henry Hudson sails up the Hudson River, exploring for the Dutch East India Company.

1626—The Dutch settle in Nieuw Amsterdam and make it a fur-trading post; Peter Minuit, governor of Nieuw Amsterdam, buys Manhattan Island from the Algonquin Indians for trinkets worth 60 florins (about $24).

1653—Dutch settlers build a wall as a fortification against the English and name the adjacent street Wall Street.

1664—English invaders take New Amsterdam from the Dutch (wooden-legged Peter Stuyvesant is the Dutch governor).

1673—The Dutch take back Manhattan.

1674—Under the Treaty of Westminster, the Dutch finally give New Amsterdam to the English, who rename it New York after James, duke of York.

1776—American colonists topple the statue of King George on Bowling Green on July 9, but by year's end New York becomes a British stronghold and remains that during the Revolutionary War.

1783—Victorious Gen. George Washington bids farewell to his troops at Fraunces Tavern in Lower Manhattan.

1789—Washington is inaugurated as the first president at Federal Hall in New York City, the first capital of the new United States.

1790—Philadelphia deposes New York City as the nation's capital.

1792—The first U.S. stock exchange is founded in New York City, making it the country's financial capital.

1811—The city north of 14th Street is laid out, using an orderly grid system.

1825—The Erie Canal opens upstate, dramatically increasing New York City's role as a major port.

1853—The World's Fair is held in New York's Bryant Park.

1858–73—Central Park is laid out by Frederick Law Olmsted and Calvert Vaux, who won the design competition.

1870—The American Museum of Natural History is founded.

1880—The Metropolitan Museum of Art opens on the east side of Central Park.

1883—The Brooklyn Bridge is completed, spanning the East River and linking Manhattan and Brooklyn.

the third rail (the rail supplying electric power to the train), and you get the feeling of descending into a mysterious underworld. Creepy and totally cool.

- **Watching One of the Parades of All Nations:** Every one of the many nationalities that share New York City gets its own day in the sun—generally a national holiday celebrated with a parade down Fifth Avenue. St. Patrick's Day is the biggie—it's celebrated more festively here than it is even in Ireland—but there are scores of others, from the German Steuben Day Parade in September to the Italian Columbus Day Parade in October to the Mexican Cinco de Mayo Day in early May and the Puerto Rican Day parade in June; Greeks, Israelis, Poles,

1885–86—The Statue of Liberty is delivered from France and erected in New York Harbor.

1887—Electric street cars begin to run on elevated railways.

1892—Ellis Island opens as an immigration station.

1898—The newly consolidated New York City incorporates all five boroughs.

1904—Construction begins on the first line of the New York City subway system.

1920s—African-American literary culture flowers with the Harlem Renaissance.

1925—*The New Yorker* magazine is founded.

1939—New York's second World's Fair is held in Flushing Meadows, Queens.

1952, 1953, 1955—Baseball's three "Subway Series" are held between the New York Yankees and the Brooklyn Dodgers.

1964–65—New York's third World's Fair is held in Flushing Meadows, Queens.

1969—The New York Jets win the Super Bowl; the "Miracle" Mets win the World Series.

1970s—New York nearly declares bankruptcy.

1973—The World Trade Center opens.

1976—The entire city experiences a power blackout.

1977–78—The Yankees beat the L.A. Dodgers in the World Series 2 years in a row.

1983—The restoration of South Street Seaport takes wing with the opening of the Seaport Museum and a festival marketplace.

1986—The Statue of Liberty's centennial is celebrated with a fireworks extravaganza; the Mets win another World Series.

1987—The Giants win the Super Bowl (and again in 1991).

1990—Ellis Island reopens as a museum after a spectacular 6-year renovation.

1993—Terrorists bomb the World Trade Center.

1996—The city endures the heaviest winter of snowfall in its history; the Yankees win another World Series.

1997—The restored New Amsterdam Theater opens, a milestone in the rehabilitation of West 42nd Street.

1998—The restoration of Grand Central Terminal is completed; the Yankees take the World Series in a four-game sweep.

and more all have their own celebrations, complete with floats, marching bands, and loads of costumes from the old country. If crosstown traffic seems tied up on a fair-weather Saturday, hurry on over to Fifth—chances are there's a parade in progress.

- **Hanging Out at Rockefeller Plaza:** The sunken plaza beneath the golden *Prometheus* statue truly is a locale for all seasons: In winter it's a tiny ice rink lively with the clash of blades and the tinny blare of piped-in music; in summer it's an open-air cafe with big umbrellas. In December it's an especially thrilling holiday sight, with the city's biggest Christmas tree (a real doozy) twinkling with lights.

A railing surrounds the plaza at street level, where onlookers hang over and take in the scene; overhead, flags of all the United Nations countries fly from a tall rank of flagpoles. You really feel at the heart of the Big City.

- **Eating a Piece of New York Pizza:** Thin-crust pizza may have been invented in Naples, but New Yorkers know it was brought to perfection right here: oversize triangles with flat, crisp bread crusts, dripping with tangy tomato sauce and sloppy melted mozzarella. Even the most basic corner pizza stands usually have a couple of tables where you can sit down, and the open glass counters let kids watch the pizza being made—toss the dough, smear the sauce, scatter on some cheese, fling on a few rounds of pepperoni, and presto! For some suggestions, see chapter 8.

- **Shopping on Fifth Avenue:** With kids? Yes, indeed, because it's not all Tiffany's and Bergdorf's anymore. FAO Schwarz, the top-end toy store, has long been at 58th and Fifth, but in the mid-1990s the huge glitzy Warner Bros. Store opened a block south at the corner of 57th Street; a spectacular Disney Store, the largest in the chain, soon arrived at 55th Street, followed soon after by NikeTown, around the corner on 57th Street between Fifth and Madison avenues. And a big NBA Store debuted at 666 Fifth Ave. at 55th Street in fall 1998. Both Disney and Warner Bros. also popped up in 1998 at Times Square, turning the formerly seedy 42nd Street into the city's newest retail destination, but it'll never supplant Fifth Avenue. See chapter 6 for details.

2 A Few Practical Words of Wisdom

I can understand how intimidating it must be to families who come here as tourists, not knowing a single local soul, trying to navigate and negotiate around the sights. In New York's heavy tourist areas, the prices are high, the traffic is dense, and the crowds are pushy and rude. Outside those areas, certain pockets of town may be dingy and even downright scary. And when you're traveling with kids, one bad experience can send you home to Nashville or Indianapolis or Dubuque, shaking your head and wondering why anybody would live in a place like New York City.

So let's deal with some of the negatives head-on. First of all: Yes, there's crime in New York. It's by no means America's Crime Capital, however—perhaps the biggest coup of Rudolph Giuliani's mayorship has been the city's plummeting crime rate in all categories. TV cop shows and gritty action movies may paint New York as a town of mean streets, but face it, one big reason they set their stories here is that this city's such a super location, with instantly recognizable landmarks.

Of course, it's possible to get mugged at night on the sidewalks of New York—to avoid such an incident, stay on well-lighted, well-populated streets as much as possible and *know where you're going.* If you're in dense crowds—rush-hour buses or subways, the pre- and postcurtain crush in the Theater District—be on the alert for pickpockets. Keep your wallet in a front pocket and hold your purse in front of you; tell your kids to carry backpacks over one shoulder, not strapped onto their backs. Keep a firm grip on your cameras too. Don't leave purses or backpacks or cameras hanging on the backs of your chairs in restaurants. With kids in tow, you may not stay out all that late, but it's wise after dark to take taxis if you're going any distance. All this is just plain common sense.

Traffic is another problem, which is why I heartily advise you not to drive in the city if you don't have to. New York pedestrians get pretty cocky about darting off the curb into traffic, but don't let your kids follow their example: My under-6s know they have to hold my hands when crossing a street, and we don't step into the

Three Invaluable Tips

- **Eat outdoors whenever you can.** If a restaurant has tables in a courtyard or on the sidewalk, grab them (your fellow diners won't hear your kids' racket and the passing show will distract your restless offspring). If the weather's decent, pick up food from a deli or hot-dog stand and eat in a park—you'll save money and have more fun.

- **Never be shy about asking directions.** New Yorkers may look like they're in a rush, but most are such incurable know-it-alls they're always happy to tell you where to go. Even lifelong Manhattanites can get disoriented when emerging from a subway station, so verifying that you're headed the right way doesn't brand you as a tourist. Don't wear your kids out with any needless walking—ask.

- **Spend as little time as you must in Midtown.** Granted, most visitors' hotels are in Midtown, and there are some boffo attractions for kids here—the Empire State Building, the Sony Wonder Technology Lab, FAO Schwarz—but you can't really understand New York City unless you get out to the neighborhoods. They're quieter, safer, cheaper, and more kid-friendly. The Upper West Side, the Upper East Side, Greenwich Village, Chelsea, and Brooklyn Heights—this is where New Yorkers with children live. Go thou and do likewise.

intersection until we get a white "Walk" signal. (We hold hands even in mid-block in congested pedestrian areas like Midtown. My kids know this isn't even a negotiable point.) Just about all intersections have traffic lights and most streets are one-way, which means it's fairly straightforward even for a kid to see where traffic is coming from and to know when it's safe to cross.

Yet another reality of life in New York is the street people. The number of beggars, homeless people, and scruffy loiterers has fallen drastically since the late 1980s; panhandlers aren't allowed to hassle people on the subways anymore (though a few still do). Nevertheless, you and your kids are bound to spot a few die-hard vagrants sleeping in doorways or pawing through corner trash bins. What do you say to your children when you see a wino relieving himself against a building wall or when a red-eyed junkie weaves past you on a subway platform? My kids are still pretty young, so my husband and I just try to steer them away from such sights. But it means keeping your wits about you to anticipate such scenes.

The reason folks are more likely to run into desperate characters like this in New York is really not because New York has a such a high percentage of weirdos, wackos, and wastrels. It's simply because you're always out walking on the streets here, not whizzing around in the isolation of your car. With so many million human beings coexisting in a relatively small area, you're bound to come into contact with lots of people in the course of a day, and the law of averages dictates that some of those people will have more of an edge to them than you'd like.

But to my mind that's just the flip side of one of this city's great pluses: Everybody, from the Wall Street banker to the greengrocer to the starving actor waiting tables, shares the streets. The rich can't ignore the poor, the young can't ignore the old, the Republicans can't ignore the Democrats, and vice versa. My kids are well aware of how tough it is for people in wheelchairs to get around, because they've often watched such folks persistently hauling themselves onto city buses. They know that not everyone in the world speaks English, because there's a constant counterpoint of Spanish, Greek, Urdu, or Japanese swirling around them.

A million different agendas clash every day in the Manhattan mélee, and it keeps us all honest; it keeps us all in touch with reality. Kids who grow up in New York City tend to have street smarts—not a bad thing to have, in my opinion. If you want a sanitized version of America, you go to Walt Disney World.

Now that I've gotten the negatives out of the way, I'll go back to the positives. The pulse and tempo of New York City can be dizzying at first if you're not used to it, I'll grant you that, but once you attune yourself you'll find it tremendously exciting, even for youngsters. When my kiddos return to the city after an idyllic 2-week vacation at the beach, I've seen them sit up in their strollers and look around eagerly, glad to be back in a place where there's something happening every few yards. They love the fact that when they go to a playground there's always someone else to play with. Driving through Times Square, they don't see the traffic jams—they just oohh and aahh at the neon gaudiness. The West Side subway is their own homegrown thrill ride, racketing through tunnels and running races with the trains on neighboring tracks. World-class museums are their after-school classrooms, where they encounter more art, science, and history than I'd been exposed to by the time I graduated from college. Central Park is their backyard, all 840 acres of it, and it provides them with nature ponds, tennis courts, horseback riding, ice skating, and on and on and on.

Let me tell you about one Sunday we spent a while ago. Right after breakfast, from our own apartment windows, we heard via loudspeakers the Pope—*the Pope!*—saying mass in Central Park. Walking outside afterward, we saw legions of the faithful trooping home, festooned with Pope pennants and badges and memorabilia. As we rode the subway downtown, we had an earnest conversation about who the Pope is and why so many people wanted to see him—that is, until we changed trains and got distracted by the Asian guy who plays electric harmonica on the N/R platform in Times Square. We went on to a SoHo furniture store where we saw performance artist Eric Bogosian busy trying out the rocking chairs (my kids weren't impressed, but my 5-year-old admitted that Bogosian's young son's leather jacket was pretty cool). When we ran into Bogosian and Bogosian Jr. minutes later down the street at the Fire Museum, we all smiled at one another with recognition. ("Your kids bugging you to buy souvenir fire engines too?" Bogosian's weary chuckle seemed to say to us.) Then on the subway ride home we sat next to actress Sarah Jessica Parker, who kept sneaking eye contact with our baby. By the time we got home, it was too late to cook so we ordered in Chinese food; my older son, whom we've nicknamed the Bok Choy Boy, snarfed down Buddhist Delight with his chopsticks like an old pro, while our toddler delicately dismantled an egg roll on her plate and smeared her face with cold sesame noodles. A whole family of satisfied customers.

And that wasn't even an unusual day—we hadn't planned anything more glamorous than furniture shopping. Serendipity is the name of the game in New York City, all the more so if you've got kids. So many things are coming at you all the time, you can't help but stumble onto something interesting.

At a luncheon for new mothers I went to shortly after my youngest was born, one young mom wistfully said to me that she felt shut out of Manhattan life. "This city is totally oriented toward singles," she sighed. "That's what Manhattan is all about. People in Manhattan think babies should be kept in a closet until they reach the age of twenty-one." I nodded my head, but even though there's a kernel of truth to what she was saying, I couldn't really agree with her.

I thought of her complaint constantly while writing this book. I made it my mission to help people like her get up and running. I do know how she felt—I've been there. But, like the kids in *A Wrinkle in Time* or the Narnia Chronicles, I've discovered a parallel universe: New York City with Kids. It's a grand, goofy, glorious place. And there isn't anywhere else on the planet I'd rather live.

2

Planning a Family Trip to New York City

New York City is much more kid-friendly than most visitors anticipate—the trick lies in planning your trip to take advantage of it. Timing is everything, as is fortifying yourself with all the printed information you can snare.

1 Visitor Information

Once you decide to visit Manhattan, write to the **New York Convention & Visitors Bureau's Visitors Information Center**, 810 Seventh Ave., 3rd floor, New York, NY 10019, for maps, hotel lists, brochures, and sightseeing suggestions. The bureau's 24-hour information hot line at ☎ **800/NYC-VISIT** (212/397-8222 from outside North America) offers similar info by phone; via the Internet, contact the bureau at **www.nycvisit.com**.

You may want to send away for the local parents' monthlies: the $29-per-year *Big Apple Parents' Paper*, 36 E. 12th St., New York, NY 10003 (☎ **212/533-2277;** fax 212/475-6186; www.bigappleparents.com); the $19.95-per-month *ParentGuide,* Parent Guide Network Corp., 419 Park Ave. S., New York, NY 10016 (☎ **212/213-8840**); or the $22-per-year *New York Family,* 141 Halstead Ave., Suite 3D, Mamaroneck, NY 10543 (☎ **914/ 381-7474;** www.nyfamily.com). Once you're here, you can pick up free copies of these publications at toy stores, children's clothing and shoe stores, and indoor playgrounds all around town.

2 When to Go

New York buzzes every day, with pretty much everything open year-round. All school vacation seasons—late December, spring vacation, and summer—tend to be busy times; lots of museums schedule special programs then, since New York schoolchildren are looking for something to do too. December is particularly jam-packed, with lots of annual holiday entertainment (*The Nutcracker,* the Big Apple Circus, the Radio City Christmas Spectacular, a musical version of *A Christmas Carol*). Fall is traditionally the prime season for culture, with new plays opening on Broadway and classical-music venues booked solid, but even in summer, music series at Lincoln Center and star-studded limited-run plays fill the boards. Spring and

What Things Cost in New York City	U.S. $
Hot dog at corner umbrella cart	1.00–1.25
Hot pretzel at corner umbrella cart	1.25–1.50
16-oz. soft drink in a deli	1.00
16-oz. apple juice in a deli	1.25
Take-out bagel with cream cheese	60¢–1.25
Slice of plain pizza	1.00–2.00
McDonald's Happy Meal with Chicken McNuggets	3.49
Weekday *New York Times*	60¢
Weekday *Daily News* or *New York Post*	50¢
Local telephone call	25¢
Movie ticket	8 or 9 adult, 4 child
Taxi ride from the Empire State Building to FAO Schwarz	4 (plus $1 tip)
Taxi ride from the World Trade Center to Rockefeller Center	10, depending on traffic (plus $2 tip)
Package of Pampers	9.99
Package of Luvs	6.99
32-oz. can prepared Similac formula	4.59

summer weekends really bustle, with street fairs all over town and what seems like an endless succession of parades, one for every ethnic group in the city, filing down Fifth Avenue.

There's no "high" or "low" season as far as hotel rates go, though it may be a little harder to get a reservation around Christmas or Labor Day (when the U.S. Open is in town) or during the fall and spring fashion shows. Hotels are slightly less crowded on weekends, when business travelers clear out of town; many even offer weekend package rates.

In terms of weather, winter tends to be cold but not intolerably so, while July and August can be sweltering and muggy—but that never stops hordes of visitors from descending on the city every summer.

KIDS' FAVORITE NEW YORK CITY EVENTS

February

- **Black History Month** is observed with some very good programs for kids at museums around town.
- The **Chinese New Year** rattles the streets of Lower Manhattan with dragon parades, firecrackers, and fun.
- The **Westminster Kennel Club Dog Show** at Madison Square Garden (☎ 212/465-6000) brings champion pooches of every breed to the city. Besides watching the judging, it's fun just to walk around outside the ring, where the dogs and handlers hang out.

March

- The **International Cat Show** at Madison Square Garden (☎ **212/465-6000**) draws hosts of cat fanciers and their felines to a world-class competition.
- The **Radio City Music Hall Spring Spectacular** (☎ **212/247-4777**) runs for several weeks, an annual treat of music and entertainment geared to youngsters.
- The **St. Patrick's Day Parade** rolls down Fifth Avenue on March 17.
- The **Ringling Bros. and Barnum & Bailey Circus** begins its annual month-long run at Madison Square Garden (☎ **212/465-6000**).

April

- The annual **Central Park Easter egg hunt** is held on Easter Sunday near the Bandshell, with activities, giveaways, and visiting celebrities.
- The **Easter Parade** on Easter Sunday morning is a stroll down Fifth Avenue that anyone can join—the bigger the bonnet, the better.

May

- The Theater at Madison Square Garden (☎ **212/465-MSG1**) mounts an annual musical production of *The Wizard of Oz* in early May.
- The Brooklyn Botanic Garden's annual **Cherry Blossom Festival** (☎ **718/622-4433**) takes a cue from Japanese tradition in celebrating the flowering pink trees around its pond.
- The **Ninth Avenue International Food Festival** lines the avenue from 37th to 57th streets, with open-air stalls selling an amazing array of snacks, nibbles, and noshes.
- **Fleet Week** (☎ **212/245-0072**) welcomes a host of U.S. and foreign naval ships to the Hudson River piers, highlighted by a parade of ships.

July

✪ **Macy's July 4 Fireworks Extravaganza** explodes in the skies over the East River.

August

- The **Lincoln Center Out-of-Doors Festival** (☎ **212/546-2656**) turns the plaza around the arts complex into one big street fair, with crafts and food stalls and loads of free performances.

September

- The **U.S. Open Tennis Championships** (☎ **718/760-6200**) are played in Flushing Meadows, Queens, for 2 weeks starting just before Labor Day.
- The **San Gennaro festival** fills the streets of Little Italy with carnival booths and Italian food stands for a week around the saint's day, September 19.

October

✪ The Cathedral of St. John the Divine overruns with animals for its **Blessing of the Animals** on the Feast of St. Francis, the first Sunday of the month.
✪ The **Christmas Spectacular** at Radio City Music Hall (☎ **212/247-4777**) ushers in the holiday season early, beginning a 2-month run.
- **Halloween** activities include the outrageous Greenwich Village Halloween Parade up lower Sixth Avenue.

November

✪ The **Big Apple Circus** (☎ **212/268-2500**) settles in for its annual 2-month run at Lincoln Center's Damrosch Park.
✪ The **Macy's Thanksgiving Day Parade** runs from 77th Street and Central Park West down to Broadway and 34th Street; sidewalk viewing along the route is

first-come, first-served. The evening before, the parade's mighty balloons are blown up on 77th and 81st streets, around the Museum of Natural History, but it's a mob scene; come by at 8am Thanksgiving morning and you can view the whole parade lying in wait, with no one else around but Macy's elves and Santa.

December

- The **Christmas Tree Lighting** at Rockefeller Center is early in December.
- ✪ The **Christmas Spectacular** continues at Radio City Music Hall (☎ **212/ 247-4777**), bringing music, dancing, Santa, and the Rockettes together on one enormous stage.
- ✪ More **Big Apple Circus** (☎ **212/268-2500**) at Lincoln Center's Damrosch Park.
- A live musical version of *A Christmas Carol* (☎ **212/465-MSC1**) takes the stage at the Theater at Madison Square Garden.
- ✪ The New York City Ballet's annual *The Nutcracker* (☎ **212/870-5570**) is a perpetual delight at Lincoln Center.
- The **Lighting of the Giant Hanukkah Menorah** at Grand Army Plaza (Fifth Avenue and 59th Street) is on the first night of Hanukkah.
- **New Year's Eve** is celebrated famously in Times Square, though that's hardly an event for kids; older kids, however, could participate in the alcohol-free **First Night** festivities (☎ **212/922-9393**), which include a party that takes over Grand Central Terminal. As New Year's Eve 1999 approaches, there should be some bang-up events scheduled to celebrate the end of the millennium (though technically it's New Year's Eve 2000 that ushers in the 21st century); the New York City Visitors Bureau should have a schedule of these in the fall of 1999.

3 What to Pack

If you plan to go out to a fancy dinner or the theater, you'll want at least one dressy outfit, which means a jacket and tie for men (boys may be able to get by without the tie). Most restaurants have no dress code, though.

It's more important to remember that this is preeminently a walking city. There's almost always a bit of a walk from the subway to wherever you're going, and even if you intend to cab it everywhere, you'll have to sprint for a taxi or two or trudge a few blocks when no cabs are in sight—which will happen. So bring sturdy low-heeled shoes and don't skip socks unless you're wearing well-broken-in sneakers. Sandals, however, aren't smart, since the streets can be dirty and your bare toes are vulnerable to being run over by a kamikaze bicycle messenger, a rolling dress rack or hot-dog cart, or any of a dozen other urban vehicles.

Walking a lot also makes strollers a must for any young children who can't hike at least a mile without complaining. Strollers can be a hassle, though, when getting in and out of cabs or up and down subway stairs; make sure you've got one that folds easily. If you have an infant, a soft carrier is a better idea.

July and August can be miserably hot and sticky, conditions worsened by the fact that subway platforms are like saunas, thanks to the heat thrown off by the subway trains' air-conditioning (subway cars are glacially cool, by the way). Short-sleeved T-shirts and shorts are best, the baggier the better. Sunhats are a help, and a folding hand fan is a great idea—if nothing else, it could distract the kids from how hot it is. If you don't own such a thing, buy one in Chinatown while you're here.

Top Kids' Books Set in New York City

For Preteens

- *The Adventures of Taxi Dog* by Debra and Sal Barracca (Dial; ages 2–6). This, or any of the Barraccas' books about Maxi the Taxi Dog, is a lovable look at the city from the seat of a yellow cab.

- *Tar Beach* by Faith Ringgold (Crown; ages 2–5). Evocative memories of a Harlem childhood and hot summer nights up on the roof.

- *Hillary and the Lion* by Frank Desaix, illustrated by Debbi Durland Desaix (Farrar Straus Giroux; ages 3–7). A young girl separated from her parents is befriended by the stone lions outside the New York Public Library. Magical, once you get past the stressful idea of getting lost.

- *The Little Red Lighthouse and the Great Gray Bridge* by Hildegarde H. Swift and Lynd Ward (Harcourt Brace; ages 4–7). A Hudson River lighthouse feels superceded by the new George Washington Bridge, until one dark and stormy night. . . . Kids can still see both landmarks today.

- *The House on East 88th Street* by Bernard Waber (Houghton Mifflin; ages 4–7). The book that introduced Lyle the Crocodile, the benign hero of a whole series of books about an unflappable East Side family and their unorthodox pet. Not particularly strong on New York color, but a good read.

- *Eloise* by Kay Thompson (Simon & Schuster; ages 4–8). This irrepressible 6-year-old growing up in the Plaza Hotel definitely has an exotic view of life. Perfect for the precocious.

- *The Cricket in Times Square* by George Selden (Farrar Straus Giroux or Yearling paperback; ages 6–10). A Connecticut cricket winds up in the Times Square subway station and becomes the toast of Manhattan.

- *Stuart Little* by E. B. White (Harper & Row; ages 7–10). The Little family's mouse-sized young son has adventures in and around Central Park.

- *The Pushcart War* by Jean Merrill (Dell Yearling; ages 7–10). Tongue-in-cheek chronicle of a prolonged fight between the city's pushcart vendors and delivery trucks.

- *Harriet the Spy* by Louise Fitzhugh (HarperTrophy; ages 8–11). Spunky sixth-grader Harriet M. Welch keeps tabs on her East Side friends and neighbors.

- *From the Mixed-Up Files of Mrs. Basil Frankenweiler* by E. L. Konigsburg (Simon & Schuster or Aladdin paperback; ages 8–12). A 12-year-old Connecticut girl and her younger brother hole up in the Metropolitan Museum and become involved in an art mystery.

- *It's Like This, Cat* by Emily Neville (Harper; ages 8–12). Although somewhat dated, this coming-of-age novel paints a memorable picture of the Gramercy Park area of Manhattan during the late 1950s.

For Teens

- *It's Okay If You Don't Love Me* by Norma Klein (Fawcett). Upper West Side teenagers deal with life, love, and sex.

- *Cher Negotiates New York* by Jennifer Baker (Archway). This title in a series based on the movie *Clueless* follows the Beverly Hills teen trendoid to Manhattan for a series of hip escapades. As if!

January and February may be cold, but all the buildings around you in Manhattan retain heat, so it's never as cold here as it is outside the city. Still, this is the Northeast, so gloves and hats and scarves are advisable if you come from November to March. If it does snow, the streets are plowed swiftly and sidewalks get shoveled fast: It takes a really big blizzard to stop Manhattan in its tracks—like the Blizzard of '96. Plowed banks of snow can stand for weeks, while getting filthier and filthier. Boots are a good idea in winter, just in case, because sewers quickly back up and lake-sized puddles form at curbs—too big for kids to jump over.

If you're bringing an infant, call ahead to your hotel to check what baby equipment it can provide—besides a crib, it may help to have a bathing ring and a high chair in your room. You may want to pack a few outlet covers so you can childproof your room when you arrive. Of course you can buy diapers, wipes, formula, and no-tears shampoo here, but it might be handier to bring your own bottles, spout cups, feeding dish, and infant spoon, which you can bring to restaurants. You don't want to waste your entire first day locating the right items in baby stores here.

Accidents do happen, so bring extra changes of clothes for your children—for infants and for toddlers who haven't mastered the fine art of using the potty, you should probably bring two or three changes of clothes per day. You'll also want a tote bag full of toys, for travel time and for down time in your hotel room. Toys without lots of separate pieces are best (imagine trying to pick up dozens of spilled Lego pieces off the floor of an airplane!). Older kids may want to carry their own backpacks with books, colored markers and pads, a deck of cards, handheld electronic games, personal stereo, or whatever keeps them happy.

4 Getting the Kids Interested

Send away in advance to the **New York Convention and Visitors Bureau** (see "Visitor Information," earlier in this chapter) for a Big Apple packet, which should include a city map with subway lines that kids can study. The very idea that Manhattan is an island may fascinate them.

Several corny old songs come in handy as memory guides for New York City geography: Start with "I'll take Manhattan / the Bronx and Staten Island too" to teach your kids about the city's five boroughs, which besides the three listed in that song also include Brooklyn and Queens. (Fun fact: Brooklyn on its own has a big enough population to be the sixth-largest city in the United States.) Then there's "New York, New York, a wonderful town / The Bronx is up and the Battery's down/ The people ride in a hole in the ground." Discuss the subway lines—rendered in different colors on the map—and talk about the neighborhoods and sights they pass through. New York's subways have been cleaned up incredibly since the early 1980s, and it's perfectly safe to promise your kids rides on these underground trains when you get to New York.

Current TV shows tend to present New York either as a hangout for self-involved singles or as a gritty battlefield for cops and psycho-killers. For a more accessible image of Manhattan, let your kids view *Home Alone 2, Ghostbusters,* or *Big;* among vintage movies, *Miracle on 34th Street* is a winner. Teens may like Woody Allen's *Everybody Says I Love You,* which features a fairly authentic cluster of upscale NYC teens, or the perennially lovely *Breakfast at Tiffany's.* For the younger set, Disney's animated *Oliver and Company* has a Manhattan setting, as do *The Cricket in Times Square, A Troll in Central Park,* and Jim Henson's *The Muppets Take Manhattan. Sesame Street,* of course, is more or less set in New York City, but don't promise your toddlers they'll actually meet Big Bird.

New York City's skyline is a famous sight—prime your youngsters for that first glimpse of it. Buildings to identify include the World Trade Center, twin rectangular towers at the southern tip of Manhattan, which the Dino de Laurentis King Kong scaled; the Empire State Building, with its tall antenna tower up which the original King Kong climbed; the Chrysler Building's chrome-tipped art-deco spire, looking for all the world like a hood ornament; the riverside United Nations, a vertical plane of sheer glass anchored by the dome of the General Assembly; the slant-roofed white Citibank Building; the Chippendale-style crest on the Sony Building. The Statue of Liberty is another indelible New York landmark to show your kids pictures of ahead of time. Yet another is Rockefeller Plaza, where a giant gilded *Prometheus* statue overlooks an ice-skating rink in winter and an outdoor cafe in summer—and where the even-more-giant Rockefeller Center Christmas tree sparkles during the holiday season.

Older kids may be interested in New York's battery of sports teams—depending on the season, watch some innings of Yankees or Mets baseball, a Jets or Giants football game, a Rangers or Islanders hockey match, or a Knicks basketball game.

To give kids a taste of the city's sights ahead of time, the nifty guidebook *New York City* by Deborah Kent (Children's Press) offers a clear and comprehensive introduction to the city, written at a second-grade reading level. *My New York* by Kathy Jakobsen (Little Brown), a great picture book for kids 3 to 7, is written in the form of a letter from a young New Yorker to a friend from the Midwest who's coming to visit. In *Amy Elizabeth Explores Bloomingdale's* by E. L. Konigsburg (Atheneum; ages 4–8), a little girl from Houston visits her grandmother in the city, setting out every day to visit the famous department store and always getting wonderfully sidetracked. *Be-Bop-a-Do-Walk* by Sheila Hamanaka (Simon & Schuster) works well for the same age group, illustrating a lively walk from the Lower East Side up to Central Park in 1950s New York. *Citybook* by Shelley Rotner and Ken Kreisler (Orchard Books) may be better for toddlers, with great color photos of the city and only a few well-chosen words per page. Also for preschoolers, *The Escape of Marvin the Ape* by Caralyn and Mark Buehner (Dial Books) portrays a fugitive gorilla happily losing himself in New York City's parks, museums, stores, and ballparks. George Selden's *Chester Cricket's Pigeon Ride* may be hard to find, but this chapter book for young readers, by the author of the classic *The Cricket in Times Square,* gives a soaring bird's-eye view of Manhattan.

5 Getting There

BY PLANE

Almost every major domestic carrier serves the New York area. Here's a handy list of toll-free numbers and Web sites: **America West** (☎ 800/235-9292; www.americawest.com), **American** (☎ 800/433-7300; www.americanair.com), **Continental** (☎ 800/525-0280; www.flycontinental.com), **Delta** (☎ 800/221-1212; www.delta-air.com), **Northwest** (☎ 800/225-2525; www.nwa.com), **TWA** (☎ 800/221-2000; www2.twa.com), **US Airways** (☎ 800/428-4322; www.usairways.com), and **United** (☎ 800/241-6522; www.ual.com).

In recent years there has been rapid growth in the number of no-frills airlines serving New York. These smaller, sometimes struggling airlines may offer lower fares—and all that that implies. You might check out **AirTran** (☎ 800/247-8726;

Cyber Deals for Net Surfers

It's possible to get great information as well as great deals on airfare, hotels, and car rentals via the Internet. So grab your mouse and start surfing before you head to New York. A good place to start is Macmillan Travel's site, **Arthur Frommer's Budget Travel Online (www.frommers.com),** where you'll find lots of up-to-the-minute information—including the latest bargains and candid articles updated daily by Arthur Frommer himself.

Microsoft Expedia (www.expedia.com)   The best part of this multipurpose travel site is the Fare Tracker: You fill out a form on the screen indicating that you're interested in cheap flights to New York from your hometown, and once a week, they e-mail you the best airfare deals. The site's Travel Agent will steer you to bargains on hotels and car rentals, and you can book everything, including flights, right on-line. This site is even useful once you're booked: Before you go, log on to Expedia for oodles of up-to-date travel info, including weather reports.

Preview Travel (www.reservations.com and www.vacations.com)   Another useful site, **Reservations.com** has a Best Fare Finder that'll search the Apollo computer reservations system for the three lowest fares for any route on any days. Say you want to go from San Francisco to New York and back between December 6 and 13: Just fill out the form on the screen with times, dates, and destinations, and within minutes, Preview will show you the best deals. If you find an airfare you like, you can book your ticket on-line—you can even reserve hotels and car rentals. If you're in the preplanning stage, head to Preview's Vacations.com site, where you can check out the latest package deals by clicking on Hot Deals.

Travelocity (www.travelocity.com)   This is one of the best travel sites out there. In addition to its Personal Fare Watcher, which notifies you via e-mail of the lowest airfares for up to five destinations, Travelocity will track in minutes the three lowest fares for any routes on any dates. You can book a flight then and there, and if you need a rental car or hotel, they'll find you the best deal via the SABRE computer reservations system (a huge database used by travel agents). Click on Last Minute Deals for the latest travel bargains.

E-Savers Programs   Several major airlines offer a free e-mail service known as **E-Savers,** via which they'll send you their best bargain airfares on a weekly basis. Once a week (usually Wednesday), subscribers receive a list of discounted flights to and from various destinations. Now here's the catch: These fares are available only if you leave the very next Saturday (or sometimes Friday night) and return on the following Monday or Tuesday. It's really a service for the spontaneously inclined and travelers looking for a quick getaway. But the fares are cheap, so it's worth taking a look. If you have a preference for certain airlines (in other words, the ones you fly most frequently), sign up with them first. Another caveat: You'll get frequent-flier miles if you purchase one of these fares, but you can't use miles to buy the ticket. See above for a list of airlines and their Web sites.

Epicurious Travel (travel.epicurious.com), another good travel site, allows you to sign up for all these airline e-mail lists at once.

—Jeanette Foster

Jeanette Foster is co-author of *Frommer's Hawaii from $60 a Day* and *Frommer's Honolulu, Waikiki & Oahu*

www.airtran.com), **Carnival** (☎ 800/824-7386; www.carnivalair.com), **Frontier** (☎ 800/432-1359; www.frontierair.com), **Kiwi** (☎ 800/538-5494; www.jetkiwi. com), **Midway** (☎ 800/446-4392; www.midwayair.com), **Midwest Express** (☎ 800/452-2022; www.midwestexpress.com), **Tower Air** (☎ 800/34-TOWER or 718/553-8500; www.towerair.com), and **Vanguard** (☎ 800/826-4827; www.flyvanguard.com).

Most of the major international carriers also fly into New York (see the appendix for details).

One way to find the lowest fare is to call a discount travel agency like **Travel Avenue** in Chicago at ☎ **800/333-3335.** Unlike most travel agencies, this one doesn't offer advice or itinerary planning; it does, however, offer cash rebates on fares from major airlines (over $300) and hotels.

If you decide on a trip to New York at the last minute, give a call to **1-800/ FLY-ASAP,** a national reservation service that uses a new computer program to find the lowest fares available. You could realize substantial savings here.

A highly praised organization called **FreeFlier,** P.O. Box 844, Bowling Green Station, New York, NY 10274-0844 (☎ **212/727-9675**), may be able to save you travel dollars—even if you're a relatively "infrequent flyer." For a small fee ($9.95 adults; $7.50 seniors, retirees, students, and groups of four or more), it forwards the applications of travelers to more than two dozen frequent-flyer, car-rental, and hotel-stay programs. Owner Robert Reiner points out that many programs provide instant benefits and don't require long-term loyalty. Frequent-flyer programs often offer insider discounts or advance notice of lower fares that only members may obtain. Many car-rental programs offer free upgrades or an extra day's usage. Several hotel-stay programs reward members with a free weekend night when they stay on a weekday night. Reiner advises that they often receive extra coupons for frequent-traveler bonuses that they'll pass on to anyone sending a stamped, self-addressed no. 10 envelope.

NEW YORK AREA AIRPORTS

New York City has three major airports: **La Guardia** (☎ **718/533-3400**), **John F. Kennedy (JFK) International** (☎ **718/244-4444**), and **Newark International** (☎ **973/961-6000**) in New Jersey. JFK, in southeastern Queens about an hour's drive from Manhattan, is largely served by international flights, though some domestic flights are routed through. La Guardia, chiefly for domestic flights, is also in Queens, though not as far from Manhattan—it's a shorter ride (30–45 minutes) into Midtown. Newark Airport serves both domestic and international flights; it takes about 45 to 60 minutes to drive into Manhattan from Newark. If you need to make connections at another airport, **Carey Airport Express Buses** at ☎ **718/706-9658** or 718/632-0500 shuttle travelers between La Guardia and JFK for $11 one-way.

With young kids in tow, it's best to take a **cab** from the airport into the city. All three airports have orderly taxi stands where you line up until it's your turn for the uniformed dispatcher to help you into a licensed cab (yellow cabs only from JFK and La Guardia; New Jersey cab companies work from Newark). Cab fares from JFK are set at $30, which comes out at around $40 once you've added bridge and tunnel tolls and a 15% to 20% tip; the total from Newark, including tolls and tip, is also about $40, and from LaGuardia it's more like $25. There's no charge for extra people or for luggage, though yellow cabs add a 50¢ surcharge on weekends and from 8pm to 6am; New Jersey cabs are allowed to tack on a $10 fee for crossing the state line (stay alert, for New Jersey cab drivers have been known to get lost on the way to Midtown). Passengers are expected to pay bridge and tunnel tolls, though the driver may pay the toll and then add it to your fare.

If your kids are older and you don't have loads of luggage, you can save money by taking a **Carey Airport Express** bus (☎ **718/706-9658** or 718/632-0500), running from either JFK or La Guardia to Manhattan. Buses leave clearly marked stops at the terminals every 20 to 30 minutes. The trip in from JFK costs $13 and takes about an hour; from La Guardia to Midtown costs $10 and takes 45 minutes. Carey buses stop at Grand Central Terminal (Park Avenue and 42nd Street). Carey then provides a free shuttle service between Grand Central and many Midtown hotels; if you hail a cab from Grand Central, the fare should be $5 to $7 to most Midtown hotels, though catching a cab at either of these busy terminals can be stressful. Both have taxi stands; never let a local hustler get a cab for you—they can get abusive if you don't pay them as much as they feel they deserve for this illegal service.

From Newark Airport, **Olympia Trails Airport Express** (☎ **212/964-6233**) operates a 30-minute bus ride to Pennsylvania Station (between Seventh and Eighth avenues and 31st and 33rd streets), Port Authority Bus Terminal (Eighth Avenue between 40th and 42nd streets), Grand Central Terminal, or the World Trade Center downtown; the ride costs $10 and buses leave every 20 to 30 minutes. **Gray Line Air Shuttle** (☎ **212/315-3006**) operates a minibus service between all three airports and a number of Manhattan hotels for $16 from JFK, $13 from La Guardia, and $18 from Newark.

To have a limousine (actually, a luxury sedan—don't promise the kids a stretch limo) pick you up, call before you fly (at least a day in advance) to arrange pickup from private car-service companies like **All State Car and Limo** (☎ **212/741-7440**) and **Sabra** (☎ **212/777-7171**); the cost is about $33 from La Guardia, $44 from JFK, and $47 from Newark, not counting tolls and tips. **Carmel** (☎ **212/666-6666**) charges even lower rates, provided you book an ordinary car rather than a luxury sedan—$19 from La Guardia, $29 from JFK, and $28 from Newark, not counting tolls, parking, and tips.

If you're determined to save money and have lots of time, the cheapest way to get into the city from JFK is to take the free **Port Authority Shuttle Bus** to the Howard Beach subway station, where you can catch an "A" train into Manhattan. From La Guardia, you can take a local **Q33 bus** to the subway's Roosevelt Avenue station, where you can catch the no. 7 train to Midtown; or the local **Q48 bus** to the 111th Street station, also on the no. 7 line to Manhattan. The **M60 bus** goes directly from La Guardia to Manhattan, where it makes stops along 125th Street and then down Broadway, terminating at 106th Street; you can catch the no. 1 or 9 train at 116th or 110th street and head down the Upper West Side from there. Any of these trips can take well over an hour, though the second two routes from La Guardia are generally quicker. Except for the JFK shuttle bus, which is free, you'll have to pay regular bus and subway fares, $1.50 per person (children under 44 inches ride free). Note that you can transfer free from a bus to the subway, but only if you use a MetroCard, sold at subway station fare booths; without a MetroCard, you'll have to pay a second fare when you enter the subway.

If you take a weekday flight to La Guardia on Delta's Boston or Washington shuttle, the **Delta Water Shuttle** (☎ **800/53-FERRY**) between La Guardia's Marine Air Terminal and Manhattan's East 90th Street (10 minutes from the airport), East 62nd Street (15–20 minutes), East 34th Street (25–30 minutes), and Wall Street's Pier 11 (40–45 minutes) can be a fun ride. It costs $15 one-way or $25 round-trip. To get on to your hotel, you'll need to hail a cab once you disembark.

BY TRAIN

The major long-distance rail terminal in Manhattan is **Pennsylvania Station,** known to all as Penn Station, between Seventh and Eighth avenues and 31st to 33rd streets. **Amtrak** trains (☎ 800/872-7245) come through Penn Station from all across the country. Two commuter train lines, **New Jersey Transit** (☎ 973/762-5100) and the **Long Island Rail Road** (☎ 718/217-5477), also come into Penn Station, so it can be a madhouse at rush hour, especially on the lower level LIRR platforms. **Grand Central Terminal,** at 42nd Street and Park Avenue, is the city's other train station, used today only by **Metro North** commuter trains (☎ 212/532-4900), serving Connecticut and New York State. **Path** commuter trains (☎ 800/234-PATH) from New Jersey have their own underground stations in Manhattan: World Trade Center, Christopher Street, West 9th Street, West 14th Street, West 23rd Street, and 33rd Street and Eighth Avenue; fare is $1, children under 5 free. There are taxi stands at both Penn Station and Grand Central. Penn Station has subway stations on the A, C, E, 1, 2, 3, and 9 lines. Grand Central subway station serves the 4, 5, 6, and 7 lines, and the S shuttle to Times Square.

Even if you don't catch a train from Grand Central, take your kids to see the gloriously restored main hall, a grand marble cavern with a star-spangled ceiling. The old Penn Station was just as handsome, but it was torn down in the 1960s and replaced with the soulless modern pile detailed above. Plans are to convert the neoclassical main post office on Eighth Avenue between 31st and 33rd streets (across from the current Penn Station) into a new Penn Station. Stay tuned.

BY BUS

The **Port Authority Bus Terminal,** at Eighth Avenue between 40th and 42nd streets (☎ 212/564-8484), still has its grubby corners, despite the remarkable transformation of the nearby Times Square area. On the whole, however, this cheerless big station is well lit and well patrolled, with lots of discount shops and fast-food restaurants lining the main hall. In the great tradition of urban bus stations, it also has more than its share of derelicts and panhandlers. Greyhound, Trailways, and other long-distance bus lines stop here, along with various commuter bus lines. Upon arrival, head straight for the taxi stand on Eighth Avenue, where a dispatcher can get you a cab. The A, C, and E subways make a stop at the Port Authority, and a long underground tunnel leads you to Times Square and the 1, 2, 3, 7, N, R, and S trains. But these are some of the city's dingiest subway stops—take a cab if you can. The fare won't be more than $5 or $6 to most Midtown hotels, barring traffic jams.

BY CAR

Having a car in Manhattan isn't an asset. *Drive here only if you must.* If you do, my best advice is to get to your destination, put your car in a garage, and keep it there. Yes, hotel and independent garages charge exorbitant rates, but street parking can be a nightmare and you don't want to deal with having your car broken into while you're on vacation.

North-south **I-95** runs up through New Jersey, jogs across the northern tip of Manhattan and the Bronx, and heads on up to New England. From the south, you can exit I-95 (the New Jersey Turnpike) at I-78 in Jersey City, which takes you to the **Holland Tunnel** ($4 toll) into Downtown; at I-495 in Union City, which takes you to Midtown's **Lincoln Tunnel** ($4 toll); or after crossing the **George Washington Bridge** ($4 toll), where N.Y. 9A (the **Henry Hudson Parkway**) goes down the West Side of Manhattan. I-278 branches off I-95 south of Elizabeth, N.J., crossing east to Staten Island, then into Brooklyn across the **Verrazano Narrows Bridge** ($7.00 toll westbound into Staten Island; no toll eastbound into Brooklyn).

From the north, I-95 connects with the **Bruckner Expressway** (I-278), which swings down to the **Triborough Bridge** ($3.50 toll), leading you into Manhattan on the East Side's **FDR Drive.** If you're going to the West Side of Manhattan, stay on I-95 as it becomes the **Cross Bronx Expressway** and take the last exit in Manhattan to the **Henry Hudson Parkway (N.Y. 9A).** Other useful routes from the north include the **Merritt Parkway/Hutchinson Parkway/Cross County Expressway** from New England and the **Taconic Parkway** from upstate New York, both of which feed into the **Saw Mill Parkway,** which crosses into Manhattan at the **Henry Hudson Bridge** ($1.75 toll) and becomes the Henry Hudson Parkway (N.Y. 9A). **I-87** also leads down from upstate New York; either exit south onto the **Palisades Parkway** into New Jersey and take that down to the George Washington Bridge or stay on I-87/287 as it turns east and crosses the Hudson at Tarrytown, N.Y., then exit onto the Saw Mill Parkway and contine south across the Henry Hudson Bridge into Manhattan.

If you're coming from the west, **I-80** feeds into the George Washington Bridge. **I-280** branches off I-80 out near Morris Plains, N.J., heading southeast to join **I-95;** from there, you can pick up I-78 to the Holland Tunnel or **I-495** to the Lincoln Tunnel. **I-78** is another Interstate highway coming into New York from the west; it leads into the Holland Tunnel downtown.

3

Getting to Know New York City

At first glance New York can be a very intimidating town, especially when you have a flock of youngsters under your wing. Take time from the outset to get a grasp of the city's layout and the best methods of navigating around.

1 Orientation

VISITOR INFORMATION

New York City Visitor Centers are scattered around Manhattan, including booths at **Times Square** (Seventh Avenue between 46th and 47th streets), **Grand Central Terminal** (42nd Street between Lexington and Vanderbilt avenues), **Macy's** department store (34th Street between Sixth and Seventh avenues), **Bloomingdale's** department store (Lexington Avenue between 59th and 60th streets), and the **World Trade Center** (2 World Trade Center, the same building where the observation deck is located). There's also a booth at **JFK Airport.** Stop by to pick up maps, brochures, and sightseeing suggestions, along with "two-fers" for savings on Broadway and Off Broadway plays.

The **New York Convention and Visitors Bureau**'s 24-hour information hot line at ☎ **800/NYC-VISIT** (212/397-8222 from outside North America) offers similar information. Pick up info on the Internet at **www.nycvisit.com**. In January 1999, the bureau is scheduled to open a new **public information office** at 870 Seventh Ave., between 52nd and 53rd streets (☎ **212/484-1222**); hours weren't yet determined at press time.

For recorded listings of Lincoln Center events, call ☎ **212/546-2656** or visit its Web site at **www.lincolncenter.org**. For upcoming events in city parks, call ☎ **888/NY-PARKS** or 212/360-3456.

CITY LAYOUT

MAJOR ARTERIES IN MANHATTAN   The limited-access **FDR Drive** runs along Manhattan's East River shore, from the Brooklyn Battery Tunnel (which links to Brooklyn) north to the Triborough Bridge (which links to Queens and to I-95). The **West Side Highway** goes from Battery Park up along the Hudson, eventually becoming the limited-access **Henry Hudson Parkway**

A Street by Any Other Name

When the Street Sign Says . . .	It's the Same as . . .
Amsterdam Avenue	Tenth Avenue (above 59th Street)
Avenue of the Americas	Sixth Avenue
Cathedral Parkway	West 110th Street (from Central Park West to Riverside Drive)
Central Park North	West 110th Street (between Fifth Avenue and Central Park West)
Central Park South	59th Street (between Fifth and Eighth Avenues)
Central Park West	Eighth Avenue (from 59th to 110th streets)
Columbus Avenue	Ninth Avenue (above 59th Street)
Fashion Avenue	Seventh Avenue (from 34th to 42nd streets)
Park Avenue	Fourth Avenue (above 14th Street)
St. Luke's Place	Leroy Street (from Seventh Avenue to Hudson Street)
St. Mark's Place	8th Street (from Third Avenue to Avenue A)
West End Avenue	Eleventh Avenue (from 59th to 107th streets)

running all the way to Manhattan's northern tip and on through the Bronx (Riverdale), where it finally becomes the Saw Mill Parkway.

Broadway is Manhattan's spine, beginning at Battery Park and angling north all the way through Washington Heights (from there on, as U.S. 9, it continues all the way to Albany). Since Manhattan's axis is skewed to the northeast, Broadway—which runs due north—seems to run at an angle, and every time it crosses a major avenue in the Manhattan grid, there's a significant traffic junction: **Union Square** at 14th Street, **Madison Square** at 23rd Street, **Herald Square** at 34th Street, **Times Square** at 42nd Street, **Columbus Circle** at 59th Street, **Lincoln Square** at 66th Street, **Verdi Square** at 72nd Street, and **Straus Park** at 106th Street. Above 59th Street, where Central Park divides Manhattan, Broadway is the West Side's main drag.

The other big avenues in the grid are one-way, with the exception of the East Side's **Park Avenue**, which is mostly high-rent residential north of 57th Street (between 14th and 34th streets it's known as **Park Avenue South**). The avenues that run uptown (north) are **First Avenue, Third Avenue, Madison Avenue, Sixth Avenue** (also called **Avenue of the Americas**), **Eighth Avenue** (called **Central Park West** between 59th and 110th streets and **Frederick Douglass Boulevard** above 100th Street), and **Tenth Avenue** (called **Amsterdam Avenue** above 59th Street). To go downtown (south), take **Second Avenue, Lexington Avenue** (to 21st Street), **Fifth Avenue, Seventh Avenue, Ninth Avenue** (called **Columbus Avenue** above 59th Street), or **Eleventh Avenue** (called **West End Avenue** from

107th Street, where it begins, to 59th Street). In the older areas of town, below 8th Street, the grid doesn't apply and you'll need a map to navigate. **Hudson Street** is a major north-bound thoroughfare on the West Side; on the East Side it's **Fourth Avenue** (the southern section of Park Avenue South below 14th Street), which is created when **The Bowery** splits into Third and Fourth avenues.

Most cross streets in the grid are one-way; generally, even-numbered streets are east-bound and odd-numbered streets west-bound. You'll find two-way traffic on a few major cross streets: **Canal Street,** which cuts across the island from the Manhattan Bridge to the Holland Tunnel; **Houston Street,** which funnels traffic from the Williamsburg Bridge to the Holland Tunnel; and **14th Street, 23rd Street, 34th Street, 42nd Street,** and **57th Street.** Central Park bisects the city between **59th Street** and **110th Street** (which are also called, respectively, **Central Park South** and **Central Park North**). You'll find two-way traffic on 72nd Street, 79th Street, 86th Street, and 96th Street. To cut across Central Park **from the Upper East Side to the Upper West Side,** choose either 66th Street, 72nd Street (open weekday rush hours only), 79th Street, 85th Street, or 97th Street. If you're going **from the Upper West Side to the Upper East Side,** your options are 65th Street, 81st Street, 86th Street, and 96th Street. All other car entrances to the park feed into the circular drive, open only during weekday rush hours. Above the park, **125th Street** is Harlem's major two-way commercial street.

Note: Consult the front of a Yellow Pages telephone directory for details on how to find the cross street for an avenue address and/or the avenues a street address is between.

MAJOR ARTERIES IN THE OUTER BOROUGHS The **Grand Central Parkway** leads from the Triborough Bridge to La Guardia Airport, in northern Queens, and on to Long Island. The **Long Island Expressway** (I-495) goes from the Queens Midtown Tunnel across Queens, through Forest Hills and Flushing, and out to Long Island. The **Brooklyn–Queens Expressway**—known as the BQE—runs north-south linking Brooklyn and Queens; you can get on it from the Grand Central Parkway, from the 59th Street Bridge (also called the Queensboro Bridge), from the Queens–Midtown Tunnel, and from the three Brooklyn–Manhattan bridges—the Williamsburg, the Manhattan, and the Brooklyn.

At the southern end of Brooklyn, the BQE links with the **Verrazano Bridge** (toll $7 westbound only) from Staten Island, then (as the **Belt Parkway**) swings around the coast past Coney Island and the Rockaways, feeding into **Southern Parkway,** which heads out to Long Island. **Northern Boulevard** is one of Queens's major commercial thoroughfares. Radiating out from Brooklyn Heights, **Atlantic Avenue, Flatbush Avenue,** and (starting near Prospect Park) **Ocean Parkway** fan out across Brooklyn. The **Cross-Bronx Expressway** (I-95) is the major highway cutting across the Bronx; the **Bronx River Parkway** runs up through Bronx Park, where you'll find the Bronx Zoo and the Botanical Garden.

MANHATTAN NEIGHBORHOODS IN BRIEF

Manhattan was settled from its southern tip northward, so the oldest area is **Lower Manhattan,** roughly everything south of Canal Street. Within this, the **Financial District,** centered around Wall Street and lower Broadway, has pretty much obscured traces of the early colonial settlement with its battery of skyscrapers, but you'll still find a few venerable churches tucked away, and some of the skyscrapers themselves are early 20th-century landmarks. The only really historic quarter left is

Manhattan Neighborhoods

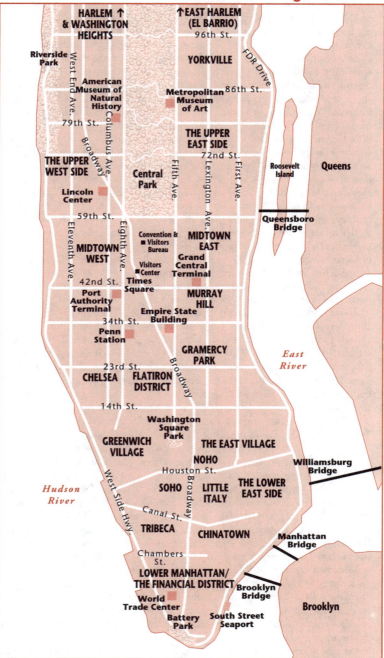

HARLEM ↑
& WASHINGTON
HEIGHTS

↑EAST HARLEM
(EL BARRIO)

96th St.

Riverside
Park

YORKVILLE

FDR Drive

West End Ave.

American
Museum of
Natural
History

Metropolitan
Museum
of Art

86th St.

79th St.

Columbus Ave.

Broadway

THE UPPER
EAST SIDE

THE UPPER
WEST SIDE

Central
Park

72nd St.

Roosevelt
Island

Queens

Fifth Ave.

Lexington Ave.

First Ave.

Lincoln
Center

59th St.

Queensboro
Bridge

Eighth Ave.

Eleventh Ave.

MIDTOWN
WEST

Convention &
Visitors
Bureau

MIDTOWN
EAST

Visitors
Center

Grand
Central
Terminal

42nd St.

Times
Square

Port
Authority
Terminal

MURRAY
HILL

Empire State
Building

East
River

34th St.

Penn
Station

GRAMERCY
PARK

23rd St.

Broadway

CHELSEA

FLATIRON
DISTRICT

14th St.

Washington
Square
Park

GREENWICH
VILLAGE

THE EAST VILLAGE

NOHO

Houston St.

Williamsburg
Bridge

Hudson
River

West Side Hwy

SOHO

Broadway

LITTLE
ITALY

THE LOWER
EAST SIDE

Canal St.

TRIBECA

CHINATOWN

Manhattan
Bridge

Chambers
St.

LOWER MANHATTAN/
THE FINANCIAL DISTRICT

Brooklyn
Bridge

World
Trade Center

Battery
Park

South Street
Seaport

Brooklyn

NA-0361

25

on the East River waterfront at South Street Seaport, a 19th-century district that has been mallified, but not out of recognition. North of the Seaport, you'll find City Hall, other municipal buildings, and an imposing set of courthouses (clustered around Foley Square). Over on the Hudson side of the narrow island, you get some open green space at Battery Park, with its ferries and harbor views; the sleek planned community of Battery Park City just north of the park has a great riverside promenade and connects via walkway to the immense World Trade Center. The nickname **TriBeCa** derives from the *Tri*angle *Be*low *Ca*nal Street, but the label is used for only the northwestern chunk of that triangle, a hypercool neighborhood of converted industrial lofts dotted with trendy restaurants and a few galleries.

Above South Street Seaport and the courts, **Chinatown** occupies the East River side of the below-Canal area, but it burst its traditional boundaries long ago and now also spills north of Canal Street, engulfing the vestiges of **Little Italy,** which still clings to Mulberry Street as its main drag. The tenement buildings lining these streets should clue you in to the fact that these neighborhoods were the 19th century's immigrant slums. East of Little Italy lies the **Lower East Side,** for years the Jewish immigrant district and more recently a Hispanic area; it's still a fairly rough neighborhood, though increasingly colonized by young urban "bohos." To the west of Little Italy, a derelict 19th-century industrial zone was converted in the 1970s to artsy **SoHo** (*So*uth of *Ho*uston Street—pronounced, by the way, "*how*-stun," never "*hew*-stun"). Its commercial streets are now lined with art galleries, boutiques, and restaurants, but some of the back streets still look grim and forbidding.

Above Houston Street, you enter the Villages—**Greenwich Village,** from Broadway west to the Hudson River; and the **East Village,** from Broadway on east, though the rougher neighborhoods along Avenues A, B, C, and D are sometimes set apart under the tag "Alphabet City." Greenwich Village still has a certain bohemian cachet, and its quiet side streets, with their redbrick town houses, make a good place to ramble when the city gets on your nerves. The East Village is funkier and grittier, just the place to bring teenagers who think their parents are so uncool they don't want to be seen with them. Teens may also want to hang out in the New York University area, which sprawls around the Village's focal point, Washington Square Park, and spills over into the fringes of the East Village.

Above 14th Street, the Manhattan grid falls into place, and the city starts to get more buttoned-down. Between 14th and 30th streets, **Chelsea** occupies the area from Sixth Avenue west. This is now a very hot area for art galleries, fashion industry *poseurs,* and gays; at its far west end, the Chelsea Piers' sports complex on the river is a major draw for families. East of Sixth Avenue is what's called the **Flatiron District** (named after the famous Flatiron Building at 23rd Street and Broadway), a trendy area for restaurants and nightlife, and the quiet older neighborhoods around **Gramercy Park,** the city's only private park; north of Gramercy lies **Murray Hill,** a largely residential neighborhood of limited interest for families.

Midtown is the major business district, sprawling across the island from about 34th Street to 59th Street. Big department stores and elegant shops march up Fifth Avenue, with a handful of museums set on side streets; looming skyscrapers (notably the Empire State Building and the Rockefeller Center buildings) draw hundreds of thousands of workers every day. The **Theater District** clusters around Times Square (42nd Street and Broadway); the United Nations anchors 42nd Street at the East River. By far the greatest number of Manhattan's hotels are in Midtown, and many restaurants as well. But with its crowded sidewalks and restaurants packed with impatient workaday New Yorkers, it's not necessarily where families want to concentrate their time. Come here to shop and to gawk at the tall buildings; at

Christmastime, Rockefeller Center and the store windows are so magical they shouldn't be missed. But venture away from Midtown and you'll get a better idea of how New York families experience the city.

The **Upper West Side** occupies the part of Manhattan directly west of Central Park—here you'll find the city's best museums for kids, lots of kid-friendly restaurants, toy stores, and playgrounds in both Central and Riverside parks. The **Upper East Side,** everything east of Central Park, is also very child-oriented but less casual; you'll see packs of uniformed kids from tony private schools gathering in its pizza parlors and GAPs. The East Side is rich in museums, especially along the park on Fifth Avenue, but many of them are either too stuffy or too dull for children (the beautiful Frick Museum, in fact, won't even allow kids under 10 to enter).

Above Central Park to the west is **Morningside Heights,** dominated by Columbia University and two magnificent churches—Riverside Church and the Cathedral of St. John the Divine; it's a casual, friendly area with some good family restaurants. East of Morningside Park, **Harlem** takes over the island north of Central Park. Many tourists visit Harlem as part of a guided tour, though you can certainly check it out on your own. However, your kids' interest in the social-history aspects of a Harlem guided tour may lag if they're under 10. Unless you're visiting the Cloisters (the Metropolitan Museum's medieval art branch in Fort Tryon Park), there's not much reason for you to tour **Washington Heights,** which lies above Harlem.

MANHATTAN'S BRIDGES & TUNNELS

Manhattan's an island—to get on or off it you have to go over or under the water. Going clockwise around the island, starting from the northern tip, you can take the **Henry Hudson Bridge** (on the Henry Hudson Parkway; $1.75 toll); the **Triborough Bridge** ($3.50 toll); the **59th Street/Queensboro Bridge;** the **Queens–Midtown Tunnel** (part of I-495; $3.50 toll). A trio of bridges into Brooklyn—the **Williamsburg,** the **Manhattan,** and the **Brooklyn**—all connect handily with the Brooklyn–Queens Expressway, as does the **Brooklyn Battery Tunnel** ($3.50 toll) at the island's southern tip. Two big tunnels cross the Hudson on Manhattan's West Side—the **Holland Tunnel** ($4 toll into Manhattan), which funnels from Canal or Houston Street; and the **Lincoln Tunnel** ($4 toll into Manhattan), which funnels from 40th Street—and the **George Washington Bridge** (part of I-95; $4 toll into Manhattan) crosses above the water up at 175th Street.

THE OUTER BOROUGHS IN BRIEF

New York City's other four boroughs surround the island of Manhattan. To the north and east lies the **Bronx,** which only partly deserves its bad rap as a crime-infested slum. Parts of the Bronx are rotten indeed, but then there's suburban Riverdale, along the Hudson, and the middle-class Fordham area, anchored by Fordham University and Bronx Park (where the zoo and the botanical garden are). The New York Yankees are called the Bronx Bombers because Yankee Stadium is at 161st Street in the Bronx (though owner George Steinbrenner is forever threatening to move them elsewhere); it's a bad area, but crowds of baseball fans make it safe around game time and the subway takes you directly to the stadium.

The landmass directly east of Manhattan—the western end of Long Island—contains the two most populous boroughs: Brooklyn and Queens. Immortalized (rightly or wrongly) as Archie Bunker territory, **Queens** is the city's great middle-class borough, where hard-working immigrant groups have colonized various neighborhoods from Astoria (Greek and Irish) to Flushing (various Asian nationalities). Directly across the river from Manhattan, Long Island City has become a haven for young artists, while Forest Hills in the middle of Queens is a manicured residential area. Further-out areas of Queens, like St. Albans and Little Neck, are basically suburban neighborhoods.

Brooklyn on the whole is more urban and edgy, though it has some of the city's loveliest residential areas, notably brownstone-lined Brooklyn Heights, right across the Brooklyn Bridge from Manhattan, and nearby gentrified neighborhoods packed with 19th-century rowhouses, such as Cobble Hill, Carroll Gardens, and Park Slope (the last has the advantage of bordering Prospect Park, Central Park's Brooklyn cousin). Facing Staten Island across the Narrows, Bay Ridge is a vast middle-class enclave; Brighton Beach, on Brooklyn's southern shore, is a former Jewish area now heavily colonized by immigrant Russians. But other Brooklyn neighborhoods, like Bedford-Stuyvesant, Brownsville, and East New York, aren't for the uninitiated. If you visit Brooklyn, know where you're going.

That leaves **Staten Island,** the most suburban of the boroughs, the one that's always threatening to secede from the city—which actually makes sense, since Staten Island is geographically more like part of New Jersey. Staten Island's attractions for visitors—the restored historic village at Richmondtown, a zoo, a children's museum, a couple of historic houses—don't manage to lure many New Yorkers across the water, which suits most Staten Islanders just fine. Still, the Staten Island Ferry ride is one of those classic New York things to do, a pleasant way to spend an hour or so crossing the harbor—and it's free.

2 Getting Around

BY SUBWAY

The **MTA–New York City Transit** (☎ 718/330-1234) operates the city's buses and subways, which run 24 hours. Even mildly adventurous visitors should feel comfortable underground from 7am to 8pm—however, the morning and evening rush hours (generally 8–9:30am and 5–6:30pm weekdays) make the trains so crowded you'd be better off not traveling then, especially with a family to squeeze in. The **fare** is $1.50, and for your buck and a half you can ride as long and far as you like, changing lines at any of more than 50 transfer points.

You can buy brass **tokens** at booths in each station for $1.50 each; you deposit them in the turnstiles to enter the train system, and once you exit the system you have to pay to get in again. But more New Yorkers these days use multiride **MetroCards,** with magnetic strips that automatically deduct one fare every time you slip them through a groove in a turnstile. MetroCards can be bought in various denominations from $5 to $80 and can be refilled at most token booths, with 10% discounts offered for buying $15 or more; unlimited-ride passes are also available, costing $63 for 30 days, $17 for 7 days, and $4 for 24 hours. Each time you run your card through a turnstile, your remaining balance is displayed. Even better, MetroCards allow riders free transfers to and from city buses, whereas token users have to pay twice. Up to four passengers traveling together can use the same MetroCard—just slide it through the turnstile once for each rider. (Unlimited-ride passes cannot be used by more than one passenger.) Children under 44 inches tall ride free; in practice, kids under 6 can just duck under the turnstile bar and no one challenges them.

Maps are posted inside stations (usually out by the token booths, so you can make sure where you're going before you enter) and in most cars. Near the token booths, many stations now also feature detailed street maps of the immediate area, so you can get oriented before you hit the street. Also check out the subway map on the inside back cover of this guide.

Most Manhattan stations have been renovated in the 1990s, and the tile walls along waiting platforms often feature work by local artists or symbols appropriate for that particular neighborhood. Not only are stations brighter and better lit than they used to be, the trains themselves are now clean, graffiti-free, and blessedly air-conditioned in summer. Rush-hour crowds can still be pushy and testy, and derelicts, panhandlers, and thugs still disturb riders' peace from time to time. And trains don't run as often as they should, either. But the subway is truly a viable alternative, especially for long daytime rides, when you'll save time as well as money by gliding under the streets instead of getting mired in city traffic.

BY BUS

Buses require a **MetroCard** (the same one you use for the subway), a **token** (ditto), or $1.50 in exact change (no pennies). You can't buy tokens on board; you'll have to get them at a subway station. To transfer to a second bus, request a transfer card from the driver of the first bus *when you pay your fare*. If you're using a MetroCard, dip it into the fare box slot; if you've just come from the subway, the machine will register this as a transfer and won't deduct additional fares from your encoded balance.

Each bus's destination is displayed above its front windshield; routes are posted at most bus stops. Children under 3 feet 8 inches tall ride free (there's a line near the driver's seat against which to measure your child), but in practice kids under 6 are usually allowed to ride free, regardless of height.

BY TAXI

The only taxis authorized to pick up passengers hailing them on the street are **yellow cabs,** which have an official taxi medallion screwed onto the hood. So-called gypsy cabs, working for car services, sometimes stop illegally for passengers on the street, but since they have no meter, you'll have to negotiate your own fare with the driver and you'll have no legal recourse if there's a problem (besides, some gypsy cabs are filthy rattletraps). To know whether a yellow taxi is available, look for the lit-up center sign on the roof of the cab; off-duty cabs (side sections of the roof sign lit) may pick up passengers at their own discretion.

Taxi meters calculate the fare: $2 when you get in, plus 30¢ for each one-fifth of a mile or 90 seconds of waiting time in traffic. The meter should "click" every 4 blocks in normal traffic or once every crosstown block. There's an extra 50¢ charge from 8pm to 6am, and passengers pay any bridge or tunnel tolls. A 15% to 20% tip is expected, unless the service is bad. For complaints or inquiries about lost property, call ☎ 212/302-TAXI.

Technically, a taxi doesn't have to take more than four passengers (with adults, this is possible only if one sits in the front seat next to the driver). But if your kids are small, most cabbies will let you all squeeze in, which is good news for families of five. All New York yellow cabs are supposed to have working seat belts, though few locals actually use them when taking quick trips around town. If your kids are car-seat size, technically you could haul around a car seat and strap it in every time you get in a cab, but the only person I've ever known to do this did it only once, when cabbing her newborn home from the hospital. Most cabbies are cool about letting kids sit on laps or even kneel on the seat to look out the cab window. Occasionally you'll get one who'll hassle you about your 2-year-old getting his sneakers on the backseat upholstery. I never fight the cabbies on this one—hey, it's their cab.

BY FERRY

The free **Staten Island Ferry** (☎ **718/727-2508**) at Battery Park remains the best way to enjoy views of the Manhattan skyline, New York Harbor, and the Statue of Liberty. The **Ellis Island and Statue of Liberty Ferry** (☎ **212/269-5755**) leaves Battery Park every 30 to 40 minutes for two of the city's most popular tourist destinations, costing $7 round-trip adults and $3 kids 16 and under. The **New York Waterway Ferry System** (☎ **800/53-FERRY**) runs a spiffy service between the World Financial Center (near the World Trade Center) and the Colgate Center in New Jersey, costing $2 each way. A free shuttle to the Liberty Science Center picks up passengers at the Colgate Center.

BY CAR

Cars are the least efficient way to get around town, but if you must drive, keep in mind that car-rental rates at the airports are often lower than those in Midtown. All the big national chains operate several locations: **Avis** (☎ 800/831-2847; at all three airports and 10 city locations), **Budget** (☎ 212/807-8700; at all three airports and three city locations), **Dollar** (☎ 800/800-4000; at all three airports and three city locations), **Enterprise** (☎ 800/325-8007; at nine city locations), **Hertz** (☎ 800/654-3131; at all three airports and 11 city locations), and **National** (☎ 800/227-7368; at all three airports and seven city locations).

Some local companies offer rates that might be lower. **Autorent** has four locations: 415 W. 45th St. (☎ 212/315-1555), 433 E. 76th St. (☎ 212/517-8900), 464 W. 18th St. (☎ 212/206-1900), and 166 Perry St., in Greenwich Village (☎ 212/206-1777). **New York Rent-a-Car** has three locations: 240 E. 92nd St. (☎ 212/ 410-3100), 230 W. 31st St. (☎ 212/268-9444), and 19 E. 12th St. (☎ 212/243-9200). **Rent-A-Wreck,** at 31-31 Greenpoint Ave. in Long Island City, Queens (☎ 718/784-3302), is a 10-minute subway ride from Manhattan.

PARKING   On the streets, look for parking signs stating what days or hours you can park curbside. In Midtown and other spots where police feel it's vital to keep traffic flowing, your illegally parked car will be towed in minutes, so don't even think of violating parking laws. In residential neighborhoods, "alternate side of the street parking" means that everybody's expected to shift their cars to the opposite curb once a day. Officers are required to complete any parking ticket they start to fill out, so pleading will do no good. If your car does get towed, call the **Borough Tow Pound** at ☎ **212/971-0770** to find out where it is; you'll have to pay $150 in cash to retrieve it.

Space is so tight in New York that some residents are willing to pay over $300 a month for parking garage spaces. Public garages dot Manhattan streets every 2 blocks or so, with rates averaging about $7 for less than 2 hours, $15 for half a day, and $30 overnight. Prices are sometimes lower at night or on weekends in business districts and during the day in residential areas; outdoor lots are less expensive, when you can find them. Few hotels offer parking. Some Midtown hotels provide valet parking at about $35 per night, often with the requirement that guests not take their car from the garage between arrival and final departure. **Kinney System, Inc.,** has more than 150 garages (for locations call ☎ **800/KNY-PARK**); **Rapid Park** has over 30 locations (call ☎ **212/866-1000**, ext 203); and **GMC** has 55 locations (call ☎ **212/888-7400**).

DRIVING RULES   Except for major crosstown streets and a few north-south avenues (Broadway, Park Avenue), most of Manhattan's streets are one-way, so sometimes you'll have to circle around a couple of blocks to get to a specific address. Right turns on red are *not* legal, and left-hand turns are prohibited in some major intersections (watch for signs). Several major avenues have designated bus lanes (marked on the pavement), which are off-limits to cars during rush hours. Every passenger is supposed to wear a seat belt, and all kids 5 and under should be in car seats of some kind.

3 Planning Your Outings

Everything is relatively close together in Manhattan, but if you're traveling by cab, traffic jams can make even a few blocks' travel take half an hour; waiting for frequent changes of buses or subways can add up to lots of wasted time; and plodding long distances on foot could tire out the kids (or yourself) before you get to the sights you want to see. Instead, plan carefully and you may be able to spend the entire day within a few blocks' radius, wasting little time on street travel. If you do have to hop from one part of town to another, don't underestimate travel time—snarled traffic or sluggish subways or buses can make a 40-block journey seem to take forever.

Prime areas for families are the **Upper West Side,** with the American Museum of Natural History and the Children's Museum of Manhattan; **SoHo,** with the Children's Museum of the Arts, the Guggenheim Museum SoHo, and the Fire Museum; **Midtown,** where you'll find the Sony Wonder Technology Lab, Rockefeller Center, the Empire State Building, the Museum of Modern Art, the Museum of Broadcasting, and the *Intrepid* Sea-Air-Space Museum; **Lower Manhattan,** with South Street Seaport and the World Trade Center; and the stretch of Fifth Avenue known as **Museum Mile.** If you're going to **Brooklyn** to see the Botanic Garden or Prospect Park zoo, take in the Transit Museum and Brooklyn Heights on the same day. The same ferry goes to both the **Statue of Liberty** and **Ellis Island,** so it's a natural to do both the same day—but after waiting in all those lines, you probably won't have time to do much else that day. The **Bronx Zoo** and the **New York Botanical Garden** are right next to each other, but it'd be pretty exhausting to do both in a day.

One thing to take into account is museum closing days—many are closed on Monday.

FINDING A REST ROOM

If you've got a recently toilet-trained toddler in tow, better think ahead, because in Manhattan it's not easy to find a bathroom at sudden notice. Rest rooms do exist in **Central Park** (see chapter 5 for locations), as well as in **Bryant Park,** at 42nd Street and Sixth Avenue behind the **New York Public Library;** the library itself has nice large bathrooms, as do most of the branch libraries throughout the city, though you may need to show a library card to use them. The atrium of the **Sony Building** at 56th Street and Madison Avenue has good bathrooms; so does **Trump Tower** at 56th Street and Fifth Avenue. Hotel lobbies and department stores are other good bets, though the latter are usually on upper floors and hard to get to in a hurry.

In a pinch, if your child looks very distressed, you may be able to talk sympathetic waiters or store owners into letting you use their facilities. (I even once got the manager of a D'Agostino's grocery store to let me take my 2-year-old down to the employees' john in the basement—a real adventure.)

Best advice: Always use the potty at your hotel before you leave, and stop in the rest room before you leave any museum or restaurant.

NURSING MOMS & INFANTS

New Yorkers are wonderfully unflappable; there are plenty of mothers who nurse in public—usually onlookers pretend not to look and everything is cool. Then, of course, there are some people who stare rudely and mutter disparagingly. Ignore them. You'll find a fairly receptive atmosphere in all playgrounds and some casual restaurants. Women's lounges in the large department stores (Lord & Taylor's is best) tend to be good havens for breast-feeding a squalling infant.

FAST FACTS: New York City

Area Codes   The area codes for Manhattan are 212 and the new 646, instituted in the fall of 1998. To call Brooklyn, Queens, Staten Island, or the Bronx (at no charge), dial 1, then the area code 718, then the phone number. (Area code 917 covers all of New York City, but it's only for beepers and cellular phones.) For directory assistance, dial ☎ **411.**

ATMs   Walk-up cash machines can be found every few blocks at various bank branches, all linked to the NYCE network, as well as to Cirrus or PLUS. Locked lobbies with electronic card access are preferable, for security reasons; some even have guards on duty after bank hours. In Times Square, which is notably short on ATMs, look for a battery of Fleet Bank ATMs in the street-level lobby of the Marriott Marquis, Broadway and 46th Street, and more across the street at the Times Square Visitor Center. Note that many ATMs now charge a $1 transaction fee over and above the fee your own bank charges you.

Business Hours   The city that never sleeps truly doesn't. Although Midtown and Downtown **stores** tend to close at 6pm, shops in residential areas often stay open to 7pm or so, with drugstores and groceries usually going strong until 9pm or later, and delis and corner produce markets trucking on into the wee hours. Most stores are open on Sunday, though they may not open until noon. **Restaurants** stay open late, usually at least until 11pm, and most are open daily. Many **museums** are closed on Monday, but several have late hours—until 9 or 10pm—on Thursday, Friday, or Saturday. **Banks** tend to keep more standard hours—Monday to Friday from 9am to 3pm—but some branches open on Saturday mornings out in the neighborhoods.

Child Care   Many New York hotels provide baby-sitting services or keep a list of reliable sitters. If your hotel doesn't, call the **Baby Sitters Guild** (☎ **212/ 682-0227**) or **the Frances Stewart Agency** (☎ **212/439-9222**). Both services provide in-room child care as well as on-request trips to the playground, the Central Park Zoo, and so on for children of all ages, with licensed, bonded, insured sitters (baby nurses are trained in CPR).

Dentists   You can get a list of dentists near you by calling the **Emergency Dental Service** (☎ **212/573-9502**). Emergency dental care is available from **ABC Dental Care** (☎ **212/888-0015**).

Disability Services   The **Community Ambulette** (☎ **718/231-6666**) provides ambulette service for the disabled. Note that the subway system remains largely inaccessible to the disabled, but 95% of the city's buses are equipped to carry wheelchairs.

Doctors   Dial-A-Doctor (☎ **212/971-9692**) sends physicians on house calls 24 hours a day; **Doctors On Call** (☎ **718/238-2100**) offers similar aid 8am to midnight.

Drugstores   Some 24-hour **Duane Reades** are at Lexington and 47th Street (☎ 212/682-5338), 625 Eighth Ave. in the Port Authority Bus Terminal (☎ 212/967-8110), Broadway and 57th Street (☎ 212/541-9708), Broadway and 91st Street (☎ 212/799-3172), Third Avenue and 74th Street (☎ 212/744-2668), and Sixth Avenue at Waverly Place (☎ 212/674-5357). **Rite-Aid** drugstores open 24 hours a day include 408 Grand St. on the Lower East Side, a block above Delancey Street (☎ 212/529-7115); 282 Eighth Ave. at 24th Street (☎ 212/727-3854); 2833 Broadway at 110th Street (☎ 212/663-3135), and 146 E. 86th St., between Lexington and Third avenues (☎ 212/876-0600).

Emergencies   Call ☎ **911** for police, fire, and ambulance service; it offers TTY service for the deaf as well. Fires can also be reported in Manhattan by dialing ☎ **212/628-2900** or 999-2222. Other emergency numbers include **Animal Bites** (☎ 212/676-2483), **Park Emergencies** (☎ 800/201-PARK), **Poison Control** (☎ 212/340-4494), and **Travelers Aid** (☎ 212/944-0013).

Hospitals   The following hospitals have full-service emergency rooms: **New York University Medical Center,** 550 First Ave., at 33rd Street (☎ 212/263-7300); **New York Hospital,** 510 E. 70th St. (☎ 212/746-5050); **Beth Israel Medical Center,** First Avenue at 16th Street (☎ 212/420-2000); and **St. Luke's Roosevelt Hospital,** 58th Street and Ninth Avenue (☎ 212/523-4000). For eye, ear, or facial injuries, go to the **New York Eye and Ear Infirmary,** 310 E. 14th St. (☎ 212/979-4000).

Hot Lines   For information on theater, music, and dance performances, call **NYC On Stage** (☎ **212/768-1818**). Review current offerings at **Lincoln Center** (☎ 212/LINCOLN). The **City Parks Special Events Hotline** (☎ 212/360-3456 or 888/NY-PARKS) gives details on outdoor concerts and performances and New York Roadrunner Club events. Sponsored by the Jazz Foundation of America, **Jazzline** (☎ 212/479-7888) will clue you in on all jazz performances happening in town. Listings of commercial films are available through **Moviefone** (☎ 212/777-FILM), which also allows you to prepurchase movie tickets via credit card. **Sports Scores** (☎ 212/976-1717) gives updates of the most recent pro sports events.

Libraries   At any branch of the **New York Public Library** you can pick up a monthly brochure listing all the kids' activities planned—films, story hours, puppet plays, and the like—at the system's many branches. These are usually wonderful programs, and they're absolutely free. The **Donnell Library,** 20 W. 53rd St. (☎ **212/621-0636**), has the main children's room for the entire system, with lots of scheduled readings and events. Branches with good children's rooms include **Jefferson Market,** 425 Sixth Ave., at West 10th Street (☎ 212/243-4334); **Yorkville,** 222 E. 79th St. (☎ 212/744-5824); **Muhlenberg,** 209 W. 23rd St. (☎ 212/924-1585); **Epiphany,** 228 E. 23rd St. (☎ 212/679-2645); and **St. Agnes,** 444 Amsterdam Ave., at 82nd Street (☎ 212/877-4380).

  The **Early Childhood Resources & Information Center** at 66 Leroy St. (☎ 212/929-0815) has lots of parenting books as well as a big indoor playspace for kids 5 and under. The **Riverside branch,** 127 Amsterdam Ave., at 65th St., near Lincoln Center (☎ 212/870-1810), has listening stations in its children's room with lots of tapes and CDs. The **central research library** on Fifth Avenue at 41st Street is worth a stop to see its magnificent main reading room; there are frequent free guided tours and fascinating exhibits, but these are usually more interesting for parents than for kids, who prefer visiting the grand stone lions—named Patience and Fortitude by Mayor Fiorello La Guardia—guarding the sweeping front steps.

Newspapers/Magazines   Pick up free copies of the local parents' monthlies, the *Big Apple Parents' Paper,* 36 E. 12th St., New York, NY 10003 (☎ **212/533-2277;** fax 212/475-6186); or *New York Family,* 141 Halstead Ave., Suite 3D, Mamaroneck, NY 10543 (☎ **914/381-7474**), at toy stores, children's clothing and shoe stores, and indoor playgrounds all around Manhattan. Less easy to find, but very helpful, is the *Family Entertainment Guide,* a quarterly calendar published by Family Publications Ltd., 37 W. 72nd St., Suite 9, New York, NY 10023 (☎ **212/595-4569**). Every Friday, the *New York Times* runs a "Family Fare" column in its Weekend entertainment section, detailing special events in the upcoming week. The weekly magazines *Time Out* and *New York* and the *Village Voice* weekly newspaper have sections on children's events in their comprehensive events listings. The weekly *New Yorker* sometimes lists children's events (if there's room) in the "Goings On About Town" section.

Post Offices   The **Main Post Office** at Eighth Avenue between 31st and 33rd streets (☎ **212/967-8585**) is open daily 24 hours. Call the Postal Answer Line at ☎ **800/725-2161** for information.

Rest Rooms   See "Planning Your Outings," earlier in this chapter.

Safety   Panhandlers have been aggressively kept off the streets in Mayor Giuliani's New York City; still, they do appear here and there. Giving them handouts isn't a good idea—you may just be supporting someone's drug habit. Also beware of fast-talking con artists who prey on tourists around the bus and train terminals. They may be well dressed and have a very persuasive story, but don't give them any money, no matter how ardently they promise to repay you later.

Not to be paranoid, but I don't recommend letting your kids wear clothes with their names on them. If your child did get separated from you, it'd be easy for a non-well-meaning stranger to gain his or her confidence by seeming to know your kid's name. A small card with your name and hotel information on it could be slipped into your child's pocket, on the other hand, to help the authorities contact you if your child were lost. Since you'll often be in crowded places, if you've got a speedy, independent toddler who might dash away, consider getting a flexible cord or harness to keep your child within arm's reach.

Pickpockets like to work crowds (particularly jam-packed buses and subways), so always keep your purse or wallet in front where you can keep an eye on it. Don't let your kids carry valuables in a backpack, either. Areas to avoid after dark if you're not a local: the deserted after-hours Wall Street area, the Lower East Side, the East Village east of Second Avenue, Midtown west of Eighth Avenue, Uptown north of 96th Street (except for the corridor along Broadway up to 120th Street). With kids in tow, you might as well just use cabs at night.

Taxes   **Sales tax** is 8.25%, charged on everything except groceries and take-out food. **Hotels** add a 13.25% hotel tax to room rates.

Telephones   There are public phones on every other street corner in Manhattan, though not all are in what you'd call working order; large hotels generally have a bank of public phones off the lobby too. A local call costs 25¢.

Useful Telephone Numbers   For directory assistance, call ☎ **411** or 555-1212. For the **time,** call ☎ **212/976-6000.** For the **weather,** call ☎ **212/976-4111** (you'll also get current winning lottery numbers).

What Kids Like to See & Do

4

Considering what a world-class sightseeing destination New York City is, it's always surprising to realize how limited its attractions for kids can be. In the first place, many of its top museums are classy art repositories not inherently suited for youngsters—the most extreme example being the Frick Museum, which won't even let in anyone under 10. Real estate is too tight here for anything like a theme park, and though there are three children's museums—one in Manhattan, one in Brooklyn, and one on Staten Island—none of them is as big and clean and stimulating as their counterparts in Boston, Chicago, and Indianapolis.

The other problem is that so much of what you can do here gets so crowded, especially on weekends and school holidays. Waiting in line is inevitable for top attractions like the Statue of Liberty, the Sony Wonder Technology Lab, and the World Trade Center's observation deck. If you're visiting from out of town during the school year, try hitting the popular museums in the mornings, when the local kids are in school. On rainy weekends, it seems every family in town heads for the American Museum of Natural History—if you want peace and quiet, you'll be better off going there on the first glorious day of spring, when the hordes have deserted it for Central Park. The park, however, only gets better when it's full of people, as it usually is every weekend—see chapter 5 for the lowdown on this great green Manhattan haven.

When all is said and done, though, this metropolis is still a great place for kids, all the more so if you're willing to get on a subway and zip out to the outer boroughs. Remember, kids love subway rides and on weekends especially it's the way to go. Spend a day out in Brooklyn's Prospect Park, dividing your time between the Wildlife Center and the Lefferts Homestead and the Carousel, or pop over to the Brooklyn Botanic Garden and the Brooklyn Museum—incredibly, these are all within a few minutes' walk of one another. Flushing Meadows is my destination of choice in Queens, where you can do both the New York Hall of Science and Queens Wildlife Center in one easy go. In the Bronx, the huge Bronx Zoo and the equally huge New York Botanical Garden are right across the road from each other. Getting to Staten Island is even more fun because you get to take a ferry ride, and the children's museum there is only a short bus ride from the ferry docks.

What's in a Name?

Here's a trivia quiz to test your kids' knowledge of New York City history:

1. Who was the Hudson River named after?
2. Who was the Verrazano Bridge named after?
3. Where does the downtown street name of Wall Street come from?
4. Where does the name Harlem, for the uptown neighborhood, come from?
5. Why is the street leading down to South Street Seaport named Fulton Street?
6. What does the name of the New York Mets refer to? (*Hint:* Think of the opera and the big art museum.)
7. What other two area sports teams have names that rhyme with the Mets?
8. Why is Times Square called Times Square?
9. Carnegie Hall, the famous concert hall at 57th Street and Seventh Avenue, is named after whom? And how do you get there?
10. Who is buried in Grant's Tomb?

ANSWERS:　1. English explorer Henry Hudson, who sailed up the river in 1609. 2. Italian explorer Giovanni da Verrazano, the first European to enter the Narrows, in 1524.　3. In the original Dutch settlement, a wall was built at that point to keep out invaders.　4. Nieuw Haarlem was a separate Dutch settlement in the mid-1600s, named after the Dutch city of Haarlem.　5. Ferry service, operated by steamship inventor Robert Fulton, crossed the river at that point, linking Manhattan to Brooklyn (until the completion of the Brooklyn Bridge in 1883).　6. It's short for Metropolitans.　7. The New York Jets football team and the New Jersey Nets basketball team.　8. Because the headquarters of the New York Times newspaper is there (an earlier paper, the New York Herald, lent its name to Herald Square a few blocks south at 34th Street).　9. It's named for the man who built it, industrialist/ philanthropist Andrew Carnegie (his home is now the Cooper-Hewitt Museum). How do you get there? Practice, practice, practice.　10. Grant, of course (that's Ulysses S. Grant, Civil War commander and U.S. president), as well as his wife, Julia.

Many museums court families by designing weekend and holiday workshops for kids—these are detailed in chapter 5, where you'll also find everything you'll need to know about having fun outdoors in New York's great parks, playgrounds, and neighborhoods.

SIGHTSEEING SUGGESTIONS

IF YOU HAVE ONLY 1 DAY　Talk to the animals at the **Central Park Zoo,** then swing over to take a spin on the **Carousel.** Grab a hot dog for lunch in the park, then head up Central Park West to the **American Museum of Natural History,** with its magnificent dinosaur bones and wildlife dioramas. If you've got enough stamina, wind up with an hour or so at the **Children's Museum of Manhattan,** a couple of blocks away on West 83rd Street.

IF YOU HAVE 2 DAYS　Spend Day 1 as above—unless the weather's gorgeous, in which case do the Day 2 itinerary, then pick up the above for your second day.

On Day 2, get up early to be first in line for the ferry to the **Statue of Liberty** and **Ellis Island.** This should take most of the day, especially if your kids want to wait in line to climb to Lady Liberty's crown. After the ferry deposits you back on Manhattan, walk a few blocks to the World Trade Center's **Top of the World** observation deck, where you can see for miles and miles, then saunter east on Fulton Street to **South Street Seaport,** where you can shop, visit maritime-history exhibits, and maybe have a seafood dinner.

IF YOU HAVE 3 DAYS   Spend Days 1 and 2 as above. On Day 3, roam around **Rockefeller Center,** hanging over the railing at Rockefeller Plaza and delving into the concourse to see the underground city in action. Go up Fifth Avenue past St. Patrick's Cathedral, visiting the Disney Store and the Warner Bros. Studio Store and FAO Schwarz (see chapter 6). Then swing over to Madison Avenue, where you can pick up a sandwich to eat while waiting in line for the **Sony Wonder Technology Lab.** (Optional Midtown alternatives, depending on your kid's tastes, are the **Museum of Television and Radio** and the **Museum of Modern Art.**) Then take the Fifth Avenue bus down to 34th Street, where you can ascend the **Empire State Building** for a late-afternoon vista.

IF YOU HAVE 4 DAYS   Spend Days 1 to 3 as above. With older kids, start out Day 4 by taking the 45-minute tour of the **United Nations,** have an early lunch in the Delegates' Dining Room, then cab it uptown for an afternoon at the **Metropolitan Museum of Art.** If you have younger kids, start out at the Metropolitan first thing in the morning (when the crowds are lighter and the guards a trifle more patient), have lunch at an East Side coffee shop, then repair to Central Park playgrounds so your youngsters can let off some steam. Work your way up Fifth Avenue to 103rd Street, where you can pop in to check out the toy gallery at the **Museum of the City of New York,** and end your day with a stroll through **Conservatory Garden.**

IF THE WEATHER'S COLD   To cram the most into 1 day with a minimum of exposure to the elements, start out at the **American Museum of Natural History,** then scoot across Central Park on the 79th Street crosstown bus (just as quick as a taxi) and dive into the **Metropolitan Museum of Art.** Or do it the other way around, depending on which you think your child will want more time for. Both have reasonable on-site cafes, so you won't have to venture outside to eat.

IF THE WEATHER'S HOT   East River breezes make **South Street Seaport** a refreshing spot in summer, and you can always duck inside the air-conditioned shops and museums when the sun beats down too strongly. When that gets stale, hop across town (there's a free trolley service) to **Battery Park City,** where you can shop and eat in the tony Winter Garden atrium, loll on the plaza by the yacht basin, or stroll down the breezy Esplanade along the Hudson. Another good warm-weather refuge is **The Cloisters,** the Metropolitan's medieval art annex located north, up in Fort Tryon Park, where you can chill out amid the dim light and cool stone of transplanted European chapels.

Don't be tempted to do the **Statue of Liberty/Ellis Island** trip if the weather's insufferably hot. The ferry ride will be a pleasant break, it's true, but waiting in line for the boat (once in Battery Park, again on Liberty Island, and again on Ellis Island) will strain your family's temper, and the wait in line to climb the statue—an indoor wait in close quarters, often for 2 hours or more—will be cruel and unusual punishment. If you want a boat ride that badly, take the **Staten Island ferry.**

IF YOU'VE GOT A SITTER   Take advantage of the opportunity to dawdle in one of the art museums kids aren't as happy in—like the **Frick,** the **Whitney**

Museum of American Art, or the **Asia Society Galleries,** all on the Upper East Side. Then window-shop along tony **Madison Avenue,** where designer boutiques cluster from the 80s on down to 57th Street. Another child-free option may be to prowl around the Wall Street area: visit the **New York Stock Exchange,** venerable **Trinity Church,** and the surprisingly small but ornate **City Hall.** Go out to dinner at an elegant restaurant, then catch either a **Broadway show** or a concert at **Carnegie Hall** or **Lincoln Center.** For complete details on all such grown-up activities, pick up a copy of *Frommer's New York City.*

1 Kids' Top 10 Attractions

✪ American Museum of Natural History   All ages
Central Park West at 79th St. ☎ **212/769-5100.** www.amnh.org. Suggested admission $4.50 kids 2–12, $8 adults, $6 students/seniors; under 2 free. Museum admission plus IMAX movie ticket $6.50 kids 2–12, $12 adults, $8.50 students/seniors. Sun–Thurs 10am–5:45pm, Fri–Sat 10am–8:45pm. Closed Thanksgiving and Christmas. Subway: B/C to 81st St.; 1/9 to 79th St.

This one isn't listed first just because it comes first alphabetically—it's the city's one real don't-miss if you're with kids. When you enter the rotunda at the top of the Central Park West steps, a rearing skeleton of a mommy dinosaur protecting her baby from a small, fierce predator clues you in that the dazzling fourth-floor **dinosaur halls** are the star attraction—especially after their early 1990s renovation, which has added interactive consoles, glass-floored walkways that bring you up to the dino's eye level, and please-touch displays illustrating key points of evolution. But for natural history veterans like my kids, the dinosaurs are only the tip of the iceberg. Walk through the rotunda into the bilevel **African Mammals Hall** and you can circle around a lumbering herd of elephants (we always sing the Elephant Marching Song from Disney's animated *Jungle Book*), then check out the giraffes browsing by their water hole. The superb dioramas in the **North American Mammals** (first floor) are perennial favorites too—the grizzly bear raking open a freshly caught salmon, majestic elks lifting their massive antlers, wolves loping through eerie nighttime snow.

A circuit of the first floor alone could take a whole day. The p.c.-but-never-preachy **Hall of Biodiversity** features an immense multimedia re-creation of an African rain forest, one of the planet's most threatened ecosystems; nine other ecosystems, from tundra to coral reef to desert, are explored in a multiscreen video installation; and the Spectrum of Life displays the entire family tree of Earth's living creatures, with more than 1,500 specimens and models spread out along a 100-foot wall. We love the dimly lit **Whale Room,** where a gargantuan model of a blue whale swims overhead, with dioramas of walruses, dolphins, and sharks along the side walls; it has informally become known as the place where toddlers can stretch their legs, racing and twirling around the vast open space. Around the corner, the less-well-visited **North American Forest dioramas** are our family secret—a peaceful part of the museum where you can hunt for bluejays in oak trees and rattlesnakes behind the cactus. Most people hurry through here to get to the interactive **Human Biology and Evolution exhibits,** which seem always full of busy grade-schoolers. Past that lies the **Mineral and Gem room,** where little kids can thrust their hands into a huge geode while older kids gape in awe at the jewels on display.

The museum is not all animals, by any means (remember that Margaret Mead was only one of many brilliant anthropologists whose research was supported by this museum over the years). Studying Native Americans? On the first floor, by the 77th Street entrance, is the astounding collection of Northwest Indian totem poles

Natural History Museum Treasure Hunt

The American Museum of Natural History is so vast, kids can easily tire if you trudge from hall to hall with no organizing purpose. Here, then, is a treasure hunt designed by my sons, Hugh and Tom, to keep your kids busy exploring. Younger kids may get through only one floor in an afternoon, but persist— I swear, it's all here.

First Floor

1. **North American Mammals**—Where is the rabbit hiding from the lynx?
2. **Ocean Life**—Who's talking back to the orca? (*Hint:* Orca is another name for a killer whale.)
3. **New York State Environment**—How many baby chipmunks are sleeping in the spring burrow?
4. **Human Biology and Evolution**—Find the cave of mammoth bones.
5. **Minerals and Gems**—Find the rocks that glow in the dark.

Second Floor

6. **African Peoples**—Find the xylophone.
7. **Birds of the World**—How many stuffed penguins are there?
8. **Asian Peoples**—Who's getting married?
9. **Mexico and Central America**—Where can you see the sun rising?

Third Floor

10. **African Mammals**—Who's watching the ostriches fight the wart hogs?
11. **Reptiles and Amphibians**—Which is the crocodile and which is the alligator?

Fourth Floor

12. **Saurischian Dinosaurs**—Find the fossil dinosaur teeth.
13. **Ornithischian Dinosaurs**—Touch the triceratops horn.

ANSWERS: *1. Behind the bush. 2. The leopard seal. 3. Four. 4. Toward the end of the exhibit, in the Earliest Architecture display. 5. In the first gem room, the southeast corner. 6. Midway through the hall, on the west wall, across from the guys in straw skirts who look like Cousin Itt. 7. Twenty in all—16 adults, 4 babies. 8. In the Chinese section, a bride in her ornate ceremonial sedan chair. 9. On the huge round Aztec Stone of the Sun, the north wall. 10. The mouselike elephant shrew, behind a dead log. 11. Facing each other by the entrance at the north end of the hall—the gator (on your right) has the snub snout, the croc (on your left) has the pointy snout. 12. On the south wall. 13. On the east wall.*

J. D. Salinger immortalized in *Catcher in the Rye*. The haunting soundtracks in the **African** and **Asian peoples sections** (on the second floor) lull you into studying the precisely detailed displays there too.

The **IMAX theater** (additional ticket required—see above) is an important part of the experience; my sons' current favorites are *Whales* and *Titanica* (warning to preteen girls: Leonardo DiCaprio isn't in it). The old **Hayden Planetarium** has

Uptown Attractions

American Museum of
  Natural History 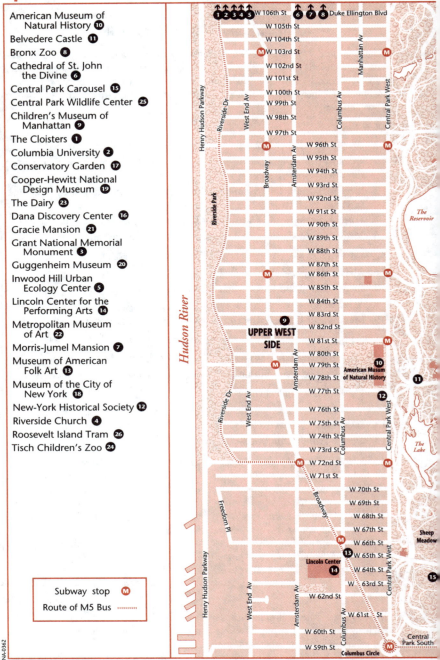**10**

Belvedere Castle **11**

Bronx Zoo **8**

Cathedral of St. John
  the Divine **6**

Central Park Carousel **15**

Central Park Wildlife Center **25**

Children's Museum of
  Manhattan **9**

The Cloisters **1**

Columbia University **2**

Conservatory Garden **17**

Cooper-Hewitt National
  Design Museum **19**

The Dairy **23**

Dana Discovery Center **16**

Gracie Mansion **21**

Grant National Memorial
  Monument **3**

Guggenheim Museum **20**

Inwood Hill Urban
  Ecology Center **5**

Lincoln Center for the
  Performing Arts **14**

Metropolitan Museum
  of Art **22**

Morris-Jumel Mansion **7**

Museum of American
  Folk Art **13**

Museum of the City of
  New York **18**

New-York Historical Society **12**

Riverside Church **4**

Roosevelt Island Tram **26**

Tisch Children's Zoo **24**

Subway stop **M**
Route of M5 Bus ·········

NA-0362

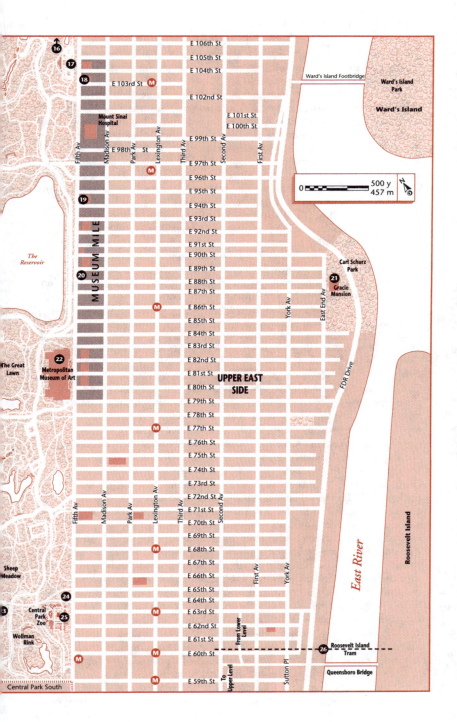

E 106th St
E 105th St
E 104th St
E 103rd St
E 102nd St
E 101st St
E 100th St
E 99th St
E 97th St
E 96th St
E 95th St
E 94th St
E 93rd St
E 92nd St
E 91st St
E 90th St
E 89th St
E 88th St
E 87th St
E 86th St
E 85th St
E 84th St
E 83rd St
E 82nd St
E 81st St
E 80th St
E 79th St
E 78th St
E 77th St
E 76th St
E 75th St
E 74th St
E 73rd St
E 72nd St
E 71st St
E 70th St
E 69th St
E 68th St
E 67th St
E 66th St
E 65th St
E 64th St
E 63rd St
E 62nd St
E 61st St
E 60th St
E 59th St

E 98th St

Mount Sinai
Hospital

Fifth Av
Madison Av
Park Av
Lexington Av
Third Av
Second Av
First Av
York Av
East End Av

MUSEUM MILE

The Reservoir

The Great Lawn

Metropolitan Museum of Art

Sheep Meadow

Central Park Zoo

Wollman Rink

Central Park South

UPPER EAST SIDE

Ward's Island Footbridge
Ward's Island Park
Ward's Island

Carl Schurz Park
Gracie Mansion

FDR Drive

East River

Roosevelt Island

From Lower Level
To Upper Level

Sutton Pl

Roosevelt Island Tram

Queensboro Bridge

0   500 y
     457 m

16
17
18
19
20
21
22
24
25
26
3

41

been razed and the new one won't be open until 2000, but in the meantime the popular weekend-night laser rock shows are screened in the IMAX theater. (For more on IMAX, see Films in chapter 7.)

Squirrelled away in a back corner of the second floor is the **Alexander M. White Natural Science Center,** a delightful hands-on workshop where kids can explore the natural life of New York City (open Tuesday to Friday 2 to 4pm, Saturday and Sunday 1 to 4:30pm). Down the same corridor, in the Leonhardt People Center, **Discovery Room** programs are held weekend afternoons once a month (ages 5 and older), and hour-long **family workshops** are held Saturday and Sunday at 11am and 3:30pm. There are several excellent gift shops too; if your kid is bugging you for a souvenir, make a beeline for the **Junior Shop** by the restaurants and rest rooms on the lower level, which has 50¢ rubber dinosaurs.

Where to Eat: The **Dinersaurus** cafeteria (open daily 11am to 4:45pm) sells sandwiches and salads, including dinosaur-shaped french fries and chicken nuggets my kids find irresistible in concept, though they often don't like the taste well enough to finish them. The sit-down **Garden Cafe** is more upscale—a better option if your kids are older. Since you can reenter the museum with your admission tag, consider popping out into the neighborhood to **Rain, Pizzeria Uno,** or the **Museum Cafe** (see chapter 8), only a block away.

✪ Bronx Zoo/International Wildlife Conservation Park   All ages

In Bronx Park, Bronx River Pkwy. and Fordham Rd. ☎ **718/367-1010.** Admission: Apr–Oct $4 kids 2–12, $7.75 adults, $4 seniors; Nov–Dec kids/seniors $3, adults $6; Jan–Mar, $2 kids/seniors, $4 adults. Free Wed and always for kids under 2. Apr–Oct Mon–Fri 10am–5pm, Sat–Sun and holidays 10am–5:30pm; Nov–Mar daily 10am–4:30pm. Stroller rental $5, with $20 deposit (inquire at park entrances). Parking $6. Transportation: See below.

The Big Kahuna of New York City's wildlife parks, the Bronx Zoo is a world-class facility in every way. It covers 265 acres and boasts more than 4,000 animals, from Siberian tigers and snow leopards to condors and vultures to naked mole-rats and meerkats. Though there's a scattered number of indoor exhibits, such as the deliciously creepy **World of Darkness** (nocturnal animals), the **World of Reptiles,** the **Monkey House,** the **Giraffe House,** and the **Mouse House,** most of the animals live outdoors in large enclosures re-creating as closely as possible the species' native environment. This is all laudably humane, but kids under 5 may get frustrated by the long walks between animals and the fact that certain creatures may be viewable only at a distance. Which doesn't mean they won't love the zoo—it just means you've got to organize your visit sensibly.

April to October, there are several rides available to help you navigate the park. An **open-sided tram** rattles in a big loop around the main part of the zoo, which should allow you to see giraffes, zebras, cheetahs, lions, and bison without exhausting your toddler. The **Skyfari cable car** soars high over the park and can be fun for older kids, though you don't exactly get a better view of the animals that way (it's handy for cutting across if you don't want to walk the whole circuit). Then there's the narrated **monorail ride** (May to October only), which is the only way you can visit the Wild Asia section, so it's a good deal—the guide points out every animal roaming around and slows down for optimum viewing. (My family still fondly remembers the guide we landed last time—his punchline for every anecdote was "Don't worry, be happy, because it's a happy day, and Jason is your driver.") There's a $2-per-person charge for these rides, however, which means that with a family of five you could spend over $50 on a full day—you might as well buy a 1-year family membership ($58), which gets you into everything free. There's also a charge for the **Children's Zoo** ($2 adults, $1.50 kids 11 and under), open April to October only, but it's worth it, with lots of learn-by-doing exhibits (like a spider web rope climb and a prairie dog burrow kids can climb through) and a petting zoo.

During winter, when many of the outdoor animals aren't on view, the park lures visitors with fanciful animal sculptures spangled with lights, as well as the indoor exhibits (still enough species on view to fill a smaller zoo); there's a certain pleasure in visiting during this uncrowded season.

The zoo has several entrances: I recommend the Southern Boulevard/Crotona entrance, which brings you in near the Children's Zoo and the elephants, or the Asia Entrance (pedestrians only, closest to the subway station), which brings you in near Wild Asia, Jungle World, and the camel rides. In any case, study the zoo map as soon as you enter and plot which animals you want to visit and the simplest route to pass them. Operate on the assumption that you can't see everything in one day, even if your kids are good walkers. Relax, take your time, and enjoy yourselves.

Getting There: By **bus,** Liberty Lines BxM11 service (call ☎ 718/652-8400) runs about every 15 minutes from stops along Madison Avenue in Manhattan: The fare is $3 per person one-way (free for a child under 45 inches riding on an adult's lap). By **train,** take Metro North from Grand Central Terminal to Fordham Road, change to the Bx9 bus, and ride to the zoo's Southern Boulevard entrance. By **subway,** take the no. 2 to the East Tremont station; then walk 2 blocks west to Boston Road and turn left, cross the intersection, and bear right to the zoo entrance. A **taxi** might cost $15 to $28 one-way, depending on your Manhattan starting point or destination.

Where to Eat: The zoo's **Lakeside Cafe** is open year-round, and three open-air cafes operate seasonally. Expect fast-foodish menus, with slightly high (but not outrageous) prices. Pack a picnic lunch if you can—there are plenty of places to sit and eat outdoors.

Central Park Wildlife Center and Tisch Children's Zoo   All ages

In Central Park, near the park entrance at Fifth Ave. and 64th St. ☎ 212/861-6030. Admission (includes both zoos) 50¢ kids 3–12, $3.50 adults, $1.25 seniors; 2 and under free. Apr–Oct Mon–Fri 10am–5pm, Sat–Sun and holidays 10am–5:30pm; Nov–Mar daily 10am–4:30. Subway: N/R to Fifth Ave.; 6 to 68th St.

Beautifully landscaped, this pair of tiny zoos is perfect for young animal lovers—there's nothing bigger than a polar bear here, you can get pretty close to every species on display, and you don't have to walk very far to see everything. The centerpiece of the main zoo is the oval **Sea Lion Pool,** which has glass sides so everyone can watch the sea lions swimming underwater. A few steps to the west is **Monkey Island,** where a troop of snow monkeys scramble over the rocks and a few swans glide on the water. To the north lies the **Polar Circle,** with a big flock of penguins indoors and a trio of polar bears outside, cavorting in and out of their rock-edged pool (the obsessive-compulsive male that used to swim in the same frantic loop day after day has been responding very nicely to therapy, thank you). Up on the hill behind Monkey Island is the **Temperate Territory,** which stars an otter, some ducks, and a shy red panda; at the south end you can stand on the bridge over a mucky turtle pond and look for frogs sunning themselves. The greatest number of species in the zoo is inside the **Tropical Zone,** a two-story enclosed aviary with plenty of glass tanks arranged along the wall, featuring exciting creatures like piranhas and bats and snakes—not to mention our favorites, the golden lion tamarins, whose wizened faces look for all the world like those of the flying monkeys from *The Wizard of Oz.* Be sure to climb to the upper levels and stand out on the stairways, looking for the bright plumage of tropical birds flitting from tree to tree. Always warm and humid, the Tropical Zone is a great refuge on a chilly day. As soon as you go through the main zoo's gates, check signs near the entrance to see when the sea lion and penguin feedings are scheduled; there's often a crowd for these, but it's fun to see the animals scamper over to their keepers for their fish. (No, they don't do tricks—that wouldn't be p.c.)

The **Tisch Children's Zoo** is a short stroll north, on the other side of the Delacorte Arch. Much of this friendly hilltop spot is a walk-through aviary, which my older son, the budding ornithologist, finds incredibly cool. My kids also love the waterfall they can stick their hands through, with a dusky little grotto full of fish tanks behind it. Wooden bridges cross over a tidy central pond, cedar-chip paths circle around (strollers are useless here—park yours by the gate), and at the back is a giant spider web kids can clamber over. Children can get right up close to most of the animals here, so who cares if none of them is an exotic species?

Where to Eat: If you can, pack a picnic lunch and eat it at outdoor tables in the cafeteria courtyard. Otherwise, you'll have to go with the **zoo cafeteria** (there aren't many choices in the park), which has a limited menu, with a few sandwiches, salads, and fast-food items. At least there's a special kids' meal that may include animal crackers. There's usually also a cart selling drinks and ice cream in the central courtyard. Note that drinks are served without straws, since a straw tossed into an animal's enclosure could be harmful.

Children's Museum of Manhattan   Ages 10 & under

212 W. 83rd St. (between Broadway and Amsterdam Ave.). ☎ **212/721-1223.** www.CMOM.org. Admission $5 kids/adults, $2.50 seniors; under 1 free. Sept–June Wed–Sun 10am–5pm; July–Aug Tues–Sun 10am–5pm. Subway: 1/9 to 79th or 86th St.; B/C to 81st St.

My children are always happy to come here, though its limited installations can wear thin if we go too often. Best for the under-8 crew, it's full of things they can touch, space for them to run and jump, make-believe environments, and opportunities to experiment. New additions for 1999 are the main floor's interactive exploration of the human body and the mezzanine's Word Play exhibit, with seven activity areas cleverly designed to stimulate language development in kids 4 and under. The museum's four floors also include a playroom specially for 4-and-unders, a carpeted reading room with a puppet theater where kids can do their own impromptu shows, a few computers for older kids to mess around on, and an activity-packed basement area that's periodically remodeled, most recently with a delightful Dr. Seuss theme. The outdoor WaterWhirl and the recycling-oriented Urban Treehouse are fun too, I'm told, though they seem to be closed whenever we're visiting. Now that my older son is reading, he appreciates the fun upstairs corridor paying homage to Maira Kalman's nutty Max the Dog books.

There are always daily activities (check the posted schedules when you enter) like face painting, storytelling, and shows in the auditorium. Special weekend events focus on holidays. On rainy days and during school vacations, the joint gets pretty crowded, and the badly lit high-ceilinged spaces reverberate with noise; staff members posted in the galleries seem listless and uninvolved. It's a pity this place isn't better, but it's still worth checking out.

Where to Eat: The museum has no cafe, but there's a host of nearby restaurants that are kid-friendly: **EJ's Luncheonette, Brother Jimmy's,** the **Royal Canadian Pancake House,** and **Lemongrass Grill** (see chapter 8).

Ellis Island Immigration Museum   Ages 4 & up

On Ellis Island in New York Harbor. ☎ **212/363-3200.** Free admission (but you have to pay for the ferry—see "Getting There," below). Daily 9:30am–5pm (to 6pm in summer). Closed Christmas. Subway: 4/5 to Bowling Green; 1/9 to South Ferry.

My 5-year-old didn't want to get off the ferry—as far as he was concerned, this was supposed to be a trip to the Statue of Liberty and nothing else. Boy, am I glad I talked him into doing Ellis Island too. There's lots more to see here than there is at the Statue, from the huge pile of ragtag luggage right inside the front doors to the cramped dormitories upstairs to **Treasures from Home,** a fascinating collection of heirlooms brought to America by immigrants. The second-floor **Registry Hall** is awesome, with its soaring vaulted ceiling faced with white tile; this is where new arrivals waited in endless lines to be interviewed by immigration officials. My son even liked the first-floor **Peopling of America** exhibit, with a life-size "family tree" and huge three-dimensional bar graph tracking immigration patterns over the years. And the **Wall of Honor** outside, where some 420,000 immigrants' names are inscribed in steel, was fun even though no one in our family ever ponied up the dough to have a relative's name enshrined—we looked up two or three family names anyway. We had a good 45-minute visit, then caught the next ferry home; older kids will probably want to spend more time. To get even more out of it, you can take the self-guided audio tour, pick up handsets at various displays to hear narration, and watch the stirring documentary *Island of Hope, Island of Tears,* which runs frequently throughout the day. This place is what they mean when they talk about making history come alive.

Getting There: See the Statue of Liberty entry, below.

Where to Eat: There's a big, clean **cafeteria** on the site, as well as a snack bar on the ferry. Bring a picnic lunch if you can—there are plenty of places to sit out and eat.

✪ Metropolitan Museum of Art   All ages

1000 Fifth Ave. (at 82nd St.). ☎ **212/535-7710.** Suggested donation (includes same-day admission to the Cloisters, below) $8 adults, $4 students/seniors; 11 and under free. Tues–Thurs and Sun 9:30am–5:15pm, Fri–Sat 9:30am–8:45pm. Closed New Year's Day, Thanksgiving, Christmas. Strollers not permitted Sun (back carriers available at 81st St. entrance). Subway: 4/5/6 to 86th St.

Even though this is the city's number-one tourist attraction, many families we know never take their young kids here. Big mistake. You can have a great time at the Metropolitan, even with toddlers, so long as you remember two rules: Go at their pace, not yours (forget about standing transfixed for 10 minutes in front of that wonderfully serene Vermeer), and don't let the gruff museum guards intimidate you. They're the city's most fervent believers that children should be seen and not heard—they'll level stern, disapproving glares if your child so much as skips for joy or exclaims above a whisper. Naturally, don't let youngsters touch the precious works of art or press their fingers against glass cases, but otherwise let your own common sense prevail.

The echoing marble-clad Great Hall tells you as you enter that this is a Serious Art Museum. If there's a long ticket line at the booths in front of the entrance, go to the right, past the cloakroom—the booth at the north end is generally quicker. My kids love to climb the awesome central stairway up to the European painting galleries, the museum's prize jewel, but we generally veer off and skip those galleries—they go on forever, boring the pants off most kids.

Here are the galleries kids are more likely to enjoy: the **arms and armor** (first floor), the extensive **Egyptian rooms** (also on the first floor—make a beeline for the glorious mummies), **musical instruments** (second floor, off the American Wing's courtyard), the **Costume Institute** (ground floor), and the **European and American period rooms** (all over the place). On the first floor of the **American Wing** is a side gallery displaying vintage baseball cards, and a whole gallery of grandfather clocks ticks away on the second floor. Older kids who are beginning to appreciate art may go for the **impressionist gallery** (second floor) or the **Lehman Pavilion,** set up like the town house of a wealthy collector—it's art in small enough doses that it doesn't overwhelm.

Our favorite corner, hands down, is the **courtyard of the American Wing,** a light-filled open space with plantings, benches, and statues kids can actually relate to (a mountain lion and her cubs, a pensive Indian brave). Bring lots of small change for them to throw into the pool here and in the pool in front of the Egyptian Wing's momentous **Temple of Dendur** (but *not* in the Chinese scholars' court goldfish pool in the second-floor Asian art galleries!). In the Japanese galleries, there's a little-known room actually overlooking the Temple of Dendur, a perspective my kids prefer. They also like the balcony off the musical instruments gallery overlooking the mounted knights in armor and a second-floor balcony overlooking a transplanted Spanish courtyard. Get the idea? Wander around this immense museum, keep your eyes open, and be willing to walk away from anything that interests you if it doesn't interest your children.

The huge museum gift shop up on the second floor, one of the world's best, has a lot of stuff for kids.

Where to Eat: The **museum cafe** is in a vast pink-columned salon that can be a thrill, but the cafeteria line is awfully long and the food is overpriced and not great. Since your museum badge allows reentry, with younger kids it's probably better just to go outside and sit on the splendid Fifth Avenue steps (one of the city's best impromptu grandstands) to eat a hot dog bought at a nearby pushcart. Or walk a block east to Madison and **Nectar of 82nd Street,** 1090 Madison Ave. (☎ **212/ 772-0916**)—clean, kid-friendly, and fairly priced for the usual coffee-shop menu.

✪ Sony Wonder Technology Lab   Ages 4 & up

550 Madison Ave. (entrance on 56th St.). ☎ **212/833-8100.** wondertechlab.sony.com. Free admission. Tues–Sat 10am–6pm (to 8pm Thurs), Sun noon–6pm. Subway: E/F to Fifth Ave.

Though no doubt it helps sell Sony products, this wonderful interactive exploratorium isn't annoyingly self-serving. (Leave that to the Playstation and other Sony outlets arranged around the sleek atrium here at Sony's Manhattan headquarters.) Sony Wonder actually lets people experiment with all types of high-tech equipment, from TV cameras to industrial robots to ultrasound scanners; you can play at being a recording engineer, videotape editor, or computer designer or just mess around on the Internet.

When you first enter the lab, you get your own personal card, which becomes magnetically encoded with your name and photo; as you continue through three floors of activities, every time you slide the card through the scanner on a new terminal, your name and photo are inserted into whatever program is up. On your way out, you can print out a personalized certificate recording all the activities you tried. Kids love seeing their name and face everywhere, and the activities have been pretty well designed so that even 4- and 5-year-olds can work them (though older kids can explore them to greater depth and adults are bound to get hooked too). Saturday and Sunday workshops (small fee charged, pre-registration advisable) help youngster explore different aspects of technology at greater depth.

The staff is careful not to let too many people in at one time, so it's not unusual to wait in line in the lobby for up to an hour (an awesome robot, b.b.wonderbot, chats up the crowd as they wait). Don't let the wait daunt you—once you're inside, you should always be able to get your hands on equipment. Loads of friendly young Sony staffers are around to help you figure out how stuff works. I wanted to linger on the Communications Bridge—actually a long ramp between floors where terminals and displays tell the history of communications—but as I stood trans-fixed in front of a videotape of the Beatles arriving in New York in 1964, my son kept yanking on my arm to move on. Plan for at least 2 hours here, more if you've got a really high-tech kid.

Where to Eat: Bring sandwiches in and eat at the tiny metal tables in the sleek **Sony Plaza atrium** or buy something on site at food stalls in the atrium.

South Street Seaport and the Seaport Museum   All ages

12 Fulton St. (between Water & South sts.). ☎ **212/748-8600.** www.southstseaport.org. Admission $3 kids, $6 adults, $4 students, $5 seniors. Oct–Mar Wed–Mon 10am–5pm; Apr–Sept daily 10am–6pm (to 8pm Thurs). Subway: 2/3/4/5 to Fulton St.; A/C to Broadway/Nassau St.

This collection of warehouses and maritime shops on the cobblestoned East River waterfront was a major shipping port in the days of clipper ships, but the spectac-ular renovation of these historic 19th-century buildings has often been over-shadowed by the attendant development of much of the site as a "festival market-place" (touristy urban shopping mall). You can spend a fun day here without ever paying admission to the Seaport Museum, what with all the shops and restaurants, pierside entertainers, and wide-open views of the East River and Brooklyn.

That said, when we finally forked over museum admission one steamy July after-noon, we discovered a whole new dimension to the Seaport that goes beyond the shopping-mall experience. There's a small but interesting hands-on **children's museum** at 165 John St., a 19th-century **printing shop** at 211 Water St., and a **boat-building shop** at the corner of John and South streets—each occupied us for 20 minutes or so. My sons' (and husband's) favorite part of the day was clambering all over the **historic ships** moored to the piers. There are always special exhibits, like the one we saw about tattoos (my kids thought it was gross, but older kids might've been totally fascinated); harbor cruises on the Seaport Liberty Line or the historic *Pioneer,* an 1885 schooner, also leave from here (see "Boat Tours," later in this chapter). Special children's workshops and storytelling hours are organized all over the place—pick up a schedule at the visitor center. Because the various museum buildings are scattered all over the site, you'll be mingling with the tourist crowds of shoppers, but the museum sites themselves are usually pleasantly uncrowded. What with the ocean air whipping in off the estuary, you'll feel like old salts before the day is through.

Where to Eat: The Seaport is loaded with restaurants of varying quality. With kids, your best bet is to go to the top floor of the Seaport's **Pier 17,** where there's an excellent food court with a wide choice of fast foods (not all of the greasy variety), often live music, and great East River views.

Statue of Liberty   Ages 3 & up

On Liberty Island in New York Harbor. ☎ **212/363-7620.** Free admission (but you have to pay for the ferry—see "Getting There" below). Daily 9:30am–5pm (to 6pm in summer). Closed Christmas. Subway: 4/5 to Bowling Green; 1/9 to South Ferry.

The symbol of New York is impressive enough from across the harbor, but close up—man, this chick is BIG. It gives me vertigo just to look up at her. In fact, younger kids may be frightened by the sheer scale of Lady Liberty, and they won't want to climb the 354 steps up to her crown for the prize-winning view. (And for the climb there's also a wearying wait in line that can last 2 or 3 hours in fair weather.)

Here are your alternatives: Take the elevator up to the 10th floor (the top of the statue's pedestal), where there's a pretty amazing view, or go out on the plaza around the base of the pedestal to gaze out over the harbor. The exhibit inside the base is

The While-Waiting-in-Line-at-Lady-Liberty Quiz

1. The Statue of Liberty weighs
   a. 225 tons.
   b. 25 tons.
   c. 225 pounds (when she's been to her step-aerobics class).

2. The statue's full official name is
   a. The Gatekeeper of Liberty.
   b. Liberty Enlightening the World.
   c. Liberty Looking for a Lost Contact Lens.

3. Sculptor Frédéric-Auguste Bartholdi is said to have modeled the statue after
   a. the Mona Lisa.
   b. Napoleon Bonaparte's girlfriend.
   c. his mommy.

4. Emma Lazarus's poem *The New Colossus* ("Give me your tired, your poor . . .") is engraved
   a. on the tablet Liberty cradles in her arm.
   b. on a plaque inside the base of the statue.
   c. on a tattoo on every park ranger's left bicep.

5. The engineer who designed the statue's tricky steel skeleton is also known for
   a. the Eiffel Tower in Paris.
   b. the Brooklyn Bridge.
   c. the Spaceship Earth sphere at Epcot.

more fun than you'd expect—full-scale models of her left foot and immense ear, videos of smiths hammering out copper sheathing, a cross-section to show how the copper skin was hung on her steel skeleton. Right inside the entrance, you can see her original torch (replaced at the statue's centennial in 1986). For some kids, the ferry ride over may be more fun than the statue itself, but the whole excursion is a blast, so long as you don't waste too much time waiting in line.

Getting There: The **ferryboats** make frequent trips, running a loop from Battery Park to Liberty Island to Ellis Island and back to Battery Park (from New Jersey you can board ferries in Liberty State Park). In Battery Park, you can buy tickets at Castle Clinton, where there are some interesting exhibits to help pass the time before your ferry. You can disembark at either island and board a later boat to continue your trip. Schedules vary, but the service generally runs daily starting at 9:30am (last trip starts around 3:15pm, later in summer). Boats depart every 30 or 40 minutes; sailing time is about 15 minutes to Liberty Island, another 10 minutes to Ellis Island, and 10 minutes back to Manhattan. The fare is $3 for kids 3 to 17, $7 for adults, and $6 for seniors. For information and current schedules, call ☎ 212/269-5755.

Where to Eat: There's a **cafeteria** on the site, as well as a snack bar on the ferry. Bring a picnic lunch if you can—there are plenty of places to sit and eat. (Just watch out for marauding seagulls.)

6. The French intellectual who first proposed the idea for the statue was
   a. the marquis de Lafayette.
   b. Edouard René Lefebvre de Laboulaye.
   c. Pepe Le Pieuw.

7. Once completed and shipped in sections to the United States, the statue almost wasn't erected because
   a. they lost the instructions on how to put it together.
   b. Americans hadn't raised enough money to build a pedestal for it.
   c. everybody thought it was so ugly.

8. Lady Liberty looks green because
   a. the statue's hammered-copper sheathing has oxidized as expected.
   b. pollution from New York Harbor has corroded it.
   c. she gets seasick from watching the ferries chug past all day.

9. The statue's nose is
   a. 4½ feet long.
   b. 10 feet long.
   c. 100 feet long (she could use some plastic surgery).

10. The Statue of Liberty was given to the people of the United States by the people of France
    a. because there was no room for it in Paris.
    b. in repayment of old war debts.
    c. to symbolize a special friendship between the two countries.

ANSWERS: *1. a 2. b 3. c 4. b 5. a 6. b 7. b 8. a 9. a 10. c.*

United Nations   Ages 8 & up

On the East River from 42nd to 48th sts. (entrance at First Ave. and 46th St.). ☎ **212/963-7713**. Admission $3.50 grades 1–8, $7.50 adults, $4.50 students, $5.50 seniors; kids under 5 not admitted on tours. Daily 9:15am–4:45pm. Subway: 4/5/6/7/S to Grand Central. Bus: M15, M42, M104.

When I was 13 and on my first visit to New York, the United Nations made a very deep impression on me. The idea of a world peacekeeping organization may have lost a little of its luster since then, but it's still a pretty darn impressive sight. First of all there's the location, a commanding East River site with serene lawns and gardens, cantilevered cleverly over FDR Drive. Then there's that memorable architectural design, the low dome of the General Assembly building tucked in at the base of the sheer glass plinth of the Secretariat building. Finally, the thing that struck me most as a kid was the place's international population, with African and Asian and Scandinavian and Middle Eastern and Latin American bureaucrats bustling around chattering in a Babel of different tongues; it really brought home to me how big the world is and what an amazing feat it is to get all these people to agree on *anything*.

Stop by the booth near the 46th Street entrance to get on a guided tour in English; these run about every half hour and last 45 minutes (call to find out about tours in other languages). These information-loaded talks fill you in on the

Midtown Attractions

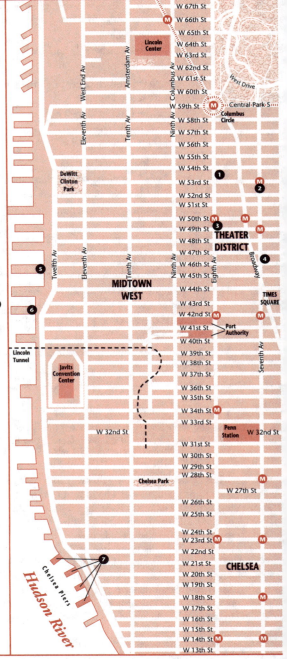

Subway stop **M**
Route of M5 Bus ········

NA-0363

organization's history while you cruise around to the complex's major highlights—the General Assembly Hall, the Security Council chamber, and other major meeting halls—and take in lots of internationally donated art and sculpture en route. A sobering exhibit of relics from the 1945 bombing of Nagasaki and Hiroshima reminds us of why the U.N. was formed in the first place.

The various U.N. agencies operate year-round, so there's always plenty of activity on the grounds. But things heat up when the General Assembly is in session, from the third Tuesday in September until sometime near the end of December. The Gift Center downstairs is great for finding unusual international handcrafts.

Where to Eat: The **Delegates Dining Room** (reservations required—call ☎ **212/963-7625** and be sure to bring a photo I.D.) is open to the public Monday to Friday 11:30am to 2:30pm. Even if it's not exactly packed with high-level diplomats, the river views are great. If that's too sedate for your kids, head away from the U.N. to the **Comfort Diner** on East 45th Street or the **Royal Canadian Pancake House** on Second Avenue (see chapter 8).

2 Best Views

Battery Park City Esplanade   All ages
On the Hudson River, between Chambers Street and Battery Place. Subway: A/C/E to World Trade Center.

The Statue of Liberty, Ellis Island, the Verrazano Bridge, and the Jersey City skyline punctuate the harbor views from this landscaped riverside walkway in a stunning residential/office complex at the lower edge of Manhattan. People loll on the benches reading the *Times,* coffee mugs in hand; dog owners walk frisky pets on leashes; in-line skaters and cyclists weave patiently through the crowd; and children hang on the inward-curved railings watching yachts cruise past on their way to the boat basin at the north end. No panhandlers, no T-shirt vendors, no ice-cream carts—it's a wonderfully civil scene, compared to tourist-thronged Battery Park just to the south.

✪ Brooklyn Heights Promenade   All ages
West of Columbia Heights, between Montague and Cranberry sts., Brooklyn Heights, Brooklyn. Subway: 2/3 to Clark St.; then follow Clark St. west to reach the Promenade.

The calm here is so palpable, you'd never know that the Brooklyn-Queens Expressway is rumbling underneath this cantilevered promenade. On one side are the back gardens of lovely Brooklyn Heights town houses; on the other, the East River and a drop-dead view of Lower Manhattan and the harbor. It faces west, which means that the view is especially terrific near sunset. Best of all if you're with little kids, there's a superb neighborhood playground at the south end, near Pierrepont Street. Combine this with a walk across the Brooklyn Bridge or a visit to the New York Transit Museum (below) and you've got a great day trip.

✪ Empire State Building   Ages 4 & up
Fifth Ave. and 34th St. ☎ **212/736-3100.** Admission $3 kids 11 and under, $6 adults. Daily 9:30am–midnight (ticket booth on concourse level, open to 11:20pm). Subway: B/D/F/N/R to 34th St.

To my mind, the Empire State Building is the classic skyscraper observation deck—after all, this is where Cary Grant and Deborah Kerr missed their rendezvous in *An Affair to Remember* and Tom Hanks and Meg Ryan made theirs in *Sleepless in Seattle.* And, of course, this is where Fay Wray and King Kong had their own kind of rendezvous. Shabby as much of the building has become, its art-deco lobby is still

The New Times Square

New York families used to strenuously avoid the Times Square area when out on the town with their kids, but now quite the opposite is true—so much so, in fact, that local curmudgeons bewail the clean-scrubbed look of the new district.

Where the Theater District once cohabited uneasily with porn shops and XXX cinemas, you'll now find **theme restaurants** (the existing Official All Star Cafe and Comedy Nation will be joined by David Copperfield's magic-themed restaurant in late 1998), **theme stores** (Disney and Warner Bros. face off across the intersection of Seventh Avenue and 42nd Street, while the Virgin Megastore sells an enormous range of recorded music at Broadway and 45th), and gloriously restored **theaters,** two of which—Disney's ornate New Amsterdam and the New Victory across the way on 42nd between Seventh and Eighth—specialize in family entertainment. A New York branch of **Madame Tussaud's** is also set to open eventually on 42nd Street, and there's now a big and flashy **Times Square Visitors Center** on Seventh Avenue between 46th and 47th streets. **MTV** has just opened a huge new studio on the mezzanine level of 1515 Broadway (between 44th and 45th streets, on the west side), with floor-to-ceiling windows and cameras trained on the passing crowd below. And of course, **David Letterman** still broadcasts from the Ed Sullivan Theater, up at 53rd and Broadway, with frequent segments filmed on the street outside.

But kids may not even need to go inside any particular attractions to enjoy the unabashed razzle-dazzle of Times Square, where immense advertising signs are designed to be as bright and as gimmicky as possible. My kids especially love the **Eight O'Clock Bean Coffee** sign, with steam rising from a giant cup of coffee, and the model of the **Concorde** that seems to have landed on a rooftop at 42nd and Seventh; the huge **video screen** that faces uptown from a skyscraper at 43rd between Broadway and Seventh is distracting to drivers but fascinating to kids. Find yourselves an advantageous street corner—or better yet, one of the pedestrian islands between Broadway and Seventh Avenue—stand back from the stream of pedestrians, and crane your necks upward. Don't be ashamed to gawk; we all do.

impressive and the location puts you squarely in the middle of Manhattan, with close-up views to all sides. The enclosed observation deck on the 86th floor (change elevators at the 80th floor) has outdoor promenades on all sides, and there's port-hole-type window viewing from the 102nd floor (1,250 feet up). Gift shops in the main lobby and on the 86th floor sell all kinds of New York City, Empire State Building, and (of course) King Kong knickknacks.

For information on the New York SkyRide attraction inside the Empire State, see "Best Rides," below.

Riverside Church Bell Tower   Ages 4 & up

120th St. and Riverside Dr. ☎ **212/870-6700.** Admission $2 adults, $1 kids/students. Mon–Sat 11am–3pm, Sun 12:30pm–4pm. Subway: 1/9 to 116th St. Bus: M5 to 120th St.

Though not nearly as high as its skyscraper competitors—only 355 feet in the air—this elegant church's bell tower has a glorious 360-degree view across and down Manhattan, not to mention jaw-dropping Hudson River vistas. It's rarely crowded, another decided plus, and the small observation deck puts you cheek to jowl with Gothic stone buttresses (sorry, no resident hunchback, but the mood is definitely dramatic). Only one thing to beware: An immense 74-bell carillon will be right beneath you, and it rings forth every 60 minutes on the hour, which can be unsettling to youngsters.

Top of the World/World Trade Center Observation Deck   Ages 4 & up
2 World Trade Center (bounded by West, Vesey, Liberty, & Church sts.). ☎ **212/323-2340.** Admission $6 kids 6–12, $12 adults, $9 seniors; 5 and under free. Sept–May daily 9:30am–9:30pm; June–Aug daily 9:30am–11:30pm. Subway: A/C/E to Chambers St.; 1/9 or N/R to Cortlandt St.

It may not be the world's tallest building anymore, but it's still New York's tallest and plenty high enough (1,377 feet) to produce a thrill. Because the World Trade Center is at the tip of Manhattan island, the views here include a sweeping vista of the harbor and the ocean beyond; the nighttime perspective is a tapestry of twinkling street lights to the north. Whiz upward in a superspeed elevator to the 107th-floor observation deck, with windows on all four sides, powerful binoculars for zooming in on details, and computer consoles for identifying the sights you're seeing. In good weather, the 110th-floor open-air rooftop deck is opened, for those who are really into heights. Admission also includes a simulated helicopter ride over New York City and a nightly laser show that'll beam visitors' messages out into space. Awesome!

3 Best Rides

Central Park Carousel   All ages
In Central Park, midpark between 64th and 65th sts. ☎ 212/879-0244. Ride 90¢. Daily 10am–5pm (to 6:30pm in summer). Subway: 1/9 to 66th St.; N/R to Fifth Ave.

The elaborate carving that graces this 1908 merry-go-round's wooden horses may be lost on your kids. No matter—it's a big, fast classic carousel with a vintage calliope (playing tunes of a decidedly different vintage, like "Rainy Days and Mondays"). The 4-minute ride is a pleasant way to top off a Central Park expedition, considering you're not far from either the zoo or the Wollman Rink. (For more on Central Park, see chapter 5.) Younger, skittish kids may want to find one of the horses that doesn't go up and down or opt for one of the gilded swan cars.

✪ The Magic Bus (M5 city bus)   All ages
Recommended starting point: 125th St. and Riverside Dr. Fare $1.50, exact change, Metro-Card, or token.

It's an ordinary city bus route, but it happens to rumble past a host of sights you'd like to see in its 90-minute loop, and if you happen to board the bus helmed by veteran driver Pee Wee Rodriguez, you'll even get some lively narration over the PA. You can board anywhere along the route, which is marked with a dotted line on the three city maps in this chapter.

I recommend catching the bus at 125th and Riverside, where you'll first wheel past **Grant's Tomb** (122nd Street) and gleaming neo-Gothic **Riverside Church** with its carillon bell tower (120th Street). You'll proceed down handsome residential Riverside Drive (Riverside Park and the Hudson lie out the right-side window) to 72nd Street, where the route jogs east to Broadway, then south past **Lincoln Center.** At Columbus Circle, it turns east and goes across 59th Street—also called Central Park South, since the park lies on your left—to the Plaza, where the **Plaza Hotel** faces **FAO Schwarz** at 58th Street. Down Fifth Avenue you'll go, past **Tiffany's** (on your left on the south side of 57th Street), **St. Patrick's Cathedral** (on your left at 51st Street), **Rockefeller Center** (on your right from 51st to 48th streets), the main research library of the **New York Public Library** with its famous stone lions Patience and Fortitude (on the right from 42nd to 40th streets), the **Empire State Building** (on the right at 34th Street), the narrow wedge-shaped **Flatiron Building** (on the left at 23rd Street), to the white triumphal arch of **Washington Square** (facing the foot of Fifth Avenue where 6th Street should cut through). After circling the square, you'll go back north up Sixth Avenue, which from 16th to 23rd streets takes you past **Ladies' Mile,** the late 19th-century department store district (many of the old stores have been recently restored for new tenants); the Herald Square shopping intersection where **Macy's** department store presides at 34th Street; **Bryant Park** (on your right from 40th to 42nd streets), the New York Public Library's backyard, which was the site of a World's Fair in 1853; more of Rockefeller Center, including **Radio City Music Hall** (on your right at 50th Street); and back to 59th Street to retrace the route back north, as far as 178th Street.

New York SkyRide   Ages 6 & up

In the Empire State Building, Fifth Ave. at 34th St. ☎ **212/279-9777.** Admission $9.50 kids 4–11/seniors, $11.50 adults. Daily 10am–10pm. Subway: B/D/F/N/R to 34th St.

For roller-coaster daredevils, this 7-minute simulation may seem tame, but I wouldn't take my 5-year-old on it. "Passengers" are seated on a large platform that begins to tilt and jolt and career wildly while a big screen shows you "crashing" your way around New York landmarks, with lots of ear-splitting recorded sound effects. Count on a long line, up to 30 minutes at times. For goofy, kitschy fun, it's worth considering if the prices don't put you off.

Roosevelt Island Tram   All ages

Manhattan terminus: Second Ave. and 60th St. Fare $1.50. Subway: 4/5/6 to 59th St.

A pair of big red cable cars swing over the East River alongside the 59th Street/Queensboro Bridge to Roosevelt Island. Though most of the trip is actually over an unglamorous wedge of East Side real estate, it does go over the river, and you're high up enough to get good views of Manhattan up and down. There are few seats—only a narrow hard bench at either end of a car that holds 30 or so—so get there early to grab a seat by the front windows.

Once you're on Roosevelt Island, site of a former smallpox hospital, you can turn right around and ride back—or you can take a ride on the red shuttle bus (fare 25¢) to loop around this island housing development. It's all forgettable modern apartment blocks, but there's lots of riverside green space and little playgrounds are tucked away everywhere. The village's main street looks like something out of the 1960s British TV series *The Prisoner*—a curved main street cutting between characterless shopfronts (one of everything: post office, library, church, deli, Chinese restaurant, bank, school). It has a middle-class, racially mixed population, and the whole place is wheelchair accessible—it would be a little utopia if only the architecture weren't so grim. Nevertheless, it's a quick, cheap trip to a place where kids can run around outside and play—and getting there on the cable car is more than half the fun.

✪ Staten Island Ferry   All ages

Departing from South Ferry in Battery Park. ☎ **718/727-2508.** Passengers free, cars $3. Subway: 1/9 to South Ferry.

Walk right on at the South Ferry Terminal and you can chug across New York Harbor, past the Statue of Liberty, to Staten Island, where you walk around the

Downtown Attractions

Battery Park City Esplanade **6**
Brooklyn Bridge **19**
Brooklyn Heights
   Promenade **28**
Castle Clinton
   National Monument **7**
Children's Museum of the Arts **14**
City Hall **18**
Columbus Park **17**
Ellis Island/
   Statue of Liberty ferry **8**
Federal Hall
   National Monument **23**
Forbes Magazine Galleries **9**
Guggenheim Museum SoHo **13**
Jefferson Market **1**
Lower East Side Ecology Center **11**
Lower East Side
   Tenement Museum **15**
Merchant's House Museum **12**
Museum of Chinese in
   the Americas **16**
National Museum of the
   American Indian **25**
New York City Fire Museum **3**
New York Unearthed **26**
Old U.S. Custom House **25**
St. Luke's-in-the-Fields **2**
St. Mark's-in-the-Bowery **10**
Seaport Liberty Cruises **22**
South Street Seaport Museum **21**
Staten Island ferry **27**
Statue of Liberty/
   Ellis Island ferry **8**
Top of the World **4**
Trinity Church **24**
Woolworth Building **20**
World Financial Center **5**
World Trade Center **4**

Subway stop **M**

Route of M5 Bus ·········

Route of Downtown ― ―
   Loop Shuttle Bus

NA-0364

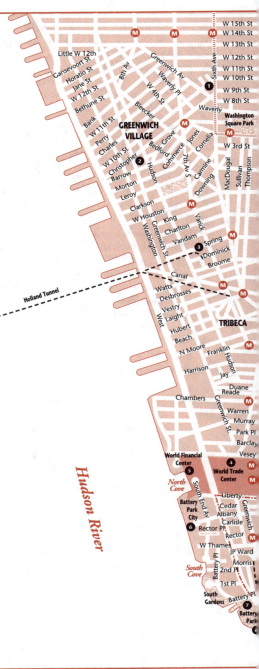

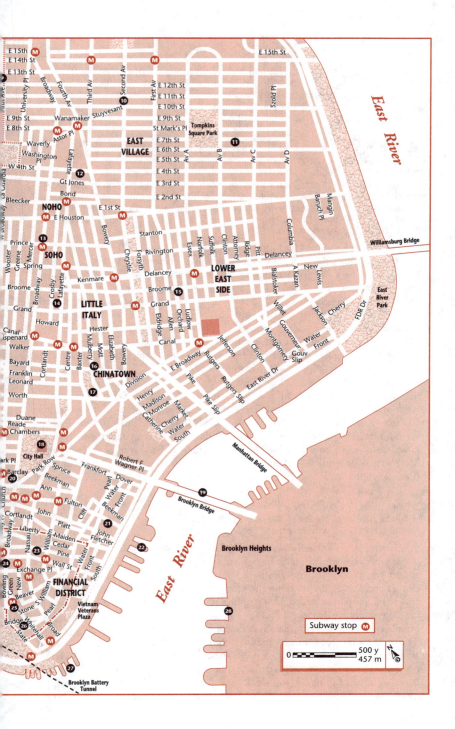

E 15th St
E 14th St M
E 13th St
E 15th St
E 15th St

La Guardia Pl
University Pl
Broadway
Fourth Av
Third Av
Second Av
First Av
Stuyvesant
E 12th St
E 11th St
E 10th St
E 9th St
St Mark's Pl
E 8th St
E 7th St
E 6th St
E 5th St
E 4th St
E 3rd St
E 2nd St

Szold Pl

M 10

East River

Wanamaker
Astor Pl M
Waverly
Washington Pl
W 4th St

Lafayette

EAST VILLAGE

Tompkins Square Park

Av B
Av A
Av C
Av D

M 11

Mangin
Baruch Pl

M 12
Gt Jones
Bond
Bleecker

NOHO
M
E Houston

E 1st St
Bowery

Stanton
Columbia

Williamsburg Bridge

Wooster
Greene
Mercer
Prince
Spring
M 13
SOHO

Broadway
Crosby
Lafayette
Kenmare
Forsyth
Chrystie

Rivington
Delancey

Norfolk
Essex
Suffolk
Clinton
Attorney
Ridge
Pitt
Delancey

Bialstoker
A Kazan
New
Lewis

East River Park

Broome
Grand
M 14
LITTLE ITALY

Howard
Hester

Broome
Grand M 15
Eldridge
Allen

Ludlow
Orchard

LOWER EAST SIDE

Willet
Gouverneur
Jackson
Cherry

FDR Dr

Canal
Ispenard M
Walker

Centre
Baxter
Mulberry
Mott
Elizabeth
Bowery

Canal

Montgomery
Clinton
Water
Front
Gouv Slip

Bayard
Franklin
Leonard
Worth

M 16
CHINATOWN
M 17

Division
E Broadway
Rutgers
Jefferson

East River Dr
Rutgers Slip

Duane
Reade
Chambers M

Henry
Madison
Monroe

Pike
Market

Pike Slip

Robert F Wagner Pl

Manhattan Bridge

Park Pl
City Hall
M 18
M
Park Row
Spruce
Frankfort

Catherine
Cherry
Water
South

Barclay
M 20
Beekman
Ann
M Fulton

Pearl
Water
Dover
Front
Beekman

Brooklyn Bridge
M 19

Cortlandt
John
Platt
M 21
John
Fletcher

Cliff

East River

Broadway
Liberty
Nassau
M 23
Maiden
Cedar
Pine

William
Water
Front
M 22

Brooklyn Heights

M 24
Exchange Pl
Wall St
South

Brooklyn

Bowling Green
New
Beaver

FINANCIAL DISTRICT
Stone
S William
Vietnam Veterans Plaza

M 25
Bridge
Whitehall
State
M 26
Pearl
Broad

M
M 27
Brooklyn Battery Tunnel

M 28

Subway stop M

0 ⊢━━━┫ 500 y
457 m

N

57

barriers and get on again for the return ride. The whole round-trip should take about an hour. Most of the ferry decks are now glassed in, alas, but the views are still great. A friend of mine tells me that his mother used to corral the kids onto the ferry on hot summer nights to sleep when their un-air-conditioned apartment got too stifling hot; that's the kind of wonderfully populist institution the Staten Island Ferry is in the hearts of New Yorkers.

4 More Manhattan Museums

The Cloisters   All ages
In Fort Tryon Park at 193rd St. and Fort Washington Ave. ☎ **212/923-3700.** Suggested donation (includes same-day admission to the Metropolitan Museum of Art, above) $8 adults, $4 students/seniors; kids 11 and under free. Mar–Oct Tues–Sun 9:30am–5:15pm; Nov–Feb Tues–Sun 9:30am–4:45pm. Closed New Year's Day, Thanksgiving, Christmas. Subway: A to 190th St. Bus: M4 to the end of line.

Of course your kids aren't into medieval art—that's not the point. For families, the point of the Cloisters, the Metropolitan's beautiful medieval art annex, is the sheer weirdness of it—a conglomeration of chapels and courtyards and refectories lifted from European convents and monasteries, brought in packing crates to America, and reconstructed here on a blufftop site in Fort Tryon Park. Wander from room to room, soaking up the time-stands-still atmosphere; go out on the terrace for splendid views of the Hudson River and the New Jersey Palisades, and poke around the monks' herb garden. Talk with your kids about unicorns before you go—there's one fascinating gallery devoted to a series of tapestries depicting a unicorn hunt (a medieval version of an adventure comic strip?).

It's a long trek up here, considering that children may not want to spend more than an hour in the museum, but they might actually enjoy the bus ride, which won't take forever if you're coming from the Upper West Side (combine the Cloisters with visits to St. John the Divine and Riverside Church for a full day of Gothic-ness). If you're doing this in the same day as the Metropolitan (which makes sense, since your admission covers both sites) compare what you see up here to the Met's first-floor medieval galleries, right next to the arms and armor department that many kids love.

Children's Museum of the Arts   Ages 10 & under
182 Lafayette St. (between Broome and Grand sts.). ☎ **212/941-9198.** Admission $4 Wed–Fri, $5 Sat–Sun; kids under 18 months free. Wed–Sun noon–5pm; closed Mon–Tues except for school holidays. Subway: 6 to Spring St.

Smaller than the Children's Museum of Manhattan (above), this is a good alternative if you're Downtown, with lots of hands-on stuff for kids. Various art projects are set up; youngsters are encouraged to explore rhythm instruments; dress-up clothes and a stage invite young thespians to create their own theater. There are a couple of computers loaded with graphics programs that my son enjoyed, though even on a noncrowded day he had to cope with a waiting line for the PC. A "ball pond" lets kids work off some physical energy; there's also a small infant play area. This is less a museum than an indoor playground with an arts emphasis, and the afternoon we went it was full of neighborhood preschoolers who acted like they owned the place and whose baby-sitters were too busy gossiping in a corner to supervise them. I think my son would've had a blast if he'd come with a playmate, though—next time we'll know. On rainy or cold weekends it's crowded to the rafters, so be warned.

Cooper-Hewitt National Design Museum   Ages 3 & up

2 E. 91st St. (at Fifth Ave.). ☎ **212/849-8300** or 212/849-8400. Admission $5 adults, $3 students/seniors; kids 11 and under free. Tues 10am–9pm, Wed–Sat 10am–5pm, Sun noon–5pm. Free Tues 5–9pm. Closed major holidays. Subway: 4/5/6 to 86th St.

Check to see what exhibit is currently running at this Smithsonian branch devoted to design and decorative arts: A surprising number of them appeal to kids (clothing, furniture, advertising posters), and the accompanying material is usually so lucid that even a young kid can grasp what's interesting about the displays. What's more, it gives you a chance to get inside industrial tycoon Andrew Carnegie's surprisingly homey neo-Georgian mansion—point out to your kids how low the doorways are, since Carnegie, a short man, wanted the house built to *his* scale. My older son fell in love with the elegant leaded-glass conservatory; there's a nice garden out back and a super gift shop (Carnegie's old music room—look at the decorative plasterwork).

Forbes Magazine Galleries   All ages

62 Fifth Ave. (at 12th St.). ☎ **212/206-5548.** Free admission. Tues–Wed and Fri–Sat 10am–4pm. Closed major holidays. Subway: 4/5/6 or N/R to 14th St./Union Square.

An obsessive collector, publishing magnate Malcolm Forbes had enough money to turn his obsessions into a strange and wonderful little museum. Basically, he collected six things: toy boats, toy soldiers, Monopoly games, medals and trophies, presidential papers, and lavishly bejeweled Fabergé eggs. Okay, younger kids may not care about the presidential papers, but that leaves plenty kids *do* love. This labyrinth of small galleries won't tax youngsters' attention spans, though they should be warned ahead that this is a sedate don't-touch kind of place. (No strollers permitted inside, either.) The display windows aren't always low enough for small children, so expect to do a lot of lifting. Don't expect your kids to linger as long as you may wish over the minutiae of the collection—remember, Forbes was a successful and influential grown-up when he collected this stuff, with a mere adult's eye to what made something valuable. But there's still enough here to make kids press their noses against the glass for a good half an hour or so, more if they're older.

Guggenheim Museum   Ages 5 & up

1071 Fifth Ave. (at 89th St.). ☎ **212/423-3500.** Admission $12 adults, $7 students; kids 12 and under free. Fri evenings pay what you wish. Sun–Wed 10am–6pm, Fri–Sat 10am–8pm. Subway: 4/5/6 to 86th St.

The Guggenheim's rotating exhibits of 20th-century art may or may not appeal to your kids—Edward Hopper maybe yes, Mark Rothko maybe no. No matter. The main reason for including this museum in your NYC itinerary is the museum building itself: Frank Lloyd Wright's glorious, streamlined, totally wacked-out inverted spiral, which displays the art along one long ramp coiling down around a huge central atrium. I mean, can you imagine doing the Guggenheim on a *skateboard?* Since kids get in for free, it may be worthwhile to pay the adult admission just so you can enjoy this visionary interior for half an hour. In any case, the side galleries display some artworks kids might enjoy, by such masters as Degas, Cézanne, and Picasso.

Guggenheim Museum SoHo   Ages 4 & up

575 Broadway (at Prince St.). ☎ **212/423-3500.** Suggested donation $8 adults, $5 students; kids under 12 free. Wed–Sun 11am–6pm (Sat to 8pm). Subway: N/R to Prince St.; 6 to Spring St.

A 1996 renovation turned this Downtown museum into a showplace for video art and other new media projects. Whether or not you think this is art, your kids probably will. A bank of synchronized TV monitors greets you in the lobby; the galleries beyond feature rotating exhibits of ultra-cool cutting-edge stuff. Kids who don't get the point of Rembrandt and Renoir may plug in happily.

✪ Intrepid Sea-Air-Space Museum   Ages 3 & up

At Pier 86, the Hudson River at the foot of W. 46th St. ☎ **212/245-0072.** Admission $1 kids 2–5, $5 kids 6–11, $7.50 kids 12–17, $10 adults; 5 and under free; $1 for each additional under 6. Daily 10am–5pm (to 6pm on summer weekends). Closed Mon–Tues Oct–Apr. Bus: M42 westbound (to the last stop) or M50 (stops directly in front of the museum).

You don't have to be a fan of the military to be fascinated by this rambling museum set on a disused aircraft carrier. It boasts of being the world's largest naval museum, but there's less exhibit space than you'd imagine in the cavernous hangar of the *Intrepid* (many areas of the ship remain off-limits—don't expect a re-creation of life on board a carrier). Still, it covers all the bases: audiovisual displays, uniforms, weapons, equipment, vintage aircraft, and memorabilia from all branches of the navy, including a handful of copters and small planes and jets up on the landing deck, some of which you can climb up into. The fighter jet simulator is a big draw for boys of a certain age; you can also prowl around a submarine and a Vietnam-era destroyer. There are special free Saturday workshops once a month.

Not a government-funded museum, the *Intrepid* has a clear patriotic bias to all its exhibits, which could be annoying but instead comes across as refreshingly honest and un-p.c. From time to time, visiting aircraft and sea vessels land here and you can tour them; during Fleet Week at the end of May, it's a beehive of activity. Call for an updated schedule of visiting ships.

Lower East Side Tenement Museum   Ages 5 & up

90 Orchard St. (at Broome St.). ☎ **212/431-0233.** Admission: Gallery, free; tenement tour $8 adults, $6 seniors/students/children; both tenement tours, $14 adults, $10 students/seniors/children; tenement tour plus walking tour, $12 adults, $10 seniors/students/children; both tours plus walking tour, $18 adults, $14 students/seniors/children. Gallery Tues–Fri noon–5pm, Sat–Sun 11am–5pm. Tenement tours Tues–Fri at 1, 2, and 3pm, Sat–Sun 11am–4:15pm; walking tours Sat–Sun at 1:30 and 2:30pm. Subway: B/D/Q to Grand St., J/M/2 to Essex St.

A narrow 1863 tenement building has been converted into this thoughtful small museum that picks up the immigrant story where Ellis Island leaves off—in the poor neighborhoods where the new arrivals landed. Once you've seen these bare, cramped living quarters, all too authentically furnished, your kids may never fight again over sharing a bedroom. (It's the perfect antidote to all those ornate period rooms at the Metropolitan Museum.) Though the gallery has some interesting artifacts and bits of social history, the tours are the heart of the experience, so schedule your visit to include one. The museum recommends the interactive tour of the Confino apartment (ca. 1916) for families; it's held only on weekends at noon, 1, and 3pm. Tours are limited to 15 people, so reserve slots in advance to avoid disappointment, especially for Sunday tours. Weekend walking tours widen the scope to include the whole neighborhood—they're wonderful if your kids are old enough to keep up with the pace.

Museum of American Folk Art   All ages

2 Lincoln Sq. (between 65th and 66th sts.). ☎ **212/595-9533.** www.folkartmuse.org. Free admission; $1 materials fee for children's workshops. Tues–Sun 11:30am–7:30pm. Closed legal holidays. Subway: 1/9 to 66th St.

For whatever reason, even young kids get the point of folk art—in fact, young kids sometimes enjoy this stuff more than older kids who think they know what "good" art is. The shows here change continually, but every time we've ventured inside, my children have been charmed by the paintings and sculptures and collages, all by untutored artists, past and present—quilts, weathervanes, bottle-cap sculptures, an immense canvas covered with obsessively tiny handwriting, whatever. It's not an overwhelming museum; you can just walk in, browse around for 20 minutes, and walk out. The excellent gift shop (nearly as large as the museum itself) sells many handmade items, including a fairly interesting selection of toys you don't see everywhere else. A much larger space is slated to open at 45–47 W. 53rd St. in spring 2000.

Museum of Chinese in the Americas   Ages 5 & up
70 Mulberry St. (at Bayard St.). ☎ **212/619-4785.** Admission $3 adults, $1 students/seniors; kids 11 and under free. Tues–Sat noon–5pm. Subway: N/R/6 to Canal St.

Nestled in the atmospheric heart of Chinatown, this museum delves into a huge collection of photographs and artifacts—tiny shoes for a Chinese woman's bound feet, tin tea canisters, brocaded Chinese opera costumes, the heavy irons used in a laundry—to document, often poignantly, the experience of Chinese immigrants. The gallery itself is stunning, with its 15 angled translucent walls creating the illusion of being inside a giant-sized Chinese lantern. Even if it holds your kids' attention for only 20 minutes, it'll give them a perspective on a very different side of New York.

✪ Museum of Modern Art (MoMA)   All ages
11 W. 53rd St. (between Fifth and Sixth aves.). ☎ **212/708-9400.** www.moma.org. Admission (includes movie admission) $9.50 adults, $6.50 students; kids 15 and under free; Fri 4:30–8:30pm pay what you wish. Thurs–Tues 10:30am–6pm (to 8:30pm Fri). Closed Thanksgiving and Christmas. Subway: E/F to Fifth Ave.

If young kids don't get the point of modern art, it's not the fault of this world-class museum in Midtown: Saturday activities here include special tours for 4-year-olds, gallery talks for ages 5 to 10, interactive activity workshops for the entire family, and programs of classic short films chosen for a family audience. The "modern" in the museum's name no longer means cutting edge, but its large bright galleries do provide a retrospective of the best in 20th-century art, from Picasso to Pollock, from Rodin to Rothko.

The very young may be blissfully happy here because they don't care whether a painting looks like anything; preschoolers who've just learned how to make a tree look like a tree may be baffled by a canvas covered with mere stripes or squares or spatters of paint—steer them instead toward the bright pop art image of Andy Warhol's Marilyn Monroe portrait, the moody intensity of van Gogh's *Starry Night,* or the surreal images by Magritte or Dalí. While the painting galleries dominate the MoMA, don't overlook the photography, architecture, and design exhibits, which kids may actually prefer. And don't miss the splendid sculpture garden, where kids can stretch their legs while parents recline on a bench and stare happily at masterpieces.

✪ Museum of Television and Radio   Ages 5 & up
25 W. 52nd St. (between Fifth & Sixth aves.). ☎ **212/621-6600.** Admission $3 kids 12 and under, $6 adults, $4 students. Tues–Sun noon–6pm (to 8pm Thurs). Subway: E/F to Fifth Ave. (53rd St.).

In this sleek Midtown museum (with a sister branch in L.A.), junior couch potatoes can gorge on all kinds of broadcast media, from vintage commercials to 1960s sitcoms to TV coverage of the first moon walk. The catch: You've got to get here early in the day to make a reservation to use the library, where you can search the database on a Mac, then call up a program on an individual console with headphones. Failing that, you can stop by the fifth-floor radio listening room to sample sound bites from timely preselected programs or attend any of several screenings running frequently in a number of cushy small theaters. Weekends are the best time for kids, when there are hands-on workshops in the morning and uncrowded screenings of top international children's TV shows in the afternoon; the staff is genuinely friendly to youngsters. If your child's hooked on Nick at Nite, plan for several hours of browsing around.

Museum of the City of New York   Ages 3 & up

1220 Fifth Ave. (at 103rd St.). ☎ **212/534-1672.** www.mcny.org. Suggested admission $4 kids/students/seniors, $5 adults, $10 families. Wed–Sat 10am–5pm, Sun noon–5pm. Subway: 6 to 103rd St. Bus: M1/M2/M3/M4.

Don't drag your kids uptown just to see this museum, but if you're on Museum Mile already, it's worth stopping in for an hour or so (and skip across the street to Central Park's lovely **Conservatory Garden** afterward—see "Gardens," later in this chapter). The biggest draw for kids is the spectacular dollhouse exhibit in the **Toys Gallery,** though some kids I know like to come here just to parade up and down the gorgeous staircase in the entrance hall. My younger son also likes the **Marine Gallery,** tricked out to look like a little wharf, with ship models all around, a few weathered figureheads from old sailing ships, and a gigantic statue of Robert Fulton. The six period alcoves on the second floor are "kinda cool" for older kids, and theater lovers will want to swing through the Broadway exhibit, displaying posters and mementoes from the Great White Way (including a costume Barbra Streisand wore in *Funny Girl*). My son tells me this is all boring girl stuff, though.

National Museum of the American Indian   Ages 5 & up

1 Bowling Green, beside Battery Park. ☎ **212/668-6624.** Free admission. Daily 10am–5pm (to 8pm Thurs). Closed Christmas. Subway: 4/5 to Bowling Green; N/R to Whitehall St.; 1/9 to South Ferry.

A branch of the Smithsonian, this museum enjoys a fabulous setting in the ornate 1907 U.S. Customs House, a beaux arts gem that was a principal site in the movie *Ghostbusters II*. To enter the exhibition galleries, you pass through the awesome Great Rotunda—don't miss looking up at the painted dome. The museum has vast holdings, only a small portion of which are on display (another branch is set to open on the Mall in Washington, D.C., in 2002), but it's presented in such a hushed, dignified, reverential way it doesn't hold kids' attention for long. Still, it's free and it's right across the park from the Statue of Liberty ferry, so wend your way through the labyrinth of small rooms looking for stuff that isn't over your children's head—a hanging bison hide they can stroke or the round glass case filled with hundreds of moccasins large and small. My kindergartener, who wouldn't know a Choctaw from a Cherokee, lingered in the two adjacent replica rooms from a contemporary reservation—one a family's living room, the other a schoolroom—and marveled over the fact that Indian kids play with Gumbys and watch TV just like he does. That cultural insight in itself was reason enough to come here.

✪ New York City Fire Museum   Ages 3 & up

278 Spring St. (between Varick & Hudson sts.). ☎ **212/691-1303.** Suggested admission $1 kids 11 and under, $4 adults, $2 students/seniors. Tues–Sun 10am–4pm. Subway: 1/9 to Houston St.; C/E to Spring St.

Though small, this two-story museum in a converted firehouse is worth the money if your kids are as much into firetrucks as my son is. Okay, nobody else is *that* much into fire trucks, but a lot of kids do love them and this place is full of antique fire engines, including several horse-drawn ones. The horses aren't on display, unfortunately, but there's a stuffed fire dog named Nig who used to be the mascot of one Brooklyn firehouse. A lot of the museum is most interesting to adults patient enough to pore over the mementoes of 19th-century firefighting, but there are enough bells, alarms, pickaxes, and nozzles to hold young interest for 45 minutes or so. Our favorite room is a little back gallery on the first floor displaying loads of color snapshots from firehouses all over the five boroughs and embroidered badges from fire companies all over the world (we like the one from Maui, with a volcano on it, and the one from Houston, with the motto "You Light 'Em, We Fight 'Em").

New York Historical Society   Ages 4 & up

2 W. 77th St. at Central Park West. ☎ **212/873-3400.** Suggested donation $5 adults, $3 students/seniors; 11 and under free. Tues–Sun 11am–5pm. Subway: B/C to 79th St.

While the general collection here isn't big on the fun factor, a new interactive exhibit called Kid City should pique children's interests. Re-created from old photographs in the society's exhaustive collection, Kid City presents a New York neighborhood from 100 years ago, full household objects and toys and the sorts of things kids notice about their world. A good three-dimensional, hands-on history lesson.

New York Public Library   Ages 6 & up

Fifth Ave. at 41st St. ☎ **212/930-0800.** Free admission. Mon and Thurs–Sat 10am–6pm, Tues–Wed 11am–7:30pm. Subway: B/D/F/4/5/6 to 42nd St.; 7 to Fifth Ave.

Though most little kids fall in love with the regal pair of lions—Patience and Fortitude—poised beside the front steps, the exhibits mounted inside the New York Public Library are usually of interest to older kids only. (But you never know—there was an exhibit on garbage in 1995 that my boys thought was totally cool.) The library does have an extraordinary collection of first editions, manuscripts, letters, prints, maps, and other treasures on paper and often puts together fascinating shows, but whether or not your youngster will be intrigued all depends on the theme. Otherwise, pop in for a few minutes just to gape at the beaux arts architecture, from the dignified marble to the extraordinary Main Reading Room, where anyone can join the scholars and writers at endless ranks of tables poring over research materials from the NYPL's famous stacks. Note that behind the library is **Bryant Park.**

The NYPL's **Donnell Branch,** 20 W. 53rd St., between Fifth and Sixth avenues, may be worth a stop too, to see the original Winnie-the-Pooh animals displayed in the Central Children's room (open Monday to Saturday noon to 5:30pm, to 8pm Thursday, early opening at 9:30am Tuesday).

New York Unearthed   Ages 8 & up

17 State St. at Battery Park (entrance on Pearl St. between Whitehall and State sts.). ☎ **212/ 748-8628.** Free admission. Mon–Sat noon–6pm. Closed Sat Christmas–Easter. Subway: 4/5 to Bowling Green; N/R to Whitehall St.; 1/9 to South Ferry.

A branch of the South Street Seaport Museum (above), this gallery shows off all sorts of stuff that got dug up when construction crews excavated Manhattan sites in preparation for building skyscrapers. It's a tangible history of all the layers of civilization that have occupied this island, from early Native American flint tools to Dutch trade goods to 20th-century junk—which means that only school kids will get the point. (Exhibits are placed too high for younger kids anyway.) But gazing at all this random detritus of human lives can have its own weird fascination, and the glass-enclosed pit where you can watch real archaeologists at work gives the place a proper field-trip aura. It makes a logical combination with the nearby National Museum of the American Indian (above); while you're here, young Indiana Joneses may want to go 2 blocks up Pearl Street to investigate the archaeological excavations of an old Dutch city hall under a transparent panel in the sidewalk, beside the office building at 85 Broad St.

Pierpont Morgan Library   Ages 8 & up

29 E. 36th St. (between Madison & Park aves.). ☎ **212/685-0008.** Admission $6 adults, $4 students/seniors; 11 and under free. Tues–Fri 10:30am–5pm, Sat 10:30am–6pm, Sun noon–6pm. Subway: 6 to 33rd St.

The Morgan Library's refined gallery space exhibits prints and drawings, which may or may not be of interest to kids—a recent show about Lewis Carroll and *Alice in Wonderland* was just the ticket, but that isn't always the case. What kids will appreciate is the wing J. P. Morgan actually used as a library, especially his elegant wood-paneled study.

Police Academy Museum   Ages 6 & up

235 E. 20th St. (between Second & Third aves.). ☎ **212/477-9753.** Free admission. By appointment only, Mon–Fri 9am–3pm. Subway: 6 to 23rd St.

If your kid's into cops and robbers, this exhaustive collection of police memorabilia—attached to the NYPD's police academy—should be mesmerizing. Confiscated weapons, counterfeit money, police uniforms and badges and radios and alarms and nightsticks . . . the mind boggles. Perhaps the coolest item on display is Al Capone's machine gun; one of the weirder exhibits shows Pretty Boy Floyd's efforts to change his fingerprints (which didn't work). The museum is probably suited better for older kids, especially since the display style is unsensational and low-tech, requiring a fair amount of reading.

5 Classic Lobbies to Look Into

MIDTOWN

UP FIFTH AVENUE   Start at the biggie: The **Empire State Building,** 34th Street and Fifth Avenue, whose streamlined 1931 interior includes murals of the Seven Wonders of the World. Then head up Fifth Avenue to the **New York Public Library** at 40th Street, where you can walk up the steps between the famous lions (Patience and Fortitude) and peek into the ornate lobby, eternally cool in white marble. The **Fred E. French Building,** Fifth Avenue at 45th Street, has a wonderfully Byzantine lobby with loads of mosaics. Up Fifth Avenue in Rockefeller Center, between 49th and 50th streets, **30 Rockefeller Plaza**—formerly the RCA Building, now the General Electric Building, still home to the NBC TV network—has another awesome deco lobby, sheathed in dark marble; check out the ceiling mural inside the Rockefeller Plaza entrance, a very pro-labor statement that must have galled the Rockefellers when they first saw it. Continue up Fifth to glitzy modern **Trump Tower,** between 56th and 57th streets, full of rosy marble, shiny brass, greenery, and a waterfall.

ACROSS 42ND STREET   Start in the **Lincoln Building,** 60 E. 42nd St., between Madison and Park avenues, whose imposing Depression-era lobby holds a replica of the Daniel Chester French statue of Lincoln that occupies the Lincoln Memorial in Washington, D.C. Then pop into **Grand Central Terminal** on the north side of 42nd Street at Park Avenue, which, though technically not a lobby, has a gloriously restored main room that'll knock your socks off. Gaze up at the constellations on the soaring ceiling. Snuggled next to Grand Central Terminal, the **Graybar Building,** Lexington Avenue at 43rd Street, has a fairly typical 1930s deco lobby. But step out to look at the awning built over the Lexington Avenue entrance

New York Movie Sites

Fans of the 1988 hit *Big* will no doubt want to check out **FAO Schwarz,** the mega–toy store at 58th Street and Fifth Avenue where Tom Hanks tap-danced on a giant keyboard in the movie's signature scene. *Home Alone 2,* the sequel to Macaulay Culkin's first big hit, takes place in New York; Kevin stays at the **Plaza Hotel,** Fifth Avenue and 59th Street, conveniently across from Central Park— the robbers (played by Joe Pesci and Daniel Stern) spot him ice-skating at the park's **Wollman Rink.** Kevin also hangs out at **Rockefeller Plaza** to gape at the giant Christmas tree and has a heart-to-heart with the Pigeon Lady who lives in the attic of **Carnegie Hall,** Seventh Avenue at 57th Street. The climax is set in a fictitious Upper West Side brownstone on West 95th Street between Central Park West and Columbus Avenue.

The 1984 comedy *Splash,* starring Tom Hanks and Darryl Hannah, features the **Statue of Liberty,** in New York Harbor, where Hannah's mermaid first comes ashore; after Hanks takes her to his bachelor apartment in the **Tudor City complex** (east of Second Avenue between 41st and 43rd streets), she makes her way to **Bloomingdale's,** 59th Street and Lexington Avenue, where a session in front of a bank of TVs quickly teaches her to speak the language of dry land. Later, Hanks and his brother, played by John Candy, smuggle the mermaid away from scientists at the **American Museum of Natural History,** on Central Park West at 79th Street.

The 1978 *Superman,* starring Christopher Reeve and Margot Kidder, features the **Daily News Building,** 220 E. 42nd St., as the headquarters of the *Daily Planet.* Superman skims down the long sleek facade of the skyscraper at **9 W. 57th St.** to catch a falling child. Lex Luthor has his subterranean lair underneath **Grand Central Terminal,** 42nd Street and Park Avenue, and Lois Lane lives in the penthouse of **240 Central Park South,** just east of Columbus Circle—the outside terrace being handy for those fly-in dates with Superman.

The classic 1947 Christmas movie *Miracle on 34th Street* kicks off with the Macy's Thanksgiving Day Parade, as Maureen O'Hara fires a drunken parade Santa and hires Kris Kringle on **West 81st Street,** just off Central Park West. O'Hara's daughter, played by young Natalie Wood, watches the parade from their apartment window in an unspecified building along Central Park West. At the **Macy's** department store in Midtown, 34th Street and Broadway, Kringle revolutionizes retailing by sending families across the street to the now-defunct Gimbel's store at 33rd and Broadway (where the Manhattan Mall is today) if Macy's didn't have the right toys. The main **U.S. Post Office** at Eighth Avenue between 31st and 33rd streets is where sacks of mail addressed to Santa Claus were collected and delivered to Kringle downtown at the **New York County Courthouse,** 60 Centre St., happily putting an end to his insanity trial.

Older kids may have seen that quintessential Manhattan movie *Breakfast at Tiffany's,* the 1961 charmer starring Audrey Hepburn and George Peppard. Prominently featured is **Tiffany & Co.,** the elegant jewelry store at Fifth Avenue and 57th Street; the Upper East Side town house where Hepburn's Holly Golightly lives is at **171 E. 71st Street** (look for the distinctive green-striped awning). Hepburn and Peppard make an excursion to the **New York Public Library,** Fifth Avenue at 42nd Street, to find a copy of his recently published book; Peppard and Buddy Ebsen (as Holly's husband) have a poignant scene later in **Central Park,** at the Bandshell, midpark just south of the Bethesda Fountain, at 72nd Street, now a popular weekend area for in-line skating.

and you'll see curious iron struts fashioned like ship's mooring ropes, with round brackets to prevent wharf rats—also fashioned in iron—from climbing aboard. On the northeast corner of 42nd and Lexington, duck into the **Chrysler Building,** whose steel-tipped spire indeed looks like a hood ornament from a 1930s Chrysler. The small lobby is surprisingly warm and rich looking (think luxury glove compartment), with black marble and inlaid wood. Continue east on 42nd Street, where you'll pass the art deco **Daily News Building,** 220 E. 42nd St., with its spinning 12-foot globe and a floor inlaid with an immense bronze compass. The modern **Ford Foundation Building,** on the north side of 42nd between Second and First avenues, is a complete contrast, with its tranquil atrium garden—a good place to sit for a few minutes and rest your weary feet.

DOWNTOWN

Begin at the corner of Broad and Pearl streets, where the modern **85 Broad St.** building pays tribute to the archaeological past: The curved lobby shows where old Stone Street used to run and the Pearl Street sidewalks outside contain glassed-over pits revealing foundations of the old Stadt Huys, the town hall of 17th-century Nieuw Amsterdam. Follow Pearl Street down to State Street and turn left. Even if you're not visiting the National Museum of the American Indian, go inside the **Alexander Hamilton Customs House** on Bowling Green, Broadway and State streets, across from Battery Park. Just past the museum's front desk (admission is free) is the glorious Grand Rotunda, with a huge circular ceiling mural celebrating New York.

Heading on up Broadway, stop in the **U.S. Post Office** at 25 Broadway to check out the painted vaulted ceilings, a glorious celebration of transatlantic travel dating from 1921, when this room was the booking office for the Cunard Lines' New York office. Head up Broadway past the venerable Gothic-style Trinity Church, tucked among the skyscrapers at the head of Wall Street. Between Dey and Fulton streets is **195 Broadway**—built from 1915 to 1922 as AT&T headquarters—looking like a wedding cake stacked with several levels of classical columns. This facade has more columns than that of any other building in the world. Go in the lobby to see even more columns. Then proceed up to the **Woolworth Building** at Park Place and Broadway, which was the world's tallest building from 1913 to 1930. In its pre-deco heyday, the Woolworth Building was a prime exemplar of Gothic skyscraper design, and the lobby's sculptured ceiling is worth several minutes' study. Ask your kids to look for the self-portrait of the architect hugging his building in his arms and a Scrooge-like caricature of Mr. Woolworth hoarding his wealth.

6 Museums in the Outer Boroughs

IN BROOKLYN

✪ **Brooklyn Museum**   Ages 4 & up

200 Eastern Pkwy., at Prospect Park, Brooklyn. ☎ **718/638-5000.** Admission $4 adults, $2 students, $1.50 seniors; kids 11 and under free. Wed–Fri 10am–5pm, Sat 11am–9pm, Sun 11am–6pm. Subway: 2/3 to Eastern Pkwy.

The superb Egyptian collection, full of over-the-top mummy cases, is the best reason to visit this big underappreciated museum in Brooklyn, near neighbor to the Brooklyn Botanic Garden and Prospect Park; even if you're going to spend only an hour or so in the museum, there are enough other things to do nearby to justify the excursion. If your kids like history, they can wander past 27 detailed American period rooms from 1675 to 1928, including an eye-popping Moorish-style smoking room from John D. Rockefeller's town house. If they're old enough to appreciate great art, the American and European galleries are strong, with lots of impressionists and a load of Rodin bronzes. There's a special gift shop just for kids and lots of weekend drop-in programs for children.

Brooklyn Children's Museum   All ages

145 Brooklyn Ave. (at St. Mark's Ave.) in Brower Park, Crown Heights. ☎ **718/735-4400.** Suggested admission $3 per person. Wed–Fri 2–5pm, Sat–Sun 10am–5pm; summer Wed–Mon noon–5pm. Transportation: See below.

This futuristic museum building—erected in 1976 to replace an earlier pair of Victorian town houses—is technically the oldest children's museum in the country, founded in 1899. But it's the modern structure the kids will remember: an Epcot-like experiment in subterranean architecture. You enter through a neon-lit tunnel and burrow into various large open spaces snuggled within a cluster of earth mounds. A terraced outdoor plaza is fun to romp around in fair weather. The exhibits stress hands-on activities, such as the MusicMix studio, where kids can experiment with how various instruments produce sounds, or the Magic School Bus Discovery Area, where the TV cartoon characters help kids explore animal bones and bugs. Other current exhibits help kids learn about animal eating habits, human sleeping habits, and plants' growing habits (in a greenhouse environment that's a collaboration with the Brooklyn Botanic Garden). If the joint isn't overrun with school groups, you can have a pleasant time here.

Getting There: By **subway,** take the no. 3 to the Kingston Avenue station, walk 6 blocks (with traffic flow) on Kingston Avenue to St. Mark's Avenue, and turn left for 1 block. Or take the no. 2 to the President Street station, go 8 blocks on Nostrand Avenue (against traffic) to St. Mark's Avenue, turn right, and go 2 blocks. Or take the A to the Kingston Avenue station, walk 6 blocks on Kingston Avenue (against traffic) to St. Mark's Avenue, turn right, and go to Brooklyn Avenue. By **car,** take Atlantic Avenue east to Brooklyn Avenue, turn right, and drive 4 blocks south; or follow Eastern Parkway east from Grand Army Plaza to New York Avenue, turn left, and go 6 blocks north to St. Mark's Avenue, where you turn right and go 1 block east. Unmetered on-street parking is nearby.

Lefferts Homestead   All ages

Flatbush Ave., Prospect Park, Brooklyn. ☎ **718/965-6505.** Free admission. Apr–Oct Thurs–Fri 1–4pm, Sat–Sun 1–5pm; Nov Thurs–Sun 1–4pm. Subway: D/Q to Prospect Park.

This Dutch colonial farmhouse has been filled with exhibits for kids—old-fashioned toys, puppets, storybook corners, art activities—and absolutely everything in it is touchable. It's a little shabby, but who cares, when your kids are allowed to run up and down the stairs and jump off the porch and just enjoy themselves. On summer Sundays, come for the early-afternoon story hours under the big tree outside and go on to visit the nearby **Prospect Park Wildlife Center** (below) and take a spin on the stunning carved animals of the vintage **Prospect Park Carousel.**

✪ New York Transit Museum   Ages 3 & up

At the corner of Boerum Place and Schermerhorn St., Brooklyn. ☎ **718/243-8601.** Admission $1.50 kids 16 and under/seniors, $3 adults. Tues–Fri 10am–4pm, Sat–Sun noon–5pm. Closed Jan 1 and Dec 24–25 and 31. Subway: 2/3/4/5 to Borough Hall; A/C/G to Hoyt/Schermerhorn sts.; F to Jay St./Borough Hall.

Another of my sons' favorite places (naturally, since it has to do with vehicles), this Downtown Brooklyn museum is a snap to get to from Manhattan. The first great thing about this museum is that it's built in a disused subway station, with exhibits sprawling down the tunnels. The second great thing is the pair of bus cabs kids can climb into and pretend to drive. The third is the set of vintage subway cars kids can lope through, hanging on straps and swinging around poles. (Meanwhile, I got a kick out of reading the vintage subway ads on a couple of cars.) The fourth is the science shows presented Tuesday through Friday 10am to 2pm.

Beyond that, the joint is full of things most kids will look at only for a minute or two—antique turnstiles and fareboxes and route maps and scale-model trolley cars and subway station mosaics and switching apparatuses. And there's only so long you can spend down in a subway tunnel without eventually starting to feel like a Mole Person. But the sheer amount of stuff makes this place good for an hour, more if you're transportation-obsessed (like my younger son). On weekdays, you may be battling school groups for that bus cab; on weekends, there are some wonderful workshops for kids—call ahead for a schedule.

IN THE BRONX

North Wind Undersea Institute   Ages 6 & up
610 City Island Ave., City Island, the Bronx. ☎ **718/885-0701.** Admission $2 kids, $3 adults. Guided tour $4.50. Tues–Sun noon–4pm. Transportation: Take no. 6 subway to Pelham Bay station, then take bus no. 29 (make sure the bus sign says "City Island"). North Wind is the first stop on City Island.

Getting here requires a bit of trek, which is why few New Yorkers (except for sailing enthusiasts and yachters) have ever visited this corner of the Bronx, a separate island with its own maritime flavor. One of its underappreciated resources is this well-regarded research institution devoted to preserving marine environments, housed in a century-old sea captain's mansion. The institute is known for its dramatic animal rescues—harbor seals, a baby diamondback terrapin, and Physty the Whale, which was spectacularly stranded on Fire Island in 1981. Exhibits not only detail these ventures but also acquaint visitors with other forms of marine life, with a mock coral reef, a humongous shell collection, a touch tank, and an 11-tank aquarium of local sea life. The antique diving equipment is pretty cool too.

IN QUEENS

✪ American Museum of the Moving Image   Ages 10 & up
35th Ave. and 36th St., Astoria, Queens. ☎ **718/784-0077.** Admission $4 kids 5–18, $5 students/seniors, $8 adults; 4 and under free. Tues–Sun noon–4pm. Subway: N to Broadway; R/G to Steinway St.

This superb resource for cinephiles is housed in the Kaufman Astoria Studio, where talkies were made long ago and *Sesame Street* and *Cosby* are filmed today. At nine interactive work stations you can fiddle with sound effects, dub in new dialogue, call up different soundtracks, and even add your face (à la Woody Allen's *Zelig*) to classic movie scenes. You can record yourself making a series of funny faces into a video camera, which is then printed out in a flip book (thumb through it rapidly to re-create your moving facial expressions). At the digital animation stands, you can move cardboard cutouts around to create your own animated short. At other stations where the equipment is especially high-tech, museum staffers helpfully demonstrate the behind-the-scenes wizardry.

Many of the historic artifacts on display—a 1910 wooden Path camera, a 1959 Philco TV set—may elicit yawns from youngsters, but the extensive costume gallery should interest kids, with recognizable items like one of Bill Cosby's sweaters from *The Cosby Show* or Robin Williams's dowdy padded housedress from *Mrs. Doubtfire*. To illustrate the history of TV and movie merchandising, there's a fun display of tie-in toys and lunchboxes. The makeup exhibition has enough ghoulish masks to satisfy young *Goosebumps* readers. There's a cafe here too, which is convenient.

If your kid liked the interactivity of the Sony Wonder Technology Lab (above), this place should be a hit; less slick and commercial than a Universal Studios Tour, it's a great way to open kids' minds to the art and science of motion pictures.

✪ New York Hall of Science   Ages 3 & up

47-01 111th St., Flushing Meadows–Corona Park, Corona, Queens. ☎ **718/699-0005.** Admission $4 kids 4–15, $6 adults, $4 seniors; 3 and under free. Free admission Thurs–Fri 2–5pm except summer. Mon–Wed 9:30am–2pm, Thurs–Sun 9:30am–5pm; summer Mon 9:30–2pm, Tues–Sun 9:30am–5pm. Parking $5. Subway: 7 to 111th St.

This is one of the great discoveries I made while researching this book—a totally hands-on museum that makes learning *really fun*. You can pedal furiously on a bicycle to turn a huge propeller; you can watch a bank of rotating electric fans create wind; you can hunt for microbes and fungi with microscopes; you can use colored Plexiglas tiles to make your own rainbow; you can watch your brother get really huge and then really tiny as he walks across an optically distorted room. Put your ear to glass pipes and you can hear different pitches; stand in front of a special light scope and you can cast three different-colored shadows at once.

The exhibits weren't over our 4-year-old's head, and yet they were plenty fascinating enough for my husband, who's no slouch when it comes to physics. Best of all, no activity takes more than a minute to execute, which means that kids sprint from one to another instead of hogging a demo station—we never had to wait our turn to try anything. Museum staffers were performing all kinds of cool demonstrations down on the main floor, but my boys were too busy to watch them. And the Science Playground is awesome—30,000 square feet of outdoor fun with 27 interactive activities, including a gigantic teeter-totter, a light-activated kinetic sculpture, windmills, and a waterplay area.

There's a limited cafe here, but you'd be better off packing a lunch—there aren't many options in the neighborhood. Definitely combine the science museum with a stop at the nearby Queens Wildlife Center (below), which won't add more than an hour to your expedition.

Queens County Farm Museum   All ages

73–50 Little Neck Pkwy., Floral Park, Queens. ☎ **718/347-3276.** Free admission. Mon–Fri 9am–5pm (grounds only), Sat–Sun 10am–5pm (house and grounds). Subway: E/F to Kew Gardens/Union Turnpike; then Q46 bus to Little Neck Pkwy.

Still a working farm, this 18th-century homestead is a bucolic spot of fields and orchards and barns full of animals, with ongoing demonstrations of agricultural arts—plowing, planting, apple picking, reaping, milking cows, birthing foals, incubating chicks, and so on. The simple three-room frame farmhouse, built in 1772, is open only on weekends.

Queens Museum of Art   Ages 8 & up

NYC Building (next to the Unisphere), Flushing Meadows–Corona Park, Queens. ☎ **718/592-5555.** Admission $4 adults, $2 students/seniors; under 5 free. Wed–Fri 10am–5pm, Sat–Sun noon–5pm. Subway: 7 to Shea Stadium—walk south over ramp into park and head for the Unisphere.

Besides the fact that it's parked next to the Unisphere, that famous stainless-steel globe from the 1964 World's Fair, the chief reason for children to visit this museum of 20th-century art is the Panorama, an awesomely huge three-dimensional re-creation of the New York skyline that's kept faithfully up-to-date. Kids will love picking out familiar landmarks; anyone who enjoys dollhouses, Polly Pockets, and MicroMachines can marvel over the incredibly detailed small-scale rendering of a city that's often all too large-scale.

ON STATEN ISLAND

✪ Historic Richmond Town   Ages 5 & up

441 Clarke Ave., Staten Island. ☎ **718/351-1611.** Admission $2.50 kids 6–18, $4 adults; 5 and under free. Sept–June Wed–Sun 1–5pm; July–Aug Wed–Fri 10am–5pm, Sat–Sun 1–5pm. From the Staten Island ferry, take bus no. S74 to Richmond Rd./Court Place.

Somewhat off the beaten track, this 100-acre re-creation includes 27 buildings spanning the 17th to the early 20th century—which may create a disjointed effect for historical purists, but kids generally don't care. Three little streets are set up like a small village, and kids can run in and out of the houses and basically just have a ball. Many buildings were moved here from other sites on Staten Island; they range from a neoclassical courthouse serving as a visitor center to a little schoolhouse dating from 1695, the oldest elementary school building in the country. Costumed interpreters are in action July and August, demonstrating crafts like basket weaving, spinning, weaving, tinsmithing, and printing. A good full day's expedition.

Staten Island Children's Museum   Ages 10 & under

1000 Richmond Terrace, Staten Island. ☎ **718/273-2060.** Admission $4 kids/adults; under 2 free. Tues–Sun and most school holidays noon–5pm; July–Aug opens at 11am Tues–Sun. From the Staten Island ferry, take the S40 bus (Richmond Terrace) to the Snug Harbor center, with its black wrought-iron gate. The museum is in Building M.

Another interactive children's museum with a raft of workshops to keep kids busy, the Staten Island contender has one advantage—a lovely setting on the lawns and gardens of the Snug Harbor Cultural Center—and one main disadvantage, which is that it's out on Staten Island, albeit only a short bus ride from the ferry terminus. Seven hands-on interactive exhibits help children explore the wonders of water, insects, computers, and animals, among other subjects, with an emphasis on fun. New museum space is currently under construction and should open by fall 2000.

7 Historic Houses

Manhattan doesn't have many full-fledged historic houses, maybe because real-estate values are too high for old homes to sit around long waiting for a preservation society to snap them up. You can see the mayor's yellow-frame home, **Gracie Mansion,** in Carl Schurz Park on the East River at 89th Street, but the public rooms on the main floor can be toured only on Wednesday by appointment—call ☎ **212/570-4751** (admission $4). Older kids who really want the experience of another era do have a few choices (beyond the extensive period rooms at the Metropolitan Museum of Art), but most are well off the beaten track and may have limited visiting hours.

Abigail Adams Smith Museum   Ages 8 & up

421 E. 61st St. (between First and York aves.). ☎ **212/838-6878.** Admission $3 adults, $2 students/seniors; 12 and under free. Tues–Sun 11am–4pm (Tues to 9pm June–July). Closed New Year's Day, July 4, Aug, Thanksgiving Day, Christmas. Subway: N/R or 4/5/6 to Lexington Ave./59th St.

This one's claim to fame is a bit dodgy—its namesake, daughter of President John Adams and his wife, Abigail, never really lived in this former carriage house, though the land did belong to her family. Nevertheless, the Colonial Dames of America have latched onto this property and use it to display furniture and decorative arts from the 1820s and 1830s, re-creating nine period rooms as they might've been in the Mount Vernon Hotel that stood here back in the days when this was a country retreat. The surrounding gardens, planted in 18th-century style, offer a welcome whiff of horticulture in the middle of the city. The location is convenient, and the curators vigorously try to attract families with theme workshops, candlelit tours, and other special events.

✪ Alice Austen House   Ages 6 & up

2 Hylan Blvd., Staten Island. ☎ **718/816-4506.** Admission $3 adults; 7 and under free. Thurs–Sun noon–5pm. From the Staten Island ferry terminus, take the S51 bus 2 miles to Bay St./Hylan Blvd.

Many things about pioneer photographer Austen's house make it a great bet for kids. First, it's really more of a cottage, a low-slung gingerbread-trimmed bungalow with rolling lawns that offer dynamite views of New York harbor. Second, Austen herself is such an appealing character, a spunky turn-of-the-century woman who started taking pictures when she was 10 and just never stopped. Lots of her work is on display, and the garden has been replanted according to her photos of the original grounds. Third, you get to ride the Staten Island ferry over. What more could you ask?

The Merchant's House   Ages 8 & up

29 E. 4th St. (between the Bowery and Lafayette St.). ☎ **212/777-1089.** Admission $3 adults, $2 students/seniors; 11 and under free. Sun–Thurs 1–4pm. Subway: 6 to Astor Place or Bleecker St.

The most interesting thing about the Tredwell family—who lived in this house continuously from 1835 to 1933—is that they weren't famous or unusual at all, just a stable prosperous upper-middle-class family whose house and furniture happened to survive intact, wallpapers and all, into the mid–20th century. The house itself is a fairly notable example of Greek Revival, but your kids will probably be more struck by the old-fashioned furnishings.

Morris-Jumel Mansion Museum   Ages 10 & up

65 Jumel Terrace (at 160th St.). ☎ **212/923-8008.** Admission $3 adults; 12 and under free. Wed–Sun 10am–4pm. Subway: B/C to 163rd St.

Dating back to 1765, this imposing mansion with its Georgian front columns had a major brush with history when Gen. George Washington used it as his headquarters in 1776. As they tour the house, however, your kids may become more interested in Eliza Jumel, the wealthy, brazen 19th-century woman who lived here for many years, during her marriage to and after her divorce from Aaron Burr. It's too bad this big, elegant mansion is off the beaten path for tourists . . . or then, again, maybe that's its saving grace. As a bit of colonial history, Manhattan's oldest house is a gem.

8 Zoos & Aquariums

Aside from the following, check out the **Bronx Zoo/International Wildlife Conservation Park** and the **Central Park Wildlife Conservation Center** (see "Kids' Top 10 Attractions," earlier in this chapter).

Aquarium for Wildlife Conservation   All ages

Surf Ave. and W. 8th St., Coney Island, Brooklyn. ☎ **718/265-3400.** Admission $4.50 kids 2–12/seniors, $8.75 adults. Daily 10am–5pm. Parking $6. Subway: D/F to W. 8th St. (Brooklyn).

After an hour-long subway ride from Manhattan—an adventure in itself—you hit the ocean at Coney Island beach, skirting the tawdry rides of Coney Island's amusement park, and walk to the left on the open part of the boardwalk (away from the cheesy stuff) to the Aquarium. I'm a veteran aquarium lover and have to admit that this place disappointed me, perhaps because we went in spring—many of the exhibits are outdoors and it was still too chilly to linger long watching the seals and walruses. But having heard how crowded this place gets in summer (and how distracting the tinselly lights of Wonderland are, once the amusement park opens for summer), I'm glad we did it out of season, with the beach deserted and the ocean misty, cold, and gray. The kids still had a ball in the **Discovery Cove,** where they could get their hands on real sea creatures. Time your schedule so you can catch the dolphin and sea lion shows too. New larger windows are slated to be installed by the whale holding pools, which should ease up viewing there. Pack a lunch if you're going in the cooler months, when the outdoor snack bar may be closed and nearby boardwalk joints are boarded up (it's several blocks to the nearest McDonald's).

✪ Prospect Park Wildlife Center   All ages

450 Flatbush Ave., Prospect Park, Brooklyn. ☎ **718/399-7339.** Admission 50¢ kids 3–12, $2.50 adults; 2 and under free. Apr–Oct Mon–Fri 10am–5pm, Sat–Sun and holidays 10am–5:30pm; Nov–Mar daily 10am–4:30pm. Subway: D to Prospect Park.

This is my kids' favorite of all New York City's zoos, probably because it's right at the level of preschoolers and young grade-schoolers. The fanciful abstract sculptures arching over the walkway from the side entrance tell you right away you're in kid territory, and on it goes, to the **Animals in Our Lives** petting zoo and the outdoor **Discovery Trail,** where kids can hop like a wallaby, squat on their own lily pads, or huddle inside a giant turtle shell. There's a miniamphitheater built in front of the glass-enclosed environment where a troop of hamadryas baboons scamper around—somebody knows which animals kids most like to watch. It's small, clean, safe, and tons of fun. Once you're out here, make it a full day by visiting nearby Lefferts Homestead (above), New York's only historic house set up just for kids, and taking a ride on the gorgeous antique Prospect Park Carousel, only steps from the zoo entrance. The subway ride from Manhattan isn't all that long, leaving you off only a block or so from the zoo.

Queens Wildlife Center   All ages

53–51 111th St. (at 54th Ave.), in Flushing Meadows Park, Queens. ☎ **718/271-1500.** Admission 50¢ kids 3–12, $2.50 adults; $1.25 seniors; 2 and under free. Mon–Fri 10am–5pm, Sat–Sun 10am–5:30pm (daily to 4:30pm Nov–Mar). Subway: 7 to 111th St. (Queens).

Though it may not rate a trip out to Queens from Manhattan on its own account, this smart little zoo is a natural add-on to a New York Hall of Science excursion (above)—a good excuse for a tramp through the old World's Fair grounds. The zoo's focus is on North American species (don't expect exotics here, though my sons considered the American bison plenty exciting) arranged along a handsomely landscaped walking trail. You feel surrounded by wilderness, yet the pathway is actually pretty short—it won't tax young legs—and the loop shouldn't take more than 15 or 20 minutes. Across the park road is a minifarm with domestic animals that'll satisfy the yen for feeding and stroking warm furry creatures.

Staten Island Zoo   All ages

614 Broadway, Barrett Park, Staten Island. ☎ **718/442-3101.** Admission $2 kids 3–11, $3 adults; 2 and under free. Daily 10am–4:45pm. From the Staten Island ferry, catch the S48 bus, get off at Broadway and Forest Ave., turn left, and go 2½ blocks up Broadway.

The little Staten Island zoo isn't under the umbrella of the Wildlife Conservation Society, as are the other zoos around here, and it's definitely a poor cousin. But you may want to combine this with a visit to the Staten Island Children's Museum (above), especially if you're into snakes—the reptile collection is a stand-out. The 8 acres also are home to a small aquarium and a fair number of birds. Feeding times are frequent attractions, and there's also a small children's zoo, for younger kids who like their nature hands-on.

9 Gardens

✪ Brooklyn Botanic Garden   All ages
1000 Washington Ave. (at Eastern Pkwy.), Brooklyn. ☎ **718/622-4433.** 50¢ kids 6–16, $3 adults, $1.50 seniors; free on Tues. Tues–Fri 8am–6pm, Sat–Sun and holidays 10am–6pm (to 4:30pm Nov–Mar). Subway: 2/3 to Eastern Pkwy; D to Prospect Park.

Every month something new is blooming at this 52-acre garden beside the Brooklyn Museum and across from Prospect Park. Starting in spring, **Daffodil Hill** dazzles the eye with a field of stunning yellow, then delicate pink cherry blossoms fringe the **Japanese Pond** (local Japanese families flock in for their annual blossom-viewing picnics). A riot of roses fills the **Cranford Rose Garden** as summer sets in, and thickets of rhododendron blossom near the Eastern Parkway entrance. There's also a **Fragrance Garden** for the blind and a sweet little **Shakespeare Garden** featuring all sorts of plants mentioned in Shakespeare's plays. Year-round, you can stroll through the **Steinhardt Conservatory,** with its outstanding bonsai collection, orchids, water lilies, and **Trail of Evolution,** a pathway lined with increasingly sophisticated plant forms. You'll also find a cafe, a lovely gardening gift shop, and frequent weekend programs for children and families. Kids may get a kick out of the **Celebrity Path,** inlaid with the names of famous Brooklynites from Mae West to Woody Allen.

Conservatory Garden   All ages
Central Park at 105th St. ☎ **212/860-1382.** Free admission. Daily dawn–dusk. Subway: 6 to 96th St.; then walk up Fifth Ave.

Central Park's only patch of formal garden is a delightful find in Manhattan and rarely crowded because it's so far uptown. Walk through glorious wrought-iron gates (which once fronted the enormous Fifth Avenue mansion of Cornelius Vanderbilt II) and turn left to find the **Children's Garden,** with beds of flowers blooming around a wishing well with a statue of the children from Frances Hodgson Burnett's *The Secret Garden.* The central section of the garden is a long lush lawn flanked by a pair of walkways lined with flowering trees; the northern end has a circular design, with a fountain of the Three Graces surrounded by flower beds—a spectacular blaze of tulips in spring and chrysanthemums in fall. On spring and summer weekends there's nearly always a wedding party here getting photographed; with rest rooms and a fair-weather outdoor cafe, it's a welcome refuge, a perfect place to let your kids stretch their legs after a Museum Mile trek.

✪ New York Botanical Garden   All ages
200th St. and Kazimiroff (Southern) Blvd., the Bronx. ☎ **718/817-8705.** Admission $1 kids 6–16, $3 adults; 5 and under free. Wed free. Tues–Sun and Mon holidays, 10am–6pm (to 4pm Nov–Mar). Parking $4. Transportation: See below.

With the 1998 opening of the **Everett Children's Adventure Garden,** this plant-filled 250-acre park—five times bigger than the Brooklyn Botanic Garden (above)—is now a real magnet for families. The stunning 8-acre Adventure Garden (separate admission $2 adults/kids over 5, $1 kids 3–5) tempts youngsters with cunning minitrails and mazes and topiaries and fanciful sculptures, not to mention hands-on stations where they can learn about pollination and chlorophyll and root systems and all that other good stuff. My kids simply adore it. Other highlights are the **Wild Wetland Trail,** which engagingly leads kids through a natural ecosystem; the **Ruth Rea Howell Family Garden,** where young city-dwellers can plant, weed, water, and compost tidy little garden plots; the 19th-century **Snuff Mill,** perched on its riverside terrace; a **rock garden** (admission $1 adults, 50¢ kids 6 to 16)**;** a huge formal **rose garden;** a steep **rhododendron valley;** and the huge Victorian-era greenhouse complex of the **Enid Haupt Conservatory** (admission $3.50 adults, $2.50 kids 6 to 16)**,** which alone makes the Garden a delightful destination year-round.

A narrated **tram** ($1) swings around the grounds to help you cover the territory. Spring is intoxicating here, what with the huge stands of azaleas, magnolias, dogwood, and lilacs, but my younger son can't wait to get up here in winter, when the **Holiday Garden Railway exhibit** is set up—a large-scale model train wending its way through fanciful landscapes and cityscapes. Although the botanical garden is right next to the Bronx Zoo (see "Kids' Top 10 Attractions," earlier in this chapter), you'd have to be very ambitious (and very good walkers) to do both justice in 1 day, since their sites are so spread out—but if you're game, it can be done.

Getting There: Metro North trains from Grand Central Terminal make the 20-minute trip to the Botanical Garden Station; cross Southern Boulevard and you're at the entrance. One-way fare is $3.50 off-peak or $4.75 peak. By car, take the Henry Hudson Parkway to the Mosholu Parkway; at the end of the Mosholu, turn right onto Kazimiroff Boulevard and follow the garden perimeter to the entrance.

✪ Wave Hill   All ages

675 W. 252nd St., Riverdale, the Bronx (entrance at 249th St. and Independence Ave.). ☎ **718/549-3200.** www.wavehill.org. Admission $4 adults, $2 students/seniors; 5 and under free. Tues free. Tues–Sun 9am–4:30pm (mid-May to mid-Oct to 5pm, Fri to dusk). Transportation: See below.

A very suburban enclave in the Bronx, Riverdale has some fine housing stock on its Hudson River shore, notably this 28-acre estate with two mansions and extensive gardens. Over the years many famous people lived here, as tenants or as guests—writers Mark Twain and William Makepeace Thackeray, conductor Arturo Toscanini, and Theodore Roosevelt; at one time the Tudor-style house was also the official residence of Great Britain's ambassador to the U.N. But there's not much to see inside the houses—just let your kids play on the grounds, which offer one of the few unobstructed views across the Hudson to the magnificent New Jersey Palisades.

Nobody minds if youngsters run on the grass, and the formal gardens are world-famous, well worth prowling around. My kids' favorites are the Aquatic Garden, with a pair of pergolas enclosing a formal pool; the nook-filled Wild Garden; and a terraced series of small walled gardens showing off cactuses and Alpine flowers. Below the mansions' smooth lawns sprawls a 10-acre woodland with walking trails that give kids a nice bit of a hike. Excellent children's workshops are held on weekends in the learning center; make a phone call or check the Web site for a current schedule.

Getting There: Liberty Lines (call ☎ **718/652-8400**) bus no. BxM1 (from the East Side) or BxM2 (from the West Side) goes to 252nd Street; then walk west across the parkway bridge and follow the signs to the main gate. The fare is $4 one-way; children under 45 inches may sit on parents' lap for free. Or take the Metro North train (call ☎ **212/532-4900**) to the Riverdale stop, walk up 254th Street, turn right on Independence Avenue, and go to the main gate at 249th Street.

The one-way fare is $4.75 peak and $3.50 off-peak. By car, take the Henry Hudson Parkway to the 246th Street exit, drive straight north to 252nd Street; turn left to cross the parkway overpass, turn left at the light, and drive south to 249th Street, where you turn right and follow it to the Wave Hill gate.

10 Nature Centers

Note that **Central Park** is covered in depth in chapter 5 under "Green New York: The Top Parks."

The Dairy   All ages
In Central Park, midpark at 65th St. ☎ **212/794-6564.** Free admission. Tues–Sun 11am–5pm. Subway: 6 to 68th St.; 1/9 or A/B/C/D to Columbus Circle.

This charming 19th-century structure, with patterned roof tiles and gaily painted gingerbread trim, actually started life as a dairy, back in the days when people grazed cows on Central Park's meadows (children could stop in here and buy a cool cup of milk fresh from the udder). There aren't too many Guernseys left in Manhattan, so nowadays the Dairy is the park's chief visitor information center, with a roomful of displays about the park's landscape. There are always a few hands-on activities for youngsters, and it's a pleasant short stroll from either the Carousel or the zoo, not to mention the Wollman Rink.

✪ Dana Discovery Center   All ages
In Central Park at 110th St., near Fifth Ave. ☎ **212/860-1370.** Free admission. Tues–Sun 11am–5pm. Subway: 2/3 to 110th St. Bus: M2, M3, or M4 to 110th St./Fifth Ave.

After Harlem Meer was dredged out in the early 1990s and its banks beautifully relandscaped, this pretty structure on its north shore opened as a nature study center, bringing visitors uptown for the first time in years. Weekend family workshops run year-round (usually at 1pm, but call for schedules), and a room overlooking the Meer's serene waters is set up with hands-on nature exhibits. Stroll around the Meer to the neighboring Conservatory Garden (see "Gardens," earlier in this chapter).

✪ Henry Luce Nature Observatory at Belvedere Castle   All ages
In Central Park, midpark at 79th St. ☎ **212/772-0210.** Free admission. Apr–Oct Tues–Sun 10am–5pm; Nov–May Tues–Sun 10am–4pm. Subway: B/C to 79th St.

Besides studying the kid-friendly interactive exhibits on Central Park's natural habitats, young visitors to Belvedere Castle get a kick out of standing out on the rocky terrace hanging high over **Turtle Pond** and the outdoor **Delacorte Theater** or walking out onto the castle's upper-level terraces for some super views of the Upper West Side, including the American Museum of Natural History. The mere fact that it's a castle is intriguing enough, though it's an awfully tiny castle, built in 1872 as an optical illusion to make the lake to the south look bigger (the woods of the Ramble have since grown so high they nearly obscure the lake view). But this castle has a U.S. Weather Service station on top—note the twirling weathervanes on the tower. Stroll down the hillside west of the castle, a neatly planted **Shakespeare Garden** (appropriate, since the neighboring Delacorte is home to the Public Theater's free Shakespeare in the Park series), or scamper down the long slope to the east, where turtles and ducks populate the adjacent pond.

Inwood Hill Urban Ecology Center   All ages
Inwood Hill Park, 218th St. and Indian Rd. ☎ **212/304-2365.** Free admission. Wed–Sun 11am–4pm. Subway: 1 to 215th St.; then walk several blocks to Indian Rd.

This art-deco canoe house, tiled in aqua and white, holds weekend walking tours of the surrounding park, with its marsh, meadow, and steep rock cliffs. A telescope inside the center lets kids zoom in on details of the neighboring marsh and meadow; other exhibits include hands-on geology displays, an aquarium, and a flip-book of pictures of the native plants and animals. Few Manhattanites venture up to this northern tip of the island, but it's a stunning site.

Lower East Side Ecology Center   Ages 3 & up
E. 7th St. between Avenues B and C. ☎ **212/420-0621.** Free admission. Wed 4–7pm, Fri–Sun 8am–5pm. Subway: 6 to Astor Place.

Though it looks at first like another abandoned Alphabet City lot, look closer and you realize that every structure has been built from discarded materials—coffee cans, plastic laundry detergent jugs, old tires—with some inventive sculptures amid garden works in progress. The neighborhood can be funky, but the walk across East 7th Street from Tompkins Square is fairly innocuous. Green guerrillas and other plucky souls may get a charge out of such a determinedly urban spin to nature studies.

11 Kid-Friendly Tours

SELF-GUIDED TOURS

Heritage Trails   Ages 5 & up
Federal Hall National Monument, 26 Wall St. (at Broad St.). ☎ **888/4-TRAILS** or 212/ 269-1500. Free admission; guidebook $2 or map $1; walking tours with guide, $7 kids 6–12, $11 adults, $9 seniors/students. Visitor center Mon–Fri 9am–5pm. Subway: 2/3/4/5 to Wall St.; A/C to Broadway/Nassau St.

Like Boston's Freedom Trail, Downtown New York's Heritage Trails use colored dots laid out on sidewalks and streets to define pedestrian routes past a set of land-marks, which are described in an accompanying booklet ($2). There are four trails, each marked with a color. The **Red Trail** goes up Broadway from Trinity Church to City Hall, the courthouses at Foley Square, and the Brooklyn Bridge. The **Blue Trail** swings over to South Street Seaport. The **Orange Trail** leads to the pair of great modern financial towers, the World Trade Center and the World Financial Center, ending on the Battery Park City esplanade.

The **Green Trail** is the longest and, to my mind, most interesting: Starting at the New York Stock Exchange, the nerve center of Wall Street, it passes several great skyscrapers on its way to Hanover Square, heart of the old merchant New York, then takes in the Vietnam War Veterans Memorial, historic Fraunces Tavern, the Shrine of St. Elizabeth Seton (New York's only native Catholic saint), the docks for the Staten Island ferry and the Statue of Liberty/Ellis Island ferries, ending at the foot of Broadway and the old U.S. Customs House at Bowling Green.

Note that Federal Hall is open only on weekdays; on weekends look for the booklet in local bookstores. If you don't have a guidebook, however, you can still get a brief description of each site on a freestanding marker at each location. There's also an option of doing the tours with a professional tour guide ($7 kids 6–12, $11 adults, $9 students/seniors). All four trails together cover about 4½ miles, linking 50 marked sites, but each trail is short enough that a 5- or 6-year-old could walk it, given a few rest stops en route. The dots are spaced rather far apart, so they're not quite as easy to follow as the Freedom Trail's continuous red line, but the idea is still a winner, adding a sort of treasure-hunt element to sightseeing on foot. My 5-year-old had a ball just connecting the dots, even though the sights themselves weren't all that interesting to him—what a painless way for me to get in some hardcore sightseeing.

BUS TOURS

The Downtown Loop   All ages

Fare free. Mon–Fri 6:45am–10pm, Sat 9:45am–9:30pm, Sun 9:45am–8:30pm.

The Alliance for Downtown New York sponsors this air-conditioned jitney bus running a continuous loop around Downtown. From Battery Park it goes up West Street to Battery Park City, past the World Trade Center to Liberty Street, east across Liberty Street and Maiden Lane to Water Street by South Street Seaport, then down Water Street to Battery Park. No narration, but it's a handy way to hop from sight to sight, especially when young legs get tired.

Gray Line Tours Double-Decker Bus Tours   All ages

Main stop at Port Authority Bus Terminal (42nd St. and Eighth Ave.). ☎ **800/669-0051** or 212/397-2600. Full city tour: $19 kids under 12, $30 adults. Upper or Lower Manhattan loop: $12 kids under 12, $20 adults. Statue of Liberty/Ellis Island grand tour: $26 kids under 12, $37 adults. Children under 5 ride free if sitting in adult lap. Daily starting at 9am.

Though lengthy narrated bus tours can make some younger children squirm like crazy, they're convenient for helping you see a lot of sights without having to run your kids ragged. Hop-on/hop-off tours provide a happy medium—you get driven around and spoon-fed information, and when your kids get restless you just jump off at the next stop, expecting to get back on again later.

Operating both red double-decker buses and bright-red trolley buses, Gray Line offers so many options it could make your head spin—and at slightly lower prices (at least for children) than their big competitor, New York Apple Tours (below), which makes virtually the same stops. Gray Line's tour guides are a bit more reliable too. Besides the 2-day **Grand Tour,** which would take 5 hours if you didn't indulge in hopping on and off, there are a **Lower Manhattan loop** and an **Upper Manhattan loop,** the **Grand Tour plus Statue of Liberty 2-day option,** and the **Lower Manhattan plus Statue of Liberty 1-day option.** More traditional escorted sightseeing tours—the kind where you have to stick with the same groups of bus pals throughout—include both half-day and full-day Manhattan routes that involve a buffet lunch, as well as escorted Harlem tours (the Sunday version includes a gospel church service), helicopter tours, and a harbor cruise add-on to the Grand Tour loop.

New York Apple Tours   Ages 3 & up

Visitor center at Eighth Ave. between 53rd and 54th sts. Open daily 8am–6pm. ☎ **800/876-9868.** Full city tour: $18 kids under 12, $30 adults. Downtown tour: $12 kids under 12, $21 adults. Statue of Liberty Express: $23 kids under 12, $39 adults. Daily 9am–6pm.

My boys love to watch these red London-style double-decker buses trundling up Central Park West; we always wave to the tourists on board, most of whom wave back. Most passengers gamely opt for the top deck, which is roofless in decent weather. This hop-on/hop-off narrated tour service has earned some poor marks in the local press, with reports of wacky misinformation blithely promulgated by sloppily trained guides. It might not be a bad idea to rely on your own guidebook, just in case; you and your kids could even have fun spotting errors in the narration. The bus ride is still kinda cool.

The **Full City Tour** lets you bus-hop for 2 days; you only have 1 day to complete the **Downtown tour,** which goes east on 34th Street and down Fifth Avenue to Greenwich Village, hits a few key points Downtown (including a swing through Chinatown, Little Italy, and the Lower East Side), then checks out Midtown highlights—the U.N., Grand Central, the Plaza, and Rockefeller Center.

The **Statue of Liberty Express** throws in a trip to Liberty and Ellis islands along with the 2-day Full City Tour (ferry fare is included in the tour price), at $2 more than what you'd pay separately for the ferry plus the bus tour. An **Uptown tour** covers the Upper West Side, Harlem, and the Upper East Side; the **Harlem Gospel Express tour** on Wednesdays and Sundays includes a walking tour and a chance to listen to authentic gospel music; a **Hudson River Waterfront tour** stops at the *Intrepid* Sea-Air-Space Museum, various boat and helicopter tour bases on the Hudson shore, and the Chelsea Piers sports complex, then more or less duplicates the Downtown tour from the World Trade Center on.

You can buy tickets at many hotels, at any of the tour stops, or at five NY Apple outlets: 1 World Trade Center; 34th Street between Eighth and Ninth avenues; 41st Street and Seventh Avenue; 47th Street and Eighth Avenue; and Eighth Avenue at 55th Street. Buses make convenient hotel pickup stops first thing in the morning. In winter, uptown buses run every 90 minutes, downtown buses every 45 minutes, which means you might waste a lot of time waiting for the next bus if you don't time things right; April to November, buses run every half-hour uptown and every 15 minutes downtown, which is much better.

BOAT TOURS

✪ Circle Line Sightseeing Cruises   Ages 3 & up
Departing from Pier 83, at the foot of W. 42nd St. at the Hudson River. ☎ **212/563-3200.** 3-hour tour $12 kids 2–11, $22 adults; 2-hour tour, $10 kids 2–11, $18 adults. Parking 10–15. Bus: Westbound M42 to the Hudson River.

Delivering a classic New York City experience, these low-slung little steamers chug right around Manhattan on a 3-hour tour (shades of *Gilligan's Island?*) with narration that can be very entertaining. On the first leg you deconstruct the Midtown skyline, get a good look at the Chelsea Piers, pass Battery Park City and the World Trade Center, and swoop past Ellis Island and the Statue of Liberty. Then the boats cut across New York Harbor and go up the east side of the island, past Wall Street and South Street Seaport, and under the East River bridges, getting a view of the other end of Midtown, with the United Nations presiding over the river at 42nd Street. This is where the shortened Express Tour stops and turns around, but if you continue, you'll pass the Upper East Side, seeing Gracie Mansion, where the mayor lives, and you get to go through Hell Gate, where the East River merges with the Harlem River, and Spuyten Duyvil (Spite the Devil), where the Harlem River empties into the Hudson. Granted, there's not so much to see on the northern end of the island, but the guides gamely fill in with lots of trivia. And when you pass under the George Washington Bridge, you can spot the little red lighthouse featured in Hildegarde H. Swift's classic children's book *The Little Red Lighthouse and the Great Grey Bridge.*

The experience of being out on the water with the wind in your hair is marvelous by itself, but getting a minicourse in New York history and architecture is a definite bonus. On the other hand, you're a captive audience—if your kid freaks out in the middle of the trip, you have no choice but to endure the rest of the tour. (There are rest rooms and a snack bar on board, at least.) Compared to some of the bus tours, however, the Circle Line narration can really be pretty interesting, despite the sometimes corny jokes; each guide's patter is idiosyncratic, and these guys certainly know their stuff. Go early in your trip to get a firm sense of Manhattan as a whole.

The Pioneer   All ages

Departing from Pier 16 at South Street Seaport. ☎ **212/748-8590.** Admission $12 kids 12 and under, $20 adults, $15 students/seniors.

Two-hour harbor cruises aboard an historic schooner depart a couple of times a day (schedules vary) from South Street Seaport. The time-warp experience of setting sail from this old seaport is somewhat diluted by the views of very modern Downtown skyscrapers and the chug of barges, tugboats, and tour boats on the water around you, but it could still be a memorable throwback to an earlier era. New York viewed from the water is quite a sight.

Seaport Liberty Cruises   All ages

Departing from Pier 16 at South Street Seaport. ☎ **212/630-8888.** Admission $6 kids 12 and under, $12 adults.

These narrated harbor cruises last only an hour, which makes them a better alternative for younger kids than the Circle Line tours (above). You'll go from the Seaport down around Wall Street to Battery Park, swing around to pass by Ellis Island and the Statue of Liberty, then cruise past Brooklyn Heights and the Brooklyn shipyards, under the Brooklyn Bridge, and back to the Seaport. If just being out on the water is more important to you than getting a comprehensive view of Manhattan, bag Circle Line and do this one instead.

PRIVATE GROUP TOURS

Small Journeys, Inc.   All ages

114 W. 86th St., New York, NY 10024. ☎ **212/874-7300.** $200 per group for 4-hour tour.

These custom-designed group tours are too expensive for individual families, but if you can hook up with another two or three broods, go for it, because Steven Kavee and his guides really gear their tours to kids' interests. The company also designs behind-the-scenes field trips for school groups, going on-site to meet professionals in fashion, art, theater, music, interior design, whatever. Transportation may be by van, by limo, by bus, or on foot, depending on the sights involved. Arrange well in advance.

WALKING TOURS

For detailed strolls around the city and even Brooklyn, you may want to check out *Frommer's Memorable Walks in New York.* Take into account, however, that some of the walks (like the Greenwich Village literary tours) may not be of much interest to kids.

Several organizations run a number of tours; check the schedules in the *Big Apple Parents' Paper, New York Family,* or the New York *ParentGuide,* available free at children's bookstores and clothing stores all over town.

ARTime (☎ **718/797-1573**), as its name implies, runs walking tours oriented toward the fine arts, usually focusing on museums and galleries. Because they don't cover as much physical ground as some of the neighborhood and architectural tours (no more than 2 or 3 blocks between art galleries), they're quite suitable for younger kids—so long as the kids are into art. Tour guides gear their talks to children 5 to 10. Tours last about 1½ hours and cost $20 one adult plus a child and $5 each additional child (an extra adult tagging along is free). You can usually book a tour up to a day in advance—call ahead for schedules of upcoming tours.

Big Onion Walking Tours (☎ **212/439-1090;** www.bigonion.com) are designed primarily for adults, but kids 8 and up will respond to many of their lively topics, which often touch on the multiethnic dimensions of New York's mosaic. Tours can last as long as 2 hours; they cost $8 students and children and $10 adults.

The **Grand Central Partnership** (☎ **212/818-1777**) is an active coalition of business interests in the area around Grand Central Terminal that sponsors a free 1½-hour walking tour along East 42nd Street—an area that includes such Midtown classics as the Chrysler Building, the Daily News Building, the art deco Chanin Building, and the old Bowery Savings Bank. With its historical/architectural emphasis, this may be a bit scholarly for kids under 10, but the length (and the price) make it worth trying out. Tours depart Friday at 12:30pm from the Whitney Museum at Phillip Morris, 120 Park Ave. at 42nd Street.

The **Municipal Arts Society** (☎ **212/935-3960** for reservations and details, 212/439-1049 to get a schedule by mail) runs fascinating tours that explore the city's architecture and neighborhoods from an urban-design perspective. The guides are top-notch—occasionally they'll talk over a kid's head, but they're so enthusiastic it's infectious, and their depth of knowledge means they can handle just about any question thrown at them. Tours run from 2 hours up to 6- or 7-hour excursions; weekday tours cost $8 students/seniors and $10 adults, while weekend tours cost $15. One very popular option is the hour-long lunchtime tour of fascinating Grand Central Terminal (suggested donation $5), which meets every Wednesday at 12:30pm (call the society to find out where to meet). Advance reservations aren't required for weekday tours, but for some of the popular weekend tours you may need to reserve a couple of weeks in advance.

The **34th Street Partnership** (☎ **212/868-0521**) offers a free 90-minute walk weekly, covering the 34th Street territory with a noted urban or architectural historian, a good way to explore a small bit of Manhattan in depth. If your kids begin to lose interest, you can always drop out, but at least stick around for the Empire State Building segment, which comes first. Meet at the Fifth Avenue entrance of the Empire State Building at 12:30pm on Thursday.

For the Active Family

5

It's a fallacy to assume that New Yorkers are soft, flabby city people who never get any exercise. On the contrary, we end up walking much more than car-dependent suburbanites do, and the city's complement of huge parks makes it super-easy to ride bikes, play tennis, jog or stroll, toss a Frisbee, fly a kite, skate, or skateboard, not to mention feed ducks or squirrels and watch boats drift lazily past.

But New York parents as a breed tend to be more organized than that—at the drop of a hat they'll enlist their children in classes for anything from chess and computers to horseback riding and fencing. Staying active in New York is a 12-months-a-year proposition, and neither the dog days of summer nor the ice days of winter are allowed to slow down kids' activities. Though many classes and workshops are only for full series enrollment, I've listed below a number of drop-in classes, both weekday and weekend, for visiting families and for local kids who want to do something on the spur of the moment.

1 Green New York: The Top Parks

Though New York is studded with squares where you can find a patch of grass and some benches, it has only a handful of parks large enough for a real exploration. Some of these are somewhat off the beaten track: **Flushing Meadows–Corona Park** out in Queens (take the no. 7 train out to 111th Street or Willets Point/Shea Stadium) and **Van Cortlandt Park** up in the Bronx (take the no. 1 or 9 train up to 242nd Street) are both loaded with recreational facilities, but they're so big and spread out you can't just ramble around aimlessly. **Fort Tryon Park** up at the northern end of Manhattan (take the A train to 190th Street), a wooded strip of park on high ground overlooking the Hudson, is lovely if somewhat overgrown, but the surrounding neighborhood is iffy—it's not worth a special trip unless you're already coming to visit the Cloisters branch of the Metropolitan Museum of Art (see chapter 4). For other green pleasures in the city, see "Gardens" and "Nature Centers" in chapter 4.

That leaves the five parks below, but they go a long way toward keeping New Yorkers happy. The larger three—Central Park, Riverside Park, and Prospect Park—were laid out in the 19th century by the team of Frederick Law Olmsted and Calvert Vaux, which isn't just a coincidence: The ultimate architects for urban parks, these guys really knew how to maximize space, with twisting paths and artful hills and dales that make you feel as though you've left the city as soon as you're 10 paces inside the park. Later park commissioners slapped on recreational amenities like tennis courts and playgrounds that may not strictly have been what Olmsted and Vaux envisioned, but nothing has seriously marred the beauty of these detailed landscapes.

✪ Central Park

From 59th to 110th sts., between Central Park West (Eighth Ave.) and Fifth Ave. ☎ **212/ 360-3444.** Event hotline: 888/NY-PARKS or 212/360-3456. Subway: 1/9 to Columbus Circle; B/Q to 57th St.; N/R to Fifth Ave.; B/C to any stop from Columbus Circle to 110th St.; 4/5/6 to any stop from 59th St. to 103rd St.

At 840 acres, this park—one of the world's greatest—is a vital resource for the city. Set right in the middle of things, with frequent entrances cut into its low brownstone wall, it separates the Upper West Side from the Upper East Side, lying between Midtown at the south end and Harlem at the north end. It's big enough to give you a real sense of escape, and when you're walking around the park the only roads you have to deal with are the circular park drive and one cross-cut at 72nd Street; both are closed to car traffic weekdays 10am to 3pm and 7 to 10pm, as well as 7pm Friday to 6am Monday (holidays keep weekend hours too). Four other east-west streets do cross the park—66th, 79th, 86th, and 96th—but they're cunningly hidden beneath overpasses so you'll never notice them.

The section below 72nd Street is somewhat formal. Starting at 59th Street and Fifth Avenue—where **horse-drawn carriages** line up to give tourists a ridiculously overpriced ($34 for 20 minutes) ride through the park—you'll find the **Pond,** a picturesque small body of water reflecting Midtown skyscrapers. Just northwest of this lie the **Wollman Rink,** where you can ice-skate in winter and roller-skate in summer (see "Skating" under "Sports & Games," later in this chapter), and the **Dairy** visitor center (see chapter 4); from the Dairy, follow a path west under an arch to the **Carousel** (see chapter 4). The ballfields west and south of here are fun even for spectators on summer weekday evenings, when some very competitive after-work leagues slug it out. As you walk up the West Drive past **Tavern on the Green** restaurant (see chapter 8), your kids may be interested to know that it was originally built as a sheepfold in 1870 when the **Sheep Meadow,** the broad fenced-in green lawn on your right, still was used for grazing sheep; the sloping drive here is a prime spot for skateboarders and in-line skaters showing off their tricks. Midpark, east of the Sheep Meadow, is a paved road that swarms with volleyball games and in-line skaters on weekends. The **Mineral Springs Pavilion** just north of the Sheep Meadow has a **snack bar** and **rest rooms.**

Go north across 72nd Street to **Strawberry Fields,** a gem of a bit of landscape laid out in memory of Beatle John Lennon, who lived across Central Park West from here in the Dakota apartment building (he was shot out front). My sons, both of them next-generation Beatlemaniacs, love to hang out here. It seems there are always flowers laid in tribute to Lennon on the black-and-white mosaic medallion that reads IMAGINE. Across the drive to the northeast lies the **Lake,** a body of water larger than the Pond—large enough, in fact, for boating. To rent rowboats, cross the park along the 72nd Street Transverse. Along the way, though, stop off at two postcard views that even your kids may recognize from scores of movies and TV shows: Turn left at **Cherry Hill Fountain** and walk over lovely **Bow Bridge,** or take either the lakeside path or 72nd Street to **Bethesda Terrace,** a grand lakeshore plaza

Central Park Attractions

American Museum of
  Natural History **9**
The Bandshell **18**
Belvedere Castle &
  Shakespeare Garden **8**
Bethesda Fountain **15**
Bow Bridge **13**
Carousel **23**
Central Park Zoo & Wildlife
  Conservation Center **26**
Cherry Hill Fountain **16**
Chess & Checkers House **24**
Claremont Stables **1**
Conservatory Garden **3**
Conservatory Water **12**
Dairy **25**
Delacorte Theater **7**
Great Lawn **4**
Heckscher Playground **29**
Information booth **27**
The Lake **14**
Loeb Boathouse & Park View
  at the Boathouse **11**
The Mall **20**
Metropolitan Museum
  of Art **5**
Mineral Springs Pavilion **19**
The Obelisk
  (Cleopatra's Needle) **6**
The Pond **30**
Ramble **10**
The Reservoir **2**
Sheep Meadow **21**
Strawberry Fields **17**
Tavern on the Green **22**
Wollman Rink **28**

Subway stop **M**
Path of Animal
Statue Walk

NA-0365

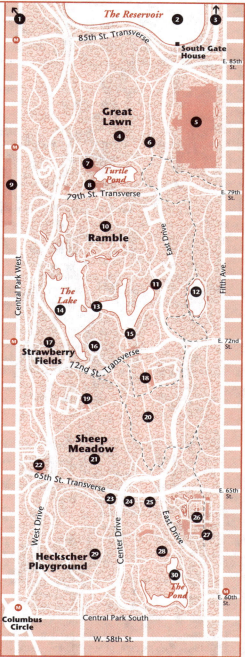

Stalking the Animal Statues in Central Park

In the course of half an hour's walk, you and your kids can bag a couple dozen animals in the wilds of Central Park—statue animals, that is.

Start on the northwest corner of East 79th Street and Fifth Avenue. A few steps into the park, on your right are **(1–3) three bronze bears,** a copy of a Paul Manship statue that's in the Metropolitan Museum directly north. Continue on the path into the park, going through a vaulted tunnel under the East Drive and veering to your left (south) to reach the east end of Turtle Pond. There you'll find King Jagiello of Poland astride a **(4) magnificent horse.** Stroll uphill to your left to the drive and walk downtown (south) on the road, keeping to the right-hand jogging path if there's car traffic in the park. About halfway down the hill, atop a massive rock outcropping on your right crouches a **(5) bronze panther,** peering out of the foliage ready to pounce on unsuspecting joggers.

Cross the East Drive at the crosswalk near the Loeb Boathouse and walk a few yards south to a dirt path cutting east over the grass; a short, steep slope brings you to a path leading south to the Conservatory Water. The Alice in Wonderland statue at the pond's north end has not only the **(6) White Rabbit** but also the **(7) Cheshire Cat,** Alice's **(8) kitten Dinah,** and **(9) assorted mice,** along with the usual number of children climbing all over the giant mushrooms. Swing around to the west side of the pond to find the **(10) Ugly Duckling** waddling past the statue of Danish storyteller Hans Christian Andersen.

Take either path leading south from the Conservatory Water up the hill to the 72nd Street Transverse; cross 72nd Street and go to the west side of the circular drive. On your right, the ground rises to the Rumsey Playground (less a playground these days than a plaza for special events). Set amid the steps rising to Rumsey's entrance gate is a big **(11) stone goose,** with who else but Mother Goose riding on its back. (Walk around to identify carved scenes from various nursery rhymes.) Go east past Rumsey and bear right, crossing the plaza in front

featuring the Bethesda Fountain. The lakeside path continues, winding north to the **Loeb Boathouse** (☎ **212/517-2233),** where you can rent boats and also get something to eat at the snack bar or the more upscale **Park View at the Boathouse** (see chapter 8). The boathouse is open March to November, depending on the weather; rowboat rental is $10 per hour (cash only, $30 deposit required), and there's also an honest-to-God gondola you can rent at night, April to October, for $30 per half hour. The boathouse is open noon to 10pm.

Across East Drive and just above 72nd Street, the **Conservatory Water** is a fun area even for the littlest ones, with its large serene formal pool—the Alice in Wonderland statue at the north end features a giant mushroom that just begs to be clambered on. April to September, you can rent 41-inch-long radio-controlled model sailboats ($10 per hour) from a stand beside the boathouse here. The cafe on the pond's east side also has **rest rooms.** Stroll back south through a shady green strip with winding paths, passing a couple of good playgrounds (see "The Playground Lowdown," later in this chapter), and you'll soon go under an arch past the **Tisch Children's Zoo** (see chapter 4). There's usually a vendor here selling windspinners and rattling balloons and other toys that can be very hard to get young ones past; hustle them along to the **Delacorte Arch,** with its delightful glockenspiel chiming every hour, and finally to the **Central Park Wildlife Center** (see chapter 4).

of the Bandshell (watch for rollerskaters on weekends!). At the western edge of the plaza you'll find a **(12–13) pair of eagles** devouring a hapless **(14) mountain goat.** Continue west on 72nd Street. On your left, just before 72nd Street meets the West Drive, look up on another big outcropping to find the **(15) falcon** lighting on the glove of *The Falconer.*

Retrace your steps east on 72nd Street until you reach the Dead Road, that broad asphalt lane bordering the Sheep Meadow, where skaters and volleyball games proliferate on warm-weather weekends. Follow the Dead Road south to find the Indian hunter with his faithful **(16) dog.** Turn left, following the circular drive past the foot of the Mall; go under the drive via a brick-vaulted tunnel (try out the echoes). The path swings uphill on the east side of the drive to reach one of the most famous animal statues in the park, **(17) Balto the sled dog,** hero of a 1995 animated film.

From here the path leads south through another underpass past the gates of the Children's Zoo; look for a **(18–19) pair of goats** prancing atop the zoo's wrought-iron entrance arch. On through a second underpass, you'll come up to the redbrick Delacorte Arch. In a niche to the right of the arch is a bronze **(20) dancing bear,** while the glockenspiel on top of the arch features **(21–26) a hippo, a goat, a penguin, a kangaroo, an elephant,** and **a bear**—plus a **(27–28) pair of monkeys** squatting on top, hammering the bells. The musical clock performs on the hour and half hour; stick around to watch if possible. Then proceed south on the walkway past the Central Park Zoo; at the southern end of the zoo's redbrick structures, turn to your right to see another niche with a **(29) dancing goat** inside.

After stalking all this sculpted prey, your kids may well feel as mine did: "Mom, can we see some live animals now?" And here you are, right near the gates of the zoo, ready to answer their wish.

North of the Lake, the **Ramble** is a compact wilderness that's easier than you'd think to get lost in; navigate with care and stick to daylight hours when there are plenty of other folks around (unsavory types know it's the best place in the park for a mugging). Above 79th Street, a pair of museums dominate the park: the **Metropolitan Museum of Art,** inside the park at East 82nd Street, and the **American Museum of Natural History,** facing the park at West 79th Street and Central Park West (see chapter 4). Midpark, between them, lies the **Great Lawn,** a huge stretch of grass and ballfields where crowds happily congregate in summer for events ranging from Metropolitan Opera concerts to the 1995 premiere of *Pocahontas.* At the south end of the Great Lawn, **Turtle Pond** protects a habitat for turtles, ducks, and dragonflies. To the west of it lie the **Delacorte Theater,** home of summer's free Shakespeare in the Park (and another essential set of **rest rooms**); the picturesque wooden **Swedish Cottage,** where daily marionette shows are held (see chapter 7); and, up on the hill, the **Shakespeare Garden** (see chapter 4) and **Belvedere Castle** with its nature center.

Between 86th and 96th streets, the major feature of the park is the **Jacqueline Kennedy Onassis Reservoir,** named in 1995 in honor of the presidential widow who lived for years nearby at 1040 Fifth Ave. (at 85th Street). A gravel path makes a 1.6-mile loop around the reservoir, much of it lined with cherry trees that are breathtaking in spring; there's also a bridle path circling the reservoir, where experienced riders can bring their mounts from the **Claremont Stables** on West 89th Street (see "Horseback Riding" under "Sports & Games," later in this chapter). Take a walk along here and you've got a very good chance of sighting horses, if that's a treat for your kids. My boys like following the bridle path on the south end of the reservoir because it runs through the parking lot of Central Park's **police precinct station,** housed in an old set of redbrick stables along the 86th Street transverse road. North of the reservoir is the green stucco **Tennis House** (see "Tennis" under "Sports & Games," later in this chapter), which also has **rest rooms.**

Above 96th Street, the east side of the park has two big attractions: the **Conservatory Garden,** at 105th Street and Fifth Avenue (see chapter 4), which has **rest rooms,** and **Harlem Meer,** the graceful pond at the northeast corner of the park, where the **Dana Discovery Center** (see chapter 4) runs nature workshops and hands out fishing poles so even youngsters can try their hand at angling in the Meer. On the west side, a stroll above 96th Street will take you to a picturesque and little-known area at West 100th Street: the **Pool,** a willow-fringed pond with a lively waterfall at the east end; our kids love to hang over the railing on the bridge and watch the cascading waters beneath. North of here, the **Great Hill** has a high, broad lawn perfectly suited to picnics. Midpark are more ballfields and, at 110th Street, the **Lasker Rink,** which converts in summer into the **Lasker Pool.** Be wary about going too deep into the park this far north, however, since it's less populated and the surrounding neighborhoods include some risky elements. I readily take my kids to the Pool and Harlem Meer on weekend days and lots of families we know skate at Lasker Rink, but the social scene is rougher in summer when the rink turns into a pool.

Riverside Park

Between the Hudson River and Riverside Dr., from 72nd to 153rd sts. ☎ **212/408-0265** or 870-3070. Subway: 2/3 to 72nd St. or 96th St.; 1/9 to any stop from 72nd St. to 125th St.

Long, narrow Riverside Park really shows off designer Frederick Olmsted's ingenuity: Beneath it lie miles of underground railroad tracks, while the Henry Hudson Parkway, a major thoroughfare out of the city, bisects it lengthwise. You can't always get to the river shore as a result; the section of the park between the highway and the Hudson is overgrown and deserted in some spots and totally given over to playing fields in others. But between West 83rd and West 96th streets, Riverside features a wide straight **promenade** with stone railings where you can lean over and gaze west over the Hudson; the pavement here makes it super for leisurely biking and skating, though you'll have to weave through strolling crowds on summer Sundays. The **dog run** near 86th Street always manages to entertain children even if they don't have a pooch to exercise, and the **community garden** along the median strip at 91st Street is simply glorious.

At 72nd Street, 79th Street, and 86th Street, you can find paths going under the highway to the riverside promenade, a wide path leading past the **79th Street Boat Basin**—a marina full of bobbing houseboats that don't all necessarily look seaworthy. Most of the docks are private, but Pier A, the northernmost (just above 79th Street), is open to the public on weekends; stroll to the end and you'll get wonderful wide-open Hudson views, as well as close-up glimpses of the houseboats. The grassy shade behind the esplanade makes a good place for a picnic, or you can stop for a casual meal at the **West 79th Street Boat Basin Cafe** (see chapter 8).

The southern end of Riverside Park, from 72nd to 83rd streets, is flatter and more open and unbelievably beautiful in spring, when all the flowering trees come out. If you want to fly a kite, this may be a good place for it, with breezes blowing in from the river. The playground at 76th Street includes basketball courts where you can often watch some fierce hoop action. Above 96th Street the park gets more rustic and uncrowded, with some very steep paths plummeting down the slope from Riverside Drive. Up at 116th Street and in the lower section of the park at 96th Street, there are tennis courts (see "Tennis" under "Sports & Games," later in this chapter). Go all the way to 125th Street and you can visit the **Grant National Memorial Monument,** familiarly known as Grant's Tomb (see chapter 4). Nearby, at about 123rd Street, hunt for a much smaller and very touching memorial—a stone urn surrounded by iron palings, erected in memory of St. Clair Pollock, who died in 1797 at the age of 5.

Prospect Park

In Park Slope, Brooklyn. Bounded by Prospect Park West (Ninth Ave.), Eastern Pkwy., Flatbush Ave., Parkside Ave., and Prospect Park South. ☎ **718/965-8961.** Events hotline: ☎ 718/965-8999. Subway: 2/3 to Grand Army Plaza or Eastern Parkway; D to Prospect Park or Parkside Ave.; F to 15th St./Prospect Park.

Designers Frederick Law Olmsted and Calvert Vaux considered this park their crowning achievement, though it hasn't been kept up as well as Central Park. The main draws for kids are the super trio of attractions on the park's east side, along Flatbush Avenue: the **Prospect Park Wildlife Center,** the **Lefferts Homestead** house museum for children, and the **Prospect Park Carousel** (see chapter 4). Across Flatbush you'll find the **Brooklyn Museum** and the **Brooklyn Botanic Garden** (see chapter 4), which aren't part of the park proper but were always considered part of the overall scheme. On weekends and holidays noon to 5pm, a free hourly **trolley** runs continually among all these attractions (call ☎ **718/965-8999** for information).

If outdoor activities are on your agenda, you may well want to head for the **Long Meadow,** 90 acres of rolling greensward just inside the park's ornate entrance on Grand Army Plaza. Warm-weather weekends always see plenty of picnic action on the meadow, with lots of families tossing Frisbees and working on little sluggers' pitching arms; it's not so great for kite-flying, since the meadow is set down in one huge gentle hollow. Brooklyn's sizable Middle Eastern and Caribbean populations give cookout hours here a special spicy aroma. In winter, the slopes along the edges of the meadow are just the ticket for trying out that new sled or pair of cross-country skis. The park's circular drive follows a 3.45-mile loop that's great for biking or in-line skating; follow it to the park's southern end, skirting the tangled woods and ravines in the middle of the park, and you'll find a 60-acre lake where you can rent four-person pedalboats (11am to 6pm Thursday to Sunday and holidays; $10 per hour); Prospect Park's own **Wollman Rink** sits on its northern shore.

Carl Schurz Park

Along the East River from East 84th to East 90th sts. Subway: 4/5/6 to 86th St.

Though not as extensive as its West Side counterpart, Riverside Park, Carl Schurz Park—named after a prominent 19th-century German immigrant who was a newspaper editor, senator, and cabinet member—offers some very good East River views and, behind them, a few delicious green landscaped dells to wander through. Along the river, **John Finley Walk** (which actually continues south for several blocks past the park) is a paved promenade with wide-open views of the Triborough Bridge to the northeast, the railroad bridge spanning the rough waters of Hell Gate (a name that never fails to titillate my boys), and, across the river, the small lighthouse on the northern tip of Roosevelt Island; otherwise it's just warehouses and boxy modern apartment complexes across the water. No bikes or skating are allowed, but there's a dynamite enclosed dog run just inside the park about halfway up; come right before dinnertime and watch the dogs romp. Walk to the north end of the promenade, where it loops around **Gracie Mansion,** the mayor's yellow clapboard residence (built as a country house in 1799, when this still was country); stand by the railing and face south to see how this tranquil park actually is built over four lanes of car traffic, on the busy FDR Drive. Just another example of New York City maximizing its real estate.

✪ Hudson River Park / Battery Park City / Battery Park

West of West St., from Chambers St. to the end of Manhattan. ☎ **212/267-9700.** Subway: 1/2/3/9 to Chambers St.; C/E to World Trade Center; 4/5 to Bowling Green; 1/9 to South Ferry.

Although these three parks aren't yet totally connected, Battery Park City's master plan calls for eventually extending all the way to Battery Park, creating a continuous strip of park along the river's edge from Chambers Street on south. Don't expect to find the big green fields and woods the other parks offer; this is a narrow strip of landfill, much of it devoted to a broad paved riverside esplanade with in-ward-curving iron railings. But bicyclists and in-line skaters and joggers make good use of that esplanade, which connects to the 2-mile bike path running along West Street up to the Village, while droves of other people lounge on the benches and stroll along gazing at the river and the harbor.

The oldest section, city-run **Battery Park,** is southernmost, occupying the tip of Manhattan Island. An expanse of grass with some fine old trees, it's crisscrossed by paved paths and dotted with statues; round brownstone **Castle Clinton** stands here, selling ferry tickets to the **Statue of Liberty** and **Ellis Island** (see chapter 4); the ferries embark from Battery Park's waterfront pilings. Battery Park is generally thronged with tourists; hot-dog carts, T-shirt vendors, and street musicians are allowed in Battery Park but not in the other two, which are privately operated. **Battery Park City** is a large mixed-use development, built in the early 1980s, with tony office/retail towers as well as some pleasant residential buildings. Its Esplanade connects the whole. In the lovely gardens around **South Cove,** kids may enjoy scampering over a small bridge and up into a postmodern gazebo echoing the Statue of Liberty's crown. The **North Cove,** at the other end of the Esplanade, has a yacht harbor where some impressive white ships are moored; a pink granite plaza accented with fountains leads up from the yacht basin into the **Winter Garden Atrium** of the World Financial Center, an upscale retail development with stores and restaurants.

North of the World Financial Center, the Esplanade runs on into **Hudson River Park,** which has a really excellent playground (see "The Playground Lowdown," below). There's a stunning waterfall pool, a large green lawn at the north end, and an outstanding **sculpture garden** so deliriously full of fancy that kids are bound to love it. Bronze figures run riot, perched atop lampposts and walls and even over-taking the drinking fountain: oversize pennies, human feet, frogs, cats, immense earthworms, and weird little round-headed people, all of which invite kids to climb on them. In the middle of this small paved wonderland is a railed-off centerpiece sculpture with a ring of rushing water for youngsters to wade in—sheer delight.

2 The Playground Lowdown

CENTRAL PARK

Central Park's "adventure playgrounds," most built in the 1980s, feature imagina-tive designs incorporating lots of places to climb, jump, slide, and hide out, as well as lots of sand to dig in or land safely on. In the 1990s, a new generation of playground began appearing, with rubber mat ground surfaces (as opposed to asphalt) and large, complex structures of metal bars coated with tough plastic, usually in primary colors. The playgrounds are surrounded by iron palings so kids don't wander away unsupervised; they all have drinking fountains, operational from Memorial Day to Labor Day, though none has rest rooms, and many have sprinklers to make summertime play a whole lot cooler. (Which makes up somewhat for the appalling lack of decent public pools.)

The playgrounds below have bucket swings for toddlers and babies and either tire swings or flat swings for older kids. The Parks Department keeps playground equipment decently well maintained, often with the help of neighborhood parents who join in for monthly clean-up days.

THE WEST SIDE   The large **Heckscher Playground,** midpark at 62nd Street, could use renovation; surrounded by chainlink fence, it's a relic of an era when gray brick pyramids, metal slides, concrete ledges and tunnels, and a few brown timber climbing contraptions were the be-all and end-all of playground design. One area is set in a shallow expanse of rather dirty sand, but most of the rest of the playground is asphalt paved, and very little is shaded by trees. There are a few straightforward swings and seesaws at one end, which seem to be used mostly by sullen teenagers hanging out. There are working rest rooms here, but they're often locked up.

Just north of Tavern on the Green, the **West 67th Street Playground** has two sections: a 1960s-era playground atop a small hill and a smaller fenced area across the path with some newer primary-colored climbing structures and a set of bucket swings. The hilltop area is deliciously shady and better than most of this vintage, with undulating concrete forms, a nice bilevel brown timber treehouse, and sprinklers set in a little concrete amphitheater that spills running water into a long raised basin. The sight lines aren't too bad, but the sand could be cleaner.

The well-shaded **Diana Ross Playground** at West 81st Street—so named because the singer donated money to the park after violent incidents marred her Central Park concert in the early 1980s—was one of the first adventure playgrounds and now it could use some refurbishment. The weathered wood structures, set in sandpits, are complex enough to inspire some really fun games, with webs of chains to climb on, suspension bridges to bounce on, and fireman's poles to slide down. But the design isn't geared to younger kids, who may have some trouble climbing where they want to go (which means you'll have to climb up after them to give them a boost). There are two hulking climbing structures set right in the middle; the sight lines can be a problem. Two giant pluses: There are public rest rooms nearby (next to the Delacorte Theater—usually dirty but infinitely preferable to soiled undies), and you're only a block north of the American Museum of Natural History.

Set atop a rise of land with lots of picnickable grass around it, the **Spector Playground** at West 85th Street features a very nice fenced-off toddler area (baby swings, sandbox, sprinklers) and a rambling wooden treehouse with chain nets to scramble over and a giant rope to swing on. Many of the playground's structures are set in sand; a long wooden bridge arches over the middle of the immense sandpit, which makes the sight lines problematic if you're in the toddler area and trying to keep an eye on older kids down by the treehouse. Though many of the climbing structures are weather-beaten, near the gate a newer construction of rubber-coated steel is scaled just right for preschoolers. The paved sprinkler area

Manhattan Playgrounds

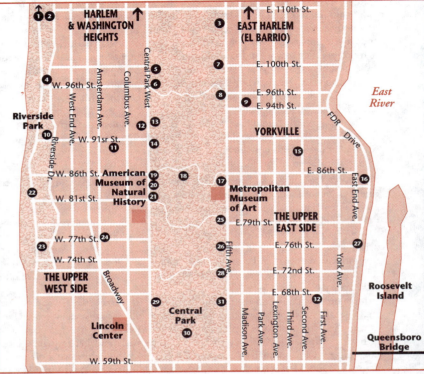

CENTRAL PARK PLAYGROUNDS
West Side
Diana Ross Playground ㉑
Heckscher Playground ㉚
Pinetum ⑱
Rudin Playground ⑥
Safari Playground ⑭
Spector Playground ⑲
West 67th Street Playground ㊴
West 84th Street Playground ⑳
West 99th Street Playground ⑤
Wild West Playground ⑬
East Side
Ancient Playground ⑰
Bernard Family Playground ③
East 72nd Street Playground ㉘
East 96th Street Playground ⑧
East 100th Street Playground ⑦
James Michael Levin
　Playground ㉖
Pat Hoffman Friedman
　Playground ㉕
Rustic Playground ㉛

RIVERSIDE PARK PLAYGROUNDS
Claremont Playground ①
Dinosaur Park ④
Elephant Park ㉓
Hippo Park ⑩
West 83rd Street Playground ㉒
West 110th Street Playgrounds ②

OTHER MANHATTAN PLAYGROUNDS
The Upper West Side
Amsterdam Avenue & 77th St. ㉔
St. Gregory the Great
　Playground ⑪
Sol Bloom Playground ⑫
The Upper East Side
Carl Schurz Park Playground ⑯
Hunter School Playground ⑨
John Jay Park ㉗
Ruppert Park ⑮
St. Catherine's Playground ㉜
Midtown
Sutton Place Park ㉝
Tudor City Playground ㉞

Chelsea & the Flatiron District
Augustus Saint-Gaudens Park ㊱
Clement Clarke Moore Park ㉟
Union Square Playgrounds ㊲
Greenwich Village
32 Carmine Street Playground ㊴
Bleecker Street Playground ㊳
Mercer Playground ㊷
Washington Square Park Playground ㊵
The East Village
Tompkins Square Park ㊶
SoHo
Thompson Street Playground ㊸
Little Italy
De Salvio Playground ㊹
Chinatown
Columbus Park ㊺
TriBeCa & Lower Manhattan
Battery Park City ㊽
Hudson River Park Playground ㊼
Pearl Street Playground ㊾
Washington Market Park ㊻

A BROOKLYN HEIGHTS PLAYGROUND
Pierrepont Street Playground ㊿

NA-0366

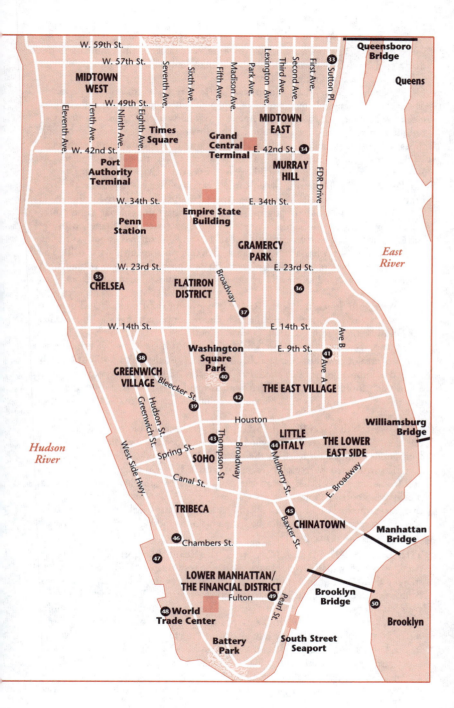

gets very active in summer. Across the drive are some bucket swings midpark in the shady cool of the **Pinetum,** and the older playground at West 84th Street was reconstructed in the summer of 1998.

The delightful **Safari Playground** at West 91st Street is an imaginative playscape where children scramble over a herd of hippo sculptures and hop in and out of a green rowboat embedded in the pavement. It has no swings or slides and only two rudimentary climbing structures, but kids hardly notice, they're so busy with jump ropes and hopscotch and sidewalk chalk and running in and out of the sprinklers. With picnic tables and lots of shade, it attracts swarms of preschoolers. At West 93rd Street, the **Wild West Playground** is extremely popular with Uptown families, especially in summer, when sprinklers send water rushing down the long central gully into a circular wading pool at the far end. Four square fortlike wood towers at the center make this a great spot for playing all sorts of war games; three of the towers anchor big sandpits surrounded by low wooden palisades, with tire swings, slides, a bouncy suspension bridge, and weathered wood climbing structures (the fourth has a rubber mat surface that's better for playing ball). The towers in the center make the sight lines a bit of a problem, and the combination of water gully and sandpit means lots of wet gravelly muck in your kids' shoes when you get home.

At West 96th Street, the newer **Rudin Playground** is set on an island between two busy transverse roads, meaning a bit more noise and exhaust than other playgrounds; the gate leads straight out to Central Park West, which can also be a problem. But in other respects it's a pleasant place, with a central paved sprinkler area, a vine-hung pergola shading a set of benches, and a trio of brightly colored climbing gyms that modulate from low toddler-friendly structures to a fairly demanding set of parallel bars and swinging rings. There's only one small concrete-edged sandbox, but there are lots of bucket swings (well shaded too) for babies.

The **West 99th Street Playground** is past its prime and looks it, but athletic kids can have a blast on its weathered wood structures, especially the concrete mountain with interior tunnels for reaching the top of a big metal slide. Essentially one large sandpit surrounded by asphalt, it's rarely crowded, but the sight lines can be a problem since the benches are on the perimeter. The gang here is fairly mixed, mostly neighborhood folks, but for whatever reasons it seems to be kept less tidy than playgrounds farther south and the park here is a bit wilder and more overgrown. There are good lawns nearby for picnicking, and right across the drive are the North Meadow playing fields.

THE EAST SIDE   At East 67th Street, the **Rustic Playground** is one of the park's most imaginative play spaces. You enter through a leafy wooden arbor; straight ahead is an arched stone bridge that looks very much like the famous Bow Bridge over the Lake to the north, connecting a pair of lushly planted islands. On your left is a midsize sandpit with a slide, on your right a terrace with picnic tables. Best of all, behind the stone bridge, steps lead up a steep rock outcropping to the top of a long curved metal slide actually set into the face of the rock; daredevil kids in the know bring a square of corrugated cardboard to sit on to make the slide super-fast, sort of like a waterless log flume ride. The big problem with the Rustic Playground is you can't see past the bridges and islands in the center; if one of your children is doing repeat trips down that slide—it can be addictive—you can't monitor the rest of the playground if your other children are elsewhere. Still, it's a wonderful place for a pre- or post-zoo frolic.

The **East 72nd Street Playground** is another dinosaur from the era of brown timber, brick pyramids, metal slides, and concrete. These hulking shapes make the sight lines pretty bad, and the ground surface, mostly sand, looks a bit dirty. It's quite shady, though, and the entrance is set safely inside the park. Kids in this neighborhood prefer to go to the **James Michael Levin Playground,** set well inside the park near East 76th Street, with a small iron entrance gate everyone conscientiously keeps latched. The centerpiece of this graceful wide-open playground is a lovely fountain featuring scenes from classic fairy tales; there's a lively new climbing structure near the gate and picnic tables and a decent-sized concrete sandbox at the other end, with plenty of open pavement in between for skating and hopscotch and the like. The sight lines are super, and the crowd is pretty well behaved, yet it does get crowded after school. On the north side of East 79th Street, the **Pat Hoffman Friedman Playground** is a well-sheltered small area behind a replica of the Metropolitan Museum's American Wing's statue *Three Bears* by Paul Manship; there's not much here except bucket swings, a tiny concrete sandbox, a metal slide, and a few climbing bars. It's a handy place for a quick stop right after a visit to the Metropolitan, though only the 4-and-under set will be satisfied.

With its series of glazed-brick pyramids, the **Ancient Playground** at East 84th Street pays homage to the neighboring Metropolitan Museum's Egyptian Temple of Dendur, visible through the glass wall right across the road. The concrete banks around the edges do give this playground a bunkerlike quality, and, wedged between two busy transverse roads, it somehow lacks any bucolic feeling. Most of the benches are set up at one end, grouped around handy concrete chess tables, which means baby-sitters congregating there have a hard time supervising their charges. Older kids have a ball leaping all over the pyramids, thundering up and down the metal slides, and taking furious spins on the rope swings; a segregated area at the far end makes a safe haven for little tots, with a sandbox and bucket swings.

The popular **East 96th Street Playground** sits at the top of a short, steep rise from Fifth Avenue. A good-size toddler area is set off by iron palings in the center; other separately defined areas include a rubber-matted zone with tire swings and wooden pilings to climb on; a large modern metal-bar structure with all sorts of bridges, ladders, towers, and plastic slides; a cool little treehouse platform in a shady back corner; and a paved expanse surrounding a big water sprinkler. The sight lines are very good, and the Carnegie Hill crowd is pleasant to play with. The well-shaded **East 100th Street Playground** has a coil of red steel that becomes a run-through tunnel of spraying water in summer; the climbing structure is particularly imaginative, with lots of inspiring nooks for all sorts of make-believe. Best of all, this playground is wheelchair-accessible. It's adjacent to an extensive lawn that sees lots of ball playing and picnic action on weekends. On the east shore of Harlem Meer, at 108th Street, the **Bernard Family Playground** is a very civilized area featuring a large steel-bar climbing apparatus, painted maroon and forest green, mounted on black rubber matting. It also has a small, clean sandbox, a paved sprinkler section, and a few bucket swings. Few white families make it up this far, which is their loss; only a few yards south of the playground is a marvelous tiny sand beach where small children can happily dig, sift, and mold sand beside the lapping Meer water.

RIVERSIDE PARK

The **Henry Neufield Playground** at West 76th Street is commonly known as the **Elephant Park** after a set of five plump little stone pachyderms set around an open expanse of asphalt. This pleasant playground also has two modern climbing structures, a fenced swing area, a small fenced sandbox with very clean sand, and rest rooms (hallelujah!) actually kept decently clean. There's an active set of basketball courts next to it. The only drawback is that traffic roars on the West Side Highway right past the bushes on the other side of the back fence. The **West 83rd Street Playground** was renovated in the summer of 1998, with new surface, swings, climbing equipment, a sandbox, and a sprinkler feeding into a river; the 35-foot sandbox here is a whimsical wonder, with sculptural forms of castles, classical gods, and woodland animals frolicking around its run.

The so-called **Hippo Park** (down a steep hill from Riverside Drive, at West 91st Street) derives its nickname from the wonderful hippopotamus sculptures in the middle, which children can climb on. It has swings for both tots and big kids, smallish sandboxes, and sprinklers in summer. An energetic group of neighborhood parents that banded together to raise money to renovate the park now organizes drop-in arts and crafts classes in summer. Best of all, the Hippo Park has rest rooms—and clean ones at that. A few blocks north at 97th Street and Riverside Drive, the **Dinosaur Park** has similar sculptures (dinosaurs, naturally) and a huge sprinkler area, great for cooling off in summer, but the secret is out and the playground gets super-crowded after school. Set alongside the Riverside Drive promenade on the park's upper level, the **West 110th Street Playground** has smaller climbing structures, bucket swings, and small sandboxes that make it especially good for toddlers. The farthest north, the shady **Claremont Playground**, at West 124th Street (right behind Grant's Tomb), has spouting porpoise sprinklers and a sandbox shaped like a huge rowboat.

THE UPPER WEST SIDE

Sandwiched between Central Park and Riverside Park, the Upper West Side doesn't need as many playgrounds of its own as the wider Upper East Side does—yet it seems to have more. Along **Amsterdam Avenue at 77th Street** (northeast corner), helpfully near the American Museum of Natural History, is a small fenced-in playground whose wooden structures had just been razed for reconstruction as this book went to press—check it out in the spring of 1999 to see what new clever design the Parks Department wizards have wrought. On West 90th Street, between Columbus and Amsterdam avenues, you'll find the **St. Gregory the Great Playground**, a small rubber-floored playground with a sprightly set of climbing structures built in 1995; the **community garden** just to the east of it (with gates on both 90th and 89th streets) offers a lovely place to sit and enjoy a riot of flowers from April to November. On West 92nd Street between Central Park West and Columbus Avenue, the **Sol Bloom Playground** not only has two great climbing structures (one toddler-scaled) on a soft red-and-black checkerboard surface but also is the focus of lots of neighborhood athletics, with basketball hoops, a paved softball diamond, and a handball court.

THE UPPER EAST SIDE

St. Catherine's Playground, on the west side of First Avenue between 67th and 68th streets, is unrelentingly urban—chainlink fence, asphalt paving, traffic churning past on three sides—but the construction crews had just moved in the fall of 1998, and the renovated playground will no doubt be less grim than its predecessor. It's definitely a welcome spot in this near-Midtown neighborhood: It's roomy and fairly shady and has a couple of terraced levels for interest, not to mention a set of happening basketball and handball courts on the other side of that fence. **John Jay Park,** on 76th Street east of York Avenue, has some nice up-to-date climbing structures for toddlers in the shady outer area and some for older kids inside the chain-link fence. There are also wide-open asphalt surfaces to run (and fall) on, a small East River lookout near the entrance, and an outdoor pool open in summer (see "Swimming" under "Sports & Games," later in this chapter).

The **Carl Schurz Park Playground,** at 84th Street and East End Avenue, is my top choice on the East Side: This well-shaded playground has several multilevel climbing structures of red-and-green plastic-coated steel and weathered wood—ladders, slides, bridges, steering wheels, climbing chains, and sliding poles provide plenty of playtime interest. It also has a separate sprinkler area and lots of open pavement in the middle that just cries out for a rousing game of Red Rover or Prisoners All. The well-behaved Upper East Side crowd flows in and out of adjacent Carl Schurz Park with its superb riverside promenade (see "Parks," earlier in this chapter). Not far away is **Ruppert Park** (89th to 90th streets along Second Avenue); despite its limited playground equipment, kids love to frolic on the park's landscaped series of terraces, with lots of curved paths, flowerbeds, and benches for playdate tête-à-têtes. Another Upper Upper East Side playground with some interest is the **Hunter School Playground** on Madison Avenue between 94th and 95th streets; its Madison Avenue entrance incorporates a redbrick castlelike facade preserved from a demolished turn-of-the-century National Guard armory. (A similar armory, still intact, is down Park Avenue between 66th and 67th streets.) Though this playground is open to the public only after school hours, it may be worth a special detour to let your kids scamper up and down the steps between the stout brick towers, through a wide arch that just cries out for a moat and drawbridge.

MIDTOWN

At the east end of 42nd Street, the **Tudor City** residential complex is set on a terrace above First Avenue; halfway up the stairs that rise on the south side of 42nd Street just past Second Avenue is a small fenced playground with a rubberized surface and primary-colored climbing structures. Overlooking the river, **Sutton Place Park** is set in a quiet cul-de-sac where East 57th Street dead-ends just past Sutton Place. This tiny brick-paved play area is a few steps down from street level, on a terrace above the FDR Drive, with lots of shade and some great views of the 59th Street Bridge arching over the East River. It's best for infants and toddlers, though, since there's no playground equipment to speak of—nothing but wooden benches, one absurdly small iron-fenced sandbox, and a large bronze wart hog (Pumbaa!) on a pedestal.

CHELSEA, THE FLATIRON DISTRICT & GRAMERCY PARK

Named for the clergyman who wrote *A Visit from St. Nicholas* (better known as The Night Before Christmas), **Clement Clarke Moore Park,** in western Chelsea (southeast corner of Tenth Avenue and 22nd Street), isn't much—a paved corner lot with a few benches and concrete sculptures, with one rubberized-steel climbing structure at the far end—but it's decently shady and quiet enough.

In the Flatiron District, the most centrally located are the two small but heavily populated playgrounds in **Union Square,** side-by-side near Broadway and

16th Street. The fenced-in one has a smart rubber-coated steel climbing gym in happy primary colors, with hordes of toddlers swarming all over it; outside the fence, many kids still insist on clambering over an older playground's outmoded metal structures, which look like geodesic dome skeletons. The Union Square Greenmarket, operating Monday, Wednesday, Friday, and Saturday, is only a few steps away, which makes playground picnics very handy. Somewhat off the beaten track in the Gramercy Park area is **Augustus Saint-Gaudens Park** (19th Street and Second Avenue), which has shade, good climbing structures, and lots of open pavement, some with basketball hoops.

GREENWICH VILLAGE & THE EAST VILLAGE

The focal point of the Village, **Washington Square Park,** at the foot of Fifth Avenue (between Sixth and Fourth streets, though the names are changed here for a couple of blocks), has on the north side a bustling playground with lots of up-to-date climbing structures, set off by a fence from the rest of the park. Farther west, at Sixth Avenue and Bleecker Street, the **32 Carmine Street Playground** is buffered by a redbrick wall from the surrounding traffic; go through the iron gate and you'll find swings and wooden climbing structures in an asphalt-paved yard. Or follow Bleecker Street west to the point where it dead-ends at Hudson Street to find the always-hopping **Bleecker Street Playground,** fenced off with iron palings. It's got swings, a sandbox, picnic tables, and a stretch of asphalt just big enough for hopscotch or a round of double-dutch jump-roping. Older kids may be attracted more to the **Mercer Playground,** a long narrow strip on the west side of Mercer Street between Bleecker and West 3rd streets; instead of climbing equipment, it features a long skating path, a spray shower, plantings, and benches for socializing. The under-8 crowd is served with a small playground a short way down Mercer Street, in front of NYU's sports center.

Once-derelict **Tompkins Square Park** has become a leafy haven in the increasingly gentrified East Village, and it has no less than three good-sized fenced-off playgrounds with black rubberized ground surfaces and rubber-coated metal play structures in bold primary colors (my kids are downright envious of such an abundance). The biggest and busiest is along Avenue A at East 9th Street; the other two are along East 7th Street. After a vigorous play session, head down the avenue for pizza at Two Boots (see chapter 8).

SOHO, LITTLE ITALY & CHINATOWN

The **Thompson Street Playground,** on the east side of Thompson Street between Prince and Spring streets, is a welcome romping spot in oh-so-urban SoHo; it has large red timber climbing structures on an asphalt surface. Good for stretching limbs in fair weather, it's about halfway between the New York Fire Museum and the Children's Museum for the Arts, both on Spring Street. Check first for derelict types, though, who sometimes camp here.

At the corner of Mulberry and Spring streets in Little Italy, the **De Salvio Playground** has a couple of bright modern climbers set in a pleasant fenced-in corner lot, neatly paved with a few benches under the trees. Let's just hope the graffitists who messed the place up right after its renovation have been persuaded to leave it alone since neighborhood forces cleaned and repainted things. In tree-shaded **Columbus Park,** at Worth Street between Baxter and Mulberry streets in Chinatown, hordes of Asian and Asian-American children scramble over the climbing structures and dangle on the swings, while elderly men play chess nearby.

TRIBECA & LOWER MANHATTAN

One of Lower Manhattan's few really inviting green spaces is **Washington Market Park,** on Greenwich Street between Chambers and Duane streets, a 2½-acre lawn sprouting up where the city's rough-and-tumble wholesale food markets used to be. The gentle rises of the grassy area, punctuated with a delightful gazebo, are perfect for picnics and Frisbee games, and there's a fanciful maritime-themed wrought-iron fence at the south end, where P.S. 234 sits. The tidy playground is a small enclosed strip along the park's eastern wall.

The **Hudson River Park Playground,** at the west end of Chambers Street, is a thriving enclosed area across the esplanade from the river. The super climbing structures, made of weathered wood and royal-blue steel, provide bridges and platforms where kids can scamper above ground; on ground level are three good-size sand areas, one wheelchair-accessible. The northern section is set aside for toddlers, with a delicious bronze dodo set in a tiny splashing area; there's another sprinkler area for older kids, with a stone elephant and hippo. At the southern end is one of the coolest pieces of playground equipment in the city: a red steel whirligig seating eight, powered by pedals mounted beneath every other seat. Though most of the playground is unshaded, several wooden arbors along the sides allow parents and sleeping babies to duck out of the sun. While it isn't technically a playground, the same park's esplanade also features a fanciful **sculpture park** with a wade-in fountain that's irresistible to children (not to mention adults, who grin goofily as they inspect the whimsical bronze figures swarming over every available surface). Adjacent **Battery Park City** has a handful of other tiny fenced play areas tucked in around its residential buildings, many of them with no more than a yard-square sandbox and a couple of weathered-wood blocks for climbing on; the slightly larger one at the south end of the Yacht Basin is scaled nicely for toddlers.

Across the street from South Street Seaport, iron fences surround a triangular lot at Fulton and Pearl streets, where the **Pearl Street Playground** has a delightfully complicated climbing structure where kids can let off steam.

BROOKLYN

At the south end of the Promenade in Brooklyn Heights, the excellent **Pierrepont Street Playground** has rest rooms (dirty, but still a blessing in times of toilet emergency), a separate yard for the very young, lots of shade trees, and loads of slides. Add to that plenty of neighborhood buzz and a peerless view across the East River to Manhattan. **The Imagination Playground** in Prospect Park (east side of the park, near the Lincoln Road entrance) is as fanciful as its name promises: a bronze dragon spouts water, a black-and-white-striped bridge twists like a helix, child-sized masks are mounted for children to peek through, and a central sculpture features the little boy Peter and his dog Willie from Ezra Jack Keats's beloved children's books.

3 Indoor Playgrounds

The winter play scene in Manhattan is relieved by several indoor playgrounds, huge rooms with innovative, brightly colored structures encouraging all sorts of active and fantasy play. While these can be lifesavers on a cold or rainy day when the kids are climbing the walls, when you arrive you may find that everybody else in town has had the same bright idea. They're popular party locales too, which makes for sardinelike crowds on weekends.

Chelsea Piers Field House

Pier 62 at Chelsea Piers, 23rd St. and the West Side Hwy., at the Hudson River. ☎ **212/336-6500.** Admission $8 to Toddler Gym, $15 to Open Gym & Climb, $7 for soccer field or basketball courts, $1 per 10 balls in batting cages. Call for schedule. Subway: 1/9, C/E, or F/N/R to 23rd St. stations. Bus: M23 across 23rd St.

Calling this recreation facility an indoor playground is kind of like calling the Superdome a football field. What a fabulous resource this is: batting cages, basketball courts, artificial turf fields that can be adapted for soccer or volleyball or lacrosse, an indoor climbing wall scaled perfectly for young climbers, and a gymnastics area you have to see to believe—spring floors, in-ground trampolines, deep foam pits for practicing dismounts, and loads of bars, beams, rings, horses, and vaults. Most of the facility is booked up with ongoing classes and league play, but kids 4 and older can check out the Field House at an Open Gym session, while children 1 to 4 can occupy themselves happily in the Toddler Gym, a separate playroom with soft climbing structures.

Early Childhood Resources & Information Center

66 Leroy St. (between Hudson St. and Seventh Ave. South). ☎ **212/929-0815.** Free admission. Mon–Wed and Fri 1–6pm, Thurs 1–8pm, Sat 1–5pm. Subway: 1/9 to Houston St.

This public library branch in the West Village has a little-known bonus: a large indoor area set aside for infants and toddlers, with small slides and other equipment for stretching those muscles. Best of all, it's free.

Hackers Hitters and Hoops

123 W. 18th St. (between Sixth and Seventh aves.). ☎ **212/929-7482.** Admission $3 per person Wed–Thurs after 5pm, $4 Fri–Sat after 5pm; free rest of the time. Sun–Mon 11am–7pm, Tues–Thurs 11am–midnight, Fri–Sat 11am–2am; no one under 18 admitted after 8pm. Subway: 1/9 to 18th St.

In a different league from the other indoor playgrounds, this joint is totally sports oriented and not a bit childish—in fact, the evening sessions are primarily for adults. Miniature golf, batting cages, basketball, volleyball, Ping-Pong, and soccer are offered, as well as various arcade games; once in the door, you buy 50¢ tokens to spend on various activities. Birthday parties invade on weekends, but the minigolf, the batting cages, and the games arcade should still be open.

Kidmazeum

80 East End Ave. (at 83rd St.). ☎ **212/327-4800.** Admission $8 kids 8 months–8 years (half price after 5pm), free for adults; $4 in summer whenever temperature is over 75°. Sept–Mar Mon–Fri 9am–5pm, Sat–Sun 10am–6pm; Apr–Aug Tues–Fri 10am–5pm, Sat–Sun 10am–6pm. Subway: 4/5/6 to 86th St.

Maybe it's the stiff admission price that leaves so many parents looking grumpy here; maybe it's the fact that once you've paid up at the gate you still have to fork over quarters for a handful of rides and video games, including the all-too-popular tiny carousel. Maybe it's the prominent placement of the vending machines, which kids are constantly begging for snacks from. Or maybe it's just the adult's response to the mood set by the humorless staff. But this bilevel center certainly offers kids plenty to do. Upstairs are three play areas decorated in the usual primary colors: a small toddler play area with cushioned gym mats, a slide, a mini–ball pit; a plastic climbing structure with a couple of slides and tunnel overpasses; at the far end is a Discovery Zone–style ball maze. Downstairs you'll find a series of imaginative play areas—a bank, a grocery store, a tiny stage with lots of costumes for dressing-up—plus an inflated trampoline, a set of percussive pads for making music, and a whole room with plastic-pegged walls for Lego constructions. Sounds great, doesn't it? Then why don't I enjoy it more?

My Favorite Place

265 W. 87th St. (between Broadway and West End Ave.). ☎ **212/362-5320.** Admission $8 kids 5 and under; free for adults. Mon–Thurs 9:30am–5:30pm, Fri 9:30am–3pm; Fri afternoon and weekend times vary. Subway: 1/9 to 86th St.

Beneath this winning West Side toy store (see chapter 6) is an excellent carpeted toddler playroom, decorated in soft, soothing colors (not primary colors, for a change) and equipped with Brio trains, Duplo blocks, wooden building blocks, a play kitchen, a dress-up area, and a small climbing area. The low ceiling and carpet make it nicely soundproofed, in contrast to the vaulting spaces of most of the other indoor playgrounds, and it's generally not crowded. A lovely, gentle place to spend time with wee ones.

Party Palace

1158 Second Ave. (near 61st St.). ☎ **212/935-9577.** Admission $10 children; free for adults. Daily 10am–6pm. Subway: 4/5/6 to 59th St.

The Midtown location may give this lackluster playground an edge for visiting families, though the admission price is pretty steep for the kind of unimaginative stuff you get. Areas are segregated for the 1-to-8 age group and the 5-to-15 set; all the usual Discovery Zone–clone equipment is here—your ball pit, net climb, slides, moon walk—and there's a game arcade as well.

✪ PlaySpace

2473 Broadway (at 92nd St.). ☎ **212/769-2300.** Admission $5.50 per person (second parent admitted free). Daily 9am–6pm (to 7pm Thurs). Subway: 1/2/3/9 to 96th St.

This large colorful playroom is custom-designed for the 6-and-under crowd, with a special carpeted area set aside for infants and their grown-ups. Large windows let in plenty of light, making it feel less claustrophobic than some of the other indoor playgrounds. There's a huge sand area with lots of digging toys and incredibly white sand (you could never keep sand this clean outdoors in the parks); a wide-open area of blond hardwood floor allows toddlers to trundle around on sturdy little bikes and minicars, and there are a couple of waist-high troughs for water play. Best of all is the imaginative bilevel structure running along the north wall, incorporating little nooks and crannies for block-building and dress-up and puppet play with a series of ladders and tunnels and towers and bridges. There's also a small cafe where kids can refuel and parents can prop themselves up with coffee and a newspaper. Everything is spick-and-span and well supervised, and nothing seems too hokey or contrived—no ball mazes for small children to get lost and frightened in, either. When this place first opened, I thought it was overpriced, but now that I've seen all the competition I realize how superior PlaySpace is.

Rain or Shine

115 E. 29th Street (between Park Ave. South and Lexington Ave.) ☎ **212/532-4420.** Admission $8.95 per child under 13 ($7.95 for additional siblings); free for adults. Daily 10am–6pm. Subway: 6 to 28th St.; N/R to 28th St.

Best for children 6 and under, this rain forest–themed play space is a godsend in this between-neighborhoods part of town. Dramatic play is encouraged in the main area with a curtained stage, dress-up costumes, puppets, and a good-sized playhouse (complete with a picket fence), as well as a few slides and tunnels to work off energy. My children were drawn like magnets to the mini–roller coaster—a riding toy on a track with very gentle hills—which is extremely popular (giving rise to lots of impromptu lessons on sharing). It also has a super sandbox, a big walk-in pit with a slide, lots of big plastic dump trucks, and sparkling white sand. The enclosed infant area is small but cozy, and a open art room provides an outlet

The *Ghostbusters* Tour

One of the great Manhattan movies of all time, the 1984 film *Ghostbusters* really used the city well. It starts out in Midtown at the **New York Public Library,** Fifth Avenue at 42nd Street, where a little old lady librarian flips her card catalog at an onslaught of spooks and specters. The team of paranormal researchers played by Dan Aykroyd, Harold Ramis, and Bill Murray has been teaching way uptown at **Columbia University,** Broadway and 117th Street, but after setting up shop as Ghostbusters they move their **Ghostbuster headquarters** into an old fire station at 14 Moore St., at Hudson Street, down in TriBeCa.

An urgent call from an attractive cellist, played by Sigourney Weaver, brings them to **55 Central Park West** at 65th Street, where a spirit named Gozer has taken up residence in her refrigerator; looking up at this varicolored art-deco building, however, you'll note that the top looks significantly different from the way it did it the movie—an elaborate rooftop was matted in. Bill Murray has a rendezvous with Sigourney later after she leaves a rehearsal at nearby **Lincoln Center,** by the fountain on the central plaza, Columbus Avenue at 64th Street. Once the spooks have erupted full force from 55 Central Park West, the nerdy accountant down the hall, played by Rick Moranis, becomes possessed and roams glassy-eyed outside **Tavern on the Green,** the festively lit restaurant across the street in Central Park at West 65th Street. And when the evil spirit turns into a giant Stay-Puf Marshmallow man, it wades up Central Park West from **Columbus Circle,** 59th Street and Central Park West, looking for all the world like a Macy's Parade balloon (the parade passes through Columbus Circle every Thanksgiving Day).

for kids at the older end of the spectrum. This long, narrow space is easily flooded by arriving birthday parties, but once they vanish to the downstairs gym and party room, things calm down. There's a limited selection of snacks for sale, with a cafe counter running the length of the main space so noshing parents can keep an eye on their kids.

4 Neighborhood Strolls

ROCKEFELLER CENTER

The heart of Midtown is **Rockefeller Center,** a huge streamlined office/retail complex of pale limestone built in the 1930s by the famously wealthy Rockefeller family. Start on Fifth Avenue between 49th and 50th streets at the so-called **Channel Gardens,** which lie between the British building on the north and the French building on the south just as the English Channel lies between Britain and France. The Channel Gardens slope down to **Rockefeller Plaza,** the center's heart. Beneath the colossal gilded statue of the Greek god Prometheus, in winter there's a jewel of an ice-skating rink, in summer an open-air cafe; all the flags of the U.N. member nations flap in the breeze from their flagpoles around the upper railings. Behind *Prometheus,* where the giant Christmas tree stands every December, rises **30 Rockefeller Plaza,** home of the NBC TV network; step inside to see about taking the **NBC Studio Tour** and to buy souvenirs of your favorite NBC shows at the gift shop. Or if you're here between 7 and 9am, stop outside the big glass windows on the south side of 49th Street to watch the *Today Show* being broadcast live; hosts Katie Couric and Matt Lauer often take to the streets outside as well to film various segments.

Various concourses and tunnels snake under Sixth Avenue (excuse me, Avenue of the Americas) connecting all the Rockefeller Center buildings in an underground world of shops and restaurants; you may want to take the escalators down from the lobby in 30 Rock and prowl around. Study the monumental lobby murals inside 30 Rock's Rockefeller Plaza entrance, then exit the building on Sixth Avenue and turn around to see the glittering mosaics decorating that entrance. Walk north to 50th street to see the neon-accented streamlined facade of the great art-deco theater **Radio City Music Hall,** which still has some live stage shows as well as a continual lineup of pop concerts.

Return to Fifth Avenue along 50th Street and turn left to pass the **International Building,** with its famous bronze statue of Atlas carrying the world. Across the street is Rockefeller Center's famous neighbor, **St. Patrick's Cathedral,** seat of the Archdiocese of New York. You may want to step inside for a look at this graceful late-19th-century Gothic-style church—if you're lucky there may be a wedding to watch.

TUDOR CITY & THE UNITED NATIONS

If you're staying in Midtown, sightseeing in Midtown, and dining in Midtown, you may crave a quick shot of residential calm—and you'll find it in Tudor City, a protected mock-Tudor enclave built in the 1920s on the East River end of 42nd Street. From Second Avenue and 41st Street, walk east up a steep hill to **Tudor City Place,** where you can turn left. Stand at the railings across the street, look east to the East River, and then down to see the traffic of 42nd Street thunder through the underpass, while all up here on the terrace remains calm. Linger in the neatly planted gardens on the west side of Tudor City Place, visit the playground (go down the steps on the south side of 42nd Street), or proceed north on Tudor City Place to 43rd Street, where you can look straight across First Avenue to see the **United Nations** complex. A flight of stairs takes you down into tiny paved Ralph Bunche Park, from which you can cross the street to the United Nations (technically, you're no longer on U.S. soil here—like the Vatican, the U.N. is its own nation). Even if you're not doing a tour (see chapter 4), walk around the U.N.'s beautiful Rose Garden, with broad paved walkways overlooking the East River.

GREENWICH VILLAGE

Start in the heart of the Village, **Washington Square,** with its white triumphal arch at the foot of Fifth Avenue. The redbrick houses facing the north side of the square look totally 19th century, dating from a time when Greenwich Village really was a separate country village. Much of the rest of Washington Square is now surrounded by the modern buildings of **New York University,** but the park's crowd is a democratic melange of all sorts of New Yorkers, not just college students. Weekends usually attract street performers, and on many afternoons there are informal speed-chess competitions going on beneath the shade trees at the southwest corner of the park.

For a taste of the bohemian Village, go south from the park (down Thompson, Sullivan, or MacDougal) to **Bleecker Street,** lined with cheap ethnic restaurants and long-running music clubs. Go west on Bleecker Street across Sixth Avenue, where Bleecker takes an unpredictable angle north, like many of the West Village streets. This is a more Italian part of the village, with some great food shops selling coffee, bread, pastries, cheese, and pork and sausage. If you've got older kids who are hardy walkers, follow Bleecker all the way across Seventh Avenue, turn left on Grove Street, and go west until Grove dead-ends at the charming church of **St. Luke's-in-the-Fields.** The well-preserved 19th-century look of this quiet neighborhood makes it popular for TV and movie shots; the apartment where TV's *Friends* supposedly live is right at the crook of Grove Street between Bedford and Hudson. Go north on Hudson to West 10th Street, turn right, and return east to Sixth Avenue.

At Sixth Avenue and West 9th Street, the castlelike redbrick building on your left is **Jefferson Market,** originally a courthouse and now a branch of the public library. Turn right (east) onto West 11th Street. The brick wall on your right surrounds a tiny cemetery, one of several belonging to Shearith Israel, the oldest Jewish congregation in the country. Continue down the block, lined with classic brick town houses, until you see one that's startlingly modern—**18 W. 11th St.** Inside the large picture window, the owner's stuffed Paddington bear is usually dressed in a timely fashion, with a yellow slicker on if it's raining, a Yankees or Mets cap in baseball season, depending on which team is winning. Soon after, you'll be back at Fifth Avenue—turn right to get back to Washington Square or left to make a stop at the **Forbes Magazine Galleries** (see "More Manhattan Museums" in chapter 4) with its collections of toy soldiers, toy boats, and Fabergé eggs.

THE EAST VILLAGE

Gentrified but still urban cool, the funky East Village is a magnet for preteens and teenagers determined to prove their hipness quotient. Start on **Astor Place,** the busy intersection of Fourth Avenue, Lafayette Street, and East 8th Street, where sidewalk peddlers usually hawk everything from hammered silver jewelry to old vinyl LPs to well-thumbed paperbacks to secondhand lamps and furniture. The hulking brownstone building to the south is **Cooper Union,** a progressive school of architecture, art, and engineering founded in 1859. Head east on what should be 8th Street, here called **St. Mark's Place;** busy day and night, the block of St. Mark's between Third and Second avenues is lined with vintage-clothing stores, bookstores, coffeehouses, and cafes. Beatniks hung out here in the 1950s, hippies in the 1960s, punks in the 1970s. (Somewhat incongruously, this neighborhood also has long-established enclaves of Ukrainian immigrants, centered on 7th Street, and Russians, on 9th and 10th streets, as you can see if you stroll around farther.)

At **Second Avenue,** you may want to turn left and go 2 blocks north to the **Second Avenue Deli** (southeast corner of Second Avenue and 10th Street). Stars set in the sidewalk in front celebrate long-ago stars of the golden age of Yiddish theater, which was centered along this stretch of Second Avenue. On the northwest corner of this intersection, the fieldstone **St. Mark's-in-the-Bowery Church** is the city's oldest continually used church building—Peter Stuyvesant, the famous governor of the Dutch colony of Nieuw Amsterdam, used to worship here. In fact this area used to be his farm, and **Stuyvesant Street,** which angles south back to Astor Place, is named for him. Stroll past the early 19th-century town houses on Stuyvesant Street and try to imagine what the Village looked like back then—before the beatniks, hippies, and punks took over.

If you're looking for club-kid coolness, follow St. Mark's Place until it ends at Avenue A. (Manhattan widens here, requiring a set of lettered avenues to be added east of the numbered ones—hence the neighborhood's nickname, Alphabet City.) You'll be at **Tompkins Square** (bounded by Avenue A, East 7th Street, Avenue B, and East 10th Street), once the site of bloody confrontations in the late 1980s between the police and a resident camp of homeless people. Today it has been thoroughly spruced up—a controversial move in this politically conscious neighborhood, long the low-rent-or-no-rent domain of squatters, struggling artists, and drug dealers. Avenue A is lined with funky shops and cafes, well worth scoping out.

CHINATOWN

Begin on **Canal Street,** the major thoroughfare cutting across Manhattan at this point; Canal used to be the northern boundary of Chinatown before its burgeoning population spilled over into Little Italy and the Lower East Side. Walk east from Centre Street to the Bowery on the south side of Canal Street, where a string of produce and fish stores offer wares on the sidewalks. Point out to your kids the Chinese lettering on every sign and the pagoda-shaped pay-phone stations. Turn right (south) at the Bowery. On the Bowery's east side, a gargantuan statue of the Chinese philosopher Confucius dominates the little plaza in front of **Confucius Plaza,** an otherwise undistinguished redbrick modern residential development.

Continue south on the Bowery 2 blocks to the frantic intersection called **Chatham Square,** with its big Chinese arch in the middle. Then backtrack on the Bowery a few steps to narrow sloping **Pell Street,** where you turn left. A Hong Kong–like jumble of restaurants and neon signs, Pell leads you west 1 block to busy **Mott Street,** a crowded and decidedly unglitzy shopping street. Barbecued ducks hang in glass shopfronts, candy shops sell pastel-colored imported sweets, and twanging recorded music leaks out into the street. Turn right on Mott and go 1 block to Bayard Street, where you turn left and go 1 block to Mulberry. The **Museum of Chinese in America** (see "More Manhattan Museums" in Chapter 4) will be on your right and **Columbus Park** on your left, where Chinatown residents old and young congregate. If your kids are young enough to enjoy a swing and slide, stop in Columbus Park's playground for some closer contact with the locals.

LITTLE ITALY

There's not much left to this classic tenement neighborhood, what with Chinatown encroaching on the south and SoHo on the west; you and your kids can do the whole bit in half an hour easy, even if you stop along the way to check out the authentic little shops. From Canal Street, walk up **Mulberry Street** to Houston Street, past several Italian restaurants that thrive on the tourist trade; don't miss **Umberto's Clam House** at 129 Mulberry St., site of a famous 1973 Mafia hit, when a wiseguy named Joey Gallo was rubbed out.

On Mulberry and the streets branching off it, look for stores selling religious medals and figures and others selling glorious foodstuffs—fresh pastas, imported olive oil and vinegars, Baci chocolates, tangy gelati (Italian ices). At the intersection of Broome Street, **Caffè Roma,** 385 Broome St., is a great old-fashioned tile-floored pastry shop where you can stop for cannoli and espresso. Look above the shop signs to see the tracery of iron fire escapes hanging out over the street, a distinguishing feature of these turn-of-the-century tenement buildings, which slumlords designed to cram in as many small rooms as possible onto the narrow lots.

Things get quieter above Spring Street—a leafy little paved park, **De Salvio Square,** on the southeast corner of Spring and Mulberry; the traditional **D & G Bakery** at 45 Spring St., with its vintage coal oven; and **Old St. Patrick's Cathedral,** the 19th-century precursor to Midtown's big Catholic cathedral, now a parish church. Behind the redbrick walls lies a tiny cemetery where some of the city's early Roman Catholic bishops are buried; scenes from Martin Scorsese's seminal Little Italy film *Mean Streets* were shot here.

MORNINGSIDE HEIGHTS

The upper end of the Upper West Side, this neighborhood is Manhattan's college town, with Columbia University, Barnard College, the Union Theological Seminary, and the Jewish Theological Seminary all clustered along Broadway from 116th to 122nd streets. The place to start, however, is at 112th Street and Amsterdam Avenue, on the front steps of the Episcopal **Cathedral of St. John the Divine.** This will be the largest cathedral in the world if they ever finish building it; they've been at it for over a century, since 1892, but if your kids have studied medieval history at all they'll know that most of the great European cathedrals took a couple of centuries to complete too. Notice how only two of the arches over the front doors have statues in them; empty niches in the other arches await future stonecarvers' work. Go inside and stroll around, stopping on the north aisle at Poet's Corner, where paving stones honor selected American poets. St. John the Divine is so huge that the Statue of Liberty could fit under the central dome, and the tiny-looking figure of Christ you see in the rose window over the front doors is actually life-size. Stop in the wonderful gift shop, which has some books and toys for kids, to a see a model of what the cathedral should look like when completed. Then go out to the garden just south of the cathedral to see the Children's Fountain, a fanciful huge sculpture surrounded by peewee sculptures created by local schoolchildren. On the lawns of the surrounding cathedral close, you can sometimes spot a pair of peacocks strutting and preening.

Go north on Amsterdam Avenue. (If your kids are good walkers, you may want to detour at 113th Street, turning right to head over to **Morningside Drive.** Walk north to 116th Street and Morningside, where a small plaza overlooks the steep slope into Morningside Park below and Harlem to the east, then return to Amsterdam Avenue.) At 117th Street and Amsterdam, pass through the wrought-iron gates into **Columbia University,** New York's entry in the Ivy League. As you cross the campus, notice the broad steps of Low Memorial Library on your right; parents may remember it as the site of the famous student protests in 1968, but kids will recognize it as the place where Dan Aykroyd, Bill Murray, and Harold Ramis decided to leave academic research and become full-time *Ghostbusters.*

Exit the campus through the matching set of gates onto Broadway and cross the street to enter the gates of **Barnard College,** Columbia's all-women sister college. Or head north on Broadway to 120th Street: **Columbia's Teachers College** is the big dark redbrick building on the northeast corner, and the **Union Theological Seminary** is the medieval-looking gray stone complex on the northwest corner. (**Jewish Theological Seminary** is a redbrick fortress up on the northeast corner of Broadway and 122nd Street.) Turn left on 120th Street and go west to Riverside Drive, where **Riverside Church** stands on your right. If its pale limestone reminds you of a Gothic version of Rockefeller Center, it's no coincidence, since John J. Rockefeller was one of its founders in 1930. Step inside to take the elevator to the top of the 356-foot-tall bell tower. Across Riverside Drive and several yards north sits the columned neoclassical **Grant National Memorial Monument,** where President Ulysses S. Grant and his wife, Julia, are buried. (Ask your kids the corny old joke: "Who's buried in Grant's Tomb?") Admission is free—step inside and peer down into the sunken chamber where their dark marble tombs are laid. It can be deliciously creepy if you think about it, though the high-ceilinged memorial has a few other distractions, including a National Parks Service information stand and some interesting exhibits about Grant's life and the Civil War he won for the Union. My kids' favorite part is actually outside, in the plaza around the tomb, with its nutty mosaic benches designed by New York's public school students. We usually repair afterward to the **Claremont Playground,** in the park just north of the memorial, then meander south down the broad sidewalk on the west side of Riverside Drive, overlooking shady **Riverside Park.**

5 Sports & Games

BASKETBALL

Several city-run playgrounds have asphalt half-courts where some pretty aggressive games of one-on-one take place. The famous courts at **Sixth Avenue and West 4th Street**—known as "The Cage"—are a breeding ground for serious hoop-dreamers; the action is so fast and furious, kids may be better off spectating than playing. Intrepid kids may, however, be able to get a pick-up game at **St. Catherine's Playground** (First Avenue between 67th and 68th streets), in **Central Park**'s courts just northeast of the Great Lawn (midpark at 85th Street), **Riverside Park** at West 76th Street, the **Sol Bloom Playground** (West 92nd Street between Central Park West and Columbus Avenue), or **Goat Park** (Amsterdam Avenue and 99th Street)—named after Earl "the Goat" Manigault, a high-jumping, high-scoring street player who watched his peers win NBA offers while his own life unraveled in disappointment and drug addiction. Manigault redeemed himself by running athletic programs for kids in this very park, for which he will be forever remembered.

BICYCLING

The circular drive in **Central Park** is probably the city's most popular biking road, a 6-mile-long circuit that includes a couple of fairly grueling hills; younger kids should probably stick to the relatively flat lower loop, which shortcuts across at 72nd Street, or even the footpath looping around the Great Lawn, midpark from 81st to 86th streets (officially off-limits to bikes, but trikes are usually tolerated).

Or try this **suggested route:** Starting at East 79th Street and Fifth Avenue, pedal up Cedar Hill to the East Drive, turn right, and follow a flat stretch of the drive past the reservoir; at the crosswalk just south of 96th Street, turn left again (west) and follow the footpath that cuts west across the park, bearing left at the fork to go past the Tennis House and exit the park at 93rd Street; turn left and ride south on the Central Park West sidewalk to West 81st Street, where you can turn back into the park and follow paths across the foot of the Great Lawn back to your starting point. Park drives are closed to traffic weekdays 10am to 3pm and all weekend long; bike traffic circles the park clockwise. The wide sidewalk bordering the park walls is also good for young riders, with few cross streets to negotiate; follow it up either Fifth Avenue or Central Park West.

The circular road in Brooklyn's **Prospect Park** is another great traffic-free place to ride on weekends; it's only 3½ miles long and has only one really tough hill. **Riverside Park** offers a flat, wide promenade from 83rd to 96th streets, as well as paths skimming down under the West Side Highway to let you ride for a few blocks right along the Hudson. (The downward path at 86th Street has the gentlest incline of the three; the 79th Street path entails negotiating around a busy West Side Highway off-ramp, while the 72nd Street path to the boat basin has a very steep hill just west of the highway. See "Green New York: The Top Parks," earlier in this chapter.) Like Central Park, Riverside is bordered by wide sidewalks, either of asphalt or of distinctive hexagonal paving stones, so you can cruise along the west side of Riverside Drive from 79th Street up to 125th Street with very few cross streets to worry about.

The **Battery Park Promenade** also runs along the Hudson, with some great harbor views, though it isn't all that long; you can extend your ride by following the 2-mile bike path through **Hudson River Park,** running up to Christopher Street and West Street. On weekends, there's little traffic in Lower Manhattan, so you may have fun going across Liberty Street or Rector Street to the Wall Street area, where you can circle around the deserted skyscrapers. Swing north on Nassau Street and go up to City Hall, where broad entrance ramps lead onto the **Brooklyn Bridge,** with broad bike/pedestrian lanes leading you over the river (see the box "Crossing the Brooklyn Bridge").

Now here's the catch: Very few of Manhattan's many bicycle rental shops stock bikes for kids; apparently the insurance costs are too prohibitive. The ones that do are **Larry & Jeff's Bicycles Plus,** 1690 Second Ave., between 87th and 88th streets (☎ 212/722-2201), charging $5 per hour for kids' bikes, $7 per hour for adults' (a full day runs $25 adults, $20 kids); **Pedal Pusher,** 1306 Second Ave., at 69th Street (☎ **212/288-5592;** closed Tues), charging $3.95 per hour, $9.95 per day; and **Central Park Bicycle Rentals,** at the Loeb Boathouse in Central Park, midpark at 72nd Street (☎ **212/861-4137**), charging $8 per hour ($6 if you're with a group of 10 or more).

BOWLING

Bowlmor Lanes
110 University Place (between 12th and 13th sts.). ☎ **212/255-8188.** $4.95 per person per game (reduced Mon–Fri before 5pm, $3.50 adults, $3 kids under 14); $12 (including shoe rental) for Night Strike, Mon 10pm–4am. Shoe rental $3. Sun and Tues–Thurs 10am–1am, Mon and Fri–Sat 10am–4am. Subway: 4/5/6/L/N/R to Union Sq.

Down in the Village, 42-lane Bowlmor survives as a sort of hip throwback, with a long sleek bar, a restaurant, a VIP lounge, and lots of postmodern date bowling (DJs, glow-in-the-dark pins, nude bowling parties, and so on), alongside some ferocious league action at night. Daytimes being less in demand, they allow kids 6 to 14 to bowl at discounted prices until 5pm; there's automatic scoring, and gutter bumpers are available to keep kids' balls in the alley. Trivia fans take note: The first *Bowling for Dollars* TV game show was shot here, and Nixon bowled here regularly in the 1950s.

✪ Chelsea Piers AMF Bowling
Pier 60 at Chelsea Piers, 23rd Street and the West Side Hwy. at the Hudson River. ☎ **212/835-2695.** $6 per person per game. Shoe rental $4. Sun–Thurs 9am–2am, Fri–Sat 9am–4am. Subway: 1/9, C/E, or F/N/R to 23rd St. stations. Bus: M23 across 23rd St.

This sparkling 40-lane facility, one of the newer additions at Chelsea Piers (it's in the building just south of the Field House), sees lots of family action on weekends. There's also a games arcade, and waiters from the on-site restaurant will bring food right to your lane. Gutter bumpers are much in demand here.

Leisure Time Bowling
625 Eighth Ave., in the Port Authority Bus Terminal, 2nd level (enter at 40th St. and Eighth Ave.). ☎ **212/268-6909.** $4.25 per person per game ($3.75 before 5pm); bumper bowling $10 extra. Shoe rental $2.50. Sun–Thurs 10am–11pm, Fri–Sat 10am–2am. Subway: A/C/E to 42nd St.

Budding bowlers should foray into the unattractive bus terminal because this surprisingly clean and modern 30-lane complex offers kids bumper bowling, with special padding to keep balls in the lane. Bumper bowling is available only 10am to 3pm.

CHESS

It's possible to play at the outdoor chessboards beside the **Central Park Chess and Checkers House,** midpark at 67th Street, just west of the Dairy; the boards are built into the stone tables and you can pick up chess pieces at the Dairy. The real scene for kids, however, is in Greenwich Village, where two chess stores sit a few doors away from each other on Thompson Street between 3rd and Bleecker streets: **Chess Forum,** 219 Thompson St. (☎ **212/475-2369**), and **The Chess Shop,** 230 Thompson St. (☎ **212/475-9580**). Loads of kids stream in to play, especially on Saturday, and the charges are minimal—officially $1 an hour per person, though the guys on staff rarely charge even that much. Either store can also arrange lessons for $25 an hour.

Kids also play free at **New York Chess and Backgammon,** 120 W. 41st St., between Broadway and Sixth Avenue (☎ **212/302-5874**). This club organizes tournaments for kids outdoors in Bryant Park (Sixth Avenue between 40th and 42nd streets) late June to September, every Saturday 11am to 2pm; there's a $7 entry fee, a lesson and lecture are thrown in, and many levels of players show up. School-age kids can also take chess lessons on Saturday 11am to 2pm and Sunday noon to 3pm at the **Manhattan Chess Club,** 353 W. 46th St., between Eighth and Ninth avenues (☎ **212/333-5888**); the cost is $5 per class.

FENCING

The Fencers Club
119 W. 25th St. (between Sixth and Seventh aves.), 5th floor. ☎ **212/807-6947.** Subway: 1/9 or E/F/N/R to 23rd St. stations.

Led by Peter Westbrook, one of the few Olympic-level American fencers, this fencing studio's youth program is outstanding.

Metropolis Fencing Club
45 W. 21st St. (between Fifth and Sixth aves.), 2nd floor. ☎ **212/463-8044.** Subway: 1/9 or E/F/N/R to 23rd St. stations.

Starting at age 7, kids—even rank beginners—can book fencing lessons at this high-ceilinged, friendly studio. Equipment provided.

FISHING

Dana Discovery Center
In Central Park at E. 110th St. ☎ **212/860-1370.** Free admission. Tues–Sun 11am–5pm. Subway: 2/3 to 110th St. Bus: M2, M3, or M4 to 110th St./Fifth Ave.

Believe it or not, you actually can fish in Manhattan, at the north end of Central Park in the Harlem Meer. Take your kids to the redbrick boathouse on the Meer's north shore and the staff will give them simple fishing poles; they'll even throw in some bait. (Don't worry, it's not live worms.) No one I know has ever successfully caught a fish up here, but fish did nibble at their lines and everyone reports having had a whale of a time.

FOLK DANCING

Central Park International Folk Dancing
In Central Park, on the east end of Turtle Pond, midpark at 81st St. ☎ **718/584-4578.** Free admission. Sun 2–6pm (weather permitting).

It's free, it's outdoors, and it's so uncool it's cool. A mismatched bunch of enthusiasts shows up every week to hop, skip, cross-step, and clap in time to various kinds of folk music, blared from Alex Quartner's tape deck; show up at 1:30pm or so and Alex will give you a little lesson. People come and go, joining in for a few dances or sitting on the base of the King Jagiello statue just to watch. Nothing is too difficult that you can't pick up the steps just by shuffling along behind the regulars, and nobody cares if you do it right—they're just happy you're participating. Though it's mostly adults, there are always a few kids hanging on the fringes until they figure out the steps (of course, the kids catch on faster than we bumbling adults do). Donations to help cover the organizer's costs are appreciated. Anyone who thinks New York is a cold, rude, overstimulated city should show up here on Sunday to see a very different face of the Big Apple.

GOLF

The Golf Club at the Chelsea Piers

Pier 59 at Chelsea Piers, 23rd St. and the West Side Hwy., at the Hudson River. ☎ **212/ 336-6400.** Minimum charge $15, which gets you 68 balls at peak times, 100 other times. Summer, daily 5am–midnight. Subway: 1/9, C/E, or F/N/R to 23rd St. stations. Bus: M23 across 23rd St.

This is truly an amazing facility: a four-level driving range, where 52 golfers at a time can slam balls out into a huge open space bounded by high-tech mesh. All the time, you're looking out at incredible Hudson River views. Modeled after multitiered ranges in Japan, where golf's popularity far outweighs the availability of land for golf courses, this is the first such facility in the United States. The stalls are heated for year-round play, and you don't have to lug around buckets of balls—a computerized system in the floor slides a new ball up on your tee as soon as you've hit the previous one. You pay for as many balls as you wish and get a magnetized card to swipe in a slot at the tee; the computer subtracts how many you hit and you can come back whenever you want to hit the rest. There's also a 1,000-square-foot practice putting green, and pros are available for lessons at the attached Jim McLean Golf Academy.

Hackers Hitters and Hoops

123 W. 18th St. (between Sixth and Seventh aves.). ☎ **212/929-7482.** Admission $3 per person Wed–Thurs after 5pm, $4 Fri–Sat after 5pm, free rest of the time; minigolf costs five 50¢ tokens per person. Sun–Mon 11am–7pm, Tues–Thurs 11am–midnight, Fri–Sat 11am–2am; no one under 18 admitted after 8pm. Subway: 1/9 to 18th St.

Among the features at this super Chelsea indoor recreational center is a nine-hole miniature golf course designed for adults as well as kids. Various holes are inspired by real-life holes at championship courses around the country, with imitation water hazards and sand traps.

Pier 25 Mini-Golf

N. Moore St. at the West Side Hwy. ☎ **212/732-7467** or 212/941-6922. Admission $2 kids, $2.50 adults. Daily noon–7pm whenever the weather is warm.

Community-based Manhattan Youth Recreation and Resources has developed this Downtown pier, just north of Hudson River Park, as a children's play area, with a sand yard, a sprinkler plaza, a snack bar, and an 18-hole miniature golf course. The layout is ungimmicky, just green outdoor turf fairways with a few mock boulders, mini–sand traps, and blue-painted water to simulate the type of hazards you'd get on an actual course. Everybody we saw there was playing with young kids, which meant that everybody was forgiving if play wasn't exactly regulation. A great place to stop off, especially if you're riding or skating on the Hudson bike path.

Crossing the Brooklyn Bridge

As thrilling a sight as this beautiful brown-hued East River bridge is from afar, with its Gothic-style towers and lacy mesh of cables, the view *from* the bridge is even more thrilling. A boardwalklike pedestrian walkway goes all the way across, raised slightly above the car traffic. One mile long, it should take about half an hour to traverse—except you'll be tempted to stop more than once to ooh and ahh at the vision of Manhattan's skyscrapers thrusting upward, with the great harbor and Verrazano Bridge beyond.

Why has the Brooklyn Bridge captured the popular imagination so much more than its neighbors to the north, the Manhattan and Williamsburg bridges? Well, for one thing, it scored one historic first—it was the first steel-wire suspension bridge in the world when it opened in 1883, sonorously hailed as the Eighth Wonder of the World. Until then, the only way to get from Manhattan to Brooklyn, at that time separate cities, had been via ferry (crossing from Manhattan's Fulton Street to Brooklyn's Fulton Street, both named after steamship inventor Robert Fulton, who operated the ferry company). You can imagine what a difference the bridge made in consolidating the New York metropolis.

As you walk over, wow your kids with some of the bridge's history. It took 16 years to build, from 1867 to 1833, and you could say it seemed to have a bit of a curse on it—the original designer, John A. Roebling, died from tetanus contracted when his foot was crushed while surveying the site, and his son, Washington, who took over the job, fell ill with the bends after diving into the river to supervise the workmen laying the pilings. A virtual cripple afterward, Washington Roebling watched the bridge going up through a telescope from his house in nearby Brooklyn Heights, while his wife actually supervised much of the completion of the project.

Since then, however, the Brooklyn Bridge has become a byword in New York lore. The standard old joke defines a con artist as a guy trying to sell rubes the deed to the Brooklyn Bridge ("Brother, have I got a bridge to sell you. . . ."). Cocky teenage hoodlums have proved their bravado by shinnying up its cables, while suicides with a flair for the dramatic have plummeted to their deaths from those same cables into the tidal currents below. The bridge has appeared in countless movies and TV shows, its outline practically synonymous with New York City.

The entrance ramps to the bridge begin by the plaza in front of the city's Municipal Building, along Centre Street just south of Chambers Street. Be aware, though, that things get awfully windy once you're over the water and the sensation of being suspended in midair, while exhilarating to some, can inspire uneasiness and even vertigo in others. The bridge's pedestrian ramps empty out into Brooklyn's downtown, which is a bit of a wasteland on weekends. It isn't a far walk from here to Brooklyn Heights, one of the loveliest brownstone neighborhoods you'll ever see—but you'd better be armed with a map and look like you know where you're going. If your kids aren't hardy urban trekkers, consider walking just halfway to get the view and then doubling back to Manhattan. If you're on bicycles (and yes, the walkway is a perfectly fine place to bike, though it's a very long ascent) going all the way to Brooklyn is a better bet.

Randall's Island Family Golf Center

On Randall's Island. ☎ **212/427-5689.** Driving range: $10 for bucket of 102 balls. Minigolf: $5 adults, $3 children under 16. Batting cages: $2 for 15 pitches. Free parking.

Randall's Island is one of the city's best-kept sports secrets; with an athletic stadium and lots of ball fields, it's a haven for amateur athletes and a quick drive across the Triborough Bridge from Manhattan. Along with a driving range, batting cages, a golf shop, and a snack bar, there's a nifty mini–golf course at this golf complex on the island. It's open daily 8am to 11pm, though on Mondays it doesn't open until 1pm. If you don't have a car, you can take a shuttle bus, leaving from Modell's sporting goods store at 86th Street and Third Avenue; it costs $7 and leaves every hour on the hour 4 to 8pm weekdays and 10am to 6pm weekends.

HORSEBACK RIDING

★ Claremont Riding Academy

175 W. 89th St. (between Columbus and Amsterdam aves.). ☎ **212/724-5100.** Mon–Fri 6:30am–10:30pm, Sat–Sun 8am–5pm. Subway: 1/9/B/C to 86th St.

Manhattan's only riding stables, Claremont occupies a charming 1892 building that should have completed a major restoration by the end of 1998. There are lots of classes for kids 6 and up, riding in an indoor ring—English saddle only, $35 for a 1-hour class (a private lesson costs $40 per half hour). Call a day or two in advance to schedule. Experienced riders can take their mounts out into nearby Central Park for $33 per hour; the bridle trail runs nearly the length of the park, looping around the reservoir. You must wear shoes with enough of a heel to catch hold in a stirrup; helmets are required, but the stable provides them free of charge.

Kensington Stables

51 Caton Place, Brooklyn. ☎ **718/972-4588.** Daily 10am–9pm for lessons, 10am–sundown for trail rides. Subway: F to Fort Hamilton Pkwy.

To me, this is one of the best horseback deals in New York City, provided the schlep to Brooklyn doesn't daunt you. For $20 per hour, you can join a guided trail ride through leafy Prospect Park, riding either English or western saddle; because there's a guide along, even inexperienced riders can join in. Lessons at the stable (English or western saddle) can be private ($40 per hour, $25 per half hour), semiprivate ($35 per hour), or in a group of three or more ($30 per hour). Call ahead if you want to book a lesson; drop-ins are welcome for the trail rides.

Riverdale Equestrian Center

In Van Cortlandt Park at W. 254th St. and Broadway, Riverdale, the Bronx. ☎ **718/548-4848.** Tues–Fri 8am–9pm, Sat–Sun 9am–5pm. Subway: 1/9 to 242nd St.

Private lessons in the indoor ring here cost $65 per hour, $35 per half hour; semi-privates are $47 per hour, $30 per half hour; and group lessons are $35 to $40, depending on skill level. Once you've taken a lesson to show how well you ride, you may be qualified to take a horse out onto the park's wooded trails, at a cost of $35 per hour. Call a few days in advance to book lesson time.

ICE SKATING

Ice Studio

1034 Lexington Ave. (at 73rd St.). ☎ **212/535-0304.** Admission $5 for hour-long sessions, $6 for 90-minute sessions. Skate rental $2.75. Closed Aug.

Somewhat smaller and more kid-friendly than some of the outdoor rinks, this East Side spot runs a steady business in skating classes and birthday parties. General skating sessions offer youngsters a good chance to try out their blades without getting overwhelmed by crowds of hot-dogging older skaters. They're scheduled as often as twice a day in summer, once a day in winter (often evenings); call for the current schedule.

Lasker Rink

In Central Park at 110th St. and Lenox Ave. ☎ **212/534-7639.** Admission $1.75 kids, $3.50 adults. Skate rental $3.25. Nov–Mar Mon–Wed 10am–3pm, Thurs–Sun 10am–10pm. Subway: 2/3 to 110th St.

Cheaper and less crowded than its Central Park cousin, the Wollman Rink, Uptown's Lasker is well populated by families on weekends. The ice here doesn't get as chewed up as Wollman's, and the rental skates are better quality.

Riverbank State Park

145th St. and Riverside Dr. ☎ **212/694-3642.** Admission $2 kids 5–11, $4 adults. Skate rental $3. Late Oct–Mar Fri 6–9pm, Sat–Sun noon–3pm and 4–7pm. Subway: 1/9 to 145th St. Bus: M11.

Built above a sewage plant on the Hudson River shore—hence its nickname "The Stink Rink"—open-air Riverbank is rarely crowded, though some fast and furious teenage skaters here don't always watch out for little ones. In summer, it converts to a roller rink.

Rockefeller Plaza Rink

Lower Plaza, Rockefeller Plaza (off Fifth Ave. between 49th and 50th sts.). ☎ **212/332-7654.** Admission Mon–Thurs $6 kids 11 and under, $7.50 adults; Fri–Sun $6.75 kids, $9 adults. Skate rental $4. Oct–Apr 45-minute sessions Mon–Thurs 9am–10:30pm, Fri–Sat 8:30am–midnight, Sun 8:30am–10pm. Subway: B/D/F/Q to 47th–50th sts./Rockefeller Center.

No doubt the most famous rink in town—and the easiest to find if you're a first-time visitor staying in a Midtown hotel—the Rockefeller Plaza rink does have undeniable charm, especially in December, when you get to skate under the gargantuan Christmas tree. The golden statue of Prometheus reclines at rinkside, and tourists crowd around the railings above, staring down as you pirouette around (though the ice is sunken far enough below street level you're hardly aware of your audience). It's expensive, the rink is so small you can't get up much speed, and there's usually a crowd, which means a wait in line to get in as well as a bit of jostling once you're on the ice. But do it once for the glamour of it.

✪ Sky Rink

Pier 61 at Chelsea Piers, 23rd St. at the Hudson River. ☎ **212/336-6100.** Admission $7.50 kids 12 and under, $10 adults. Skate rental $4.50. Subway: 1/9, C/E, or F/N/R to 23rd St. stations. Bus: M23 across 23rd St.

Open 24 hours year-round, this facility offers not one but two permanent ice rinks—the city's only permanent ice, in fact, which means the skating surface has more give than ice rinks laid down on top of other surfaces. (This is how Sky Rink justifies its higher prices.) While the East Rink is booked up pretty solid with figure-skating classes and hockey programs, the West Rink is open for general skating sessions every afternoon, more or less noon to 5pm, and some evenings to 9pm (call for the current schedule).

South Street Seaport Rink

Pier 17, at the foot of Fulton St. east of the FDR Dr. No phone at press time. Admission $5 children, $7 adults. Skate rental $4. Late Nov–early Mar daily 9am–9pm. Subway: 2/3/4/5 to Fulton St.; A/C to Broadway/Nassau St.

Opened on Thanksgiving 1998, this smallish outdoor rink on the deck outside Pier 17 offers East River views and is handy to the shops and restaurants of the enclosed South Street Seaport pier.

Wollman Rink

In Central Park—enter at E. 62nd St. ☎ **212/396-1010.** Admission $3.50 kids 11 and under, $7 adults. Skate rental $3.50. Oct–Mar Mon 10am–3pm, Tues–Thurs 10am–9:30pm, Fri–Sat 10am–11pm, Sun 10am–9pm.

Central Park's chief skating rink, at the southern end of the park nearest to Midtown, makes a super place to spin around the ice outdoors, though it's very popular and weekends can get thronged.

IN-LINE SKATING & ROLLER-SKATING

In **Central Park,** the top places for skating on weekends are the plaza by the Bandshell (just south of 72nd Street, at the end of the Mall), the Dead Road just east of the Sheep Meadow, and the West Drive near Tavern on the Green. The entire 6-mile loop of the circular drive is generally thronged with skaters on weekends, though it includes some challenging hills that may be too much for young skaters; the so-called Inner Loop, from 72nd Street down to 60th Street, is mostly level, however. At the **Wollman Rink,** midpark at 62nd Street (☎ **212/396-1010**), you can rent skates for use in the park, costing $15 for all day ($100 deposit, in cash or with a credit card).

Other favorite skating pavements around the city are the Promenade in Riverside Park, West 83rd to 96th streets; the Upper East Side's walkway on the bank of the East River from 60th Street on north; Union Square; the riverside Promenade in Battery Park City; and the pavements of Washington Square Park (bounded by Waverly Place and West 4th Street, at the foot of Fifth Avenue).

Skate-rental outlets have proliferated in Manhattan along with the in-line skating craze, but not all rent skates in children's sizes. Try **Blades Board & Skate** at one of its six Manhattan locations: 120 W. 72nd St., between Columbus Avenue and Broadway (☎ **212/787-3911**); 1414 Second Ave., between 73rd and 74th streets (☎ **212/249-3178**); 160 E. 86th St., between Lexington and Third avenues (☎ **212/996-1644** or 212/336-6199); 23rd Street and the West Side Highway (☎ **212/336-6299**); 659 Broadway, between Bond and Bleecker streets (☎ **212/477-7350**); and 128 Chambers St., at West Broadway (☎ **212/964-1944**). If you don't have your own wheels you'll have to go to the following rinks, where skates are available for use at the rink only.

Riverbank State Park

145th St. and Riverside Dr. ☎ **212/694-3642.** Admission $1. Skate rental $4. May–Sept daily 3–6pm (Fri–Sat also 7–10pm, Sat–Sun also 11am–2pm). Subway: 1/9 to 145th St.

Perched above the banks of the Hudson, this sizable roofed rink catches lots of cooling breezes in summer, though it's an uptown trek.

The Roller Rink

Pier 62 at Chelsea Piers, 23rd St. and the West Side Hwy., at the Hudson River. ☎ **212/ 336-6200.** Admission $3 kids 12 and under, $4 adults. Skate rental $7 kids, $10 adults. Subway: C/E to 23rd St.

A pair of open-air roller-skating rinks are set out on the northernmost of Chelsea's recreational piers. Though roller hockey leagues keep the rinks busy, at least one or the other is open for general skating Monday to Friday 10am to 6pm and Saturday and Sunday noon to 6pm; there's also a grooving skate disco on Saturday 8 to 11pm. In-line skating instruction is offered as well. Between the rinks is an "aggressive skate park" for those who want to do stunt skating; it's open 10am to 10pm daily, at a price of $8 per session.

Wollman Rink

In Central Park—enter at E. 62nd St. ☎ **212/396-1010**. Admission $3 kids 12 and under, $4 adults. Skate rental $6 (includes safety gear); $3 for safety gear only. Mid-Apr to mid-Sept Thurs–Fri 10am–6pm, Sat 10am–8pm, Sun 10am–7pm.

Considerably less crowded in the roller-skating season than it is in ice-skating season—probably because all the park's sidewalks and roads are also available for skating that covers more territory—in summer the Wollman hosts a hardy crew of in-liners who prefer circling around a rink with rock music blaring over the PA system. The fact that it's not crowded may make it an excellent place for beginning skaters to try out their wheels; it sure helps to have those wooden rink walls to crash into when you still haven't learned how to brake.

SKATEBOARDING

The two primo sites in Manhattan for trick skateboarders are **Central Park's West Drive,** between 66th and 70th streets (near Tavern on the Green), where hot-doggers set up jumps and obstacles to show off their moves; and the swerving concrete ramps around the **entrance to the Brooklyn Bridge,** near City Hall and the Municipal Building, Centre Street just south of Chambers Street. The sidewalks in and around **Union Square** (14th to 17th streets, Broadway to Park Avenue South) are another good option, and there are ramps set up for stunts in **Riverside Park** at about 100th Street. The primo sources for boards, either sale or rental, is **Blades Board & Skate;** of its several locations all over town, the two handiest for these skate-boarding sites are at 120 W. 72nd St., between Broadway and Columbus Avenue (☎ **212/787-3911**), and 128 Chambers St. at West Broadway (☎ **212/964-1944**).

SWIMMING

This is one severe shortage in New York's recreation facilities: There are very few clean, well-run pools open to the public. If you're visiting and a place to swim is important to you, zone in one of the hotels that has its own pool (see chapter 9). If you live here and you're dying to take a swim, enroll your child in swim classes or join a health club. Another option worth knowing about is that you can pay for a 1-day drop-in swim at the Upper East Side's **Asphalt Green,** York Avenue between 90th and 92nd streets (☎ **212/369-8890**). A 1-day pass is $15 adults and $7 kids 16 and under; public swimming sessions are Monday to Friday 5:30am to 3pm and 8 to 10pm and Saturday and Sunday 8am to 8pm. Asphalt Green has two marvelous clean pools, one 25 yards long and the other an Olympic-size 50-meter pool; the big pool is used for public swimming only on Sunday. A pricier option is a day-use pass for the atrium rooftop pool at **Le Parker Meridien hotel,** 118 W. 57th St., between Sixth and Seventh avenues; passes cost $40 per person, child or adult, and you must call the health club at ☎ **212/245-1144** to check on availability.

To be frank, I wouldn't advise taking your kids to swim in the city parks' pools, which often are overrun; conditions can be less than sanitary, and there have been some alleged incidents of sexual harassment. I wish the situation were better, but it hasn't improved yet. For the record, here are the three main city-run indoor pools: **East 54th Street,** 348 E. 54th St., between First and Second avenues (☎ **212/397-3154**); **Carmine Street,** Clarkson Street and Seventh Avenue South (☎ **212/242-5228**); and **West 59th Street,** 533 W. 59th St., between Amsterdam and West End avenues (☎ **212/397-3159**). Carmine Street also has an outdoor pool open in summer, when you can also swim at the pool in **John Jay Park,** East 77th Street and Cherokee Place, just east of York Avenue (☎ **212/794-6566**), and Central Park's **Lasker Pool,** midpark at East 106th Street (☎ **212/534-7639,** July–Aug only).

TENNIS

Very few public tennis courts are available in Manhattan, where most serious tennis players belong to private clubs. You'll find two fairly decent sets in **Riverside Park,** Riverside Drive at either 96th or 116th Street; play is first-come, first-served, but there's not usually much of a wait. At the city's premier public facility, the **Central Park Tennis Center,** midpark at West 93rd Street, matters are somewhat more complicated. Players who have bought an annual tennis permit ($50 adults, $20 seniors, $10 juniors—call ☎ **212/360-8131** for information) can make advance reservations for $5 by calling ☎ **212/280-0205** noon to 2pm. Anyone else can get a single-play ticket for $5 at the Tennis Center on the day of play, entitling you to an hour of court time. You can sign up for a specific court time—in person only—or put your name on the No Show List to take the next available court; players who don't show up 15 minutes before their booked court time get bumped, so plenty of folks from that stand-by list do get to play. When the hourly bell rings, there's a mass exodus from the courts—26 Har-Tru and 4 hard courts—except for doubles players, who can reserve 2 hours at a time. If you don't have your own racquet, you can rent one at the pro shop ($5 for 2 hours), and they do have kid-size racquets. April to November, the Tennis Center is open daily 6:30am to dusk.

It may be worth an excursion into Queens just to play on the site of the U.S. Open, the **U.S.T.A. National Tennis Center** in Flushing Meadows–Corona Park (take the no. 7 subway to the Shea Stadium stop). Call the center at ☎ **718/760-6200** to reserve a court, no more than 2 days in advance. Fees are $10 to $21 per hour for outdoor courts; for indoor courts, per-hour rates are $24 to $30 May to July and $28 to $40 September to May.

6 Classes & Workshops

ART & SCIENCE WORKSHOPS

ArtsConnection
120 W. 46th St. (between Sixth Ave. and Broadway). ☎ **212/302-7433.** Workshops $2. Subway: B/D/F/Q to 47th–50th sts./Rockefeller Center; N/R to 49th St.

Call in advance for a schedule of this useful organization's Saturday workshops for kids, usually at 12:30pm October to June. The range of interests is huge: dance, puppetry, storytelling, hands-on art, art history, music appreciation, and more.

Dana Discovery Center
In Central Park at the Harlem Meer, 110th St. at Lenox Ave. ☎ **212/860-1374.** Subway: 2/3 to 110th St. Bus: M2, M3, M4 to 110th St./Fifth Ave.

Summer weekends usually see free entertainment out on the plaza here, and arts-and-crafts workshops, science displays, puppet shows, and the like are regularly held inside this beautiful pondside facility, a short walk north of the Conservatory Garden. Call for schedules.

My Favorite Place
265 W. 87th St. (between Broadway and West End Ave.). ☎ **212/362-5320.** Sessions $15–18 each. Subway: 1/9 to 86th St.

Drop-ins can join the ongoing art classes here. Toddler Art, geared for ages 18 months to 4 years, steers the little ones to express themselves through painting, collage, and clay; kids 5 to 9 experiment with a wide range of mediums, like print-making, sculpture, modeling, and drawing. Call for a schedule.

92nd Street Y

1395 Lexington Ave. (at 92nd St.). ☎ **212/996-1100.** Subway: 4/5/6 to 86th St.

Affiliated with the YMHA (Young Men's Hebrew Association) rather than the YMCA, this is one of the city's greatest cultural resources, with loads of evening programs in music and the arts and a vast roster of sign-up classes for adults and children. On a drop-in basis, one of the Y's best offerings is the once-monthly "Sunday Spectaculars" for kids 6 to 10 and their parents. You can sign up for a half or full day, with a morning art or science workshop, lunch, and an afternoon of swim and gym.

Sony Wonder Technology Lab

550 Madison Ave. (entrance on 56th St.). ☎ **212/833-8100.** Subway: E/F to Fifth Ave.

Many Saturdays and Sundays, this super Midtown attraction runs workshops exploring different themes in communications technology—3-D effects, mirrors, animation, robotics, and so on. Most are designed for ages 5 to 8 and charge a $4 materials fee (Sony Wonder admission itself is free); call ahead for a schedule of upcoming classes. For a mere $2 fee, parents and children can drop in any Sunday at 12:30pm for a 2-hour activity session.

DROP-IN CRAFTS

The Craft Studio

1657 Third Ave. (between 92nd and 93rd sts.). ☎ **212/ 831-6626.** Subway: 4/5/6 to 86th St.; 6 to 96th St.

Plasterwork painting is a big draw here—superheroes, harlequin masks, rainbows, cars, picture frames, puppies, kittens, dinosaurs, you name it, you can paint it (with a little help from the friendly staff). You pay according to the price of the piece you choose. Terra-cotta pots are also available for painting (think Mother's Day presents), as well as assorted other ceramic items. The space is roomy and well lit, with a rain-forest decor, and the front of the shop carries a good number of excellent crafts and toys.

Little Shop of Plaster

431 E. 73rd St. (between First and York aves.). ☎ **212/717-6636.** Subway: 6 to 68th or 77th St.

Pick a piece of precast plaster from the racks lining the walls, and you can paint it whatever colors you choose, daub on designs in finger wax, sprinkle glitter all over, and just generally make it your own masterpiece. There's no charge except the price of the plaster pieces, which are $9.95 and up. My older son's favorite part was being allowed to wield a hair dryer to dry off his red brontosaurus between stages of painting. The staff helps out as much as you need; teenagers labor intently for hours over incredibly detailed curlicues, while little kids are allowed to happily slap on paint as they please. (Our assistant just grinned and winked when my 4-year-old solemnly painted his entire car yellow, then covered it all up with red, then covered it completely again with purple.) When you're done, they'll apply discreet touch-ups and give your piece a smooth, shiny shellac finish. They also do sand bottle art (a good bet for younger brothers and sisters) and custom hand-painted "tattoos." A friendly, relaxed place, and the painting is more fun than I expected; come on weekday afternoons and you might have the place practically to yourself.

Our Name Is Mud

1566 Second Ave. (between 81st and 82nd sts.). ☎ **212/570-6868.** Subway: 4/5/6 to 86th St.

The ceramic items that customers paint here must be glazed and fired in a kiln, which means you pick them up a week after you've painted them—not as good on the instant gratification score as the plaster-painting shops above. On the other hand, you'll end up with a real piece of pottery, from a mug to a piggybank to a pitcher to a platter, a real keepsake that's also functional. Pieces range from $5 to $60. If you have older kids with an artistic bent, an afternoon at one of these shops can be very satisfying.

Other locations: 506 Amsterdam Ave., between 84th and 85th streets (☎ **212/579-5575**); 59 Greenwich Ave., at Seventh Avenue (☎ **212/647-7899**).

MUSEUM WEEKEND WORKSHOPS

On weekends, a number of major Manhattan museums seek to attract families by offering children's workshops, usually free with museum admission.

The **Children's Museum of Manhattan,** 212 W. 83rd St., between Amsterdam Avenue and Broadway (☎ **212/721-1223;** admission $5, kids under 1 free), always has a continual lineup of fun workshops, often themed to holidays. The **Children's Museum of the Arts,** 182 Lafayette St., between Broome and Grand streets (☎ **212/941-9198;** admission $5, kids under 18 months free), sets up hands-on art projects every weekend, providing materials for kids to create anything from papier-mâché masks to found-art collages to giant mobiles. Midtown's **Museum of Television and Radio**, 25 W. 52nd St. (☎ **212/621-6600;** admission $5), has fun Saturday workshops, including a series in which kids can re-create old radio scripts. Up in Riverdale, **Wave Hill,** 675 W. 252nd St., the Bronx (☎ **718/549-3200;** admission $4 adults, $2 students, kids under 6 free), organizes superb hands-on children's workshops combining arts and crafts with nature study, helping children to appreciate the estate's magnificent gardens and Hudson River landscape.

The **Museum of the City of New York,** 1220 Fifth Ave., at 103rd Street (☎ **212/534-1672;** suggested donation $5 adults, $4 kids, $10 per family), has great story hours every Saturday at 1pm featuring stories about New York. The **Jewish Museum,** 1109 Fifth Ave., at 92nd Street (☎ **212/423-3200;** admission $7 adults, $5 students, kids under 12 free), is closed on Friday and Saturday for the Jewish Sabbath, but on Sunday it often offers some lively workshops based on Judaic history or holidays.

The **Fraunces Tavern Museum,** 54 Pearl St., at Broad Street (☎ **212/425-1778;** admission $2.50 adults, $1 students, kids 6 and under free), offers occasional Saturday workshops, often tied to holidays, following the museum's focus on early American history. The **Asia Society,** 725 Park Ave., at 70th Street (☎ **212/288-6400;** admission $4 adults, $2 students, kids 12 and under free), comes up with really super workshops exploring various facets of different Asian cultures—Chinese storytellers, Indonesian puppets—and, less frequently, the **China Institute,** 125 E. 65th St., between Park and Lexington avenues (☎ **212/744-8181;** suggested donation $5 adults, $3 students), offers similar workshops connected to current rotating shows in its galleries.

Among the city's art museums, the best programs for kids are probably those offered by the **Museum of Modern Art,** 11 W. 53rd St., between Fifth and Sixth avenues (☎ **212/708-9400;** admission $9.50 adults, $6.50 students, kids under 16 free), which organizes Saturday tours for 4-year-olds, gallery talks for ages 5 to 10, hands-on classes for the entire family, and family-oriented programs of classic short films. The **Whitney Museum of American Art,** 945 Madison Ave., at 75th Street (☎ **212/570-3600;** admission $8 adults, $7 students, kids 11 and under free); the **Museum of American Folk Art,** 2 Lincoln Sq., between 65th and 66th streets (☎ **212/595-9533;** admission free, $1 materials fee for children's workshops); the **National Academy of Design,** 1083 Fifth Ave., at 89th Street (☎ **212/369-4880;** admission $5 adults, $3.50 students/children); and the **Studio Museum in Harlem,** 144 W. 125th St., between Lenox Avenue and Adam Clayton Powell Boulevard (☎ **212/864-4500;** admission $5 adults, $3 students, $1 kids 11 and under), present frequent art workshops highlighting aspects of their collections or current exhibitions.

6

Shopping with Your Kids

New York City kids are trained to be conspicuous consumers, with a wide range of options for spending money—deluxe children's clothing boutiques, toy stores crammed with imported marvels, wondrous hobby shops, and comic-book and trading-card dealers stocked with rarities. Some of these can be downright overwhelming, not to mention astronomically priced (come on, what kid really needs that $450 party frock from Magic Windows or that $600 stuffed King Kong from FAO Schwarz?). And while adults can safely indulge in mere window-shopping, it's a rare kid who's content to look and not try to coerce you to buy.

One happy thing about Manhattan toy stores is that most of them (not FAO, of course) have a wall of under-$5 toys to pacify your child with if you decide against that $150 Playmobil castle. Otherwise, it's best to know what you're shopping for and head straight for the store most likely to have it.

1 The Shopping Scene

SHOPPING HOURS & SALES TAX

Neighborhood stores are generally open daily 10am to 6pm, though some of the upscale East Side boutiques are closed on Sunday. Those stores that are open on Sunday may not open until noon, however. Some small Midtown boutiques are closed on weekends, but not the tourist-dependent Fifth Avenue showcases. Street fairs and flea markets are generally weekends-only operations.

An 8.25% **sales tax** is levied on everything except food and services.

SHOPPING DISTRICTS

THE UPPER WEST SIDE Lots of families live in this neighborhood, and its toy and clothing shops tend to be down-to-earth, if occasionally too earnestly wholesome. You'll probably be here at some point anyway, visiting the American Museum of Natural History or the Children's Museum of Manhattan or PlaySpace, so check out the outstanding toy stores between 76th and 87th streets—**Unique Science, Penny Whistle Toys, West Side Kids,** and **My Favorite Place,** all of which choose toys with an eye toward durability, educational value, and reasonable price (My Favorite Place even has a toddler playroom). The West Side is good for one-of-a-kinders, like **Shoofly,** a marvelous children's hat store (it sells shoes too), and **Plain Jane,** selling adorable nursery antiques.

THE UPPER EAST SIDE   This is the best area of town, hands-down, for pricey, gorgeous kids' clothes and precious toy boutiques. If you're shopping without kids in tow, a serious Madison Avenue expedition could take all day—all the designer kids' boutiques are here, between 62nd and 96th streets (**Jacadi** and **Bonpoint** even have two Madison Avenue locations). Shops along Lexington and Third avenues are little more reasonable, but there are still some darling finds, especially in the toy realm: **Mary Arnold Toys,** the **New York Doll Hospital, Bear Hugs and Baby Dolls,** and **Big City Kites,** not to mention the **Store of Knowledge,** a gleaming PBS-affiliated emporium with loads of nifty puzzles and gadgets and science-tinkering stuff. On East 86th Street, **Barnes & Noble Jr.** is one of the city's biggest and best children's bookstores, and if you need to get your child's locks chopped, three of the four kids' hair salons I list are here, between 78th and 92nd streets.

MIDTOWN   Primarily a business area, Midtown doesn't have many children's stores, and what it does have seems designed for indulgent grandparents and foreign tourists intent on stocking up on licensed-character items. There's **FAO Schwarz,** of course, the toy store to end all toy stores; joining it along formerly chi-chi Fifth Avenue are the **Warner Bros. Studio Store** and the **Disney Store,** which between them pretty much have the lock on cartoon character–driven merchandise (you'll also find them across from each other at 42nd Street and Times Square).

At the other end of Midtown, Herald Square (34th Street and Broadway) has a cluster of less glitzy stores to attract kids: Macy's department store, a grubby multilevel **Toys "Я" Us** in a dismal vertical mall once owned by Imelda Marcos, and a handful of chain stores in **Manhattan Mall,** Sixth Avenue at 32nd Street (☎ **212/465-0500**), a surprisingly bright and busy vertical mall with glass elevators shooting up and down the central atrium—a very un-Manhattan refuge. A number of small specialty shops, mostly for collectors, are tucked into spaces around high-rent Midtown.

CHELSEA   There's one reason for shopping in Chelsea if you have kids: **Books of Wonder,** the dean of children's bookstores in Manhattan.

GREENWICH VILLAGE   Between **Forbidden Planet** and **Village Comics,** Greenwich Village is the place to interest older kids who are into comics, trading cards, vintage records, and sci-fi/fantasy stuff. It's also Chess Central on Thompson Street just south of Washington Square, where the **Chess Shop** and the **Chess Forum** sell some beautiful chess sets and let kids play for hours. Funky-but-chic clothes rule down here, in stores like **Ibiza Kids, Village Kidz, Bombalulu's,** and **Peanut Butter and Jane.** Older kids whose idea of fashion lies more at the grunge end of the spectrum may want to troll Broadway below Astor Place, where warehouselike stores sell vintage clothes and army surplus and Doc Martens.

THE EAST VILLAGE   The shops here are just plain way out, especially when it comes to toys and accessories; work your way across East 9th Street and you'll see what I mean—starting with the relatively staid **Dinosaur Hill** and getting stranger as you go east to **It's a Mod, Mod World** or down Avenue A to **Little Ricky's** and **Alphabets.** Preteens and teens will find this edgy neighborhood eye-opening, though younger ones may not be clued in.

SOHO & TRIBECA   Parents down here tend to be loft-living urban pioneers with a highly developed visual sense, and the kids' stores reflect this with a very cool, sophisticated, miniature-adult sensibility (the **Enchanted Forest** toy store is a prime example).

WALL STREET   This area is hardly a target zone for shopping for kids. The occasional children's shop is geared to guilt-ridden working parents picking up a last-minute gift/bribe. There are a couple of mall-type destinations: **South Street Seaport** features a characterless mix of mid-range chain stores and odd theme boutiques (a whole store for butterflies, for instance, or for soft sculptures), many of them under a roof in the Pier 17 pavilion. The **World Trade Center** has a concourse of shops where commuters can buy essentials before whizzing home on the PATH trains. For upscale recreational shopping, try the **World Financial Center,** across the street in Battery Park City; though few stores cater to kids, the complex's Winter Garden Atrium is a stunning space with a long cascade of marble steps toddlers seem to find irresistible, and outside is a yacht basin and long Hudson River esplanade.

STREET MARKETS

The long-running Sunday flea market on the Upper West Side at **P.S. 44,** Columbus Avenue at 76th Street, has loads of junk to sort through in the school yard, with loads of friendly West Siders jostling one another. On Saturday and Sunday the **Annex Flea Market,** Sixth Avenue at 26th Street ($1 parking/admission), has some finds if you're into nostalgia and kitsch.

The **Union Square Greenmarket,** 16th Street between Broadway and Park Avenue South, runs Monday, Wednesday, Friday, and Saturday and has some truly glorious produce from out in rural New York State, New Jersey, even Pennsylvania. There's a bustling playground directly south of the greenmarket, so pick up lunch (crisp Macoun apples, fresh cheddar cheese, hearty seven-grain bread) and eat on a bench while the kids clamber away.

May to October, various stretches of Manhattan streets are closed to traffic for **street fairs** featuring booths selling everything from T-shirts to audiotapes to potted palms and hand-knit Peruvian sweaters. The food booths are even more fun—sizzling-hot stir-fries or heaping tacos or foot-long hot dogs. Sometimes there'll be a petting zoo or one of those inflated castles kids can bounce around in. You tend to see the same vendors weekend after weekend, and little that's on sale is really special. But the main thing is the crowd, the sunshine, and the car-free strolling. Look for posters in store windows or call ☎ 212/809-4900 after 5pm for a schedule.

2 Shopping A to Z

My listings are mainly for kid-specific stores and merchandise. If you want to check out what New York offers adult shoppers, see *Frommer's New York City.*

BABY & PRESCHOOLER CLOTHES

Au Chat Botte
1192 Madison Ave. (at 87th St.). ☎ **212/722-6474.** Subway: 4/5/6 to 86th St.

In sizes newborn to 6, you'll find beautiful and dressy European imports at stiff prices—$350 for an exquisite fawn-colored velvet frock with an ivory lace collar. The nursery furnishings shop next door offers some lovely crib beddings. Closed Sunday.

The Baby Collection

1384 Lexington Ave. (between 91st and 92nd sts.). ☎ **212/828-8633.** Subway: 4/5/6 to 86th St.

Quality children's clothes in sizes newborn to 7—wearable and fun, not overly frilly—are carried in this small Upper East Side shop. Some imports, alongside good American labels like Flaphappy and Baby Guess.

Baby Gap

1037 Lexington Ave. (at 74th St.). ☎ **212/327-2614.** Subway: 6 to 77th St.

335 Columbus Ave. (at 76th St.). ☎ **212/873-9272.** Subway: B/C to 79th St.

Although there are Baby Gap departments inside several of the Gap Kids stores (see "Everyday Clothes," below), these two branches are exclusively for baby sizes. Sturdy, simple knits with a casual sense of style, like all Gap clothes.

Baby Guess

775 Madison Ave. (at 66th St.). ☎ **212/628-2229.** Subway: 6 to 68th St.

Despite the chi-chi Madison Avenue address, this spick-and-span boutique show-cases Guess Jeans's line of sensible right-priced clothes for kids (sizes up to 6X)—knit crawlers, T-shirts, jeans, and denim dresses that look like they'd fit well and wear well. Lotsa denim.

✪ Bombalulu's

101 W. 10th St. (between Seventh Ave. and Greenwich St.). ☎ **212/463-0897.** Subway: 1/9 to Christopher St.

332 Columbus Ave. (between 75th and 76th sts.). ☎ **212/501-8248.** Subway: B/C to 79th St.

Funky, casual, colorful clothing in sizes up to age 5—a nice counterpoint to all the Upper Madison Avenue frills. Lots of toys too.

✪ Jacadi

1281 Madison Ave. (between 91st and 92nd sts.). ☎ **212/369-1616.** Subway: 4/5/6 to 86th St.

787 Madison Ave. (between 66th and 67th sts.). ☎ **212/535-3200.** Subway: 6 to 68th St.

Imported from France, this lovely upscale line of baby clothes (and stuff for older kids) features stylish simplicity in muted colors and pastels, with cottons and knits that last.

Judy's Fancies

249 E. 45th St. (between Second and Third aves.). ☎ **212/681-8115.** Subway: 4/5/6/7/S to Grand Central.

Handmade by the store's owner, the clothes in this tiny Midtown shop range from christening gowns to precious smock dresses for toddlers. The prices are pretty reasonable for the craftsmanship you get. Stop in to place an order and you can pick it up 5 to 6 days later. Closed Sunday and Monday.

Julian & Sara

103 Mercer St. (between Prince and Spring sts.). ☎ **212/226-1989.** Subway: N/R to Prince St.

This tiny SoHo shop sells frilly, pretty upscale things up to 6X, mostly for girls.

Koh's Kids

311 Greenwich St. (between Chambers and Reade sts.). ☎ **212/791-6915.** Subway: 1/2/3/9 to Chambers St.

This is the TriBeCa source for funky, contemporary, casual clothes for the newborn-to-6X set, including American labels like Cozy Toes.

La Layette

170 E. 61st St. (between Lexington and Third aves.). ☎ **212/688-7072.** Subway: 4/5/6 to 59th St.

Lace, smocking, and embroidery turn these infant clothes (to size 2) into frilly fashion statements; if you don't mind seeing a newborn spit up Similac over that $150 moiré silk dress, indulge yourself. Other new-baby gifts are engraved silver picture frames, hand-painted nursery furniture, personalized pillows, and lovely ruffly crib bedding.

La Petite Etoile

746 Madison Ave. (between 64th and 65th sts.). ☎ **212/744-0975.** Subway: 6 to 68th St.

Christening gowns and flower-girl dresses head the lineup of pretty clothes—casual as well dressy—at this trim shop along the Mad Ave boutique strip. Closed Sunday.

Lester's

1522 Second Ave. (at 79th St.). ☎ **212/734-9292.** Subway: 6 to 77th St.

The layette department at this roomy East Side clothing shop features imported and designer styles, at fairly reasonable prices.

Lolli Pop

241 Third Ave. (between 19th and 20th sts.). ☎ **212/995-0977.** Subway: 6 to 23rd St.; 4/5/6/L/N/R to Union Sq.

In the Gramercy Park neighborhood, this sweet little shop has a decided tilt toward European imports (90% of the clothes are imported from France), with an emphasis on casual specialty items. The sizes range from 0 to 8, but most are between 0 and 2. There's room for strollers, kids can enjoy themselves in a play area, and occasionally the salespeople put on a juggling show. Closed Sunday.

Magic Windows

1186 Madison Ave. (at 88th St.). ☎ **212/289-0028.** Subway: 4/5/6 to 86th St.

Here you'll find East Side–conservative, traditional baby clothes (sizes up to 6X), all in pastel blues and pinks, as well as a cascade of snowy linens for bassinet and crib. The tiny white cotton sweaters are adorable.

✪ Monkeys & Bears

506 Amsterdam Ave. (between 84th and 85th sts.). ☎ **212/873-2673.** Subway: 1/9 to 86th St.

The look here is unusual, unfrilly baby clothes with a sense of casual fun.

✪ Nursery Lines

1034 Lexington Ave. (at 74th St.). ☎ **212/396-4445.** Subway: 6 to 77th St.

Lots of hand-embroidered baby clothes, much of it imported from Italy, and precious hand-knit sweaters fill this tasteful corner shop. You can also order stunning custom-designed nursery furniture, and there's even a baby-gift registry. Sizes up to 4 years.

Plain Jane

525 Amsterdam Ave. (between 85th and 86th sts.). ☎ **212/595-6916.** Subway: 1/9 to 86th St.

There are only a few baby clothes here and they're all darling, from the lacy antique christening gowns to a nutty one-piece knit that'll make your infant look like a Campbell's Soup can. Somebody here is having fun.

Wicker Garden's Children

1327 Madison Ave. (at 93rd St.). ☎ **212/410-7001.** Subway: 6 to 96th St.

The downstairs section has loads of frilly stuff, predominantly in eye-blinding white. (I had nervous visions of splattered juice and mushed peas all over those starched pique pinafores.) They carry up to size 6, for boys as well as girls, though the boys' duds are definitely only for dress-up. The shop is on the pricey end of the spectrum. Closed Sunday.

Wynken, Blynken and Nod

306 E. 55th St. (between First and Second aves.). ☎ **212/308-9299.** Subway: E/F to Lexington/Third aves.

A convenient shop for the Sutton Place crowd, this boutique with a nostalgic 1950s look carries a range of quality children's wear, from casual to dressy. It's mostly designer stuff but not too outrageously priced, for sizes newborn to 6. The shop has a significant toy section as well, including many wooden toys and puzzles. Closed Sunday; also Mondays in summer.

Z'Baby Company

100 W. 72nd St. (at Columbus Ave.). ☎ **212/579-BABY.** Subway: 1/2/3/B/C to 72nd St.

This slick West Side shop features casual clothes (sizes newborn to 7) with upscale labels like Erin's Babies, Petit Bateau, and Annie's Antics. My son saw a $200 black leather baby biker jacket here that he badgered me to buy for about 15 minutes.

BOOKS

✪ Bank Street College Book Store

610 W. 112th St. (at Broadway). ☎ **212/678-1654.** Subway: 1/9 to 110th St.

This narrow, bright Uptown store has a wonderful selection. It's connected to an outstanding education college, so there's also a great section for parents and teachers.

Barnes & Noble

120 E. 86th St. (between Park and Lexington aves.). ☎ **212/427-0686.** Subway: 4/5/6 to 86th St.

A lot of people grouse about how this big chain bookstore drove small specialty stores out of business. Yes, I miss Eeyore's and Storyland too. But get over it, folks—these megastores have great children's sections (the 86th Street one is an entire branch devoted to kids, Barnes & Noble Jr.), with some informed salespeople, plenty of room for kids to frolic, frequent story hours and author appearances, and just about any book you could ever want for your kids. Story hours (half-hours, really) at the 86th Street branch are 10:30am on Tuesday and 5:30pm on Thursday. An addition to the city at any price.

   Other locations: The branch at **2289 Broadway,** at 82nd Street (☎ **212/ 362-8835;** Subway: 1/9 to 79th St.), has a story hour Tuesday at 10:30am. The **Lincoln Square** branch, 1972 Broadway, at 66th Street (☎ **212/595-6859;** Subway: 1/9 to Lincoln Center), has a 10am story hour on Monday and one at 4:30pm on Wednesday. In Midtown, the **Citicorp Building** branch, at Third Avenue and 54th Street (☎ **212/750-8033;** Subway: E/F to Lexington Ave.), has a Wednesday story hour at 10am. The **Chelsea** branch, 675 Sixth Ave., at 21st Street (☎ **212/727-1227;** Subway: F to 23rd St.), has a weekend story hour at 2pm Saturday and often another at noon Sunday; these four locations may have music or performers instead of simply story-reading. The **Greenwich Village** branch, 4 Astor Place, between Broadway and Lafayette Street (☎ **212/420-1322;** Subway: 6 to Astor Place), has storytime on Tuesday at 3pm and Wednesday at 7:30pm. Up at **Union Square,** 33 E. 17th St. (☎ **212/253-0810.** Subway: 4/5/6/L/N/R to Union Square), story hours are Saturday and Sunday at 2pm.

Bookberries
983 Lexington Ave. (at 71st St.). ☎ **212/794-9400.** Subway: 6 to 68th St.

A cozy little carpeted nook has been partitioned off for kids in this small East Side store. The selection is fairly good, though the picture books may be haphazardly alphabetized—probably because so many little hands have pulled out books to read. A good sign.

✪ Books of Wonder
16 W. 18th St. (between Fifth and Sixth aves.). ☎ **212/989-3270.** Subway: 1/9 to 18th St.

One of the few specialty children's bookstores left in town, this great Chelsea shop has a lot of hard-to-find titles, as well as collector's items (the Oz books, original Nancy Drews). Friendly, helpful, knowledgeable staff. Story hour is Sunday at 11:30am.

Borders Books & Music
5 World Trade Center (corner of Church and Vesey sts.). ☎ **212/839-8049.** Subway: E to World Trade Center.

461 Park Ave. (at 57th St.). ☎ **212/980-6785.** Subway: 4/5/6 to 59th St.

A more recent arrival in NYC, this chain megastore was much needed in the bookstore void known as Wall Street; the fact that it has a strong and welcoming children's section is the icing on the cake. In the Wall Street branch regular story-time is Tuesday at 10am, and there are frequent Saturday events for kids including music, costumed figures, and the like. Story hours for the Park Avenue store are Tuesday and Thursday at 10am and Sunday at 1pm.

Forbidden Planet
840 Broadway (at 13th St.). ☎ **212/473-1576.** Subway: 4/5/6/L/N/R to Union Sq.

This is the store for sci-fi and fantasy titles, as well as related paraphernalia.

Gryphon Bookshop
2246 Broadway (between 80th and 81st sts.). ☎ **212/362-0706.** Subway: 1/9 to 79th St.

This excellent little used-book store—narrow, dusky, with books to the ceiling—has a strong children's section, with some real finds.

Logos Bookstore
1575 York Ave. (between 83rd and 84th sts.). ☎ **212/517-7292.** Subway: 4/5/6 to 86th St.

Near Carl Schurz Park, this pleasant shop has a good children's corner at the back, near the small but leafy outdoor garden, a delightful place for reading in fair weather. While the store's specialty is religious books, this isn't heavily emphasized in the kids' selection, which does include some interesting titles from smaller publishers.

Shakespeare and Company
939 Lexington Ave. (between 68th and 69th sts.). ☎ **212/570-5148.** Subway: 6 to 68th St.

This surviving East Side branch of the old Upper West Side literary hangout offers a decent children's section, with pint-sized chairs and a carpet for in-store reading. Definitely worth a visit if you want to park the youngsters while you browse. The selection is intelligent, if skewed toward "worthy" picture books and classics.

✪ Tootsie's Children's Books
555 Hudson St. (at Perry St.). ☎ **212/242-0182.** Subway: 1/9 to Christopher St.

A gem. This cheery West Village bookshop with white-painted wood trim has loads of books, attractively displayed—not just juvenile titles but also paperbacks of classics older kids can (and should) read, like *Great Expectations* and *The Adventures of Sherlock Holmes*. Not snobby, either, it has full shelves of all those series like

Goosebumps and the Baby Sitters Club and the Hardy Boys, plus an ever-growing selection of good toys, puzzles, and videos. Lots of special activities and drop-in classes during the week, including toddler story hour Wednesday and Friday at 10am.

CANDY, CHOCOLATE & SWEETS

✪ Elk Candy Co.

1628 Second Ave. (between 84th and 85th sts.). ☎ **212/650-1177.** Subway: 4/5/6 to 86th St.

Wonderful marzipan creations and molded chocolate entice sweet tooths here; it has a very European flavor, a holdover from the days when Yorkville was the German part of town.

Li-Lac Chocolates

120 Christopher St. (between Hudson and Bleecker sts.). ☎ **212/242-7374.** Subway: 1/9 to Christopher St.

This charming little Village shop sells handmade chocolates molded into a delightful variety of shapes.

Mondel Chocolates

2913 Broadway (near 114th St.) ☎ **212/864-2111.** Subway: 1/9 to 116th St.

This old-fashioned little shop in the Columbia University area has beautiful handmade chocolates and other gift items for the sweet tooth.

COLLECTORS' SOURCES

Future Sports and Memorabilia

659 Lexington Ave. (at 55th St.). ☎ **212/308-1144.** Subway: E/F to Lexington Ave.

A large stock of autographed sports stuff—photos, jerseys, helmets, balls, pucks, and so on.

The Red Caboose

23 W. 45th St. (between Fifth and Sixth aves.); enter the lobby and go down stairs at the back. ☎ **212/575-0272.** Subway: B/D to Rockefeller Center.

New York's most intense model railroad shop, the Red Caboose has been selling all gauges and scales of trains since 1942, as well as equipment and supplies modelers desire.

Sports Memorabilia Gallery

150 Fifth Ave. (between 19th and 20th sts.). ☎ **212/255-9230.** Subway: N/R to 23rd St.

This store sells all kinds of sports collectibles, except for trading cards.

Train World

751 McDonald Ave., Brooklyn. ☎ **718/436-7072.** Subway: F to Ditmas Ave., Brooklyn.

True electric train fanatics may want to venture out to this huge store for train sets.

COMIC BOOKS & SPORTS CARDS

It depends on what your young collector is looking for: All these stores have a wide stock of cards and/or comics, but whether they've got that rare item you're looking for is always a question. If you're really on a quest for something special, call the whole lot until you strike gold. Otherwise, drop in for a browse at whichever shop you're nearest.

Alex's MVP Cards

256 E. 89th St. (at Second Ave.). ☎ **212/831-2273.** Subway: 4/5/6 to 86th St.

This friendly neighborhood store specializes in comics and sports cards and wax packs, as well as a decent supply of nonsports toys and supplies.

Chameleon Comics

3 Maiden Lane (between Nassau St. and Broadway). ☎ **212/587-3411.** Subway: A/C to Broadway/Nassau St.; 2/3/4/5 to Fulton St.

36–59 Main St., Flushing, Queens. ☎ **718/461-4675.** Subway: 7 to Main St., Flushing.

70–11 Austin St., Forest Hills, Queens. ☎ **718/575-8815.** Subway: E/F/C/R to 71st St./ Continental Ave., Queens.

Here you'll find Marvel comics and sports cards. Closed Sunday.

Collector's Universe

124 E. 40th St. (between Park and Lexington aves.). ☎ **212/922-1110.** Subway: 4/5/6/7/S to Grand Central.

This large, sensible Midtown shop covers all ends on sports and superheroes. Closed Sunday.

Comics for Sale

166 W. 75th St. (between Columbus and Amsterdam aves.). ☎ **212/787-7943.** Subway: 1/2/3/9 to 72nd St.

A store for true aficionados, this place stocks comic books—millions of comic books.

Cosmic Comics

36 E. 23rd St. (near Madison Ave.). ☎ **212/460-5322.** Subway: 6 to 23rd St.

This is a good source for comics, in addition to action figures, nonsports trading cards, T-shirts, models, paperback books, and videos.

59th St. Comics and Cards

118 E. 59th St. (between Park and Lexington aves.), 2nd floor. ☎ **212/759-6255.** Subway: 4/5/6 to 59th St.

Come here for posters, T-shirts, fantasy model kits, and videos, as well as old and new comics. Closed Saturday and Sunday.

Forbidden Planet

840 Broadway (at 13th St.). ☎ **212/473-1576.** Subway: 4/5/6/L/N/R to Union Sq.

Besides books (above), this overwhelming store is a valuable source for comics and assorted sci-fi and fantasy paraphernalia.

Funny Business

660-B Amsterdam Ave. (at 92nd St.). ☎ **212/799-9477.** Subway: 1/2/3/9 to 96th St.

This cluttered narrow shop improbably doubles as a shop for opera fans. Small stock, but good for rarities.

It's "A" Nother Hit

131 W. 33rd St. (between Sixth and Seventh aves.). ☎ **212/564-4111.** Subway: 1/2/3/9/B/ D/F/N/Q/R to 34th St.

Close to Madison Square Garden, this store sells sports cards and autographed memorabilia, as well as some superhero comics.

Jeff's Comics & Cards

227 Sullivan St. (between W. 3rd. and Bleecker sts.). ☎ **212/533-6350.** Subway: A/B/C/D/ E/F/Q to W. 4th St.

A pleasant place to browse for cards and comics, as well as rock music magazines.

Jim Hanley's Universe

4 W. 33rd St. (between Fifth Ave. and Broadway). ☎ **212/268-7088.** Subway: B/D/F/N/Q/R to 34th St.

Comic books old and new, plus fantasy role-playing games, can be found here.

Manhattan Comics and Cards
228 W. 23rd St. (between Seventh and Eighth aves.). ☎ **212/243-9349.** Subway: 1/9/C/E to 23rd St.

A reliable source for collectibles, this store specializes in magazines, sports cards, gaming cards, *X-Files* collectibles, paperback books, and action figures.

St. Mark's Comics
11 St. Mark's Place (between Second and Third aves.). ☎ **212/598-9439.** Subway: 6 to Astor Pl.

138 Montague St., Brooklyn. ☎ **718/935-0911.** Subway: 2/3/4/5/M/N/R to Court St./ Borough Hall, Brooklyn.

Anything comic-related can be bought here, including books, magazines, action figures, and toys.

Village Comics
214 Sullivan St. (between W. 3rd and Bleecker sts.). ☎ **212/777-2770.** Subway: A/B/C/ D/E/F/Q to W. 4th St.

This is another great source for Marvel cards, action figures, and other collector's supplies, as well as comics.

World Collectible Center
18 Vesey St. (between Church St. and Broadway). ☎ **212/267-7100.** Subway: E to World Trade Center; N/R to City Hall.

This is a great source for old action figures, such as *Star Wars* and GI Joe. The abundant stock also contains old magazines, comic books, and trading cards. Closed Saturday.

DEPARTMENT STORES

Bloomingdale's
1000 Third Ave. (at 59th St.). ☎ **212/355-5900.** Subway: 4/5/6 to 59th St.

Bloomie's prides itself on glitz, which doesn't translate well into family-oriented merchandise. The layette department is extravagant, geared toward pregnant shopaholics going on a final binge before the demands of motherhood put their shopping days to an end. The kids' clothing departments are claustrophobic and overpriced, and there's no toy department to speak of.

Lord & Taylor
424 Fifth Ave. (at 39th St.). ☎ **212/391-3344.** Subway: B/D/F/Q to 42nd St.

This slightly dowdy Midtown matron stocks traditional layette stuff and children's clothes. Its meticulous window displays at Christmas are the best in town— collectors of American Girl dolls will want to linger over the detailed historic scenes with their tiny costumed moving figures.

Macy's
At the northwest corner of Herald Sq. (Broadway and 34th St.). ☎ **212/695-4400.** Subway: B/D/F/N/Q/R to 34th St.

Macy's flagship in Midtown is one of the world's biggest department stores, with a solidly middle-class orientation. The children's departments are huge and carry a broad range of merchandise, including lots of sturdy playwear for boys and girls. This is the only Manhattan department store with a significant toy department, though the selection is fairly run-of-the-mill; my kids actually get more of a kick out of the electronic games department or the sample room setups on the vast furniture floor. At Christmastime, Macy's still mounts a Santaland, a state-of-the-art extravaganza with long lines and Santa himself taking requests.

Prowling the Pet Stores

When your child decides he or she can no longer tolerate another museum or toy store, try this boredom-buster: Visit one of Manhattan's many pet stores. Whether or not you're actually in the market to buy a pet, it never hurts to drop by and take a look. Many specialize in one kind of animal, whether it be cats, birds, or fish; your family might see some exotic animals you may have previously seen only in zoos.

For instance, there's **33rd and Bird,** 40 E. 33rd St., between Park and Madison avenues (☎ **212/447-0021**), which carries not only your standard parakeets and canaries but also exotic parrots and cockatoos. If someone in your family just can't go home without one of these rare birds, the store offers worldwide shipping. **Jungle Boyz,** 2369 Second Ave., near East 21st Street (☎ **212/426-7702**), also carries exotic birds and reptiles, as well as puppies and kittens; the Upper West Side's **Amsterdam Aquarium and Pet Shop,** 652 Amsterdam Ave., between West 91st and 92nd streets (☎ **212/724-0536**), carries reptiles and exotic small animals like snakes and frogs.

New World Aquarium, 5 W. 8th St., between Fifth and Sixth avenues (☎ **212/460-9390**), is the place to go if your child is fascinated by fish. This Greenwich Village store specializes in marine fish, African chichlids, and rare and exotic freshwater fish, and it's open daily as late as 9pm. Up on the East Side, roomy **Crystal Aquarium,** 1659 Third Ave., at East 93rd Street (☎ **212/534-9003**), is not just a fish store: It also carries birds, reptiles, and small mammals, including the occasional chinchilla.

If your kids are demanding to see puppies and kittens, stop at the **International Kennel Club,** 1032 Second Ave., between East 54th and 55th streets (☎ **212/755-0100**); **American Kennels,** 798 Lexington Ave,. between East 61st and 62nd streets (☎ **212/451-0077**); **Pets-on-Lex,** 1271 Lexington Ave., between East 85th and 86th streets (☎ **212/426-0766**); or **U.S. Pets,** 83 Chambers St., between Church Street and Broadway (☎ **212/406-5555**). Upscale **Just Cats,** 244 E. 60th St., between Second and Third avenues (☎ **212/888-2287**), is a self-described East Side "feline boutique" selling pedigreed kittens and cats as well as toys, accessories, and food for your feline friends. This being Manhattan, of course, there's not just one but two stores that exclusively sell pedigreed cats: The other is **Fabulous Felines,** 657 Second Ave., between East 35th and 36th streets (☎ **212/889-9865;** closed Wednesday). This Murray Hill boutique may not be as posh as Just Cats, but the selection and variety are the same.

And then there's the Upper East Side's **Le Chien Pet Salon,** 1044 Third Ave., at East 61st Street (☎ **212/861-8100**), unique not because of the animals it carries but because of the clientele it serves: The cats and dogs that come for grooming arrive via limousine, and the puppies and kittens for sale, needless to say, are all pedigreed.

—by Jennifer Lebin

Saks Fifth Avenue

611 Fifth Ave. (at 50th St.). ☎ **212/753-4000.** Subway: B/D to Rockefeller Center.

Sleek and chic, Saks does best for the very young, with a fairly good infantwear department; for older kids, Saks's fashion sense—usually right on target when it comes to adults—is decidedly off kilter.

DOLLS & DOLLHOUSES

Bear Hugs and Baby Dolls
311 E. 81st St. (between First and Second aves.). ☎ **212/717-1514.** Subway: 6 to 77th St.

Pricey imported dolls, of the Corolle and Madame Alexander class, dominate at this pretty but precious boutique. Definitely not a hands-on place, more for older princesses and adult collectors.

Doll House Antics
1343 Madison Ave. (at 94th St.). ☎ **212/876-2288.** Subway: 6 to 96th St.

This big, sunny well-stocked store boasts loads of marvelous tiny things. They take care to carry sturdy, affordable items for kids as well as incredible miniatures for adult collectors.

Iris Brown Antique Dolls
253 E. 57th St. (between Second and Third aves.). ☎ **212/593-2882.** Subway: 4/5/6 to 59th St.

This is a long-established source for Victorian dolls and miniatures—not necessarily dolls for playing with. Closed Sunday.

✪ Manhattan Doll House Shop
236 Third Ave. (between E. 19th and 20th sts.). ☎ **212/253-9549.** Subway: 6 to 23rd St.

Besides a truly awesome selection of kits and finished dollhouses, this Gramercy store has all the furnishings, right down to electrical fixtures. Full-size dolls are also repaired and sold, with a specialty in Madame Alexander.

✪ Mary Arnold Toys
1010 Lexington Ave. (between 72nd and 73rd sts.). ☎ **212/744-8510.** Subway: 6 to 77th St.

This topnotch East Side toy shop includes a wonderful doll section—Madame Alexander, Corolle, Götz, and the like.

New York Doll Hospital
787 Lexington Ave. (between 61st and 62nd sts.), 2nd floor. ☎ **212/838-7527.** Subway: 4/5/6 to 59th St.

Since 1900, young New Yorkers have climbed the stairs to this musty space bearing their precious dolls and stuffed animals in need of repairs. You can also buy antique dolls and kitschy collectibles like a Charlie McCarthy doll, a Daddy Warbucks tie-in from the movie *Annie,* or a Pee Wee Herman doll (from back before scandal shut down *Pee Wee's Playhouse*). A wonderful jumble of dolls' heads, arms, and legs on the floor gives the place a slightly *Twilight Zone*–ish atmosphere.

Tiny Doll House
1146 Lexington Ave. (between 79th and 80th sts.). ☎ **212/744-3719.** Subway: 6 to 77th St.

In this small well-organized shop, rows of perfectly put-together miniature rooms flank the side walls, while a few empty doll mansions preside regally over the center of the room. Wallpaper, carpeting, lamps, cutlery—a tasteful selection of all the tiny furnishings you'll ever need.

EVERYDAY CLOTHING

Baby Depot at Burlington Coat Factory
At the corner of W. 23rd St. and Sixth Ave. ☎ **212/229-2247.** Subway: F to 23rd St.

Clothing up to size 12, boys' and girls', can be found on the third floor of this big discount store in the megastore shopping district wedged between Chelsea and the Flatiron District. The brands are quite respectable—Carter's, Buster Brown,

Guess—but not very appealingly displayed, jammed onto racks under fluorescent lighting.

Children's Place

In Manhattan Mall, 901 Sixth Ave. (at 33rd St.), 2nd level. ☎ **212/268-7696.** Subway: B/D/F/N/Q/R to 34th St.

173 E. 86th St. (between Third and Lexington aves.). ☎ **212/831-5100.** Subway: 4/5/6 to 86th St.

400 World Trade Concourse, World Trade Center. ☎ **212/432-6100.** Subway: E to World Trade Center.

This chain store sells its own label of casual wear in sizes newborn to 12. It's like a slightly cheaper version of the Gap, in all respects, but to fill out a wardrobe, a $10 polo shirt or plain $14 sundress isn't such a bad idea.

Conway's

201 E. 42nd St. (at Third Ave.). ☎ **212/992-5030.** Subway: 4/5/6/7/S to Grand Central.

Budget-conscious parents can be spotted all over town carrying Conway's pink plastic bags, bulging with basic clothing bought at low prices.

Other locations: Conway's has heavily colonized the 34th Street shopping district, with a cluster of no less than five stores (Subway: 1/2/3/9/B/D/F/N/Q/R to 34th St.): 11 W. 34th St. (☎ **212/967-1370**), and 49 W. 34th St. (☎ **212/967-6454**), both between Fifth and Sixth avenues; 1333 Broadway, at 35th Street (☎ **212/967-3460**); 450 Seventh Ave., between 34th and 35th streets (☎ **212/967-1371**); and 225 W. 34th St., between Seventh and Eighth avenues (☎ **212/967-7390**). There are also two Downtown among the discount stores near Wall Street: 450 Broad St., between Broadway and Beaver Street (☎ **212/943-8900;** Subway: 4/5 to Bowling Green), and 151 William St., between Fulton and Nassau streets (☎ **212/374-1072;** Subway: A/C to Broadway/Nassau St.).

Daffy's

111 Fifth Ave. (at 18th St.). ☎ **212/529-4477.** Subway: 4/5/6/L/N/R to Union Sq.

The price is definitely right at this smart discount clothing chain that has been rapidly expanding its children's departments thanks to popular demand. For straightforward play and school clothes, most items are under $20, and I'm talking perfectly acceptable quality and styles.

Other locations: 335 Madison Ave., at 44th Street (☎ **212/557-4422;** Subway: B/D/F/Q to 42nd St.); 1311 Broadway, at 34th Street (☎ **212/736-4477;** Subway: B/D/F/N/Q/R to 34th St.); and 135 E. 57th St., between Park and Lexington avenues (☎ **212/376-4477;** Subway: 4/5/6 to 59th St.).

Gap Kids

57th St. and Broadway. ☎ **212/956-3140.** Subway: 1/9/A/B/C/D to Columbus Circle.

You know the look—jeans, khakis, sweatshirts, T-shirts, denim jackets. Like it or not, the Gap provides a mix-and-match backbone for kids' wardrobes, giving the casual look a spin of adultlike cool. Wait for sale days and you can clean up.

Other locations: 2 World Financial Center (☎ **212/945-4090;** Subway: E to World Trade Center); Sixth Avenue between Washington Square and West 4th Street (☎ **212/777-2420;** Subway: A/B/C/D/E/F/Q to W. 4th St.); 17th Street and Fifth Avenue (☎ **212/989-0195;** Subway: 4/5/6/L/N/R to Union Sq.); 60 W. 34th St., at Broadway (☎ **212/643-8995;** B/D/F/N/Q/R to 34th St.); 657 Third Ave., at 42nd Street (☎ **212/697-9007;** Subway: 4/5/6/7/8 to Grand Central); 42nd Street and Broadway (☎ **212/302-1266;** 1/2/3/7/9/N/R/S to Times Square); 1066 Lexington Ave., between 75th and 76th streets (☎ **212/988-4460;**

Subway: 6 to 77th St.); 86th Street and Madison Avenue (☎ 212/517-5202;
Subway: 4/5/6 to 86th St.); 87th Street and Third Avenue (☎ 212/423-0033;
Subway: 4/5/6 to 86th St.); and 2300 Broadway, at 86th Street (☎ 212/
873-2044; 1/9 to 86th St.).

Gymboree Store
1332 Third Ave. (at 76th St.). ☎ **212/517-5548.** Subway: 6 to 77th St.

This tie-in clothing chain seems determined to turn kids into replicas of the Gym-
boree mascot, Jimbo the Clown, by dressing them in simple, durable knits in bold
colors and kindergartenish prints. Cut roomy for easy moving, they're a sensible,
reasonably stylish bet for everyday wear.

   Other locations: 1132 Madison Ave., between 83rd and 84th streets (☎ 212/
717-6702; 4/5/6 to 86th St.); 1049 Third Ave., at 62nd Street (☎ 212/688-4044;
4/5/6 to 59th St.); 2015 Broadway, at 69th Street (☎ 212/595-7662; Subway:
1/9 to Lincoln Center); 2271 Broadway, between 81st and 82nd streets (☎ 212/
595-9071; 1/9 to 79th St.).

Kids Are Magic
2293 Broadway (between 82nd and 83rd sts.). ☎ **212/875-9240.** Subway: 1/9 to 79th St.

Here you'll find substantial discounts on name-brand clothing, plus a few toys and
accessories. This store has minimal class, but sometimes you can find some perfectly serviceable items.

Morris Brothers
2322 Broadway (at 84th St.). ☎ **212/724-9000.** Subway: 1/9 to 86th St.

This is the place to go to get winter hats, umbrellas, socks, underwear, pajamas,
jeans—all the untrendy stuff you need to fill out a wardrobe (that's not to say you
can't find some trendy outfits as well). Very solid, not particularly cheap.

Old Navy Clothing Company
610 Sixth Ave. (at 18th St.). ☎ **212/645-0663.** Subway: F to 14th St.; 1/9 to 18th St.

Featuring sturdy, classic casualwear in the Gap mold, this clothing superstore along
the old Ladies' Mile in Chelsea has a big second-floor section for kids. Prices are as
down-to-earth as the super-wearable styles.

OshKosh B'Gosh
586 Fifth Ave. (between 47th and 48th sts.). ☎ **212/827-0098.** Subway: B/D to
Rockefeller Center.

The Rockefeller Center showcase for this sturdy kids' play clothes line has all the
cutest stuff for toddlers and preschoolers. A mecca for Europeans.

Wings
1519 Third Ave. (between 85th and 86th sts.). ☎ **212/628-6214.** Subway: 4/5/6 to 86th St.
2491 Broadway (between 92nd and 93rd sts.). ☎ **212/595-6662.** Subway: 1/2/3/9 to 96th St.

Despite the discount-store look, Wings is a solid source for OshKosh and Carters
and all kinds of jeans and sweats, at prices that really suit the way kids treat clothes.

FASHIONS

Bambini
1367 Third Ave. (at 78th St.). ☎ **212/717-6742.** Subway: 6 to 77th St.

This beautiful, humorless blond-wood store stocks European children's clothes
(brand names like Simonetta and Fiocco) and shoes. The clothes are indeed
handsome, but at princess prices—$49 for a dead-plain polo shirt or $375 for a
stunning smocked party frock.

Bebe Thompson

1216 Lexington Ave. (between 82nd and 83rd sts.). ☎ **212/249-4740.** Subway: 4/5/6 to 86th St.

A whiff of sophisticated style sets apart the clothes at this smart little shop. Much (but not all) is imported; I get a kick out of the tiny Geisswein boiled-wool jackets from Austria, which would make your toddler look perfectly ripe for the Junior League.

Bonne Nuit

30 Lincoln Plaza (at 63rd St.). ☎ **212/489-9730.** Subway: 1/9 to Lincoln Center.

551 Fifth Ave. (at 45th St.), inside the New York Look shop. ☎ **212/681-1100.** Subway: B/D to Rockefeller Center.

This shop carries lingerie and a choice selection of designer duds for kids (mostly for girls) in sizes up to 12 years.

Bonpoint

1269 Madison Ave. (at 91st St.). ☎ **212/722-7720.** Subway: 4/5/6 to 86th St.

811 Madison Ave. (at 68th St.). ☎ **212/879-0900.** Subway: 6 to 68th St.

This stunning boutique takes the cake—it has the most expensive and probably the most beautiful children's clothes in town. Everything sold is the store's private label, and the fabrics are gorgeous, no question about it; the styles are classic, chic, and perfectly cut. Closed Sunday.

Catamimi

1284 Madison Ave. (between 91st and 92nd sts.). ☎ **212/987-0688.** Subway: 6 to 96th St.

These French kids' clothes (up to size 14) show an ineffable sense of style, with sassy prints and deep-colored solids cut into simple, roomy clothes with real flair. The store has a bold, clean look and friendly, hip staff. The clothes aren't cheap, but they're casual and sturdy enough that you may get a fair bit of wear out of them.

Chocolate Soup

946 Madison Ave. (between 74th and 75th sts.). ☎ **212/861-2210.** Subway: 6 to 77th St.

This crowded little store has a lot of personality—hand-painted T-shirts and sweat-shirts, bold-print leggings, and hand-knit sweaters with nutty patterns, good for girls with a wacky sense of style. The front is packed with oddball toys that should make it superhard to get out of the store without spending any money.

✪ Coco & Z

222 Columbus Ave. (at 70th St.). ☎ **212/721-0415.** Subway: 1/2/3/9/B/C to 72nd St.

This friendly, adorable boutique for sizes newborn to 10 carries some very wearable duds from makers like Flooby, Metropolitan Prairie, and Baby Lulu, at prices in the $25-to-$75 range. Maybe they just have a knack for displaying things well, but I had a hard time getting out of this shop without buying anything. Its sibling store, **Co2**, 284 Columbus Ave., between 73rd and 74th streets (☎ **212/721-4966**), carries the whole aesthetic into the preteen arena, sizes 7 to 16.

G. C. William

1137 Madison Ave. (between 84th and 85th sts.). ☎ **212/396-3400.** Subway: 4/5/6 to 86th St.

Very Upper East Side boutique for Armani-bound youth. You'll find resort wear, club wear, and party wear but not school wear, since most shoppers here go to private schools that have uniforms.

Greenstones & Cie

442 Columbus Ave. (at 81st St.). ☎ **212/501-8536.** Subway: B/C to 79th St.

284 Columbus Ave. (at 73rd St.). ☎ **212/580-4322.** Subway: 1/2/3/9/B/C to 72nd St.

1184 Madison Ave. (between 86th and 87th sts.). ☎ **212/427-1665.** Subway: 4/5/6 to 86th St.

Upper-scale imported kids' clothes, with a kind of yacht-club look (every sweater has a design, it seems), are sold in sizes from 3 months to 12 years (the East Side shop carries up to size 8 only, however). Lots of items that are well-nigh irresistible.

Ibiza Kidz

42 University Place (at 9th St.). ☎ **212/505-9907.** Subway: N/R to 8th St.

Annexed to a gorgeous women's clothing boutique, this Village shop sells some dreamy children's clothes, with a bohemian sensibility. Shoes, books, and toys can be found next door.

Infinity

1116 Madison Ave. (at 83rd St.). ☎ **212/517-4232.** Subway: 4/5/6 to 86th St.

As a friend of mine says, "At a certain age all girls want to look like either a construction worker or a tramp": This is the store for both looks. T-shirts and jeans and skimpy knit dresses rule, along with lots of the huge dumpy backpacks every school kid has to have. Infinity doesn't necessarily try to be hip; it just stocks what kids like to wear, damn the parents. Bring your preteen here to prove you do indeed get it.

Jacadi

1281 Madison Ave. (between 91st and 92nd sts.). ☎ **212/369-1616.** Subway: 4/5/6 to 86th St.

787 Madison Ave. (between 66th and 67th sts.). ☎ **212/535-3200.** Subway: 6 to 68th St.

A French chain, Jacadi sells expensive, stylish, sturdy clothes, cut for comfort, for boys and girls up to age 12. Each season's line is color-coordinated, handy for mixing and matching, and the store looks tidy and very put-together as a result.

La Petite Etoile

746 Madison Ave. (between 64th and 65th sts.). ☎ **212/744-0975.** Subway: 6 to 68th St.

A top luxury children's chain from France, La Petite Etoile (formerly Tartine et Chocolat) carries sizes up to 12 at its only U.S. store. These are classic good-looking clothes, with embroidered designs on dress collars and little crests on the boys' jackets, and the concept is that everything a child wears—shirt, sweater, pants, dress, socks, hairbows, shoes, underwear—should match, which sounds fine when you see the shelves lined with color-coordinated accessories. (They even carry *parfum* for the young.) The total wardrobe idea is pretty staggering, though, when you look at the prices—I saw a $193 price tag on a simple striped cotton frock.

Lester's

1522 Second Ave. (at 79th St.). ☎ **212/734-9292.** Subway: 6 to 77th St.

This is an East Side staple for clothing and shoes, ages newborn to 12—most of the stock is imported and designer styles, but the prices aren't too wild.

M.W. Teen

1188 Madison Ave. (at 88th St.). ☎ **212/289-0181.** Subway: 4/5/6 to 86th St.

When you graduate from Magic Windows (see "Baby & Preschooler Clothes," above), you get to buy precociously chic party dresses from M.W. Teen next door. The clothes really are pretty, if a trifle too adult for my tastes—but then, my daughter's not a teenager yet.

✪ Marsha D. D.

1324 Lexington Ave. (between 88th and 89th sts.). ☎ **212/534-1800.** Subway: 4/5/6 to 86th St.

Two small neighboring storefronts—one for girls, one for boys—are stuffed with stylish casual clothes, strong on urban hipness and streetwise sophistication. These are clothes your kids will feel cool wearing. Closed Sunday.

Monkeys & Bears

506 Amsterdam Ave. (between 84th and 85th sts.). ☎ **212/873-2673.** Subway: 1/9 to 86th St.

Monkeys & Bears offers kicky clothes for newborns to size 14—lots of hand-painted stuff, hand-knit sweaters with unusual buttons, and brightly patterned fabrics.

Oilily

870 Madison Ave. (between 70th and 71st sts.). ☎ **212/628-0100.** Subway: 6 to 68th St.

Cherry red, tangerine orange, banana yellow—as you enter this spotless store, Oilily's trademark Trix-hued fabrics hit you like an LSD flashback. As a friend of mine says, Oilily is the only line of clothing that believes boys can wear flowered pants. They last absolutely forever, which may or may not be a good thing.

✪ Peanut Butter & Jane

617 Hudson St. (at Jane St.). ☎ **212/620-7952.** Subway: A/C/E to 14th St.

Packed to the rafters, this utterly wonderful small store carries real-life clothes at real-life prices—print leggings, tie-dyed T-shirts, Polartec ponchos, denim jackets, cotton dresses in dusky floral prints. The clutter of toys in the back is irresistible. My friends in the West Village look on this shop as a life-support system.

Robin's Nest

1168 Lexington Ave. (at 80th St.). ☎ **212/737-2004.** Subway: 6 to 77th St.

This small undistinguished store carries a lot of the same upscale imported clothes you'll see at the Madison Avenue boutiques—cute, casual outfits mostly.

San Francisco Clothing

975 Lexington Ave. (between 70th and 71st sts.). ☎ **212/472-8740.** Subway: 6 to 68th St.

This long-established East Side women's clothing store has a surprisingly darling line of little girls' clothing, in well-cut mini-preppie styles and top-quality fabrics. Don't let the wood-paneled decor and snooty staff put you off—with playclothes under $50 and dresses under $75, this is an upscale shop worth checking out.

Small Change

964 Lexington Ave. (at 70th St.). ☎ **212/772-6455.** Subway: 6 to 68th St.

Still more expensive children's clothing ($280 for a boy's navy blazer!). The store buyers clearly have a sense of style, though.

Space Kiddets

46 E. 21st St. (between Broadway and Park Ave. South). ☎ **212/420-9878.** Subway: 6/N/R to 23rd St.

Come here for some very cute Downtown-trendy stuff for wee ones—it can be pricey, but the sales are good.

Spring Flowers Children's Boutique

1050 Third Ave. (at 62nd St.). ☎ **212/758-2669.** Subway: 4/5/6 to 59th St.

905 Madison Ave. (at 72nd St.). ☎ **212/717-8182.** Subway: 6 to 68th St.

In the realm of upscale children's clothing, Spring Flowers strikes a healthy balance: The big-skirt party gowns run only $75 to $175. You can find some casual wear, but it's the dress-up stuff that catches the eye, round racks bulging with petticoats and pinafores. Imported brand names include Cacharel, Le Petit Bateau, Sophie Dess—all the usual suspects.

Talbots Kids
1523 Second Ave. (at 79th St.). ☎ **212/570-1630.** Subway: 6 to 77th St.

For all the country-club matron image of the adult Talbots store, this junior version is surprisingly bright and casual and cool, like a Gap without the grunge: loads of khaki pants and polos and tank tops in solid colors and traditional stripes, at prices that seem just right for simple well-made clothes. When my older son finally agreed to wear a navy blazer and rep tie, this is where we bought the blazer—it fit, it looked great, and I didn't pay through the nose for something he'll wear only three times.

Tutti Bambini
1490 First Ave. (between 77th and 78th sts.). ☎ **212/472-4238.** Subway: 6 to 77th St.

Carrying a wide range of labels—imported, made in the U.S.A., whatever—this busy little East Side shop knows its look: funky and fun. It carries sizes up to 10, with brand names like Spaghetti & Confetti and Cozy Toes, and tends toward designs adults wouldn't mind wearing. Most of the other shoppers I saw had kids in tow, which means they were picking out clothes the kids themselves like to wear—always a good sign.

Village Kidz
3 Charles St. (at Greenwich Ave.). ☎ **212/807-8542.** Subway: 1/9 to Christopher St.; F to 14th St.

Village Kids has perfectly adorable clothing for newborns to size 12s, with high-end labels like Jean Bourget, Miniman, and Skivvydoodles. Some styles are over the top, like the zipper-infested black leather biker jacket in size 4T and the sweet cross-stitched pinafores in cotton so thin it looks like it'd rip in a minute, but there's plenty here to tempt you. Good for shoes too. Closed Monday.

Zitomer Department Store
969 Madison Ave. (between 70th and 71st sts.). ☎ **212/737-2037.** Subway: 6 to 68th St.

Bursting at the seams, this drugstore's upstairs children's clothing department has some very upscale imported clothes (dresses in the $50-to-$500 range) that manage to look cheesy in the fluorescent light, jammed together on chrome racks as they are. It's worth a stop if you're on a quest for something special, though the setting is hardly conducive to leisurely browsing.

GAMES

Chess Shop
230 Thompson St. (between 3rd and Bleecker sts.). ☎ **212/475-9580.** Subway: A/B/C/D/E/F/Q to W. 4th St.

Come here for exotic chess sets, esoteric chess manuals, and a slew of related computer software, as well as clocks for speed chess.

Chess Forum
219 Thompson St. (between 3rd and Bleecker sts.). ☎ **212/475-2369.** Subway: A/B/C/D/E/F/Q to W. 4th St.

Competing head-to-head with the Chess Shop right up the street, the Chess Forum is big on chess lessons for kids, along with selling exquisite sets for chess, backgammon, cribbage, and dominoes. Celebrity customers include David Lee Roth, Sean Lennon, Yoko Ono, and Harvey Keitel.

The Compleat Strategist

630 Fifth Ave. (between 50th and 51st sts.), Concourse Level. ☎ **212/265-7449.** Subway: B/D to Rockefeller Center.

11 E. 33rd St. (between Fifth and Madison aves.). ☎ **212/685-3880.** Subway: 6 to 33rd St.

342 W. 57th St. (between Eighth and Ninth aves.). ☎ **212/582-1272.** Subway: 1/9/A/B/ C/D to Columbus Circle.

This specialist shop stocks a fairly mind-boggling array of games, from chess and backgammon to military simulations and role-playing games, but doesn't neglect board games for the younger set, including some noncompetitive games for nonreaders. Fun for browsing. Closed Saturday and Sunday.

Cybergames

2662 Broadway (between 101st and 102nd sts.). ☎ **212/666-2662.** Subway: 1/9 to 103rd St.

Nintendo and Sony Playstation games are for sale, along with trading cards, and there are a couple of in-store sets where you can try out games you're interested in. Sometimes this place has the atmosphere of an arcade, but it's a good source to know about.

Dart Shoppe

30 E. 20th St. (between Broadway and Park Ave. South). ☎ **212/533-8684** or 800/552-9830. Subway: 6/N/R to 23rd St.

This quirky little store in a Gramercy Park brownstone stocks everything relating to darts, period. Not a dart player? Not to worry—they can give you lessons.

The Game Show

1240 Lexington Ave. (at 84th St.). ☎ **212/472-8011.** Subway: 4/5/6 to 86th St.

474 Sixth Ave. (at 12th St.). ☎ **212/633-6328.** Subway: F to 14th St.

A little less specialty-oriented than the Compleat Strategist (above), this well-stocked bright store has lots of games to choose from, including a good range for kids of all ages.

Neutral Ground

122 W. 26th St., 4th floor (between Sixth and Seventh aves.). ☎ **212/633-1288.** Subway: 1/9 to 28th St.

Along with selling an eclectic array of games, especially role-playing games, this store sponsors Magic the Gathering tournaments, role-playing campaigns, and miniature battles. To get a monthly calendar of events, contact their Web site at **www.nground.com.**

GIFTS & GADGETS

Danse Macabre

263½ Lafayette St. (between Prince and Spring sts.). ☎ **212/219-3907.** Subway: N/R to Prince St.

Walk under an arch made of skulls and bones in this wacky little SoHo shop carrying ghoulish designs from all over the world, like a scale-model guillotine or an Indonesian skull box. *Goosebumps* fans alert.

E.A.T. Gifts

1062 Madison Ave. (between 80th and 81st sts.). ☎ **212/861-2544.** Subway: 6 to 77th St.

Next door to the absurdly overpriced E.A.T. cafe, this gift store isn't really designed for kids—it's crowded and there's an annoying "don't touch" factor—but somehow every time we wander in there's something one of my children can't live without. Little gift books, bath toys, tiny shaped soaps and crayons, chocolate novelties—it's like quicksand for the reluctant shopper.

Hammacher Schlemmer

147 E. 57th St. (between Lexington and Third aves.). ☎ **212/421-9000.** Subway: 4/5/6 to 59th St.

You want gadgets? They've got gadgets—high-quality gadgets to do everything under the sun, including some things you've never thought of doing before. Older kids and adults get a kick out of the unique and ingenious products, and don't worry if most items are way out of your price range—the ratio of browsers to buyers is usually pretty high.

It's a Mod, Mod World

85 First Ave. (between 5th and 6th sts.) ☎ **212/460-8004.** Subway: 6 to Astor Pl.

For lovers of Day-Glo vinyl, this East Village shop's collection is utterly 1960s. The impulse-buy toys near the door are less nostalgia-oriented than simply kitschy: wind-up robots that send off sparks, boxing nun hand puppets, and the like. Cute and a hoot.

Little Rickie

49½ First Ave. at E. 3rd St. ☎ **212/505-6467.** Subway: F to Second Ave.

A club-kid sensibility makes this wacky East village shop so cool it's hot. The kitschy hodgepodge of accessories, novelties, and nostalgic junk makes for fun window-shopping even if you don't venture inside.

New York Firefighter's Friend

263 Lafayette St. (between Prince and Spring sts.). ☎ **212/226-3142.** Subway: N/R to Prince St.

A sore disappointment to my son the firetruck lover, this is really a store for firefighters (there's a station two doors down), where they can buy adult-sized turnout gear and badges and FDNY T-shirts. There are a few items in stock for junior firefighters, like plastic red helmets and axes, but not many toy fire engines, and a whole case of what they do have is special-edition collectors' stuff at $25 to $80 (too high for something that's gonna get lost in the sandbox).

P.S. I Love You

1242 Madison Ave. (between 89th and 90th sts.). ☎ **212/722-6272.** Subway: 4/5/6 to 86th St.

Preteen girls love this neighborhood boutique, crammed with stickers, candles, T-shirts, jewelry, pogs, stampers, and other neat little gifts. Sheer impulse buys, nothing horribly expensive.

Sharper Image

4 W. 57th St. (between Fifth and Sixth aves.). ☎ **212/265-2550.** Subway: N/R to Fifth Ave.

900 Madison Ave. (at 73rd St.). ☎ **212/794-4974.** Subway: 6 to 77th St.

Pier 17 at South Street Seaport. ☎ **212/693-0477.** Subway: 2/3/4/5 to Fulton St.; A/C to Broadway/Nassau St.

Now that it has spread to malls all across the country, this high-end gadgetorium chain isn't so much of a draw—it can't beat Hammacher Schlemmer (above) for one-of-a-kind-ism. Still, it can be a fun stop for kids, since so many of the hands-on items on display move and do stuff.

HAIRCUTS

✪ Cozy's Cuts for Kids

1125 Madison Ave. (at 84th St.). ☎ **212/744-1716.** Subway: 4/5/6 to 86th St.

448 Amsterdam Ave. (between 81st and 82nd sts.). ☎ **212/579-2600.** Subway: 1/9 to 79th St.

Spanking clean and bright, Cozy's plays videos to keep kids happy in the chair—which may be a regular barber chair or a yellow Jeep. *Après*-cut, the little shavers get lollipops, balloons, favors, all the usual bribes. Cozy's has enough quality toys to double as a toy store, which unfortunately means you've got to ward off toy requests when you came in only for a haircut; but what the hey, at least you had no trouble getting the kids in the door. Closed Sunday.

Fun Cut

1567 York Ave. (between 83rd and 84th sts.). ☎ **212/288-0602.** Subway: 4/5/6 to 86th St.

Two things make Fun Cut a restful alternative for parents: the soft hues with which it's painted and the fact that there are no toys for sale to raise the "gimme" quotient. There are, however, videos to distract young haircuttees, and quick-working, low-key hairdressers. My squirmy toddler daughter got a superb short cut here after she hacked off her own hair with kindergarten scissors.

Kids Cuts

201 E. 31st St. (at Third Ave.). ☎ **212/684-5252.** Subway: 6 to 33rd St.

If you're in Midtown, this small salon may be more convenient; its slightly lower prices also reflect the fact that it's not part of the Upper East Side yup-scale hub. They cut adult hair as well, which is a real bargain. Closed Monday.

Michael's

1263 Madison Ave. (between 90th and 91st sts.). ☎ **212/289-9612.** Subway: 4/5/6 to 86th St.

The most expensive East Side haircut joint is also the oldest and dirtiest, and I've been told of occasional unpleasant incidents with Michael himself. But my husband prefers Michael's because, even though it specializes in children, it looks like a regular barbershop (except they've got hobbyhorse-shaped booster seats for the chairs and a couple of battered autos that rise on a pole for kids to sit in). The barbers are world-weary gray-haired guys who've cut so many little mops that no tantrum can faze them—and can they work *fast*. Very liberal with lollipops after the cut. No reservations; closed Sunday.

Paul Mole

1031 Lexington Ave. (at 74th St.). ☎ **212/535-8461.** Subway: 6 to 77th St.

Well-known for stylish men's cuts, the Paul Mole salon also has a thriving business in cutting the hair of those stylish men's children (mostly sons), at 10¢ less per cut than adult prices.

The Tortoise and the Hare

1470 York Ave. (at 78th St.). ☎ **212/472-3399.** Subway: 6 to 77th St.

My boys love getting their hair cut here, mostly because I cave in and buy them toys—the last couple of times it was electronic miniguitars like the ones they were handed as distractions during the cut. Kids can choose to watch a video, or older kids can opt for Nintendo and Sony PlayStation games. Besides standard haircutting, this shop offers French braiding and eyebrow sculpting. Closed Sunday and Monday.

HOBBY & CRAFT STORES

Ace Hobbies

35 W. 31st St. (between Fifth and Broadway), 4th floor. ☎ **212/268-4151.** Subway: B/D/F/ N/Q/R to 34th St.

This store is big on model kits, especially planes and naval craft. Closed Sunday.

Jan's Hobby Shop

1557 York Ave. (between 82nd and 83rd sts.). ☎ **212/861-5075.** Subway: 4/5/6 to 86th St.

This stocked-to-the-rafters shop is a wondrous source for all kinds of wooden models—in everything from balsa wood to mahogany—as well as plastic model kits (loads of Revell planes and race cars) and die-cast metal items for collectors. The display cases of military models are awesome. This is currently my 5-year-old's favorite store in the world.

Mach 1 Hobbies

249-A W. 29th St. (between Seventh and Eighth aves.). ☎ **212/947-0157.** Subway: 1/9 to 28th St.

This is a serious source for model makers, juvenile and adult, with discounted prices to boot. Closed Saturday and Sunday.

The Red Caboose

23 W. 45th St. (between Fifth and Sixth aves.); enter the lobby and go downstairs at the back. ☎ 212/575-0272. Subway: B/D to Rockefeller Center.

Models of all kinds of vehicles—trains, planes, cars—are sold here. Closed Sunday.

MAGIC & GAGS

✪ Abracadabra

19 W. 21st St. (between Fifth and Sixth aves.). ☎ **212/627-5194.** Subway: F to 23rd St.

10 Christopher St. (near Greenwich Ave.). ☎ **212/627-5745.** Subway: 1/9 to Christopher St.

This magic superstore even has a stage and a cafe on site, plus several thousand feet of space stocked with every magic trick, costume, and gag under the sun. For more atmosphere, though (and what's magic without atmosphere?), I prefer the Greenwich Village shop, which looks like something out of the Halloween parade, with a front window crammed with ghoulish masks and costumes.

Flosso Hornmann Magic Co.

45 W. 34th St. (between Fifth and Sixth aves.), 6th floor. ☎ **212/279-6079.** Subway: B/D/F/N/Q/R to 34th St.

Houdini himself once owned this outfit, which claims to be the oldest magic shop in the country. There's something subtle in the air here, like a *Twilight Zone* set just waiting for creepy things to start happening. Closed Sunday.

Magic Max

205 W. 42nd St. (between Seventh and Eighth aves.). ☎ **212/921-2916.** Subway: 1/2/3/7/9/N/R/S to Times Sq.

This spanking-clean little magic boutique represents the sanitized new 42nd Street—right next to the family-oriented New Victory Theater (see chapter 7), it has nary an adult gag in sight. Staff members prestidigitate at one counter, while browsers inspect the stock of magic kits, classic gags, and a few respectable NYC souvenirs.

Tannen's Magic

24 W. 25th St. (between Broadway and Sixth aves.). ☎ **212/929-4500.** Subway: F/N/R to 23rd St.

Amateur or professional, magicians shop here, in a slightly raffish commercial neighborhood of storefronts and warehouse lofts. Closed Sunday.

MUSIC

Bleecker Bob's Golden Oldies

118 W. 3rd St. (between Sixth Ave. and MacDougal St.). ☎ **212/475-9677.** Subway: A/B/C/D/E/F/Q to W. 4th St.

This famous Village hangout still has bins full of vinyl, with some very obscure albums. Older kids who are into esoterica and nostalgia may dig it.

HMV

2081 Broadway (at 72nd St.). ☎ **212/721-5900.** Subway: 1/2/3/9 to 72nd St.

1280 Lexington Ave. (at 86th St.). ☎ **212/348-0800.** Subway: 4/5/6 to 86th St.

57 W. 34th St. (entrance on Sixth Ave.). ☎ **212/629-0900.** Subway: B/D/F/N/Q/R to 34th St.

Big, big, big store for tapes and CDs, good for browsing for the latest mainstream sounds.

House of Oldies

35 Carmine St. (between Bleecker and Bedford sts.). ☎ **212/243-0500.** Subway: A/B/C/D/ E/F/Q to W. 4th St.

Like Bleecker Bob's (above), the House of Oldies prides itself on hard-to-find vintage recordings, especially 45s and LPs. If your kids don't know what a "record" is, bring them here for a history lesson.

Manny's Music

156 W. 48th St. (between Sixth and Seventh aves.). ☎ **212/819-0576.** Subway: B/D to Rockefeller Center.

On Midtown's Music Row, Manny's is one store that welcomes kids to fiddle around on the instruments for sale. Closed Sunday.

Tower Records

1961 Broadway (at 66th St.). ☎ **212/799-2500.** Subway: 1/9 to Lincoln Center.

725 Fifth Ave. (at 57th St.). ☎ **212/838-8110.** Subway: N/R to Fifth Ave.

692 Broadway (at 4th St.). ☎ **212/505-1500.** Subway: 6 to Bleecker St.

The name's a bit of a misnomer, since no one buys vinyl anymore. But Tower is the other massive source for recorded music, rivaling HMV (above). Despite its terminal hipness, the Upper West Side branch near Lincoln Center has an especially strong classical music department. The newest branch on Broadway in Midtown feeds on its proximity to the 57th Street theme restaurants and licensed merchandise stores; the original store in Greenwich Village is perhaps a bit past its 15 minutes of utter Downtown coolness.

The Virgin Megastore

1540 Broadway (at 45th St.). ☎ **212/921-1020.** Subway: 1/2/3/7/9/N/R/S to Times Sq.

Everybody's favorite hip Brit tycoon Richard Branson moved into Times Square in a big way with this three-story megamart for recorded music—along with a bookstore, cafe, and movieplex. The music selection is good and deep, and there are lots of listening posts around so you can sample the sounds before you buy. Another Virgin Megastore is planned to open in the Union Square area sometime in 1999.

SCIENCE STUFF

Maxilla and Mandible

451 Columbus Ave. (between 81st and 82nd sts.). ☎ **212/724-6173.** Subway: B/C to 79th St.

Being a block away from the American Museum of Natural History makes sense for this odd and wonderful little shop selling collectible bones and fossils (yep, that's right). Less gruesome items include butterflies pinned under glass, rock samples, and crystals. Fun for junior naturalists.

Star Magic

743 Broadway (at Astor Place). ☎ **212/228-7770.** Subway: 6 to Astor Pl.; N/R to 8th St.

275 Amsterdam Ave. (at 73rd St.). ☎ **212/769-2020.** Subway: 1/2/3/9 to 72nd St.

1256 Lexington Ave. (at 85th St.). ☎ **212/988-0300.** Subway: 4/5/6 to 86th St.

New Agers, Trekkies, and kids alike love this space-themed gift store, which takes its mission pretty loosely—stuff like wind chimes and lava lamps and crystals and tarot cards and Rubik's cubes go along with the astronomy books and telescopes and star charts. Both parents and kids can browse happily for a long time.

✪ Store of Knowledge WNET

1091 Third Ave. (at 64th St.). ☎ **212/223-0018.** Subway: 6 to 68th St.

My family has long loved Boston's WGBH Store of Knowledge in Harvard Square, so we were thrilled when the local PBS station, WNET, got its own branch. Lots of magnets, building toys, flying toys, dinosaur stuff, planetary models, and nature-study kits, along with a small computer section, make this a great source for budding scientists.

✪ Unique Science

410 Columbus Ave. (between 80th and 81st sts.). ☎ **212/712-1899.** Subway: B/C to 79th St.

Slightly more upscale than Star Magic (above), Unique Science has a quality selection of intriguing toys, books, and gift items with a scientific bent—globes, crystals, gyroscopes, experiment kits. Great location right by the Natural History museum, so you can stop in while your kids are still buzzing with interest.

SHOES

East Side Kids

1298 Madison Ave. (between 92nd and 93rd sts.). ☎ **212/360-5000.** Subway: 6 to 96th St.

Free popcorn is dispensed to shoe-shopping kids, which means the place looks like a pigsty by the end of the day. But the range of shoes is wide, some chic and some totally playground-friendly.

Great Feet

1241 Lexington Ave. (at 84th St.). ☎ **212/249-0551.** Subway: 4/5/6 to 86th St.

Carrying the StrideRite standard on the Upper East Side, Great Feet looks like a super treehouse, with separate areas (each decked out with boredom-fighting activities) for different age groups. An essential stop for durable midpriced shoes and for wider feet.

Harry's Shoes

2299 Broadway (at 83rd St.). ☎ **212/874-2034.** Subway: 1/9 to 86th St.

A West Side institution. The kids department is strong on StrideRites; moms and dads buy boots and sandals and casual shoes here too. It's always a zoo and hardly a bargain, but the weary staff is pretty professional. Fashion is less the point here than solid quality.

Ibiza Kidz

42 University Place (at 9th St.). ☎ **212/505-9907.** Subway: N/R to 8th St.

Next door to its sibling clothing store, this Village kids boutique sells shoes, books, and animals, and the stock shows some real flair.

Lester's

1522 Second Ave. (at 79th St.). ☎ **212/734-9292.** Subway: 6 to 77th St.

This all-purpose children's clothing store (see "Fashions," above) provides one-stop shopping with a full-service shoe department in the back.

Little Eric

1331 Third Ave. (at 76th St.). ☎ **212/288-8987.** Subway: 6 to 77th St.
1118 Madison Ave. (at 83rd St.). ☎ **212/717-1513.** Subway: 4/5/6 to 86th St.

Style is the watchword—get your 4-year-old shod here if you want to wow the admissions officer at your Brearley or Buckley interview. Yes, they've got plain patent-leather Mary Janes and classic penny loafers in peewee sizes, but also cowboy boots and other trendy styles.

✪ Shoofly

465 Amsterdam Ave. (between 82nd and 83rd sts.). ☎ **212/580-4390.** Subway: 1/9 to 79th St.

42 Hudson St. (between Duane and Thomas sts.). ☎ **212/406-3270.** Subway: 1/2/3/9 to Chambers St.

A whimsical collection of designer hats for kids hangs from tree branches poking out of one wall; low shelves and bins and steamer trunks overflow with a wild assortment of shoes, sandals, socks, mittens, hairbows, belts, and ties, running the gamut from goofy to glam. It's always fun shopping here, even if you don't buy. The prices aren't outlandish, but the sense of style is—just what little New Yorkers need to look really cool.

Village Kidz

3 Charles St. (at Greenwich Ave.). ☎ **212/807-8542.** Subway: A/B/C/D/E/F/Q to W. 4th St.

Come here for Downtown shoe styles that are very with it, like little brown leather lace-up boots and patent-leather hightops. No bargains.

SHOWER & BABY GIFTS

Art & Tapisserie

1242 Madison Ave. (between 89th and 90th sts.). ☎ **212/722-3222.** Subway: 4/5/6 to 86th St.

Make sure you bring the correct spelling of the new baby's name: The cheery jumble here is geared to items that can be personalized—picture frames, footstools, clocks, bookends, and other nursery accents. There are some other toys, but nothing to die for.

✪ Little Extras

550 Amsterdam Ave. (between 86th and 87th sts.). ☎ **212/721-6161.** Subway: 1/9 to 86th St.

Though there are a few toys here for older kids (pacifying gifts for displaced older siblings, perhaps), baby gifts reign: music boxes, picture frames, picture albums, nursery lamps, soft wall hangings, baby towel sets, silver cups and spoons and rattles, personalized footstools, and toy chests. This place never lets me down when I'm en route to a shower, christening, or bris and need a present in a hurry.

Tiffany's

727 Fifth Ave. (at 57th St.). ☎ **212/755-8000.** Subway: N/R to Fifth Ave.

Wanna score points? A silver spoon, rattle, teething ring, or baby cup from Tiffany's is still the classy way to celebrate a new arrival, and no new parent minds duplicates of these classics. Get the spoon or cup engraved for an extra touch; you can do it all by phone, though visiting this fabled store is usually a pleasure. All except the cup are under $100, so why not go for it? A child is born only once.

SPORTS STUFF

Blades Board & Skate

120 W. 72nd St. (between Broadway and Columbus Ave.). ☎ **212/787-3911.** Subway: 1/2/3/9/B/C to 72nd St.

In-line skaters and skateboarders gear up at this chain of specialty stores, where you can have your own board custom-built for $500 or so. Get yer helmets and kneepads here as well. Rentals are available. See chapter 5 for skateboarding info.

Other locations: 659 Broadway, between Bond and Bleecker streets (☎ **212/477-7350**); 128 Chambers St., at West Broadway (☎ **212/964-1944**); Chelsea Piers, West 23rd Street and the West Side Highway (☎ **212/336-6299**); 160 E. 86th St., between Lexington and Third avenues (☎ **212/996-1644**); 1414 Second Ave., between 73rd and 74th streets (☎ **212/249-3178**).

Crosstown Sports

2308 Broadway (between 83rd and 84th sts.). ☎ **212/875-1767.** Subway: 1/9 to 86th St.

Every time one of our sons takes up a new sport, this is our first stop. They're great for sports equipment (mitts, skates, sticks, balls, shinguards) as well as clothing—they have a good stock of pro team jerseys my boys lust after. They also sell shoes, though the endearing jocks who work here don't always know how to fit a child's foot. The batting gloves we bought here helped my older son hit two home runs in a crucial Little League game (or so he's convinced).

Other locations: 1574 Third Ave., between 88th and 89th streets (☎ **212/410-9356;** Subway: 4/5/6 to 86th St.); 2901 Broadway, at 113th Street (☎ **212/531-3012;** Subway: 1/9 to 116th St.); 455 World Trade Center, WTC #4, at the Liberty Street entrance (☎ **212/912-9701;** Subway: E to World Trade Center).

Eastern Mountain Sports

20 W. 61st St. (between Broadway and Columbus Ave.). ☎ **212/397-4860.** Subway: 1/9/A/B/C/D to Columbus Circle.

611 Broadway (at Houston St.). ☎ **212/505-9860.** Subway: B/D/F to Broadway/Lafayette St.

This place is big on camping gear and outdoor wear, along with equipment for climbing walls. The ideal place to buy a sleeping bag that doesn't have Mickey Mouse or Batman all over the lining.

Mets Clubhouse Shop

575 Fifth Ave. (at 47th St.). ☎ **212/986-4887.** Subway: E/F to Fifth Ave.

Mets fans stock up on blue-and-orange team paraphernalia and memorabilia here. You can buy game tickets here, too.

Modell's

1535 Third Ave. (between 86th and 87th sts.). ☎ **212/996-3800.** Subway: 4/5/6 to 86th St.

When you gotta go to Mo's, you gotta go. Though not totally kid oriented—Crosstown Sports (above) actually handles local Little Leaguers better—Mo's is an important destination for any family harboring a young athlete, because of its sheer size and its attention to some of the less mainstream sports as well.

Other locations: 200 Broadway, between Fulton and John streets (☎ **212/964-4007;** Subway: 2/3/4/5 to Fulton St.); 280 Broadway, at Chambers Street (☎ **212/962-6200;** Subway: A/C to Chambers St.); Manhattan Mall, 901 Sixth Ave., at 33rd Street (☎ **212/594-1830;** Subway: B/D/F/N/Q/R to 34th St.); 51 E. 42nd St., between Vanderbilt and Madison avenues (☎ **212/661-4242;** Subway: 4/5/6/7/S to Grand Central).

NikeTown

6 E. 57th St. (between Fifth and Madison aves.). ☎ **212/891-6453.** Subway: N/R to Fifth Ave.

This glitzy temple to sports and sneakers is more of a museum/attraction than a place to buy shoes, with several interactive stations where kids can measure their feet, test their reach and reflexes, and generally try to be like Mike.

Paragon Sports

867 Broadway (at 18th St.). ☎ **212/255-8036.** Subway: 4/5/6/L/N/R to Union Sq.

Paragon's good for rugged sports clothing and total gear.

Sports Memorabilia Gallery
150 Fifth Ave. (between 19th and 20th sts.). ☎ **212/255-9230.** Subway: N/R to 23rd St.

Here you'll find all kinds of sports collectibles, except for trading cards.

The Sports Authority
401 Seventh Ave. (at 33rd St.). ☎ **212/563-7195.** Subway: 1/2/3/9 to 34th St.

51st St. and Third Ave. ☎ **212/355-9725.** Subway: 6 to 51st St.

57th St. and Sixth Ave. ☎ **212/355-6430.** Subway: B/Q to 57th St.

Though not quite as comprehensive as Mo's, this is another good clean Midtown source for sports equipment and apparel.

Yankees Clubhouse Shop
393 Fifth Ave. (between 36th and 37th sts.). ☎ **212/685-4693.** Subway: 6 to 33rd St.

110 E. 59th St. (between Park and Lexington aves.). ☎ **212/758-7844.** Subway: 4/5/6 to 59th St.

Bronx Bomber fans can indulge their merchandise-buying addictions here. Also a good source for tickets.

STROLLERS, CRIBS & FURNITURE

Albee Baby Carriage Co.
715 Amsterdam Ave. (at 95th St.). ☎ **212/662-5740.** Subway: 1/2/3/9 to 96th St.

This store may be crowded and a little grimy and disorganized, but what these folks don't know about nursery equipment ain't worth knowing. There's always an unwieldy mother-to-be collapsed in a glider rocker, looking glassy-eyed as she (and her mother and/or husband) order a couple thousand dollars' worth of baby stuff—I wonder how many labors have started here over the years.

Baby Depot at Burlington Coat Factory
116 W. 23rd St. (entrance on Sixth Ave.). ☎ **212/229-2247.** Subway: F to 23rd St.

Toil up to the third floor of this discount emporium to find a Toys "я" Us–ish collection of layettes, cribs, strollers, car seats, and clothing. The prices are fairly low—just don't expect top-of-the-line furnishings for your nursery.

Baby Palace
1410 Lexington Ave. (between 92nd and 93rd sts.). ☎ **212/426-4544.** Subway: 6 to 96th St.

This friendly store is a well-stocked solid option for everything from cribs to strollers to toys and babywear. Closed Saturday.

Bellini
1305 Second Ave. (between 68th and 69th sts.). ☎ **212/517-9233.** Subway: 6 to 68th St.

110 W. 86th St. (near Columbus Ave.). ☎ **212/362-3700.** Subway: 1/9/B/C to 86th St.

At this expensive baby furniture boutique, the service can be offhand (unless, of course, you're dropping a bundle). The look is pretty with an edge of fun, nothing too unusual. If you want to start your infant off with upscale tastes, this is where to do it.

Ben's for Kids
1380 Third Ave. (between 78th and 79th Sts.). ☎ **212/794-2330.** Subway: 6 to 77th St.

Ben's is to the East Side what Albee's (above) is to the West, the main difference being that Ben's is actually pretty clean and has a substantial toy department.

Boston & Winthrop
No address. ☎ **212/410-6388.**

This firm designs some really wonderful custom-painted children's furniture; call for an appointment. They come to you, not you to them.

Bunnies

116 W. 14th St. (between Sixth and Seventh aves.). ☎ **212/989-9011.** Subway: F to 14th St.

100 Delancey St. (between Ludlow and Essex sts.). ☎ **212/529-7567.** Subway: F to Delancey St.

The downmarket locations reflect this store's mission to sell baby equipment (makers like Century and Evenflo) and clothing up to size 16 (labels like OshKosh and Guess) at very reasonable prices.

The Children's Room

140 Varick St. (at Spring St.). ☎ **212/627-2006.** Subway: 1/9 to Canal St.

Here you'll find bunk beds galore, as well as kid-size desks, dressers, toy chests, and the like. Nothing tremendously flashy, but everything is well designed and high quality, with prices to match.

Kids Supply Co.

1325 Madison Ave. (between 92nd and 93rd sts.), 2nd floor. ☎ **212/426-1200.** Subway: 6 to 96th St.

This boutique sells some intriguing children's furniture, featuring warm woods and bold colors and a sophisticated sense of style. Quality stuff, built to withstand children.

Little Folks Shop

123 E. 23rd St. (between Park and Lexington aves.). ☎ **212/982-9669.** Subway: 6 to 23rd St.

Little Folks sells a solid range of nursery outfittings, plus layettes and clothes up to size 14. Closed Saturday.

Plain Jane

525 Amsterdam Ave. (between 85th and 86th sts.). ☎ **212/595-6916.** Subway: 1/9 to 86th St.

This kicky little West Side boutique specializes in antique nursery furniture, country-look bedding, quilts, and some newer stuff with a retro sensibility—truly one-of-a-kind items like a $500 découpaged toy chest accented with kids' faces straight from some Dick and Jane primer.

Schneider's

20 Avenue A (at 2nd St.). ☎ **212/228-3540.** Subway: F to Second Ave.

This Downtown source for baby equipment, on a rundown East Village block, is a lot cleaner than the surrounding neighborhood. A staple for below-14th-Street new moms.

Wicker Garden's Children

1327 Madison Ave. (at 93rd St.). ☎ **212/410-7001.** Subway: 6 to 96th St.

While the baby clothes downstairs are lovely, the upstairs section is the real heart of this shop—nursery furniture that puts the cheap white laminated crap utterly to shame. Decorate your baby's nest with these country-house reproductions (it's not all wicker) and even Mark Hampton would approve. Closed Sunday.

THEME STORES

Just opened at press time, the three-story **NBA Store,** 666 Fifth Ave., at 52nd Street (☎ **212/515-6221;** Subway: E/F to Fifth Ave.), is the latest player in the Fifth Avenue Parade of Theme Stores, which many New Yorkers lament as imposing a mall sensibility on the big city.

Coca-Cola Fifth Avenue

711 Fifth Ave. (between 55th and 56th sts.). ☎ **212/418-9260.** Subway: E/F to Fifth Ave.

The first of Fifth Avenue's brand-name stores, this boutique sells kitschy Coke collectibles.

The Disney Store

711 Fifth Ave. (at 55th St.). ☎ **212/702-0702.** Subway: E/F to Fifth Ave.

This three-story studio store brings to Manhattan the world's largest selection of Disney merchandise under one roof: images of Mickey, Donald, and the gang painted, embroidered, and embossed on every imaginable item, from baseball hats to bedside lamps—and, of course, wristwatches. If you think this is cheap stuff, the top floor's collectibles department will set you straight, a veritable gallery of animation art, glass art, and exquisite ceramics. The first floor is dedicated to clothing, for children and adults; make a beeline for the second floor, where all the toys and games are in stock. There's always a captivating video clip playing on a huge screen somewhere, to mesmerize your children while you shop.

Other (smaller) locations: 210 W. 42nd St., at Seventh Avenue (☎ **212/221-0430**; Subway: 1/2/3/7/9/N/R/S to Times Sq.); 39 W. 34th St., between Fifth and Sixth avenues (☎ **212/279-9890**; Subway: B/D/E/F/N/Q/R to 34th St.); 141 Columbus Ave., at 66th Street (☎ **212/362-2386**; Subway: 1/9 to Lincoln Center.).

NikeTown

6 E. 57th St. (between Fifth and Madison aves.). ☎ **212/891-6453.** Subway: N/R to Fifth Ave.

Eye-popping design and lots of sports videos build the buzz at this sneaker palace.

Warner Bros. Studio Store

1 E. 57th St. (at Fifth Ave.). ☎ **212/754-0300.** Subway: N/R to Fifth Ave.

One Times Square (at 42nd St., Seventh Ave., and Broadway). ☎ 212/840-4040. Subway: 1/2/3/7/9/N/R/S to Times Sq.

The intersection of Fifth Avenue and 57th Street has become known as the Four Carats since carrot-chompin' Bugs Bunny joined the high-end jewelry stores here; in 1997, Warner Bros. also cornered a very prime piece of Times Square real estate, right below where the ball drops on New Year's Eve (not coincidentally catercorner from a Disney Store). Both megastores occupy three floors and are usually crowded to the gills. There's absolutely nothing New Yorkish about them, but they're indubitably loads of fun for little cartoon hounds, with endless cartoon videos on the huge monitors and pictures of the Looney Tunes crowd painted, embroidered, and embossed on every kind of clothing and gift item.

TOYS

Alphabets

115 Avenue A (at 7th St.). ☎ **212/475-7250.** Subway: 6 to Astor Pl.

2284 Broadway (between 82nd and 83rd sts.). ☎ **212/579-5702.** Subway: 1/9 to 79th St.

47 Greenwich Ave. (between Sixth and Seventh aves.). ☎ **212/229-2966.** Subway: 1/2/3/9 to 14th St.

The East Village branch of this wacky gift-a-torium has an annex full of campy kids' stuff—Etch-a-Sketch and Mr. Potato Head, yes, but also some truly goofball stuff like a chess set with the Simpson family (Homer and Bart, that is). Loads of one-of-a-kind T-shirts and a very big line of Hello Kitty stuff from Japan (hot with Downtown club kids).

A Bear's Place

789 Lexington Ave. (between 61st and 62nd sts.). ☎ **212/826-6465.** Subway: 4/5/6 to 59th St.

For some reason, this strikes me as a girl's toy store, maybe because it has the biggest stock I've seen of equipment for mothering baby dolls, along with wooden toys, games, puppets, big teddy bears, dolls, and the entire line of imported Battat toys for babies and toddlers. You can order some hand-painted nursery furnishings here.

Bear Hugs and Baby Dolls

311 E. 81st St. (between First and Second aves.). ☎ **212/717-1514.** Subway: 6 to 77th St.

For collectible teddy bears—your Steiffs, Gunds, Muffy Vanderbears—come to this pretty but precious East Side doll boutique. Don't expect any other kinds of toys, though—and don't touch.

Ben's for Kids

1380 Third Ave. (between 78th and 79th sts.). ☎ **212/794-2330.** Subway: 6 to 77th St.

Though principally for nursery equipment, Ben's has enough toys in the front to qualify as a toy store. The emphasis is on playthings for babies and toddlers, with lots of Fisher Price and such standard brands.

Big City Kites

1210 Lexington Ave. (at 81st St.). ☎ **212/472-2623.** Subway: 4/5/6 to 86th St.

Beyond all the great wind-worthy kites promised in the name, this handy little shop stocks loads of other flying toys, from Frisbees to balsa-wood gliders; a serious collection of yo-yos and juggling equipment rounds out the inventory. A good stop if you're on the way to Central Park on a windy spring afternoon. Closed Sunday September to March.

Breadsoul Toy Cafe

1169 Second Ave. (between 61st and 62nd sts.). ☎ **212/759-7228.** Subway: 4/5/6 to 59th St.

The toy store half of this place actually is stronger than the restaurant half (see chapter 8); I was very impressed by the number of unusual wooden toys and imports and books on its shelves. There are several decent items for under $10, though most of the stock is best for ages 8 and under.

✪ Children's General Store

Grand Central Terminal, Lexington Passage. ☎ **212/682-0004.** Subway: 4/5/6/7/S to Grand Central.

2473 Broadway (at 91st St.). ☎ **212/580-2723.** Subway: 1/2/3/9 to 96th St.

This charming toy boutique is a welcome addition to the shopping at Grand Central Terminal; the West Side original, handily downstairs from Playspace, has won customer loyalty for offering some unusual handmade and imported toys you won't see in most other stores. The emphasis is on well-made toys with a certain imagination-sparking value. The West Sider crams an awful lot into its small space; thank goodness the Grand Central space will give them room to show what they can really do.

Classic Toys

214 Sullivan St. (between Bleecker and 3rd sts.). ☎ **212/674-4434.** Subway: A/B/C/D/E/F/Q to W. 4th St.

The "classic" in the name works both ways: both vintage toys (wind-ups, trains) and the kinds of solid, quality new toys that'll endure. Closed Monday.

Cozy's Cuts for Kids

1125 Madison Ave. (at 84th St.). ☎ **212/744-1716.** Subway: 4/5/6 to 86th St.

448 Amsterdam Ave. (between 81st and 82nd sts.). ☎ 212/579-2600. Subway: 1/9 to 79th St.

Besides haircuts (above), Cozy's deals in a small stock of well-chosen toys, including lots of arts and crafts.

The Craft Studio
1657 Third Ave. (between 92nd and 93rd sts.). ☎ **212/831-6626.** Subway: 6 to 96th St.

The rain forest–themed site for plaster-painting parties has an excellent front section with lots of crafts kits, art materials, puzzles, and other toys.

Dinosaur Hill
306 E. 9th St. (near Second Ave.). ☎ **212/473-5850.** Subway: 6 to Astor Pl.

Selling imported toys, mobiles, wooden blocks, art supplies, and puppets—notably an extensive line of handmade marionettes—this airy East Village shop also has a battery of under-$1 stuff so no child will have to leave empty-handed.

Enchanted Forest
85 Mercer St. (between Spring and Broome sts.). ☎ **212/925-6677.** Subway: N/R to Prince St.; 6 to Spring St.

Befitting its SoHo location, this is a boutique for the Toy as Art—handmade wooden song flutes from the rain forest, exquisite hand-sewn stuffed animals and hand puppets, phantasmagorical pop-up books. The fanciful decor makes it more or less a gallery, highly browseable, and about as far away from Toys "Я" Us as a toy store can get.

✪ FAO Schwarz
767 Fifth Ave. (at 58th St.). ☎ **212/644-9400.** Subway: N/R to Fifth Ave.

What can I say? Vacationing families are duty-bound to visit this mecca, though locals rarely venture inside. This huge place isn't just a toy store, it's a destination— the immense mechanical music box/clock on the ground floor is worth at least 10 minutes of staring and marveling in itself. Larger-than-life stuffed animals, the FAO trademark, dominate the ground floor; upstairs (via escalator or glass-walled elevator) are incredible toy cars, a Barbie boutique, an overwhelming Lego department, an immense Brio train set-up, and more electronic robots and toys and games than you've ever seen. Not everything is imported, by any means—Fisher Price and Playskool take their place alongside the somewhat precious toys made exclusively for FAO. (Remember, this place is now a chain, with all the mass-market mentality that implies.) Grandmas with big bucks are the prime audience for all this conspicuous consumption, but persevere and you'll no doubt find some toys you could justify buying.

Geppetto's Toybox
101 Seventh Ave. So. (at Waverly Place). ☎ **212/620-7511.** Subway: 1/9 to Christopher St.

Kids and collectors alike shop at this precious Greenwich Village boutique, its ceiling festooned in luminous wooden lanterns. The selection tends toward high-end dolls, collectible bears, and artist-designed toys, less for playing with than for admiring on a shelf. Older girls may be thrilled.

Hombons
1500 First Ave. (between 78th and 79th sts.). ☎ **212/717-5300.** Subway: 6 to 77th St.

Crowded into this storefront is a deep selection of stuff to play with, best for its art-and-crafts materials, puzzles, board games, Playmobils, and other small-motor activities. It's definitely a place that rewards a long, slow browse.

Just Jake
40 Hudson St. (at Duane St.). ☎ **212/267-1716.** Subway: 1/2/3/9 to Chambers St.

In TriBeCa, Jake's mom has opened this light-filled little store where kids can play with nearly everything on the shelves. There's a sort of purity to the toy selection: No items need batteries, and nothing has a TV tie-in.

Kay-Bee Toys

In Manhattan Mall, 901 Sixth Ave. (at 33rd St.). ☎ **212/629-5386.** Subway: B/D/F/N/Q/R to 34th St.

Sometimes you need a chain toy store to get that Malibu Barbie or G.I. Joe your kid is pining for. Utterly mass market, very dependable.

Kidding Around

60 W. 15th St. (between Fifth and Sixth aves.). ☎ **212/645-6337.** Subway: 4/5/6/L/N/R to Union Sq.

68 Bleecker St. (between Broadway and Lafayette St.). ☎ **212/598-0228.** Subway: 6 to Bleecker St.

This pair of shops brings the Uptown toy-buying aesthetic to Downtown—imports and educational toys in a clean well-lighted space. Lots of rugged plastic wildlife in baskets on the floor.

Little Extras

550 Amsterdam Ave. (between 86th and 87th sts.). ☎ **212/721-6161.** Subway: 1/9 to 86th St.

Alongside some lovely baby gifts, this West Sider has a pleasant stock of painted wooden toys, hand puppets, backpacks, puzzles, and art kits, not to mention personalized little-boy yarmulkes and nifty junior jewelry. A fun place to browse.

✪ Mary Arnold Toys

1010 Lexington Ave. (between 72nd and 73rd sts.). ☎ **212/744-8510.** Subway: 6 to 77th St.

A 1997 renovation doubled this East Side store's floor space, and now it's one of the best in town, intelligently laid-out with nooks where children can fiddle and browse without clogging the aisles. Quality toys—Legos, Brios, Playmobils—many shelves of board games, lots of dress-up costumes, and a very impressive doll department make this a never-fail destination to satisfy kids of any age or interest.

My Favorite Place

265 W. 87th St. (at Broadway). ☎ **212/362-5320.** Subway: 1/9 to 86th St.

The name sums up my kids' feeling about this store, a smartly stocked little emporium that's the front for a whole kaboodle of kid-friendly activities, from a toddler playroom downstairs to art classes in the back room to birthday parties after school and on weekends. (See the end of chapter 5 for details on the toddler playroom and drop-in classes.) For Brio trains and Playmobil sets and Ravensburger puzzles and games, this store can't be beat, though it also has a handy corner of bins offering loads of totally cool little toys for $5 and under, which is a blessing for parents—great stuff for party favors, quick rewards, and bribes.

Noodle Kidoodle

112 E. 86th St. (between Park and Lexington aves.). ☎ **212/427-6611.** Subway: 4/5/6 to 86th St.

Face it: Who has time to browse delightedly for toys these days? Your kid's heart is set on a certain Brio component, or you've got two cooped up with chicken pox who are climbing the walls. Where do you go to get relief fast? Try Noodle Kidoodle, a reliable place for efficient toy shopping. Though it may lack the kind of personality and charm a small independently owned shop might have, this large chain store is positioned neatly midway between Toys "Я" Us and FAO Schwarz—it has a broad-ranging stock of quality toys, without any snobbery against commercial stuff like Barbies and Nerf guns. The prices are decent (at least by Manhattan standards), and the space is clean and bright. The selection of children's audiotapes and CDs is particularly extensive, and there's a generous section of arts-and-crafts kits, as well as good board games and puzzles. Beanie Baby collectors note: This is one of the city's best sources for current Beanies, where the prices remain fair.

✪ Penny Whistle Toys

448 Columbus Ave. (at 81st St.). ☎ **212/873-9090.** Subway: B/C to 79th St.

1283 Madison Ave. (at 91st St.). ☎ **212/369-3868.** Subway: 4/5/6 to 86th St.

This outstanding shop has more or less defined what upscale New York parents want in a toy store: imported, quality, educational toys, well made but with a sense of fun. Nothing too precious, nothing too commercial. Mechanical bears outside both stores blow soap bubbles in fair weather, which makes it very hard to get your kids past without stopping.

Promises Fulfilled

1592 Second Ave. (between 82nd and 83rd sts.). ☎ **212/472-1600.** Subway: 4/5/6 to 86th St.

This narrow, crowded, slightly tacky little toy shop is handy only if you're in the neighborhood.

Quest Toys

2 World Financial Center, 225 Liberty St. ☎ **212/945-9330.** Subway: E to World Trade Center.

Though painfully tiny, this shop in this upscale Battery Park City mall crams in a lot of carefully chosen, sometimes unusual toys. I'm always afraid my kids are going to knock over something, though, and the prices are a bit high for impulse buying. The target audience seems to be parents who work in the World Financial Center or World Trade Center across the way and have to buy a toy, any toy, in a hurry. Which isn't to say that there aren't some fun things here.

Stationery & Toy World

125 W. 72nd St. (between Columbus Ave. and Broadway). ☎ **212/580-3922.** Subway: 1/2/3/9 to 72nd St.

There's a delightfully unpretentious clutter of mass-market toys amid the spiral notebooks and ballpoint pens at this West Side storefront (which, my kids never fail to remember, is just down the street from the Krispy Kreme Doughnuts shop). A good place for reward and bribe toys and fun little surprises.

Store of Knowledge WNET

1091 Third Ave. (at 64th St.). ☎ **212/223-0018.** Subway: 6 to 68th St.

Along with awesome stuff for junior physicists, astronomers, entomologists, and paleontologists (see "Science Stuff," above), this large PBS-sponsored store has lots of good baby toys and tie-in toys to all those great PBS kids' shows.

Toys "Я" Us

1293 Broadway (at 34th St.). ☎ **212/594-8697.** Subway: B/D/F/N/Q/R to 34th St.

24–32 Union Sq. East (at 15th St.). ☎ **212/674-8697.** Subway: 4/5/6/L/N/R to Union Sq.

I'm not a snob, and there certainly have been times when I've trekked here to get that Fisher Price trike or Hot Wheels set the high-end Manhattan toy stores don't stock. But frankly, in the context of New York toy shopping, these immense toy-o-ramas are a pretty lackluster alternative; the stock looks battered, customers wander around in a shell-shocked daze, there's hardly any sales help, the toys don't even have price tags (you have to lug them over to a scanner to have the bar code read electronically), and, for all the miles of shelves, sometimes you still can't find that mass-market toy your son saw advertised on the Cartoon Network and is bugging you for. The prices aren't even significantly lower. I prefer to save my Toys "Я" Us excursions for branches in the 'burbs when we visit Grammy.

✪ West Side Kids

498 Amsterdam Ave. (at 84th St.). ☎ **212/496-7282.** Subway: 1/9 to 86th St.

This superb West Side store room enough to stock every toy a parent could want—lotsa Legos, T.C. Timber, Playmobils, every crafts kit known to youth, an impressive board game selection, and a whole wall of great imported infant and toddler items, as well as one of those great bin corners where the toy equivalent of penny candy is handily laid out (there have been days when I'd never have gotten my kids safely out of the store if I hadn't been able to buy each of them a $1 sop from the bins). When I've got a birthday or Christmas coming up and have no time to troll the stores, I can count on one-stop shopping here.

Zittles

969 Madison Ave. (between 70th and 71st sts.). ☎ **212/737-2040.** Subway: 6 to 68th St.

This East Side drugstore's toy department just kept expanding and crowded out the second floor; now it's got its own name and a floor to itself. It may be the most crowded retail space in all Manhattan, and that's saying something. Still, for completely unsnobby mainstream toys, it's a source worth knowing about.

7

Entertainment for the Whole Family

Being the theater capital of the United States doesn't necessarily make New York City the children's theater capital—most of those struggling actors and playwrights and directors are too intent on breaking into the Big Time to pay much mind to kid stuff. On the other hand, the major classical-music venues—Lincoln Center and Carnegie Hall—have in the past few years seen the wisdom of introducing children to music *early*, perhaps because impresarios realize (with panic) that their core audience is rapidly aging and needs to be replaced. In any case, there's a lot of talent hanging around this city, and when enterprising organizers decide to put on a show for young audiences, the production values are generally high.

Two important players entered the scene in the 1990s. The Disney organization has waded into New York theater in a big way, topping its live stage version of the animated hit *Beauty and the Beast* with an even more successful *Lion King* production in the stunningly renovated New Amsterdam Theater on West 42nd Street (see "The Big Venues"). The New Victory Theater, another 42nd Street rehab, opened well before Disney, paving the way with a vigorous series of family-oriented productions that has already improved the cultural life of the under-14 set (see "The Big Venues").

New York parents tend to be culture hounds, so plays and concerts for children are usually well attended—which means that, as for adult productions, you've got to reserve in advance. Compared to the $75 you can pay for orchestra seats in the big Broadway theaters, ticket prices for kids' events aren't usually outrageous, though a few major annual events—like the Big Apple Circus and *The Nutcracker*—get away with higher prices.

FINDING OUT WHAT'S ON The three local parents' monthlies—the **Big Apple Parents' Paper,** 36 E. 12th St., New York, NY 10003 (☎ **212/533-2277;** fax 212/475-6186; www.bigappleparents.com); **New York Family,** 141 Halstead Ave., Suite 3D, Mamaroneck, NY 10543 (☎ **914/381-7474;** www.nyfamily.com); and **ParentGuide,** Parent Guide Network Corp., 419 Park Ave. South, New York, NY 10016 (☎ **212/213-8840**)—carry invaluable calendars of upcoming cultural events kids would enjoy. You can usually pick up free copies at public libraries, toy stores, and kids' clothing stores. Less easy to find, but very helpful, is the **Family Entertainment Guide,** a quarterly calendar published by Family Publications Ltd., 37 W. 72nd St., Suite 9, New York, NY 10023 (☎ **212/595-4569**).

Call to get recorded listings of events for **Lincoln Center** at ☎ **212/875-5400** or **Central Park** at ☎ **888/NY-PARKS.**

Every Friday, the ***New York Times*** runs a "Family Fare" column in its Weekend entertainment section, detailing special events in the upcoming week. Three week-lies—***New York*** magazine, ***Time Out New York,*** and the ***Village Voice***—include sections on children's events in their comprehensive listings. The weekly ***New Yorker*** magazine sometimes lists children's events if there's room in the "Goings On About Town" section, but not usually.

GETTING TICKETS   In marked contrast to the adult entertainment scene, children's events in New York City don't tend to sell out far in advance. The Radio City shows and seasonal runs like *The Nutcracker,* the Big Apple Circus, and the Ringling Brothers and Barnum & Bailey Circus should be reserved a few weeks in advance, but for most other events you'll be fine calling a week ahead or even walking in the day of the show. For pro sports events, ticket availability is a matter of how well the team's been doing lately (Knicks tickets are impossible, but you can just about always walk into a MetroStars game). There are usually flocks of scalpers hovering around Madison Square Garden, if seeing a Knicks game is the most important thing on your youngster's agenda. You'll pay through the nose and might be sold bogus tickets, but it may be worth the gamble for you.

Madison Square Garden events and major theater productions offer their tickets through **Ticketmaster** (☎ **800/755-4000,** 212/307-4100, or 212/307-7171; www.ticketmaster.com) or through **Tele-Charge** (☎ **800/432-7250,** 212/239-6200; www.telecharge.com). **Madison Square Garden events** also have their own box office (☎ **212/465-MSG1;** www.thegarden.com). For smaller children's theater companies and puppet shows, contact the box office numbers in separate listings below (some are simply answering machines where you leave your number so the organizer can call you back).

Same-day tickets for many Broadway and Off Broadway events can be bought in person at the **TKTS booths** (☎ **212/768-1818**): in Midtown on the pedestrian island called Duffy Square at 47th Street and Broadway (open daily 3–8pm for evening performances, Wed and Sat 10am–2pm for matinees, Sun noon–6:30pm) or Downtown on the mezzanine of Two World Trade Center (open Mon–Fri 11am–5pm, Sat 11am–3:30pm). Most tickets are sold at half price, though some are discounted only 25%, but you'll have to have cash or traveler's checks—no plastic. A $2.50 TKTS service charge is added. The Times Square booth often has long lines, which move fairly fast but not fast enough for restless small kids. The surrounding assemblage of wild lit-up signs can provide some distraction while you're waiting, and sometimes mimes and jugglers and street musicians work the crowd. But if you can, one parent should take the youngsters for a walk while the other hangs out in line.

1 The Big Venues

Brooklyn Academy of Music (BAM)
30 Lafayette Ave., Brooklyn. ☎ **718/636-4100**. Tickets $8–12. Subway: 2/3/4/5/D/Q to Atlantic Ave., Brooklyn; G to Fulton St., Brooklyn; B/M/N/R to Pacific St., Brooklyn.

Theater, dance, music, puppetry—an impressively international selection of productions rolls through BAM in the course of a year, with a decided tendency toward the avant-garde. In the lineup you can count on a handful of reasonably priced performances suited to youngsters, always worth a trek out to Brooklyn. Age levels are specified for each performance.

Madison Square Garden

Seventh Ave. between 31st and 33rd sts. ☎ **212/465-MSG1.** Subway: A/C/E to Penn Station; 1/2/3/9 to 34th St.

B-ball, hockey, WWF wrestling, ice shows, the big-top circus, and megarock concerts occupy this large arena in a grubby part of Midtown. It can be an intimidating space for a small child, but older kids will recognize it for what it is: a big-league venue with lots of urban electricity. Tickets for most events here are also handled through Ticketmaster. The **Theater at Madison Square Garden**, part of the Garden complex, hosts concerts and live touring stage shows like *Sesame Street Live.*

New Amsterdam Theater

214 W. 42nd St. (between Seventh and Eighth aves.). ☎ **212/282-2900** or 212/307-4747 (Ticketmaster) for tickets. Subway: 1/2/3/7/9/N/R/S to Times Sq.; A/C/E to 42nd St.

Ornate and gilded to the max, this classic Broadway theater re-opened in spring 1997 with the brilliantly inventive stage version of *The Lion King,* which won a slew of Tony awards. This Disney production is practically sold out until the millennium, but same-day tickets are often released; line up outside the box office around noon to try your luck.

New Victory Theater

209 W. 42nd St. (between Seventh and Eighth aves.). ☎ **212/382-4020** or 212/239-6200 (TeleCharge). Subway: 1/2/3/7/9/N/R/S to Times Sq.; A/C/E to 42nd St. Tickets $10–$25.

Opened in December 1995, this lovely renovated theater on 42nd Street has an impressive lineup of entertainment totally for kids—international circus troupes, operas, mimes, storytellers, movies—with some high-profile talent attached, like filmmaker Martin Scorsese, new vaudevillians Bill Irwin and the Flying Karamazov Brothers, actor Patrick Stewart (*Star Trek*'s Captain Picard), and the Muppets. Groups like Theater for a New Audience, Theaterworks/USA, and the Metropolitan Opera Guild use the theater for various projects throughout the year as well. Target age groups vary, but there's a good deal of stuff for kids 8 to 12—too old to get a thrill out of puppet shows but too young still to really enjoy most Broadway shows. The lineup of shows keeps the place hopping most of the year, except August.

Radio City Music Hall

1260 Sixth Ave. (at 50th St.). ☎ **212/247-4777** or 212/307-1000 (Ticketmaster). Subway: B/D to Rockefeller Center.

The art-deco interior of this Rockefeller Center showcase is a marvel in itself, but kids probably won't notice—they'll be too busy gaping at the vast proscenium of the stage. Besides mounting its own live stage shows twice a year (see "Seasonal Events," below), Radio City hosts concerts, including the occasional family show. (We went to the Barney stage show a couple of years ago, packed with jabbering toddlers and vendors hawking licensed merchandise. Never again.) Note that Radio City will be closed 6 months for a major renovation in 1999, most likely March to September.

Symphony Space

2537 Broadway (at 95th St.). ☎ **212/864-5400.** Subway: 1/2/3/9 to 96th St.

Besides the Just Kidding series (see "Weekend Shows," later in this chapter), this Upper West Side theater hosts an eclectic variety of events: international dance troupes, Gilbert & Sullivan operettas, and, in spring, a really great series of short-story readings by famous actors and writers. Decidedly shabby and very p.c., Symphony Space is a vintage piece of the West Side community as it was before yuppies moved into the nabe in the 1980s.

2   Seasonal Events

Madison Square Garden, Seventh Avenue between 31st and 33rd streets (☎ **212/ 465-6741**), hosts various ice shows when they skate through town—**Disney on Ice, Sesame Street on Ice,** and others of that ilk. Tickets are usually available through Ticketmaster.

✪ **Big Apple Circus**   All ages
In Damrosch Park at Lincoln Center, Broadway and 64th St. ☎ **212/268-2500.** (Mailing address: 35 W. 35th St., New York, NY 10001.) Tickets $12–$55 (kids under 2 free). Subway: 1/9 to Lincoln Center.

Kids too young for clamorous Ringling Bros. and Barnum & Bailey delight in this wonderful one-ring circus that performs in a tent (heated, of course) at Lincoln Center from October to January. In 2¼ hours the Big Apple Circus manages to pack in clowns, elephants, trapeze artists, bareback riders, and something for everyone. Skilled circus artists and a sophisticated sense of humor make this a good show for adults who'd rather be charmed than stunned. A splendid time is guaranteed for all.

A Christmas Carol   Ages 6 & up
The Theater at Madison Square Garden, Seventh Ave. between 31st and 33rd sts. ☎ **212/ 465-MSG1.** Tickets $19–$49. Subway: A/C/E to Penn Station; 1/2/3/9 to 34th St.

Street Performers

The cream of New York's street performers may be the Crowtations puppet ensemble (see "Puppet Shows," later in this chapter), which has been playing Central Park on weekends for years. Top spots for catching jugglers are at South Street Seaport, by the Statue of Liberty ferry line in Battery Park, by the TKTS line in Duffy Square, by the steps of the Metropolitan Museum of Art, by the fountain in Washington Square Park, and near the Tisch Children's Zoo in Central Park (near 65th Street).

The subways see their fair share of freelancers—there's actually a great space set up for them in the Times Square station, near the Times Square shuttle platform, where jazz combos gravitate for the great acoustics. The 34th Street station for the B, F, N, and R trains often attracts good musicians as well, including an Andean pipe band that's really primo.

There's no guarantee these people will be any good, of course. Standouts in my mind include the guy who plays electric harmonica on the IND platforms in Midtown; a juggler my husband and I nicknamed Bope, who used to work the crowds at movie houses around 57th Street on weekend nights; and a totally wacked-out saxophonist who used to play the *Twilight Zone* theme over and over on the West Side IRT (memorable more for his crazy patter than for his musical technique—people used to pay him to *stop* playing). Remember, you're under no obligation to give these people money, but if you think they're good, you should. Unlike panhandlers, these people are at least doing something for their money.

With songs by perennial Oscar-winner Alan Menken (*Aladdin, Beauty and the Beast*), this glossy holiday musical based on the Dickens chestnut arrives for an annual run, late November to December. A trifle slick and you know how it's gonna end, but hey, this story didn't become a classic for nothing—it still pulls in the crowds.

The Nutcracker   Ages 10 & up
At the New York State Theater in Lincoln Center, Broadway and 64th St. ☎ **212/870-5570.** Tickets $20–$74. Subway: 1/9 to Lincoln Center.

This is where the city's best *Nutcracker* is staged every December by the New York City Ballet, with several stunning effects (like a Christmas tree that grows up out of the stage to gi-normous proportions).

Radio City Music Hall Holiday Shows   Ages 3 & up
1260 Sixth Ave. (at 50th St.). ☎ **212/247-4777,** or 212/307-1000 (Ticketmaster). Tickets $25–$60. Subway: B/D to Rockefeller Center.

The Rockettes gotta perform somewhere, and this is it. Radio City's elegant art-deco interior, with its immense stage, cries out for a stage extravaganza like this—lots of music, lavish stage effects, corny holiday motifs (Santa's workshop, the Easter Bunny egg factory), and that classic precision kickline. The Christmas Spectacular runs early November to the first week in January, usually one show a day until the holidays loom close, when up to five shows a day are performed. It's an annual tradition, and the magic still works, dazzling the Nickelodeon generation. The Spring Spectacular runs for 2 weeks in April, though in April 1999 Radio City should be closed for a major renovation.

Ringling Bros. and Barnum & Bailey Circus   Ages 6 & up
At Madison Square Garden, Seventh Ave. between 31st and 33rd sts. ☎ **800/755-4000,** or 212/465-MSG1 or 212/307-4100 (Ticketmaster). Tickets $10–$22.50 (VIP boxes $42.50). Subway: A/C/E to Penn Station; 1/2/3/9 to 34th St.

This glitzy, humongous circus takes up residence at the Garden for 6 weeks every spring, beginning in late March, starring death-defying aerialists, wild animal acts, lumbering elephants, snarling bears, hordes of clowns, the whole shebang. Smaller kids may be overwhelmed by the sheer size of the Garden, not to mention the flashing lights and eardrum-blasting music. Adults may be overwhelmed by the barrage of vendors selling junk food and junky souvenirs, at wildly inflated prices. Still, it's the Greatest Show on Earth and pretty darn impressive.

The Wizard of Oz   Ages 6 & up
The Theater at Madison Square Garden, Seventh Ave. between 31st and 33rd sts. ☎ **212/465-MSG1.** Tickets $19–$59. Subway: A/C/E to Penn Station; 1/2/3/9 to 34th St.

A durable piece calculated to suck in family audiences year after year, cleverly timed for early May, when the school year is winding down and no other big events are on the horizon. Like *A Christmas Carol* (above), this annual production casts big stage personalities as the Wicked Witch and the Wizard and lets the cast ham it up royally. Not as magical as the old MGM film, but then what could be?

3 Weekend Shows

Henry Street Settlement Abrons Arts Center   Ages 4 to 12
466 Grand St. (at Pitt St.). ☎ **212/598-0400.** Tickets $4 kids 4–12, $6 adults. Subway: F to Delancey St.; B/D/Q to Grand St.

On weekends, this Lower East Side cultural center—a longtime mainstay of the neighborhood—runs a series for kids and their parents at 2pm, with performances twice a month. The company does a wide variety of shows, including dance performances, plays based on updated fairy tales, improv sessions, and puppet shows, all nicely multicultural and very professional. I recommend you call for reservations a week in advance.

Museum of Television and Radio   Ages 3 & up

25 W. 52nd St. (between Fifth and Sixth aves.). ☎ **212/621-6600**. Tickets $3 kids 12 and under, $6 adults, $4 students. Subway: E/F to Fifth Ave.

What's called the International Children's Television Festival runs November to May, offering screenings on Saturday and Sunday afternoons. Each month has a different theme; the museum selects outstanding live and animated kids' TV shows from around the world and shows them in screening rooms in the museum.

West End Kids Productions   Ages 3 to 9

Mailing address: 173 W. 78th St., Suite 4A, 10024. ☎ **212/877-6115**. Tickets $8–15.

October to April, this invaluable organization sets up weekend shows at two sites: the **West End Cafe**, 2911 Broadway between 113th and 114th streets (Saturday at 1:30pm, tickets $8 to 10); and **Caroline's Comedy Club,** 1626 Broadway between 49th and 50th streets (Saturday and Sunday at 2pm, tickets $10 to $15). All sorts of performers show up on the schedule—musicians, clowns, storytellers, puppeteers—and there's usually a fair amount of audience interaction. At Caroline's there are monthly Kids 'N' Comedy shows, a pint-sized version of the "open mike" comedy club concept when 8- to 15-year-olds can do stand-up comedy—I shudder to think of the obnoxious stage kids who might sign on, but to be fair, I haven't seen it. My kids' favorites at the West End are magician Arnie Kolodner, Circus Minimus, and wacky scientist Professor Putter, all three stars of the Manhattan birthday party circuit. Call a week or so in advance if you can, but tickets are usually available at the last minute.

Symphony Space   Ages 5 & up

2537 Broadway (at 95th St.). ☎ **212/864-5400**. www.symphonyspace.org. Tickets $4 kids, $8 adults. Subway: 1/2/3/9 to 96th St.

One Saturday a month, November to April, the Just Kidding series here presents 11am performances by and for kids—anything from live theater to children's movie screenings. Eclectic, multicultural, fun.

4 Theater

LONG-RUNNING SHOWS

It's always hard to predict which Broadway and Off Broadway shows will still be running by the time you read this (much less by the time you get to New York), but these six are a pretty safe bet—they've been running for a long time with no sign of letting up. Most of them (except *The Lion King*) are usually available for half price at the TKTS booth at 47th Street and Broadway and the World Trade Center.

Beauty and the Beast   Ages 5 & up

At the Palace Theater, Broadway and 47th St. ☎ **212/730-8200**. Tickets $22.50–$75. Subway: 1/9 to 50th St.

The beloved Disney film has been turned into a hit Broadway musical (2½ hours long) that keeps regular Broadway hours—8pm shows Wednesday to Sunday, 2pm matinees on Wednesday and Saturday, a 1pm Sunday matinee and an early-bird 6:30pm Sunday night show (June through September there's only a 3pm matinee on Sunday). Tickets should be reserved in advance, but it may be possible to get them at the TKTS booth or at the box office an hour before the start of the show.

Blue Man Group: Tubes Ages 10 & up

At the Astor Place Theater, 434 Lafayette St. (between E. 4th and E. 8th sts.). ☎ **212/254-4370.** Tickets $39 and $49. Subway: 6 to Astor Place.

Faces painted blue, this trio has been committing weird mayhem on stage since 1992, with lots of flashing strobes and percussion effects. The hip performance-art elements are directed to adults, but preteens dig the show too—there are often birthday parties in the audience. The show runs slightly under 2 hours.

Cats Ages 4 & up

At the Winter Garden Theater, Broadway between 50th and 51st sts. ☎ **800/399-5334** or 212/239-6200 (TeleCharge). Tickets $37.50–$70. Subway: 1/9 to 50th St.

Actors dressed in furry catsuits have been prowling around the Winter Garden's stage for more than a decade, providing endless fodder for Letterman jokes and making composer/producer Andrew Lloyd Webber a very rich man. The music is haunting, though, and the total effect is right up a kid's alley. The "cats" do creep out to interact with the audience, so don't sit too close if your child is easily spooked. The show's 2½ hours long.

The Fantasticks Ages 5 & up

At the Sullivan Street Playhouse, 181 Sullivan St. (between Bleecker and Houston sts.). ☎ **212/674-3838,** or 212/307-4100 (Ticketmaster). Tickets $37.50. Subway: A/B/C/D/E/F/Q to W. 4th St.

Why has this show been running since 1960? Well, it's a sweet fable about young lovers, with very hummable tunes (the showstopper is "Try to Remember"), and in this intimate Village playhouse it's a good way to introduce kids to live grown-up theater. Call well in advance, since the theater's small and fills up quickly.

✪ *The Lion King* All ages

At the New Amsterdam Theater, 214 W. 42nd St. (between Seventh and Eighth aves.) ☎ **212/282-2900** or 212/307-4747 (Ticketmaster). Tickets $75–$25. Subway: 1/2/3/7/9/N/R/S to Times Sq.

One of the hottest tickets in town, improbably enough, is for this adaptation of a Disney animated movie. Why all the fuss? Because Tony-winning director Julie Taymor discarded glitzy special effects and made stage magic instead with puppets, dancers, masks, billowing cloths, and imagination. Drawing strongly on African folk traditions, this production is genuinely moving, even—dare I say it?—*better* than the movie. Call for tickets many months in advance, line up outside for same-day returns, or splurge on a ticket agent, but somehow get your children to see this play.

Stomp Ages 8 & up

At the Orpheum Theater, 126 Second Ave. (between 7th and 8th sts.). ☎ **212/477-2477** or 212/307-4100 (Ticketmaster). Tickets $$45–$24.50. Subway: 6 to Astor Pl.

What kid hasn't made music by tapping a broom handle on the floor or crashing two pot lids together? This troupe of eight athletic-looking dancers does the same sort of rhythmic stuff with everyday objects for an hour and a half, and it's undeniably captivating. Kids with short attention span may weary, but others will be fascinated by the endless variations. Early evening performances Saturday and Sunday make it possible to see this without being out too late.

CHILDREN'S THEATER COMPANIES

Grove Street Playhouse Ages 2 to 12

39 Grove St. (between Bedford and Bleecker sts.). ☎ **212/741-6436.** Tickets $8. Subway: 1/9 to Christopher St.

Miss Majesty's Lollipop Playhouse presents adaptations of classic tales like *The Gingerbread Man, The Three Little Pigs, Aladdin,* and *The Little Mermaid* on weekends at 1:30 and 3:30pm September to June. All performances are audience-participation comedies, and a rollicking time is usually had by all.

Here   Ages 4 & up
145 Sixth Ave. (near Spring St.). ☎ **212/647-0202.** Tickets $5–10. Subway: C/E to Spring St.

This multiarts collaborative in SoHo runs programs for kids on Saturday throughout the year—works like a spirited retelling of *Beowulf* and a popular *Pied Piper.*

New York Youth Theater   Ages 5 & up
594 Park Ave. (at 64th St). ☎ **212/242-2822.** Tickets $12. Subway: 6 to 68th St.

Pretty much year-round, this company presents a string of family performances, mostly large musicals, with not only the usual Saturday and Sunday matinees but also nighttime performances Thursday to Saturday. Kids as well as adults perform; past productions have run the gamut from an acclaimed retelling of *Charlotte's Web* to a boffo rendition of *The Wiz.* Call for a schedule.

✪ Paper Bag Players   Ages 4 to 9
At the Sylvia and Danny Kaye Playhouse, Hunter College, 68th St. between Park and Lexington aves. ☎ **212/772-4448** or 212/362-0431. Tickets $15. Subway: 6 to 68th St.

January to March, this veteran troupe presents original plays with a pleasant edge of nuttiness, on Saturday at 2pm and Sunday at 3pm. The company's trademark is using everyday materials like paper bags and corrugated cardboard for all the costumes, sets, and props, giving the productions a home-grown look that somehow makes them very appealing to kids.

Shadow Box Theater   Ages 4 & up
30 Third Ave. (at Atlantic Ave.), Brooklyn. ☎ **212/724-0677** or 877-7356. (Mailing address: 325 West End Ave., New York, NY 10023.) Tickets $6. Subway: 2/3 to Nevins St., Brooklyn.

The children's theater-in-residence at the Brooklyn YWCA specializes in original musicals with multicultural themes, featuring singing, dancing, and puppetry. November to May, they present four to five productions, each running about a month, with weekday and weekend performances. Call ahead for a schedule.

Theater for a New Audience   Ages 8 & up
At St. Clements Church, 423 W. 46th St. (between Ninth and Tenth aves.). ☎ **212/229-2819.** (Mailing address: 154 Christopher St., New York, NY 10014.) Tickets $18–$37.50. Subway: A/C/E to 42nd St.

This top-notch Off Broadway company devotes itself to the classics, mostly Shakespeare. By no means for children only, its vigorous productions do attract lots of school groups, because they're a great way to introduce youngsters to the Bard. January to April, there are two or three productions, playing Tuesday to Saturday nights, with a Saturday matinee.

✪ Theatreworks USA   Ages 5 & up
At the Promenade Theatre, 2162 Broadway (at 76th St.). ☎ **212/627-7373** or 212/239-6200 (TeleCharge). www.theatreworksusaorg. Tickets $18.50. Subway: 1/9 to 79th St.

One of the city's top choices for kids, this long-running troupe presents witty, vivid musical versions of classic books—real books like *The Lion, the Witch, and the Wardrobe* and *Oliver Twist* and *Treasure Island,* not just fairy tales. They put on a dozen or so plays each year, with several performances of each, so you can count on something every weekend at 12:30pm September to March. Babes in arms aren't allowed.

Thirteenth Street Repertory Theater   Ages 4 & up

50 W. 13th St. (between Fifth and Sixth aves.). ☎ **212/675-6677.** Tickets $7. Subway: F to 14th St; 4/5/6/L/N/R to Union Sq.

This company puts on two original shows on Saturday and Sunday at 1 and 3pm year-round. With recorded music and special effects, shows like *Danger Dinosaurs* are perfectly calibrated for a young audience, with healthy doses of humor. Reservations are recommended a couple of days in advance of the performance.

Tribeca Performing Arts   Ages 5 & up

199 Chambers St. (between Greenwich St. and the West Side Hwy.). ☎ **212/346-8510.** Tickets $8 kids 12 and under, $13 adults. Subway: 1/2/3/9/A/C to Chambers St.

Offering a mixed bag of events—some starring kids, others with adult performers, others with puppets or dancers or actors performing in sign language—this Downtown arts center brings to town a full season of children's entertainment with its Family, Folk, and Fairy Tale series (October to May, Saturday or Sunday at 1:30pm). Past productions have included musical versions of classics like *Hans Brinker* and *The Reluctant Dragon* as well as retellings of award-winning children's books.

Wings Theater Company   Ages 4 & up

154 Christopher St. (between Greenwich and Washington sts.). ☎ **212/627-2961.** Tickets $7.50. Subway: 1/9 to Christopher St.

The resident troupe, the Bill Solly Children's Theater, performs a variety of lively original musicals, and the theater fills in between with touring companies—dance, mime, magicians, what have you. On most weekends September to June (and weekdays during school breaks), Wings has something running for kids, with decent production values and no heavy-handed educational agenda.

KIDS ON STAGE

City Lights   Ages 4 & up

130 W. 56th St. (between Sixth and Seventh aves.). ☎ **212/262-0200.** Tickets $5. Subway; 1/9 to 28th St.

Twice a year, students 7 to 18 who've taken classes at the City Lights school perform—one is an original play, the other a musical. There are also three stage readings for family audiences throughout the year. Call ahead for schedules.

New Media Repertory Company   Ages 3 to 7

512 E. 80th St. (between York and East End aves.). ☎ **212/734-5195.** Tickets $6 kids, $8 adults. Subway: 6 to 77th St.

These performances are by and for kids, with lots of participation for the kids in the audience. Each season (late December to May) there's a new original nonmusical adventure story written by New Media's director, Miranda McDermott. Performances are on Saturday at 3pm. Between the young performers (students at the program's acting workshops) and the interaction with a young audience, the shows stay fresh throughout the 5-month run. Make reservations.

✪ TADA!   Ages 3 & up

120 W. 28th St. (between Sixth and Seventh aves.), 2nd floor. ☎ **212/627-1732.** www.tadatheater.com. Tickets $6 kids, $12 adults. Subway: 1/9 to 28th St.

The most energetic and successful of NYC's theater schools for kids, TADA! has even performed at the White House. A diverse group of professional kid performers, ages 8 to 17, stars in TADA!'s sprightly original musicals. They play weekends in December, January, and March (including one Friday-night show, unusual for children's companies; two Saturday matinees; and two Sunday matinees). In July and August—when most other children's entertainment dries up—TADA! comes to the rescue with weekday shows as well. The annual new play project, performed in April, varies from year to year but might not be musical and might be for slightly older audiences. Even adults without children have been known to go see TADA!'s shows, which tells you something about how lively they are.

5 Concerts

Brooklyn Center for the Performing Arts   Ages 4 & up
At Brooklyn College, a block west of Flatbush and Nostrand aves., Brooklyn. ☎ **718/951-4500.** Tickets $9. Subway: 2 to Flatbush Ave., Brooklyn.

The center's FamilyFun Series presents six productions a year, plus an annual November *Nutcracker* ($10 kids, $20 adults) on Sunday at 2pm. The programs are a grabbag of cultural events appealing to kids—circuses, puppet shows, jugglers, classical-music concerts, and ballet, with many events of a multicultural flavor.

Carnegie Hall Family Concerts   Ages 7 & up
At Carnegie Hall, at the corner of 57th St. and Seventh Ave. ☎ **212/247-7800.** Tickets $5. Subway: N/R to 57th St.

Three Saturdays a year, Carnegie Hall presents hour-long concerts at 2pm, preceded by 1pm activities like demonstrations, craft workshops, and storytelling. There are also concerts by such classical-music stars as cellist Yo-Yo Ma and clarinetist Richard Stoltzman. Advance reservations are recommended.

Growing Up with Opera   Ages 6 & up
At the Metropolitan Opera Guild in Lincoln Center, Broadway and 64th St. ☎ **212/769-7008.** Tickets $10–$15. Subway: 1/9 to Lincoln Center.

The Metropolitan Opera Guild sponsors this series as a way to get young people hooked on opera; they start out with First Stop Opera, a sampler program presenting a mix of scenes from operas, then work up to an entire opera—usually a crowd-pleasing choice like *The Barber of Seville,* with easy-to-follow action and tunes any cartoon fan will recognize. Three or four productions are staged annually, with four public performances of each, on Saturday and Sunday afternoons November to March. Performances are in various venues around town rather than in the overwhelming Metropolitan Opera House.

Haydn Seek   All ages
At the Greek Orthodox Church of the Annunciation, 302 W. 91st St. (at West End Ave.). ☎ **212/877-4475.** Tickets $20 (children free with an adult), including music cassette. Subway: 1/2/3/9 to 96th St.

Four 45-minute concerts a year—fall through spring—bring small chamber-music ensembles to a family audience. The great innovation here is that your ticket price includes a cassette of the music you'll be hearing at the concert, so that parents and children can become familiar with the music ahead of time. Ticket prices are actually a bargain, when you figure you get the kids in free *and* get the tape.

Jazz for Young People   Ages 5 & up
At Alice Tully Hall in Lincoln Center, Broadway and 64th St. ☎ **212/721-6500** or 212/875-5599. Tickets $10 kids, $15 adults. Subway: 1/9 to Lincoln Center.

Under the aegis of superstar trumpeter Wynton Marsalis, this series is part of Lincoln Center's embrace of jazz as a serious art form. There are three Saturday performances a year, sometime from September to June.

✪ Little Orchestra Society   Ages 3 to 12

At Avery Fisher Hall in Lincoln Center, Broadway at 64th St., or Florence Gould Hall, 55 E. 59th St. ☎ **212/704-2100.** (Mailing address: Box 2624, Times Square Post Office, New York, NY 10108.) Tickets $15–$32. Subway: 1/9 to Lincoln Center.

Two series—Happy Concerts for Young People (ages 6 to 12) and Lolli-Pops Concerts (ages 3 to 5)—are designed to introduce kids to classical music, using first-class professional musicians (moonlighting Philharmonic members, New York City Ballet stars, and the like). This organization has been around since the 1950s, and the quality is top-notch. There are four Happy Concerts a year, held on Saturdays (two performances each) at Lincoln Center's **Avery Fisher Hall.** The Lolli-Pop series, which uses cutesy costumed figures to help teach wee ones about music, is more extensive, with three 3-concert series (fall, winter, spring) and four performance times for each; these are held at **Florence Gould Hall.** You pretty much have to buy a whole series (at $90 a pop) for the Lolli-Pops, but there are some nonsubscription events every year, like *Peter and the Wolf* and the annual Menotti's *Amahl and the Night Visitors,* a fully staged opera with live animals, the works.

Meet the Music   Ages 6 to 12

At Alice Tully Hall in Lincoln Center, Broadway and 64th St. or at Merkin Concert Hall, 129 W. 67th St. (between Broadway and Amsterdam Ave.). ☎ **212/875-5788.** www.chamberlinc.org. Tickets $12; $30 for 3-concert subscription. Subway: 1/9 to Lincoln Center.

The Chamber Music Society of Lincoln Center puts in its bid for young audiences with this three-concert Sunday-afternoon series. Not all the chamber music performed dates back to the baroque era—modern pieces by Aaron Copland or even Andrew Lloyd Webber might qualify, so long as they're played by a small group of musicians, one player to a part. With narrators, props, and audience participation, the concerts engage fidgety youngsters admirably.

Young People's Concerts   Ages 6 to 12

At Lincoln Center, Broadway and 64th St. ☎ **212/721-6500** or 212/875-5656. Tickets $6–$21. Subway: 1/9 to Lincoln Center.

Want to turn your kid into a hardcore classical-music fan? Four Saturdays a year, the New York Philharmonic trots out musicians like violin prodigy Sarah Chang and conductors Kurt Mazur and Leonard Slatkin to introduce kids to major selections from the classical repertory—not just the chestnuts like *Eine kleine Nachtmusik* but pieces by moderns like George Gershwin and Charles Ives. Topping it off, free 12:45pm Children's Promenades precede the 2pm concerts, with hands-on demonstrations and workshops with orchestra members. Older kids (12 to 17) can graduate to Young Friends of the Philharmonic, which gives them discount seats to the orchestra's weekday Rush Hour Concerts (at 6:45pm), along with free pre- and postconcert meet-the-artist events.

6 Films

If it's standard feature-film fare you want, Manhattan is packed with cinema screens, including the busy 12-screen **Sony Lincoln Square complex** at 68th and Broadway, where each theater entrance evokes a different classic New York movie palace; many first-run children's films play at the **Guild Theater,** 33 W. 50th St., which lies handily between Rockefeller Plaza and Radio City Music Hall. A humongous 29-screen **AMC movie house** on 42nd Street is also in the works. For more unusual films, geared for a young audience, here are your choices:

Family Films   Ages 6 to 12

At the Metropolitan Museum of Art, Fifth Ave. at 82nd St. ☎ **212/570-3932.** Tickets free with museum admission ($8 adults, $4 students/seniors; kids 11 and under free). Subway: 4/5/6 to 86th St.

On Saturday at 12:30 and 2pm, September to May, the museum shows short films from around the world in the Uris Auditorium. If you're going to be visiting the museum anyway, this provides a good break from gallery strolling.

Movies for Kids   Ages 5 & up

At the Walter Reade Theatre in Lincoln Center, 165 W. 65th St., plaza level. ☎ **212/875-5610.** Tickets $3. Subway: 1/9 to Lincoln Center.

This special series run by the Lincoln Center Film Society (the same folks who run the top-drawer New York Film Festival) shows movies on Saturday and Sunday at 2pm throughout the year. The selection each month is organized along a specific theme—a recent one on cars, for instance, included *Chitty Chitty Bang Bang* and *The Phantom Tollbooth*. Most are full-length features, with some shorts or cartoons thrown in; generally these are American films, but occasional series focus on international movies from anywhere from Africa or Iran to Scandinavia.

IMAX Theater   Ages 3 & up

At the American Museum of Natural History, Central Park West at 79th St. ☎ **212/769-5100.** Tickets $6.50 kids 2–12, $12 adults, $8.50 seniors/students (includes museum admission). Subway: B/C/ to 79th St.

The screen here isn't quite as huge as the one at the Sony IMAX (below), but unless you get out your measuring tape you'd never know. The main thing is that your whole field of vision is occupied, which somehow doubles the sensory impact of a movie—something to consider before you take young, skittish children inside. You have a choice of IMAX movies every day, some more intense than others, though all have an educational bent. Whether you're in outer space, underwater, or deep in the rain forest, the sights and sounds tend to include a speeding camera taking you on a visual thrill ride that swoops over rising and falling terrain, the hallmark of the IMAX experience.

Buy the combination ticket when you enter—if you didn't or if you entered free as a member, stop by the ticket counter near the museum's 77th Street entrance to buy tickets. There's a movie every 45 minutes or so, though school groups get first dibs on seats weekday mornings (the public is then admitted on a first-come, first-served basis). The laser-light rock-and-roll films shown on weekend nights are popular with teens. The museum is open daily year-round, except on Thanksgiving and Christmas.

Sony IMAX Theater   Ages 3 & up

At Broadway and 68th St. ☎ **212/336-5000.** Tickets $6 kids 12 and under, $9.50 adults. Subway: 1/9 to Lincoln Center.

Not just IMAX but *3-D IMAX*—awesome. The screen is 8 stories high, and you get this cool headset that puts in the extra spatial dimension. Needless to say, there isn't a lot of film material for this format and some of the offerings aren't 3-D. But Sony has managed to get movies that go beyond documentaries into actual story-telling features—like *Across the Sea of Time*, which tells of a young Russian immigrant boy searching for relatives in Manhattan (think of it as a live-action *An American Tale*). Most shows run about 45 minutes to an hour.

New York Public Library   Ages 3 to 8

Various branches around Manhattan.

Along with story hours, children's rooms at several Manhattan branch libraries may run once a month an hour-long program of short films, many of them made from children's books—*Madeline, Curious George, Doctor deSoto,* and so on. For a monthly schedule ahead of time, contact the NYPL at 8 W. 40th St., New York, NY 10018 (☎ **212/221-7676**), or stop by any branch when you get to town.

7 Dance

American Ballet Theatre   Ages 8 & up
At the Metropolitan Opera House in Lincoln Center, Broadway and 64th St. ☎ **212/ 362-6000.** Tickets $18–$115. Subway: 1/9 to Lincoln Center.

On this enormous stage, the spring season (May to June) features both modern works and some classic story ballets like *Swan Lake* and *Coppelia*—just the thing for budding ballerinas.

Dance Theater Workshop   Ages 4 & up
219 W. 19th St. (between Seventh and Eighth aves.). ☎ **212/924-0077.** Tickets around $8 kids, $15 adults. Subway: C/E to 23rd St.; 1/9 to 18th St.

One of the city's leading promoters of modern dance, the Workshop presents among other things a Family Matters series, with events appropriate for parents and kids of all ages (not necessarily purely dance). The season usually runs September to June, with Saturday matinee performances. I recommend you call the box office for ticket availability.

Ice Theatre of New York   Ages 5 & up
At Rockefeller Plaza skating rink, Riverbank State Park (145th St. and Riverside Dr.), or Sky Rink at the Chelsea Piers, 23rd St. at the Hudson River. ☎ **212/929-5811,** or 212/307-7171 (Ticketmaster). Tickets around $20.

Unlike typical ice-show companies, Ice Theatre leads figure-skating strongly in the direction of dance, even commissioning noted nonskating choreographers to create new pieces for their lyrical, intriguing performances. With guest artists like Nancy Kerrigan and Paul Wylie, the skaters take to the ice in free lunchtime shows January to March at Rockefeller Center or public rinks including Riverbank State Park; other performances (not free) are at the Sky Rink at Chelsea Piers.

✪ Joyce Theater   Ages 6 & up
175 Eighth Ave. (at 19th St.). ☎ **212/242-0800.** www.joyce.org. Tickets $10 kids, $26–$35 adults. Subway: C/E to 23rd St.; 1/9 to 18th St.

This Chelsea theater devoted to modern dance does an admirable job of bringing in young audiences. The 40-member Kids Dance company, made up of young dancers in the Feld Ballet school, performs weekend matinees throughout the Feld's 6-week season, a mainstay in the Joyce's annual schedule. On 10 other Saturdays throughout the year, touring dance companies booked into the Joyce are asked to design special family matinees as well. After these matinees, dancers in the cast—still in costume—show up in the lower lobby to meet audience members and give autographs.

New York City Ballet   Ages 10 & up
At the New York State Theater in Lincoln Center, Broadway and 64th St. ☎ **212/870-5570.** Tickets $23–$68. Subway: 1/9 to Lincoln Center.

For technique, this troupe surpasses its Lincoln Center cousin, the ABT (above), but young balletomanes may not get the point of the more abstract pieces the NYCB presents, following the tastes of founder George Balanchine. However, this is where the city's best *Nutcracker* is staged every December. The ballet offers two seasons with nightly performances (except Mondays) and weekend matinees: the spring season runs April to June and the winter season Thanksgiving to February.

8 Puppet Shows

★ The Crowtations All ages

At Bethesda Fountain in Central Park (midpark at 72nd St.). Free admission (pass the hat). Subway: B/C to 72nd St.

Since 1977, this sassy quartet of puppeteers has been charming crowds in Central Park on fair-weather Saturdays and Sundays 1 to 6pm with their Muppet-sized crow puppets performing to vintage Motown tunes. The four crows (Otis, John Jay, Junior, and Fast Eddie) have delightfully different personalities, and the byplay among them is truly funny, for adults as well as kids. Best of all, you can just stroll by, watch for a few minutes, then leave when your young ones' attention span has run out (but don't forget to drop some money in the hat).

Leni Suib Puppet Playhouse Ages 2 to 5

At Asphalt Green, 555 E. 90th St. (between York and East End aves.). ☎ **212/369-8890.** Tickets $5 kids, $6 adults. Subway 4/5/6 to 86th St.

The Leni Suib Puppet Playhouse has been running for years and years; Leni Suib is a major player in the puppet world, up there with Bill Baird and Burr Tillstrom. Every weekend September to May, kids can take in a different show, with different puppets and a different theme (nonpuppet antics, like juggling and mime, are often thrown in, just to keep things hopping). Showtimes are on Saturday and Sunday at 10:30am and 12:30pm. Reservations aren't accepted (except for groups of 10 or more), so get there 20 minutes before show time to be sure of a seat.

The Puppet Company Ages 2 to 10

31 Union Sq. West (at 16th St.), Loft 2B. ☎ **212/741-1646.** Tickets $7.50. Subway: 4/5/6/L/N/R to Union Sq.

With a touch of New Vaudevillian humor, this puppet theater uses marionettes, handpuppets, even finger puppets to tell lively musical stories. Puppetmaker Steve Widerman—a protégé of Bill Baird—handcrafts each puppet and demonstrates how they're made to his young audiences. The season runs October to April on weekends only. The theater has only 35 seats, so reservations are required, but you may be able to call as late as the day before the show.

Puppetworks–Park Slope Ages 3 to 7

219 Sullivan St., Manhattan; 338 Sixth Ave., Brooklyn. (Mailing address: 338 Sixth Ave., Brooklyn.) ☎ **718/965-6058** or 718/965-3391. Tickets $5 kids, $7 adults. Subway: B/D/F to Broadway/Lafayette; F to Seventh Ave.

Using both hand puppets and marionettes, these puppeteers retell classic children's stories. The season runs year-round, with performances on weekends at 12:30 and 2:30pm. Reservations are recommended only if the weather is bad—the worse the weather, the busier they'll be.

Swedish Cottage Marionette Theatre Ages 3 to 10

In Central Park (West Dr. at 81st St.). ☎ **212/988-9093.** Tickets $4 kids, $5 adults; reservations required. Subway: B/C to 79th St.

This alpine-looking cottage holds a small stage where near-life-size marionettes prance and caper in hour-long productions of classic fairy tales—recorded soundtrack, spot lighting, full scenery, the works. A puppeteer prefaces performances with a helpful miniseminar on the kinds of puppets (the *Cinderella* we saw included a shadow puppet interlude as well as a couple of stick puppets). The pace is a little slow, the sense of humor gentle. Call 3 or 4 weeks in advance for a reservation—there are usually two shows a day, Tuesday to Saturday, but they fill up fast with school groups.

9 Spectator Sports

New Jersey Devils   Ages 8 & up

Continental Airlines Arena, East Rutherford, N.J. ☎ **201/935-6050.** Tickets $20–$65. Parking $7. For game time bus service from Manhattan's Port Authority Bus Terminal, call New Jersey Transit, 800/772-2222.

Winners of the 1995 Stanley Cup, the Devils have been in and out of the running ever since, frustrating their fans mightily. Though much of the arena gets sold out with season tickets, individual tickets for cheaper seats may be available, and it's always worth checking the day of a game to see if some seats have been released.

New York CityHawks   Ages 7 & up

At Madison Square Garden, Seventh Ave. between 31st and 33rd sts. ☎ **212/465-MSG1** or 212/307-7171 (Ticketmaster), 212/465-CITY for team info. Tickets $10–$40. Subway: A/C/E to Penn Station; 1/2/3/9 to 34th St.

The metropolitan area's arena football team has yet to secure a foothold in the public interest, so CityHawks tickets should be much more available than Giants or Jets seats. Arena football is played on a smaller scale—eight-player teams, a 50-yard-long field, padded sideline barriers—though the scoring is the same as in the NFL game. With its summer season (8 home games, May to July, with August playoffs) and controlled weather conditions, arena football may be better for young spectators, though it hasn't yet developed trading-card-caliber stars (a few players' names may be recognizable from their former NFL careers, though).

New York Giants   Ages 8 & up

At Giants Stadium in the Meadowlands, East Rutherford, N.J. ☎ **201/935-8222.**

With a seeming revolving door of coaches, the Giants dance in and out of contention. Because football teams play only once a week, there are fewer home games in the course of their September-to-December season, and just about the whole stadium goes with season ticket holders—to get tickets you have to know somebody or be Somebody or spring for a scalper. On game days there's a New Jersey Transit bus from Port Authority Terminal, Eighth Avenue between 40th and 42nd streets—call ☎ **212/564-1114** for information.

Warning: It's an open-air stadium, so it gets bitterly cold by the end of the season.

New York Jets   Ages 8 & up

At Giants Stadium in the Meadowlands, East Rutherford, N.J. ☎ **516/560-8200.**

Playing in the same stadium as the Giants, the Jets—who have had some loser seasons in the recent past—have been re-energized under Bill Parcells (formerly the Giants' coach), but not without some dissension. But Jets fans are die-hards, and season tickets are pretty well sold out. On game days there's a New Jersey Transit bus from Port Authority Terminal, Eighth Avenue between 40th and 42nd streets—call ☎ **212/564-1114** for information.

New York Islanders   Ages 8 & up

At Nassau Coliseum, Hempstead Turnpike, Uniondale, N.Y. ☎ **516/794-4100** or 516/888-9000 (Ticketmaster). Tickets $19–$60.

A lively force in recent NHL seasons, the Islanders skate on their home ice out on Long Island, hence the name. Take the Long Island Rail Road from Penn Station, Seventh Avenue between 31st and 33rd streets.

New York Knicks   Ages 8 & up

At Madison Square Garden, Seventh Ave. between 31st and 33rd sts. ☎ **212/465-MSG1** or 212/465-JUMP. Tickets $20–$200 and up. Subway: A/C/E to Penn Station; 1/2/3/9 to 34th St.

The Knicks play 41 regular-season home games a year, November to mid-April. An aging team that has suffered from injuries the past few seasons, under coach Jeff Van Gundy the Knickerbockers have still proven their mettle in the NBA playoffs, and getting tickets is next to impossible, unless you're Spike Lee. Seats usually sell out for the season within an hour of the time they go on sale. There's still hope: On the day of the game, the box office sometimes releases a small number of tickets (call ☎ **212/465-6040**), and there are always scalpers who'll be happy to let you pay top dollar for tickets.

New York Liberty   Ages 6 & up
At Madison Square Garden, Seventh Ave. between 31st and 33rd sts. ☎ **212/465-MSG1** or 212/307-7171 (Ticketmaster), 212/564-WNBA for info. Tickets $8–$50. Subway: A/C/E to Penn Station; 1/2/3/9 to 34th St.

The success of professional women's basketball has surprised all the pundits, who never expected the public to respond so immediately to its brand of clean, fast, non-trash-talking basketball. Kids, especially girls, have been an important part of the Liberty's audience all along (it helps that its June to August season coincides with school vacation), and the team's strong first seasons bode well for the future.

New York MetroStars   Ages 6 & up
At Giants Stadium in the Meadowlands, East Rutherford, N.J. ☎ **888/4-METROTIX,** 201/583-7000, or Ticketmaster (212/307-7171 and 201/507-8900). Tickets $11–$22. For game time bus service from Manhattan's Port Authority Bus Terminal, call New Jersey Transit, 800/772-2222.

Playing March to October, the MetroStars are busy building an audience from all those kids and parents who've been bit by the soccer bug through youth leagues. Games are usually Wednesday nights or weekend days or evenings. Major league soccer offers plenty of action on the field, though not a lot of scoring, but it's reasonably easy for a kid to follow even if he or she hasn't played. And sitting outdoors in the Meadowlands is a lot nicer in summer than in November.

New York Mets   All ages
At Shea Stadium in Flushing, Queens. ☎ **718/507-METS.** Tickets $9–$24. Subway: 7 to Shea Stadium.

Baseball can be awfully slow-moving for a young kid, but Shea does what it can to jazz things up, what with the loud taped music and the big DiamondVision screen broadcasting pictures of the audience (no back-flipping mascot yet, thank goodness). It's an open-air stadium, which somehow makes matters less overwhelming for younger kids and makes a fine summer afternoon a real treat. Seats cost considerably less than they do for the other sports, and unlike the theater, you don't have to worry about keeping your child quiet. Even night games are a distinct possibility—if your kids get bored or sleepy, you can always leave early. The regular season for New York's National League team runs mid-April to early October; throughout this stretch, 81 home games are played at Shea. Tickets can be purchased in advance, but even given the Mets' recent success, you may still be able to get tickets at the stadium on game day. The food is typical arena fare: nachos, hot dogs, and soda. Take the no. 7 subway to the Shea Stadium stop and you'll be right there.

New York Rangers   Ages 6 & up
At Madison Square Garden, Seventh Ave. between 31st and 33rd sts. ☎ **212/465-MSG1** or 212/307-7171 (Ticketmaster), 212/308-NYRS for info. www.newyorkrangers.com. Tickets $22.50–$140. Subway: A/C/E to Penn Station; 1/2/3/9 to 34th St.

The Rangers play 41 hockey games, mostly at night, at Madison Square Garden during their season September to June. Celebrities and CEOs pay as much as $500 for prized behind-the-bench seats, but in "Blue Heaven"—the cheap seats high above the ice—true hockey fans make Rangers games an audience-participation sport. Rangers tickets usually sell out a couple of months before the season starts, so buy in advance.

New York Yankees   All ages
At Yankee Stadium in the Bronx. ☎ **718/293-6000** or 212/307-1212 (Ticketmaster). www.yankees.com. Tickets $6–$19. Subway: D to 161st St. Subway: 4 or C/D to 161st St.

Yankees fans have never minded watching their team roll effortlessly over all the competition, and after a lean decade or so, the Bronx Bombers are once again keeping them very happy indeed; the team's handy four-game sweep of the 1998 World Series was no less than what their legions of supporters expected. Our family was lucky enough to attend pitcher David Wells' perfect game in May 1998, and it's an experience none of us will ever forget. There's a long-running soap opera over whether owner George Steinbrenner will let them continue to play at this grand old ballpark in the Bronx—as the fanfares play on an electric organ, you almost expect to see the scoreboard changed by hand. New York's American League team plays 81 home games at Yankee Stadium mid-April to early October; order tickets in advance or buy them at the stadium ticket office on game day (when they're playing well, ticket availability gets tight toward fall). The refreshments here run in the traditional peanuts and popcorn and Crackerjack vein, along with hot dogs and jumbo sodas. Show up a couple of hours early and you may be able to watch batting practice. Take the no. 4 or the C or D subway train, all of which have Yankee Stadium stops.

10 Story Hours

Bank Street College Bookstore   Ages 2 to 6
2871 Broadway (at 112th St.). ☎ **212/678-1654.** Free admission. Subway: 1/9 to 110th St.

This intelligent Upper West Side bookstore runs story hours for preschoolers at 10:30am on Wednesday.

Barnes & Noble   Ages 2 to 7
120 E. 86th St. (between Park and Lexington aves.). ☎ **212/427-0686.** Free admission.

Story hours at various branches of this big bookstore chain often feature the authors themselves. The 86th Street Barnes & Noble Jr. has two story hours, 10:30am on Tuesday and 5:30pm on Thursday. On the Upper West Side, the branch near Lincoln Center (66th Street) runs its storytimes Monday at 10am and Wednesday at 4:30pm, while the Broadway and 82nd Street branch has a Tuesday story hour at 10:30am. In Midtown, the Citicorp branch has Wednesday story hours at 10am. In Chelsea, the Sixth Avenue and 21st Street branch has children's events (not only story hours) at 2pm on Saturday and, occasionally, at noon on Sunday. Down in the Village, the Astor Place branch offers story hour Tuesday at 3pm and Wednesday at 7:30pm; the Union Square ones are at 2pm Saturday and Sunday.

   Other locations: 2289 Broadway, at 82nd Street (☎ **212/362-8835**); Citicorp Building, at Third Avenue and 54th Street (☎ **212/750-8033**); 675 Sixth Ave., at 21st Street (☎ **212/727-1227**); 4 Astor Place, between Broadway and Lafayette Street (☎ **212/420-1322**); Union Square, 33 E. 17th St. (☎ **212/253-0810**); and 1972 Broadway, at 66th Street (☎ **212/595-6859**).

✪ Books of Wonder   Ages 3 to 7
16 W. 18th St. (between Fifth and Sixth aves.). ☎ **212/989-3270.** Free admission. Subway: 1/9 to 18th St.

This great Chelsea shop runs friendly story hours on Sunday at 11:45am.

Borders Books   Ages 2 to 8

461 Park Ave. at 57th St. ☎ **212/980-6785.** Subway: 4/5/6 to 59th St.

The Midtown branch of this superstore book chain has three weekly story hours: Tuesday and Thursday at 10am and Sunday at 1pm. The Downtown branch at 5 World Trade Center, at the corner of Church & Vesey streets (☎ **212/ 839-8049**), also has a 10am Tuesday storytime, as well as frequent Saturday events for kids.

Central Park   Ages 2 to 8

At the Hans Christian Andersen Statue, on the west side of Conservatory Water (at 74th St.). Free admission. Subway: 6 to 77th St.

On summer Saturdays, there are story hours here at 11am; New York Public Library librarians also run story hours in July, on Wednesday at 11am. The park organizes a Sandbox Stories program that rotates around various playgrounds in summer; look for schedules posted on bulletin boards at the larger playgrounds.

Lefferts Homestead Children's Museum   Ages 3 to 8

In Prospect Park, Brooklyn. ☎ **718/965-6505.** Free admission. Subway: D to Prospect Park, Brooklyn.

July and August, this restored farmhouse next to the zoo and carousel in Prospect Park holds cozy storytelling hours, outside under a tree, at 2 and 3pm on Sunday (call to see if some Saturday dates have been added as well).

Museum of the City of New York   Ages 4 & up

1220 Fifth Ave. (at 103rd St.). ☎ **212/534-1672.** Museum admission $4 kids, $5 adults, $10 family. Subway: 6 to 103rd St.

Great story hours every Saturday at 1pm feature stories about New York.

New York Public Library   Ages 2 to 8

Various branches around Manhattan. Free admission.

Nearly every weekday, some Manhattan branch library holds a story hour or shows short films about children's books or holds some kind of cool workshop—and it's all free. You can contact the NYPL at 8 W. 40th St., New York, NY 10018 (☎ 212/221-7676), for a monthly brochure of events for children. Better yet, stop by the **Donnell Library,** 20 W. 53rd St. (☎ 212/621-0636), the main children's branch for the system, and pick up a brochure—while you're there, don't miss the original Pooh animals and Mary Poppins' umbrella on display.

Nightlight for Kids   Ages 4 to 8

At the Drawing Center, 35 Wooster St. (between Broome and Grand sts.). ☎ **212/219-2166.** Free admission. Subway: A/C/E to Canal St.

Once a month, this SoHo arts center presents Sunday illustrated storytelling performances, usually at 3pm. It's hip, it's Downtown.

✪ Tootsie's Children's Books   Ages 3 to 7

555 Hudson St. (at Perry St.). ☎ **212/242-0182.** Free admission. Subway: 1/9 to Christopher St.

Come down to this warm West Village bookshop for weekday story hours; call for exact times.

11 Arcades

Chelsea Piers AMF Bowling   Ages 7 & up

Pier 60 at Chelsea Piers, 23rd St. and the West Side Hwy. at the Hudson River. ☎ **212/ 835-2695.** Subway: 1/9, C/E, or F/N/R to 23rd St. stations. Bus: M23 across 23rd St.

A well-lighted, clean space at the back of this bowling alley has a dozen or so relatively wholesome games involving car-driving or shooting or ball-throwing skills. A good amusement stop if you're at the Piers anyway.

Cybergames   Ages 9 & up
2662 Broadway (between 101st and 102nd sts.). ☎ **212/666-2662.** Subway: 1/9 to 103rd St.

Way uptown, on the way to Columbia University, this neighborhood storefront selling Nintendo and Playstation games (as well as trading cards) has several consoles for in-store play as well as a few big arcade-type games near the front door. Generally a nonthreatening place to hang out, but it all depends on the crowd who's there at the moment.

Hackers Hitter and Hoops   Ages 7 & up
123 W. 18th St. (between Sixth and Seventh aves.). ☎ **212/929-7482.** Subway: 1/9 to 18th St.

This multisport indoor playspace has a sizable arcade in back, with a fairly wholesome selection of electronic and nonelectronic games (simulated driving, air hockey, ball shooting). Admission ($3 to $4) is charged after 5pm, and no one after 18 is admitted after 8pm.

Lazer Park   Ages 8 & up
163 W. 46th St. (at Seventh Ave.). ☎ **212/398-3060.** Subway: 1/2/3/7/9/N/R/S to Times Sq.

Somewhat more state-of-the-art than your typical arcade, Lazer Park offers laser tag and a virtual-reality ride simulator as well as a battery of arcade games. The destination of choice for third- and fourth-grade boys' birthday parties.

Playland   Ages 10 & up
1565 Broadway (near 47th St.). ☎ **212/944-9894.** Subway: 1/9 to 50th St.

Behind a cheesy T-shirt shop lies this dimly lit small gallery with a number of up-to-date arcade games. The atmosphere is scruffy and not too inviting.

XS New York   Ages 8 & up
1457 Broadway (between 41st and 42nd sts.). ☎ **212/398-5467.** Subway: 1/2/3/7/9/N/R/S to Times Sq.

Like Lazer Park (above), this is a high-tech version of the old arcades; various activities (priced $1 to $6) include laser tag and virtual reality, as well as video games. Way cool.

Family-Friendly Restaurants

8

In the gastronomic universe, New York has a fair number of star-quality restaurants, but are they worth it if you're eating out with your kids? Forgeddaboudit. Le Cirque 2000 and Lutèce be damned—what I look for these days is a restaurant that's noisy and casual, where the service is relatively speedy, and where the menu includes at least one or two items from my kids' major food groups: chicken fingers, pasta, pancakes, and pizza. If your child likes burgers, then you're ahead of the game (in burger joints, my kids get by with just french fries). You can find plenty of such restaurants in New York, and they won't cost you an arm and a leg.

DINING OUT WITH YOUR KIDS   You know a restaurant welcomes kids when they've printed up a placemat for young customers to color and when you get to keep the crayons you're given to color it with. If they've gone to the trouble of developing a specific children's menu, you've hit gold. A number of tourist-dependent restaurants around Times Square have gone this route, and we're grateful for them in a pinch. For us adults, however, the food is generally mediocre and the only thing that's relaxing about the ambience is that we don't have to do the dishes afterward.

Because we don't want to be limited to these family restaurants, we try to venture beyond the round of Pizzeria Uno and Houlihan's. Stressful as it can be to eat out with children, we do it at least every other week, and as a result our kids have become relatively restaurant savvy. Ethnic restaurants are one good option—our kids will always eat pasta and rice—and New York, this great immigrant city, is rich in these. Coffee shops are another option, and I don't mean just the corner Greek joints with the revolving showcase of whipped-cream-topped desserts. A number of trendy retro coffee shops have opened in the 1990s, adding upscale parent-pleasing food to the traditional menu of burgers and omelets and grilled cheese sandwiches.

I'm not a big fan of eating out at sidewalk tables, just because I've got a rowdy toddler who might toddle out into the street, but as soon as the weather warms up many families brunch alfresco at restaurants that have room to expand their seating out onto the pavement. The open-air arrangement minimizes your child's noise, provides endless distraction, and makes messes less important (there's always a pigeon or two around to peck up dropped french fries after you've cleared off).

Most Manhattan restaurants serve continuously—you can generally order dinner as early as 5pm if that's what you're used to, though most New Yorkers eat around 7 or 8pm. If you're dining anywhere in the Theater District (the West 40s) or near Lincoln Center (the West 60s), you'll be competing with lots of other people trying to finish dinner before an 8pm curtain time; unless you're trying to make that curtain too, delay your arrival until 7:30 or so, when most of these restaurants seem just about ready to draw a sigh of relief and relax. Similarly, lunch hours at Midtown and Lower Manhattan restaurants can be very busy about 11:30am to 2:30pm.

I've noted in this chapter if a given restaurant doesn't take reservations or if reservations are generally necessary to ensure a table. If there's no notation about reservations, assume you have a fair chance of being seated even if you haven't called ahead, though making a reservation is always smart. Though some posh Manhattan restaurants still cling to formal dress codes, requiring men to wear a jacket and tie, none of the restaurants I list here does.

I should make it clear that my kids are all still under age 8, so, knowing how many Manhattan restaurants are *not* for wee ones, I've tried to address the more pressing needs of families with smaller children. That's not to say all the restaurants I've included in the following list are for preschoolers only—I've also suggested some restaurants that would appeal only to older kids. If your youngsters are well behaved, adventurous eaters, your choice of eating places is obviously much broader.

Because we do keep eating out regularly, I have high hopes for the future. Our 7-year-old is getting a little more adventurous in his tastes—he'll at least try something new to see if he likes it—and our kindergartener no longer needs me to bring toys to keep him occupied at the table (especially not if the restaurant has a jukebox or big streetside picture window to view the passing show). As soon as our daughter gets to that stage, we may be ready to try Tavern on the Green.

A NOTE ABOUT PRICES   The following reviews include a range of specific menu prices as often as possible; I've also categorized the restaurants as Expensive, Moderate, or Inexpensive, based on rough estimates of what it would cost to feed a family of four—two parents and two children, assuming that one of the kids is young enough to be satisfied with either a kids' meal or a half portion or just an appetizer-size portion. If this mythical family would have to spend $75 or more for dinner (excluding any bar tab), I've classed that restaurant as **Expensive;** between $50 and $75, **Moderate;** under $50, **Inexpensive.** I haven't included in these price categories those places I recommend for afternoon tea, ice-cream sundaes, or pastries, since you won't be eating a full meal there; I also haven't given a price category to the various fast-food spots and food courts I've suggested, since prices there are uniformly low.

THE CHAIN GANG   Besides the restaurants covered in detail below, there are a number of kid-friendly chains—some local, some national—with several properties in New York City that can be very handy if you're in the neighborhood anyway; I've given them abbreviated listings at the end of each neighborhood section.

Among the local burger restaurant chains, **Jackson Hole** stands out, with burgers so thick and juicy they'll make your buns soggy (whatever that means), as well as grilled chicken sandwiches, some salads, and less successful Mexican dishes. Another decent choice for burgers and fries is **Burger Heaven,** a coffee shop–ish chain with long counters dishing out flavorful hamburgers a notch above fast food. Geared toward the office crowd, they close at 8pm and all day Sunday.

The local Mexican food chain **Mary Ann's** serves homemade-on-premises dishes that go way beyond burritos and tamales and chimichangas, embracing grilled meats and seafood, as cooked in Acapulco or the Yucatàn or Puerta Vallarta (warning: there's no gringo menu). No reservations are necessary, and they don't take American Express. Another local ethnic chain worth seeking out is **Lemongrass Grill,** for Thai food. The **Royal Canadian Pancake House** keeps long hours, 7am to midnight, as befits its pancakes-all-day menu (sort of like a hip IHOP). It's known for gargantuan servings, including the "Kiddies' Pancake"; even adults are well advised to share orders. No credit cards or reservations are accepted on weekends. Bargain-hunters like the casual **Dallas BBQ** restaurants, where you can get big portions for under $10. The menu holds no surprises: barbecued chicken, barbecued baby back ribs, barbecued sliced beef, half-pound burgers (turkey or beef). Just beware if you see a tour bus parked out front.

Pizzeria Uno is a known commodity: Swift, cheery service, child-friendly amenities (kids' menu, crayons, flimsy activity booklet, drinks served in plastic lidded cups), and a saloonish decor with wooden booths, black-and-white tiled floors, and exposed brick walls. Both the deep-dish and the thin-crust pizzas are decent; it's when they go beyond pizzas that you can't always be sure of what you'll get. **Houlihan's** and **T.G.I. Friday's,** both owned by the same organization, are dimly lit bar-and-burger joints with several super-convenient locations, mostly in Midtown and Downtown. The service is fast, the regular menu spans everything from stir-fries to pastas to burritos, and the $6.95 kids' menu rivals a Happy Meal any day—a choice of hamburger, chicken fingers, spaghetti, or grilled cheese, served with not only fries and a drink but also veggies and dip, ice cream for dessert, and a toy. Prices run a bit higher than at the other chains I've mentioned—expect entrees to cost $11 to $27.

A NOTE ABOUT FAST FOOD   The reality of eating out with small children is that fast-food joints are sometimes a blessing. Most of those in high-traffic areas of Manhattan are spanking clean and recently renovated; somehow, there's always a McDonald's or a Burger King or a Sbarro's just where you need one. There's also a **McDonald's delivery service** operating in Manhattan (how New Yorkers do love to phone out for their food): Call ☎ **212/337-3278** to get your Happy Meals and Big Macs brought to your door.

1 Best Bets

- **Best Views:** You can gaze out over Central Park's lake from the terrace of **Park View at the Boathouse,** East Park Drive and 73rd Street (☎ 212/517-2233), while the **American Festival Cafe,** 20 W. 50th St. (☎ 212/332-7620), features a movie-perfect view of Rockefeller Plaza's lower plaza—in winter you can watch ice skaters through the windows and in summer you can dine at tables set out on the plaza. The **Crab House** at the Chelsea Piers (☎ 212/366-4111) overlooks the Hudson River, offering a view that's especially spectacular at sunset; Uptown, the **79th Street Boat Basin Cafe,** West 79th Street at the Hudson River in Riverside Park (☎ 212/496-5542), gives you much the same glorious horizon, along with houseboats bobbing charmingly in the foreground. Get a table by the windows at **Cafe SFA** in Saks Fifth Avenue, 611 Fifth Ave., 8th floor (☎ 212/940-4080), and you'll have a pigeon's-eye view of Rockefeller Center and the spires of St. Patrick's.
- **Prettiest Decor:** The famous **Tavern on the Green,** in Central Park at West 67th Street (☎ 212/873-3200), looks positively enchanting day or night, with

its lushly planted Garden Room, its many windows overlooking the park, and its surrounding thicket of tiny white lights. The Plaza Hotel's **Palm Court,** Fifth Avenue and Central Park South at 59th Street (☎ 212/546-5350), dazzles with its rococo setting of marble, mirrors, and gilt.

- **Funniest Decor:** The East Side's **Pig Heaven,** 1540 Second Ave. (☎ 212/744-4333), features whimsical little pigs as a decorative motif, while the East Village's funkier **Two Boots,** 37 Avenue A (☎ 212/505-2276), does the same with cowboy boots. The roadhouse/frathouse clutter of the three **Brother Jimmy's** restaurants, 428 Amsterdam Ave. (☎ 212/501-7515), 1461 First Ave. (☎ 212/288-0999), and 1644 Third Ave. (☎ 212/428-2020), makes for lively fun as well. The Statue of Liberty crown outside **El Teddy's**, 219 Broadway (☎ 212/941-7070), is a fun TriBeCa landmark.

- **Best Outdoor Eating:** At the **79th Street Boat Basin Cafe,** in Riverside Park on West 79th Street at the Hudson River (☎ 212/496-5542), you can sit on a terrace overlooking the marina, with wide-open river vistas and no nearby car traffic. The **Cloister Cafe,** 238 E. 9th St. (☎ 212/777-9128), has a charming courtyard off a quiet East Village side street. And down in Battery Park City, **Pipeline,** 2 World Financial Center (☎ 212/945-2755), sets up tables on the pink granite plaza overlooking the yacht basin whenever the weather's the least bit fair.

- **Most Kid-Friendly Service:** Kudos to these four family favorites, where every waiter and waitress I've ever encountered is friendly, uncloying, and unflappable: **Bubby's,** in TriBeCa at 120 Hudson St. (☎ 212/219-0666); **Two Boots,** in the East Village at 37 Avenue A (☎ 212/505-2276); **Ellen's Stardust Diner,** just north of Times Square at 1650 Broadway (☎ 212/956-5151); and the Upper West Side stalwart **The Boulevard,** 2398 Broadway (☎ 212/874-7400).

- **Best Kids' Menu:** To most Manhattan restaurants, a kids' menu means burgers, chicken fingers, and spaghetti and meatballs, with maybe a hot dog or a grilled cheese sandwich thrown in. But the Upper West Side's **Mimi's Macaroni,** 718 Amsterdam Ave. (☎ 212/866-6311), also includes an array of decent Italian dishes like chicken parmagiana and pappardelle Alfredo; **Gabriela's,** 685 Amsterdam Ave. (☎ 212/961-0574), makes kids' tacos and roast chicken that are wonderfully savory and free of spicy sauces; and **Friend of a Farmer,** near Gramercy Park at 77 Irving Place (☎ 212/ 477-2188), adds some comfort foods like macaroni and cheese and chicken with pasta.

- **Best Burgers:** Wood-grilled and 7 thick ounces, the burgers at **Hamburger Harry's,** 145 W. 45th St. (☎ 212/840-0566), are dependably delicious. But my top favorite just might be the perfectly grilled burgers at the Upper East Side's **Luke's Bar and Grill,** 1394 Third Ave. (☎ 212/249-7070). And if you're partial to "sliders," those moist miniburgers steamed with onions, know that **Sassy's Sliders**, 163 First Ave. (☎ 212/228-2900), put the White Castle version to shame.

- **Best Barbecue:** Whether it's the thick cuts of meat, the hickory smoke, the sauce, or just the divey roadhouse atmosphere, **Brother Jimmy's BBQ,** 1461 First Ave. (☎ 212/288-0999), and its two branches, **Brother Jimmy's Bait Shack,** 1644 Third Ave. (☎ 212/428-2020), and the West Side's **Brother Jimmy's BBQ & Booze,** 428 Amsterdam Ave. (☎ 212/501-7515), score big with transplanted Southerners. In the Theater District, **Virgil's Real BBQ,** 152 W. 44th St. (☎ 212/921-9494), does a meticulous imitation of a down-home barbecue joint, only on a bigger, cleaner, brassier scale—and the food more than lives up to the stage set. A longtime SoHo favorite, **Tennessee Mountain,** 143 Spring St. (☎ 212/431-3993), has brought its savory BBQ to the Theater District at 121 W. 45th St. (☎ 212/869-4545), to give Virgil's a run for its money.

- **Best Retro Diners:** The TV-era kitsch at **Ellen's Stardust Diner,** 1650 Broadway (☎ 212/956-5151), is a hoot. **EJ's Luncheonette** bustles at three locations—on the Upper West Side at 447 Amsterdam Ave. (☎ 212/873-3444), on the Upper East Side at 1271 Third Ave. (☎ 212/472-0600), and in the Village at 432 Sixth Ave. (☎ 212/473-5555). But I prefer the chrome-trimmed **Comfort Diner,** in Midtown at 214 E. 45th St. (☎ 212/867-4555) and on the Upper East Side at 142 E. 86th St. (☎ 212/426-8600), for their cheerful attention to kids.

- **Best Breakfast:** TriBeCa's **Bubby's,** 20 Hudson St. (☎ 212/219-0666), welcomes kids for breakfast until 4pm daily; the weekend brunches are especially popular. The secret's not yet out about **NoHo Star,** 330 Lafayette St. (☎ 212/925-0070), where breakfasts are blissfully relaxed and uncrowded.

- **Best Brunches:** Cookie baking is part of the brunchtime fun at the leafy **Treehouse,** in the west Village at 436 Hudson St. (☎ 212/989-1471). Brunch is a popular time for kids at **Ernie's,** 2150 Broadway (☎ 212/496-1588)—try to snag a table in the garden room in the back. **Elephant and Castle,** 68 Greenwich Ave. (☎ 212/243-1400), is a longtime Village favorite for leisurely weekend brunches that won't break the bank. And **Cafe Botanica,** 160 Central Park South (☎ 212/ 484-5120), lays out a groaning buffet for weekend brunch.

- **Tops for Tea Parties:** The **T Salon,** in the Flatiron District at 11 E. 20th St. (☎ 212/358-0506), feels very artsy, grown-up, and restrained—no one in your party will suffer a sugar overload. And if you're in Midtown, try **Cafe SFA** at Saks Fifth Avenue, 611 Fifth Ave. (☎ 212/940-4080), which has a harpist playing and serves real scones and Devonshire cream.

- **Best Ice Cream:** For sheer old-fashioned soda shoppe ambience, my vote has to go to the East Side's **Peppermint Park Ice Cream Co.,** 1225 First Ave. (☎ 212/288-5054). **Moondog Ice Cream,** in the Village at 378 Bleecker St. (☎ 212/675-4540) and the East Village at 147 Avenue A (☎ 212/328-0167), has small-town charm and creamy homemade flavors to match.

- **Best Milkshakes:** The **Barking Dog Luncheonette,** 1678 Third Ave. (☎ 212/831-1800), way up on the Upper East Side, has a great retro soda fountain and the sodas, sundaes, and shakes to go with it. The **Lexington Candy Shop,** 1226 Lexington Ave. (☎ 212/288-0057), has shakes that are nearly as good, in an authentic vintage coffee-shop setting.

- **Best Chinese:** Taking into account factors like cleanliness, service, and kid-friendliness as well as the flavors of its food, Chinatown's **20 Mott Street,** at (naturally) 20 Mott St. (☎ 212/964-0380), has the edge over its neighbors.

- **Best Dim Sum Chinese:** While many Chinatowners roll out the dim sum carts only on Sunday, **HSF,** at 46 Bowery (☎ 212/374-1319), makes every day a dim sum day: Waiters offer a selection of small servings of dumplings, skewers, rolls, and other delectables right at your table.

- **Best Chinese Outside Chinatown:** That reliable Uptowner, **Hunan Balcony,** on the Upper West Side at 2596 Broadway (☎ 212/865-0400), presents a menu much like all the Chinese restaurants in New York but adds noodles and grilled seafood and steamed diet dishes as well.

- **Best Pizzas:** I'm treading on controversial ground here, in this pizza-loving city, but I'll have to give the nod to **John's Pizza;** the original Greenwich Village location at 278 Bleecker St. (☎ **212/243-1680**) is still the best, but the three other branches at 408 E. 64th St. (☎ **212/935-2895**), 48 W. 65th St. (☎ **212/721-7001**), and 260 W. 44th St. (☎ **212/391-7560**) serve up thin-crust brick-oven pies that are pretty darn close to perfection. John's longtime rival is **Patsy's Pizzeria,** with four locations: 67 University Pl. (☎ **212/533-3500**), 509 Third Ave. (☎ **212/689-7500**), 1312 Second Ave. (☎ **212/639-1000**), and 64 W. 74th St. (☎ **212/579-3000**).

- **Best Pastas:** Forget Little Italy: The best Italian pastas I've found, outside of a couple of expensive places I could never take kids, are at **Presto's,** up near Columbia University at 2770 Broadway (☎ **212/222-1760**), and **Mangia e Bevi,** 800 Ninth Ave. (☎ **212/956-3976**). Pizza at both places is also superb. Sleek **Bella Luna,** 584 Columbus Ave. (☎ **212/877-2267**), is in a more sophisticated class, but for friendliness to kids it beats all other designer pasta restaurants hands-down.

- **Best Mexican:** The Upper West Side's **Gabriela's,** 685 Amsterdam Ave. (☎ **212/961-0574**), has to be tasted to be believed, *and* the staff is lovely to kids. If you like Mexican, pick a time when you can beat the weekend-night lines.

- **Grandma's Favorites:** For a very dressed-up special meal, linen and china and all, I'd pick **Cafe Botanica,** 160 Central Park South (☎ **212/484-5120**). Or do afternoon tea Downtown, either in the West Village at **Anglers and Writers,** 420 Hudson St. (☎ **212/675-0810**), or in the Flatiron District at the **T Salon,** 11 E. 20th St. (☎ **212/358-0506**).

- **Grandpa's Favorite:** Take the progeny for an ice-cream pig-out at fun and friendly **Serendipity,** 225 E. 60th St. (☎ **212/838-3531**). At 42 Central Park South, **Mickey Mantle's** (☎ **212/688-7777**) celebrates the sports stars Granddad has actually heard of—plus, it's handsome, the food's pretty darn good, and there are lots of big TVs so you won't miss the big game.

- **Jock Heaven:** While some kids, especially collectors of vintage baseball cards, may get a kick out of the sports lore at **Mickey Mantle's,** 42 Central Park South (☎ **212/688-7777**), young fans and wanna-be athletes are more likely to fall for the pro-name glitz of the **Official All Star Cafe** theme restaurant on Times Square at 1540 Broadway (☎ **212/840-8326**).

- **Cyber Geek Heaven:** In the East Village, seek out the friendly on-line ambience of the **Internet Cafe,** 82 E. 3rd St. (☎ **212/614-0747**).

- **Most Fun Menu:** At **America,** 9 E. 18th St. (☎ **212/505-2110**), you'll find a gargantuan menu that links every one of its regional dishes with a different town in the U.S.A. For sheer goofy tongue-in-cheek menu descriptions, I get a kick out of the card at **Chat 'n' Chew,** 10 E. 16th St. (☎ **212/243-1616**). Both are family-friendly exceptions in the Flatiron District, that haven of restaurant hipness.

- **Best Floor Show:** If most waiters in Manhattan are really actors waiting for their break, the guys and gals at **Ellen's Stardust Diner,** 1650 Broadway (☎ **212/956-5151**), at least get to belt out their favorites to a karaoke machine in this Times Square cafe's weekend dinner shows. A couple of the recent crop of theme restaurants mount a floor show: Live performers at the **Motown Cafe,** 104 W. 57th St. (☎ **212/489-8030**), re-create the music of Motown. For sheer unpretentious fun, try the nightly sing-alongs at **Asti,** in the Village at 13 E. 12th St. (☎ **212/741-9105**), where the waiters all do their operatic turn.

• **Best Cooking Show:** The flying knives of the teppanyaki chefs at **Benihana West,** 47 W. 56th St. (☎ **212/581-0930**), are pretty hard to beat. But for some do-it-yourself cooking action, try the Korean tableside barbecuing at **Won Jo,** 23 W. 32nd St. (☎ **212/695-5815**).

2 Restaurants by Cuisine

CAJUN

Two Boots (p. 222)

CALIFORNIAN

California Pizza Kitchen (p. 193)
Planet Hollywood (p. 208)

CHINESE

China Fun (pp. 186, 194)
China Shalom (p. 222)
HSF (p. 227)
Hunan Balcony (p. 187)
Kelley & Ping (p. 224)
New York Noodletown (p. 227)
NoHo Star (p. 217)
Ollie's Noodle Shop (p. 188, 204)
Pig Heaven (p. 192)
20 Mott Street (p. 227)
Wong Kee (p. 227)

CONTINENTAL

Cafe Botanica (p. 196)
Cloister Cafe (p. 220)
Fraunces Tavern (p. 228)
Palm Court (p. 208)
Tavern on the Green (p. 179)
The Treehouse (p. 217)

CUBAN-CHINESE

Bayamo (p. 216)
La Caridad Luncheonette (p. 187)

DELI

Carnegie Deli (p. 197)
Second Avenue Deli (p. 220)
Stage Deli (p. 205)

ECLECTIC

America (p. 211)
Bodega (p. 229)
Brooklyn Diner U.S.A. (p. 205)
Cafe SFA (p. 197)
Comedy Nation (p. 205)
Ellen's Stardust Diner (p. 200)
Houlihan's (pp. 189, 209, 229)
Jekyll & Hyde Pub (p. 216)
Pipeline (p. 228)
Pizzeria Uno (p. 189, 196, 220, 224, 229)
Tavern on the Green (p. 179)
The T Salon (p. 213)
The Treehouse (p. 217)

FAST FOOD

California Burrito Co. (p. 229)
Chirping Chicken (pp. 189, 196, 213)
Gray's Papaya (p. 189)

ICE CREAM

Ciao Bella Café (pp. 195, 209)
Moondog Ice Cream (pp. 220, 224)
Peppermint Park (p. 195)
Serendipity (p. 192)

INTERNATIONAL

Brooklyn Diner U.S.A. (p. 205)
Fashion Cafe (p. 206)

ITALIAN

Asti (p. 213)
Angelo's of Mulberry Street (p. 226)
Arturo's Restaurant-Pizzeria (p. 213)
Bella Luna (p. 179)
Carmine's (p. 183, 197)
Ernie's (p. 183)
Mangia e Bevi (p. 200)
Mimi's Macaroni (p. 184)
Park View at the Boathouse (p. 190)
Presto's (p. 185)
Tony di Napoli (p. 193)
Two Boots (p. 222)
V & T Pizzeria (p. 189)
Vinnie's Pizzeria (p. 189)

JAPANESE

Benihana West (p. 196)
Kelley & Ping (p. 224)
Tsunami (p. 217)

KOREAN

Kelley & Ping (p. 224)
Won Jo (p. 202)

KOSHER

China Shalom (p. 222)
Dougie's BBQ and Grill (p. 223)
Great American Health Bar (p. 223)
Joseph's Cafe (p. 222)
Kosher Delight (p. 222)
Ratner's (p. 222)
Second Avenue Deli (p. 220)

MEXICAN

Benny's Burritos (pp. 218, 221)
El Teddy's (p. 228)

3 The Upper West Side

EXPENSIVE

Tavern on the Green

In Central Park at West 67th St. ☎ **212/873-3200.** Kids' menu, sassy seats. Lunch entrees $13.75–$27.50; dinner entrees $21.50–$33.75; kids' menu $8.50–$10. AE, CB, DC, DISC, MC, V. Mon–Thurs noon–3:30pm and 5–10:45pm; Fri noon–3:30pm and 5–11:30pm; Sat 10am–3pm and 5–11:30pm; Sun 10am–3pm and 5–10:45pm. Subway: 1/9 to 66th St.; B/C to 72nd St. AMERICAN/CONTINENTAL/ECLECTIC.

Local wisdom has it that only tourists go to Tavern on the Green, drawn by scores of movies featuring this huge Central Park site with its Tiffany glass lamps, crystal chandeliers, surrounding gardens, and twinkling outdoor lights. To celebrate a special event, however, even New Yorkers find themselves considering this undeniably enchanting place. The menu features such wonderful American dishes as grilled salmon, roasted rack of lamb, and aged sirloin, along with a handful of Italian dishes (risotto, gnocchi, frittata) and all sorts of variations on the mashed potato; presentation is dramatic, and accompaniments like braised fennel and vegetable ragout show gourmet flair. The children's menu is surprisingly ordinary—fish and chips, grilled cheese, chicken fingers, pasta—but it does indicate a commitment to family business. I'd save this place for a special celebration, and only with kids old enough to appreciate the glitz and glamour, because the service can be deadly slow and sloppy—and you know how fatal that is when you've got restless children.

MODERATE

✪ Bella Luna

584 Columbus Ave. (between 88th and 89th sts.). ☎ **212/877-2267.** Kids' menu (5–6:30pm only), high chairs, boosters. Reservations advised. Main courses $8.95–$16.95; kids' menu $5.95. AE, MC, V. Daily noon–midnight. Subway: 1/9 or B/C to 86th St. ITALIAN.

This cool and sophisticated restaurant with art-hung white walls and dreamy blue lights rimming the plate-glass windows looks like it'd be strictly for grown-ups—and

Uptown Dining

UPPER WEST SIDE

Subway stop **M**

NA-0367

180

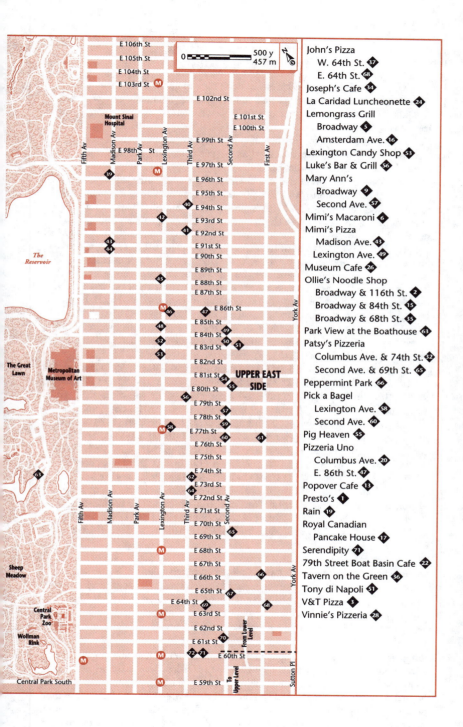

E 106th St
E 105th St
E 104th St
E 103rd St

0   500 y
     457 m

E 102nd St
E 101st St
E 100th St

Mount Sinai
Hospital

E 99th St
E 98th St
E 97th St
E 96th St
E 95th St
E 94th St
E 93rd St
E 92nd St
E 91st St
E 90th St
E 89th St
E 88th St
E 87th St
E 86th St
E 85th St
E 84th St
E 83rd St
E 82nd St
E 81st St
E 80th St
E 79th St
E 78th St
E 77th St
E 76th St
E 75th St
E 74th St
E 73rd St
E 72nd St
E 71st St
E 70th St
E 69th St
E 68th St
E 67th St
E 66th St
E 65th St
E 64th St
E 63rd St
E 62nd St
E 61st St
E 60th St
E 59th St

The Reservoir

The Great Lawn

Metropolitan
Museum of Art

Sheep
Meadow

Central
Park
Zoo

Wollman
Rink

Central Park South

UPPER EAST
SIDE

Fifth Av
Madison Av
Park Av
Lexington Av
Third Av
Second Av
First Av
York Av
Sutton Pl

From Lower Level
To Upper Level

John's Pizza
    W. 64th St. 37
    E. 64th St. 68
Joseph's Cafe 34
La Caridad Luncheonette 24
Lemongrass Grill
    Broadway 5
    Amsterdam Ave. 16
Lexington Candy Shop 53
Luke's Bar & Grill 56
Mary Ann's
    Broadway 9
    Second Ave. 57
Mimi's Macaroni 6
Mimi's Pizza
    Madison Ave. 43
    Lexington Ave. 49
Museum Cafe 26
Ollie's Noodle Shop
    Broadway & 116th St. 2
    Broadway & 84th St. 15
    Broadway & 68th St. 35
Park View at the Boathouse 63
Patsy's Pizzeria
    Columbus Ave. & 74th St. 32
    Second Ave. & 69th St. 65
Peppermint Park 66
Pick a Bagel
    Lexington Ave. 58
    Second Ave. 60
Pig Heaven 55
Pizzeria Uno
    Columbus Ave. 20
    E. 86th St. 47
Popover Cafe 13
Presto's 1
Rain 19
Royal Canadian
    Pancake House 17
Serendipity 71
79th Street Boat Basin Cafe 22
Tavern on the Green 36
Tony di Napoli 51
V&T Pizza 3
Vinnie's Pizzeria 28

181

The Best of the Bagels

Why is it that bagels in other cities just don't taste as good as New York bagels? There can't be such a mystery, after all, to baking what's essentially a chewy bread doughnut. Yet we know many transplanted New Yorkers who beg us to bring real bagels with us when we come to visit. (Even New Jersey suburbanites make special treks into the city to get their bagels.) And bagels are such a great kid-pleasing food—New Yorkers even use them to pacify teething infants—that we'd hardly know what to do without them.

In my opinion, the premier outlet is **H&H Bagels,** 2239 Broadway, at 80th Street (☎ **212/595-8000**), and 639 W. 46th St., between Eleventh Avenue and the West Side Highway (☎ **212/595-8000;** call ☎ 800/NY-BAGEL for shipping anywhere). Besides selling bagels hot out of the oven to the public, H&H supplies bagels to delis and grocery stores all around the city, so look for signs boasting WE HAVE H&H BAGELS. The only problem with H&H is that it has no seating and doesn't serve bagels with any spread (in local parlance, a "schmear"), though you can separately buy little tubs of cream cheese, chopped liver, egg salad, herring in cream sauce, whatever. At least the store has finally installed a coffee machine so you can get a cup of coffee to go. **H&H Bagels East**, 1551 Second Ave., near 80th Street (☎ **212/734-7441**), is a former branch still litigating over the right to use the name; it too has wonderfully chewy bagels, with the added convenience of a deli counter where countermen can cut and dress your bagels.

I know many people who'd award the crown to **Ess-a-Bagel,** 359 First Ave., at 21st Street (☎ **212/260-2252**), and 831 Third Ave., at 51st Street (☎ **212/980-1010**), which is more of a full-service bagel deli where you can actually sit down and eat. **Pick a Bagel** is another favorite on the Upper East Side and elsewhere: 1101 Lexington Ave., at 77th Street (☎ **212/517-6590**), 1473 Second Ave., between 76th and 77th streets (☎ **212/717-4662**), 200 W. 57th St., between Seventh and Eighth avenues (☎ **212/957-5151**), 601 Sixth Ave., between 17th and 18th Streets (☎ **212/924-4999**), or 297 Third Ave., between 22nd and 23rd Streets (☎ **212/686-1414**). The **Bagelry** is another perfectly good place to buy chewy, freshly baked bagels with a limited number of accompaniments: 1380 Madison Ave., at 96th Street (☎ **212/423-9590**), 1324 Lexington Ave., at 88th Street (☎ **212/996-0567**), 1228 Lexington Ave., at 83rd Street (☎ **212/717-2080**), and 200 W. 14th St., at Seventh Avenue (☎ **212/ 352-2604**).

Don't get taken in by novelty flavors. The classics are plain, pumpernickel, whole wheat, and the slightly sweet yellow egg bagels (akin to Jewish challah bread), with various coatings of sesame seeds, poppy seeds, or nuggets of onion or garlic. If your kid is tempted by fruit flavors, go with raisin-studded bagels with cinnamon swirls—blueberry bagels are an abomination.

in fact it's the choicest dining spot above 86th Street on Columbus. But the owners have young children, and from Day One the place has been extremely easygoing about young diners. Granted, the children's menu is served only before 6:30pm and limited to pasta, pizza, or a chicken sandwich, but bring your children at any time of day and they'll be treated reasonably. The Tuscan-style pasta dishes are truly superior, as are the salads, the bruschetta, and other starters; my kids often fill up just on the crusty, dense bread. We eat here just as often without the kids as we do with them, even bringing clients—the food's that good.

The Boulevard

2398 Broadway (at 88th St.). ☎ **212/874-7400.** Kids' menu, high chairs, boosters. Reservations recommended for parties of 6 or more. Main courses $7.95–$17.95. AE, DC, MC, V. Daily 11am–midnight. Subway: 1/9 to 86th St. AMERICAN/BARBECUE.

Upper West Side families count on this friendly, casual restaurant for dinners out. The barbecue (purportedly North Carolina style) isn't bad—chicken, both beef and pork ribs, and sweet shaved pork piled high. The portions are predictably big, with a variety of nightly specials including the $15.95 all-you-can-eat deal on Pig-Out Mondays. Pastas, salads, and a few ho-hum Mexican dishes vary the menu; apple-wood-smoked pork chops, Maryland crab cakes, and basil fried chicken are some of the better choices. The waiters are unfailingly friendly to youngsters and get all the details right, down to tiny plastic animals clipped to the drinking straws; they even have enough sense to serve their grilled cheese on Wonder bread. The large, bright, busy space has fun wall murals that always entertain my kids.

Carmine's

2450 Broadway (between 90th and 91st sts.). ☎ **212/362-2200.** High chairs, boosters. Reservations accepted only for parties of 6 or more. Family-style main courses (serve 2–3 people) $14–$46. AE, MC, V. Mon–Thurs 11:30am–3pm and 5–11pm; Fri 11:30am–3pm and 5pm–midnight; Sat 11:30am–midnight; Sun 2–10pm. Subway: 1/9 to 86th St. ITALIAN.

The original location of this popular northern Italianer still is tough to get into, but reservations are accepted for parties of six or more. My advice is to get here early if you don't want to make your children wait. That said, this lively, hearty restaurant is fun, with a decor that's a 1960s throwback (dark wood trim, chrome bar stools) and a menu of superbly executed standards like shrimp scampi, rigatoni with sausage, chicken marsala, veal scaloppine, and big thick steaks. The portions are served family-style and legendarily huge, so order accordingly—insist on your children splitting orders, even if they're *extremely* big eaters.

EJ's Luncheonette

447 Amsterdam Ave. (between 81st and 82nd sts.). ☎ **212/873-3444.** Kids' menu, high chairs, boosters. Reservations not accepted. Breakfast specials $5–$6.50; lunch specials $6–$8.50; dinner specials $9.95–$16.75. No credit cards. Mon–Thurs 8:30am–11pm, Fri–Sat 8:30am–11:30pm, Sun 8:30am–10pm. Subway: 1/9 to 79th St. AMERICAN DINER.

With its blue leatherette banquettes, pressed-tin ceiling, and chrome-trimmed Formica-topped tables, this is a museum-perfect replica of a classic American diner, and the menu strives to match—burgers, omelets, salads, sandwiches—though it gives away its yup-scale 1990s character with a number of vegetarian specials. The kids' menu tries to add some class by putting the peanut butter and jelly on challah bread, which utterly violates my sons' eating codes, but they're totally content to go instead for the fluffy stack of flapjacks. A feel-good sorta place, EJ's couldn't be nicer to kids, at least at lunchtime. Halfway between the Children's Museum of Manhattan and the American Museum of Natural History, it's a natural for the family trade.

Ernie's

2150 Broadway (between 75th and 76th sts.). ☎ **212/496-1588.** Kids' menu (to 8pm), high chairs, boosters. Reservations advised. Main courses $7.95–$14.95 at lunch, $7.95–$18.95 at dinner; kids' menu $6.50. Mon–Thurs noon–midnight, Fri–Sat 11:30am–1am, Sun 11:30am–midnight. Subway: 1/2/3/9 to 72nd St. ITALIAN.

Back when I was single, I avoided Ernie's because this cool, high-ceilinged setting opening onto the Broadway sidewalk was so noisy I couldn't hear my date talk.

Now I have kids and think the noise is great—that way no one can blame my children for disturbing the peace. The smart, spare white decor may fool you into thinking this is an East Side designer pasta joint, but it's still casual and friendly enough to welcome children; not only is there a kids' menu (pizzas, pastas, burgers, chicken and chips) and crayons to color on the paper tablecloths, but also you can order any main course to be served family-style. None of the many pasta dishes is overwrought, and all are executed with flair. With those sidewalk tables and the garden room in back, it's especially great for brunch, and there aren't any frustrating long waits to get in—principally because you can (and should) make a reservation, preferably at least a day ahead. Don't even try calling after 5pm to reserve for a weekend night.

Lemongrass Grill

494 Amsterdam Ave. (at 84th St.). ☎ 212/579-0344. High chairs. Reservations accepted only for parties of 6 or more. Main courses $6.95–$14.95. AE, DC, MC, V. Sun–Thurs noon–11:30pm, Fri–Sat noon–12:30am. Subway: 1/9 to 86th St. THAI.

Succulent spring rolls and grilled skewers of chicken start you off right at this dependable Thai restaurant with its restful tropical-colonial decor (ceiling fans, bamboo, wooden rafters). Our youngsters feast on those appetizers and plain white rice, while we indulge in stir-fried beef and green-curry chicken and spicy pork chops. The tables are set close together and things can get pretty busy, but the up-side of this is that no one minds kids' mess and noise—the staff actually seems to like children, and the service is attentive if not chatty. A good bet near the Children's Museum of Manhattan.

   Another location: 2534 Broadway, at 95th St. (☎ **212/666-0896**). (See also "The Chain Gang" on p. 220.)

✪ Mimi's Macaroni

718 Amsterdam Ave. (at 95th St.). ☎ **212/866-6311.** Kids' menu, high chairs, boosters. Reservations not accepted. Main courses $6.95–$14.95; salads and sandwiches $6.50–$7.95. CB, DC, DISC, MC, V. Daily 11:30am–11:30pm. Subway: 1/2/3/9 to 96th St. ITALIAN.

From the start, Mimi's has billed itself as a family restaurant, which is a savvy move in this part of the Upper West Side. But while there's a handy bin of toys by the front door to help keep wee ones occupied, along with the requisite crayons, the nonkids' menu is geared to fairly sophisticated palates—fusilli with seared salmon and herbs; a sandwich of broccoli rape, roasted peppers, and shaved parmesan; chicken breast with artichokes and wild mushrooms in lemon-wine sauce—and everything I've ordered has been right on the money. The kids' menu is a welcome change: ravioli, baked ziti, chicken parmigiana, and pappardelle Alfredo, as well as the tried-and-true breaded chicken cutlet and spaghetti and meatballs. Despite the fact that there are always some kids on hand, the atmosphere is surprisingly quiet and relaxed, with jazz or show tunes softly playing in the background, and the dining room even looks mildly elegant, with wood trim and tile floors and a restful blue-and-white color scheme. This is a grown-ups' restaurant that accommodates kids rather than a kids' restaurant that grown-ups can barely tolerate—if they're taking me out for my birthday, this is where I'll vote to go.

Museum Cafe

366 Columbus Ave. (at 77th St.). ☎ **212/799-0150.** Kids' menu, high chairs. Reservations not accepted for weekend brunch. Main courses $9.50–$15; salads and sandwiches $4.50–$14; kids' menu $4.95. AE, CB, DC, DISC, MC, V. Mon–Fri 11:30am–midnight, Sat–Sun 10am–1am. Subway: B/C to 81st St. AMERICAN.

This glassed-in sidewalk cafe with its simple but vividly painted walls, rattan chairs, and vintage wood bar bespeaks a grown-up identity, as does the menu—pan-seared rainbow trout, ahi tuna burger, Moroccan-style chicken salad. But it's right across from the American Museum of Natural History, so children are brought here anyway; the management has finally caved in and instituted a kids' menu, with such items as chicken and chips, cheese ravioli, a muffin pizza, and squiggly noodles with butter and parmesan, which is the way half the kids I know prefer their pasta. Order swiftly and bring your own toys or art supplies to occupy younger kids. The whole tone of the place seems brunchy, but that's what everybody else thinks too, so it ends up a zoo during Brunch Prime Time on Saturday and Sunday—come on a weekday and you'll be happier.

Popover Cafe

551 Amsterdam Ave. (at 87th St.). ☎ **212/595-8555.** Kids' menu (except weekend afternoons), high chairs, boosters. Reservations not accepted. Main courses $8.95–$14.75 at lunch, $11.50–$19.95 at dinner; kids' menu $2.95–$4.50. AE, MC, V. Mon–Thurs 8am–10pm, Fri 8am–11pm, Sat 9am–11pm, Sun 9am–10pm. Subway: 1/9/B/C to 86th St. AMERICAN.

This pleasant upscale cafe's signature teddy bears lined up in the front windows have always deluded folks into thinking it's a restaurant for kids—but it's not particularly so. With an unpretentiously handsome decor (red-plaid banquettes, cadet-blue walls, granite-speckled Formica tabletops), it serves the West Side equivalent of the East Side ladies-who-lunch crowd, wholesome chic types who appreciate sprout-bedecked salads and soul-warming soups accompanied by a light-as-air baked popover. Still, the owner seems somewhat to have accepted the family fate, serving milk in a lidded paper cup and adding a kids' menu of sorts—yet a grilled cheese cooked on hearty home-baked peasant bread isn't necessarily as good as one made with Wonder bread, if you're 4 years old. The staff's patient tolerance for youngsters helps too. I find our lunches here more memorable than my kids do, but they're perfectly happy to accompany me, so long as it's not for weekend brunch, when the lines are ridiculous.

✪ Presto's

2770 Broadway (between 106th and 107th sts.). ☎ **212/222-1760.** High chairs, boosters. Reservations recommended for parties of 6 or more. Main courses $6.50–$11 at lunch, $9.95–$14.95 at dinner. DISC, MC, V. Mon–Thurs noon–11pm, Fri noon–midnight, Sat 4pm–midnight, Sun 4–11pm. Subway: 1/9 to 103rd St. or 110th St. ITALIAN.

One of my family's all-time favorites is this comfy neighborhood pasta place with big front windows opening onto upper Broadway. First off, the fresh-baked bread is so delicious my kids can go through two baskets of it before their pasta's served. Second, the pasta dishes are some of the best I've eaten anywhere: rigatoni with eggplant and artichoke, a four-cheese pasta, linguine with grilled shrimp and veggies in a sauce of basil and goat cheese. Individual thin-crust pizzas are another hit, topped with a truly tasty pizza sauce. And seafood is routinely done well, though with few fancy flourishes. The decor is simple—white walls, a couple of ficus trees, dark-wood chairs, white tablecloths—with tables spaced out decently; and the crowd is an easygoing mix of old-time West Siders, Columbia professors and grad students, and a few undergrads dining out with their parents. We don't generally see other children here, but I don't know why, since the waiters have always treated our kids with unfailing kindness and calm. It's a real winner.

Rain

100 W. 82nd St. (at Columbus Ave.). ☎ **212/501-0776.** High chairs, boosters. Reservations recommended. Main courses $5–$11.50 at lunch, $11–$22 at dinner. AE, DC, DISC, MC, V. Mon–Thurs noon–3pm and 6–11pm, Fri noon–3pm and 6pm–midnight, Sat noon–2am, Sun noon–10pm. Subway: 1/9 or B/C to 79th St. PAN-ASIAN/THAI.

The dreamy Maugham-esque decor of this upscale West Sider perfectly matches its exotic cuisine, principally Thai but borrowing accents from Malaysia and

Vietnam—peanut sauces, coconut-milk soups, grilled meats, stir fries, and lemongrass, chile, and lime flavorings. Though there's no kids' menu, many young diners are happy with the chicken skewers, noodle dishes, and rice. The place certainly is family friendly, especially at lunch, despite the romantic calm of its softly lit dining room, with lots of drapes and rattan chairs and potted plants and fringed lamp shades. An added plus: It's very handy to the Natural History Museum—repair here after a morning in the Asian animals gallery and you'll feel you've really been to the Far East.

INEXPENSIVE

Brother Jimmy's BBQ & Booze

428 Amsterdam Ave. (between 80th and 81st sts.). ☎ **212/501-7515.** Kids' menu, high chairs, boosters. Reservations accepted only for parties of 8 or more. Main courses $9.95–$15.95; salads and sandwiches $3.95–$9.95. AE, CB, DC, DISC, MC, V. Mon–Thurs 5pm–midnight, Fri 5pm–1am, Sat noon–3pm and 5pm–1am, Sun noon–3pm and 5pm–midnight. Subway: 1/9/B/C to 79th St. BARBECUE/AMERICAN SOUTHERN.

The word *booze* in the name shouldn't be taken lightly; as the evening wears on, this low-lit, cluttered joint does become a noisy, beery Southern frat party, especially on nights when UNC and Duke square off in basketball. But the three Brother Jimmy's restaurants very definitely like kids and prove it by letting the under-12 set eat free. And the barbecue is some of the city's best, with meaty, spicy ribs, pulled pork, and chicken cooked slowly over hickory wood and slathered with a tangy sauce. Add a little cornbread, candied yams, fried okra, and black-eyed peas, and it's a welcome break from pizza and burgers. (Kids may want to play it safe with corn on the cob or french fries.) Your kids' noise level won't be a problem, that's for sure.

China Fun

246 Columbus Ave. (between 71st and 72nd sts.). ☎ **212/580-1516.** High chairs, boosters. Reservations accepted only for parties of 6 or more. Main courses $6.95–$13.95; noodles and rice $4.95–$7.95; dim sum 95¢–$4.95. MC, V. Sun–Thurs 11am–midnight, Fri–Sat 11am–1am. Subway: B/C or 1/9 to 72nd St. CHINESE.

The grandniece of Gen. Chiang Kai-shek, Dorothea Wu, is now a restaurateur in New York, and she runs this smart bilevel Mandarin-style place on the Columbus Avenue restaurant row. The look is clean and modern, with a bright abstract mural splashed on the high back wall; the food is classic and delicate, with lots of barbecued meats hanging in the glass-walled kitchen and dim sum carts trundling about. This is a good place to introduce your children to wonton soups and dumplings without hauling them all the way to exotic Chinatown, though there are some more inventive dishes on the menu as well, including pineapple curry fried rice and chicken in peach sauce garnished with sesame seeds. The kids' menu, for take-out and delivery only, goes the safe route of chicken nuggets, plain lo mein noodles, jello, and a toy; at $3.25, it's a bargain—why they don't offer it in the restaurant is a puzzlement indeed.

✪ Gabriela's

685 Amsterdam Ave. (at 93rd St.). ☎ **212/961-0574.** High chairs, boosters. Reservations accepted only for parties of 6 or more. Main courses $6.95–$12.75; tacos and tortas $1.95–$4.75. AE, MC, V. Mon–Thurs 11:30am–11pm, Fri–Sat 11:30am–midnight, Sun 11:30am–10pm. Subway: 1/2/3/9 to 96th St. MEXICAN.

As much as I like the many branches of Mary Ann's (below), Gabriela's is even better, serving up astonishingly good regional dishes that go well beyond rote Mexican combo platters. On the menu is exotic stuff even adults may not want to try—roast cactus, for example—but you can't go wrong with any of the marvelous spicy stews and casseroles and pozole soups. I must confess I can vouch for only the chicken chipilo, breast of chicken cooked in divine sour-cream sauce; though I've been here several times, I never pass up the chance to order it. Whomever I'm eating with, however, usually raves equally about their food. As for kids, there are plenty of simpler tacos and sandwiches, served up with great rice and beans, as well as a number of fruit drinks and fruit shakes, not to mention chocolate milk, which you don't find on many restaurant menus. Gabriela's is fantastically popular, so there's usually a line for dinner; go instead at weekday lunch. The staff is cordial and accommodating; the clean, modern-looking coffee-shop decor (enlivened with colorful lacy doilies hanging from the ceiling) includes nice blue banquettes, which kids may prefer to chairs.

Hunan Balcony

2596 Broadway (at 98th St.). ☎ **212/865-0400.** High chairs, boosters. Reservations recommended. Lunch specials $4.75–$5.95; dinner main courses $4.75–$13.50. AE, DC, MC, V. Daily 11:30am–1am. Subway: 1/2/3/9 to 96th St. CHINESE.

The Upper West Side has long been well served by Chinese restaurants, and Hunan Balcony is the granddaddy of them all. It's a big operation, smartly run, with a menu that tries hard to meet everybody's tastes—noodles, seafood, steamed diet items, spicy Hunan dishes, even sushi, plus the classic chow meins and egg rolls that characterized another American generation's idea of Chinese food. Purists will realize that the cooking isn't as authentic as you'll find in Chinatown, but it's usually delicious (I've eaten here so often over the past 20 years that I've occasionally hit an off night, but that's rare). Everyone's happy to serve the dishes family-style; children can drop all the rice they want and no one seems to mind.

John's Pizza

48 W. 65th St. (between Broadway and Central Park West). ☎ **212/721-7001.** No reservations. Pizzas $11.90–$50. AE. Daily 11:30am–11:30pm. Subway: 1/9 to 66th St. PIZZA.

Considering how few cheap places to eat there are around Lincoln Center, this branch of the famous Village pizzeria (see below for other locations) is a welcome addition to the neighborhood. Thin-crust pizzas, baked in a brick oven—*delicioso*.

La Caridad Luncheonette

2199 Broadway (at 78th St.). ☎ 212/874-2780. Reservations not accepted. Main courses $3.25–$8.95. No credit cards. Mon–Sat 11:30am–1am, Sun 11:30am–10:30pm. Subway: 1/9 to 79th St. CUBAN-CHINESE.

There's often a line at this cheap, authentic corner storefront spot, but customers move in and out fast—a hearty meal materializes on your Formica-topped table minutes after you order. The clientele seems split pretty evenly between those ordering white-rice dishes (savory Chinese stir-fries, chop sueys, and soups) and those going for the yellow-rice side of the menu (pork chops, fried chicken crackling, and a divine Cuban pot roast my 1-year-old daughter attacked with gusto). This isn't a place for picky eaters—the mere sight of yucca and fried plantain side dishes send my boys into total appetite arrest—but anyone who's willing to try the food comes away happy. Though the place is cramped, crowded, and crazily busy, the taciturn Asian waiters never blink at a stroller blocking the aisle or a bread crust flung on the floor. What you see is what you get, and what you get is delicious.

Mary Ann's

2452 Broadway (at 91st St.). ☎ **212/877-0132.** Kids' menu, high chairs, boosters. Reservations accepted only for parties of 5 or more. Main courses $6.95–$11.95; kids' menu $2.25–$3.25. MC, V. Sun–Thurs 11:30am–10:30pm, Fri–Sat 11:30am–11:30pm. Subway: 1/9 to 86th St.; 1/2/3/9 to 96th St. MEXICAN.

The West Side branch of this Mexican chain is its most kid-friendly, with a junior menu that includes quesadillas, tacos, chicken fajitas, and a red-cheese enchilada; there's spaghetti for kids who won't try Mexican. The earth-toned decor is movie-set Mexican, with tiled-topped tables and a sombrero or two on the walls; the food is uniformly good, delicately spiced rather than fiery, with fresh tomatilla salsa and handmade tortillas. The unruffled service makes this a fine choice for families who want to sample good-as-homemade Mexican.

Ollie's Noodle Shop

2315 Broadway (at 84th St.). ☎ **212/362-3111.** Reservations not accepted. Main courses $5.95–$13.95. AE, MC, V. Sun–Thurs 11:30am–midnight, Fri–Sat 11:30am–1am. Subway: 1/9 to 86th St. CHINESE.

The roast poultry hanging in the front window is a promising sign, and the cheery bustle inside carries out on the promise of simple, filling Chinese food—nothing exotic to challenge the tastebuds. Besides the usual spring rolls, dumplings, and steamed buns for appetizers, the menu features lots of fish, grilled or steamed or braised or sautéed, and a fairly classic range of Chinese dishes (lemon chicken, double-sautéed pork, eggplant sautéed in garlic sauce). Nothing's too heavy, too greasy, or too spicy. My kids usually opt for lo mein noodles or the broader chow fun noodles, topped with chunks of chicken and a few shredded vegetables. The service is brisk and tolerant; it can get pretty crowded on a weekend night, but tables empty quickly.

Other locations: There's another Ollie's at 1991 Broadway, near 68th Street (☎ **212/595-8181**). The Ollie's Uptown near the Columbia campus at 2957 Broadway, at 116th Street (☎ **212/932-3300**), might be a better choice if your kids aren't Chinese-savvy; it adds diner standards like burgers, chef's salads, and omelets. The Midtown branch is covered later in this chapter.

Patsy's Pizzeria

64 W. 74th St. (at Columbus Ave.). ☎ **212/579-3000.** High chairs, boosters. Reservations not accepted. Pizzas $10.95–$12.95; pasta $7–$16. No credit cards. Sun–Thurs noon–11pm, Fri–Sat noon–midnight. Subway: 1/2/3/9 to 72nd St., B/C to 72nd St. PIZZA.

Given their decades-long rivalry for pizza supremacy in New York, it was perhaps inevitable that as soon as John's Pizza (above) began to expand beyond Bleecker Street, Patsy's would want to move beyond its East Harlem original location, which it has done speedily (other branches are on the Upper East Side, in Midtown, and in the Village, below). The good news is that the pizzas are still superlative, along with mouth-watering pastas, all at very reasonable prices and with a casual, family friendly atmosphere. The Upper West Side branch is only a few blocks from the Natural History Museum, an added benefit.

✪ 79th Street Boat Basin Cafe

W. 79th St. at the Hudson River, in Riverside Park. ☎ **212/496-5542.** Kids' menu. Reservations not accepted. Main courses $3–$15; kids' menu $2.50–$3.50. AE, DC, MC, V. Daily noon–11pm. Subway: 1/9 to 79th St. AMERICAN.

A stroke of genius, to put a restaurant here overlooking the houseboat marina in lower Riverside Park. Not only are there great views west over the Hudson (time it right and you'll get a sunset show to die for), the arched stone vaults of this open-air structure have a kind of Venetian charm all their own. And the food is head-and-shoulders above what you'd expect at an outdoor cafe: superb burgers, zestfully seasoned salads and sandwiches, and excellent grilled seafood. The trappings are super casual—checked vinyl tablecloths, sturdy plastic chairs, folding tables, fries heaped in a plastic basket on wax paper—and the service can dawdle, but our kids didn't seem to mind, they were so busy counting boats on the river. They're smart enough to serve the kids' menu sandwiches on white bread and not to blacken the hot dogs on the grill; the lemonade was too sour for our kids, but once they realized they could pour packets of sugar into their glasses, they were delighted.

Vinnie's Pizzeria

285 Amsterdam Ave. (between 73rd and 74th sts.). ☎ **212/874-4382.** Reservations not accepted. Pizza $1.50 (slice)–$21 (pie); pasta $5–$9. No credit cards. Mon–Wed 11am–1am, Thurs–Sun 11am–2am. Subway: 1/2/3/9 to 72nd St. PIZZA/ITALIAN.

One of the best by-the-slice walk-in pizzerias in the city, Vinnie's also provides table service if you want to go beyond the wonderful pies and order pasta, antipasti, or salads. At $1.50 a slice, the pizza is a good deal, flavorful and nicely goopy. The location is handy too.

V & T Pizzeria

1024 Amsterdam Ave. (between 110th and 111th sts.). ☎ **212/663-1708.** Boosters. Reservations recommended. Main courses $6–$13. AE, DISC, MC, V. Daily 11am–midnight. Subway: 1/9 to 110th St. PIZZA/ITALIAN.

With its brick walls, low lighting, and red-checkered tablecloths, V & T looks just like the campus pizza joint it is, the campuses in question being nearby Columbia and Barnard. The pizzas are fabulous, with thin crusts, runny cheese, and robust tomato sauce; other southern Italian dishes, like lasagne and baked ziti, are heartwarmingly good too, and the prices can't be beat. Not much on ambience, but then you don't get a lot of attitude, either.

THE CHAIN GANG

The **Houlihan's** at 1900 Broadway, at 63rd Street (☎ **212/339-8862**), is a good option when the Lincoln Center restaurants are crammed before an 8pm curtain. Handy to the American Museum of Natural History is the **Pizzeria Uno** branch at 432 Columbus Ave., at 81st Street (☎ **212/595-4700**). There's a **Dallas BBQ** at 27 W. 72nd St., between Central Park West and Columbus Avenue (☎ **212/ 873-2004**).

The **Royal Canadian Pancake House** at 2286 Broadway, between 82nd and 83rd streets (☎ **212/873-6052**), is often mobbed at weekend brunch. The **Jackson Hole** at 517 Columbus Ave., at 85th Street (☎ **212/362-5177**), has sidewalk seating and lots of parked strollers on weekends.

FAST FOOD

Kids may not go for the milky, sweet, refreshing papaya juice at **Gray's Papaya,** 2090 Broadway, at 72nd Street (☎ **212/799-0243**), but there's also fruit punch and soda; as far as food goes, your best bet is a plump, succulent hot dog, costing about a buck. Prices are low low low and you're handed your food in a jiffy, but don't expect to sit down—a few high stools at a counter is about the extent of it. My favorite of the city's many grilled-chicken take-outs is **Chirping Chicken,** 350 Amsterdam Ave., at 77th Street (☎ **212/787-6631**), where they throw a pita bread on the grill atop the chicken to absorb some juices (okay, to absorb the flavorful grease). Corn on the cob and fries are among the sides you can order.

4 The Upper East Side

EXPENSIVE

Park View at the Boathouse

In Central Park's Loeb Boathouse, near E. 72nd St. ☎ **212/517-2233.** Kids' menu, high chairs. Reservations recommended. Main courses $18–$30; kids' menu $8.95. AE, DC, DISC, MC, V. Daily 11am–4pm and 5:30–10pm. Live music Mon–Thurs 6–9pm. Subway: B/C to 72nd St.; 6 to 68th St. AMERICAN/ITALIAN.

On a summer evening with the long-rayed sunlight glinting off the lake, this terrace restaurant with crisp white table linens is a wonderful place to be, with kids or without. It's a bit of a dress-up place, but the open-air setting, with flowered umbrellas and a white canvas canopy, throws a casual twist on the elegance, and the live jazz on weeknights keeps things from getting too sedate. The menu, which changes seasonally, has real flair—like grilled seafood, pasta, risotto, and luscious roast chicken. The kids' menu is decently upscale as well, offering chicken, pasta, and sirloin steak. At these prices, make sure your children are prepared to behave, but if the weather's right you could all have a dreamy time.

MODERATE

Barking Dog Luncheonette

1678 Third Ave. (at 94th St.). ☎ **212/831-1800.** Boosters, sassy seats. Reservations not accepted. Main courses $10.50–$14.50; sandwiches and salads $4.50–$8.95. No credit cards. Daily 8am–11pm. Subway: 6 to 96th St. AMERICAN.

The Barking Dog isn't automatically a family restaurant, but that's what I like about it. Convenient to the 92nd Street Y and Carl Schurz Park, this sleek retro diner is suffused with a mellow glow from golden walls, wood-trimmed booths, and parchment-shaded lamps at every table. The dog motif amuses my daughter: Posters, cookie jars, and even bulldog hood ornaments from Mack trucks put dogs all around the room, and there's even a dog bar outside, a blue-tiled corner trough with a polished spigot. But what really makes this place work for families is that it serves breakfast until 4pm—kids can feast on waffles or blueberry pancakes while parents get a chance to eat something suitably grown-up, like a salad of field greens with goat-cheese croutons or grilled lamb sandwich on a baguette with olive tapenade. Dinner selections might be more problematic, but there's a good fried chicken with real mashed potatoes (grown-ups might gravitate to the horseradish-crusted salmon filet or knock-out jambalaya). Bribe your children with old-fashioned ice-cream sodas and sundaes, served from a shiny vintage soda fountain.

Brother Jimmy's BBQ

1461 First Ave. (at 76th St.). ☎ **212/288-0999.** Kids' menu, high chairs, boosters. Reservations accepted only for parties of 8 or more. Main courses $9.95–$15.95; salads and sandwiches $3.95–$9.95. AE, CB, DC, DISC, MC, V. Sat–Sun noon–3pm; daily 5pm–midnight. Subway: 6 to 77th St. BARBECUE/AMERICAN SOUTHERN.

If God was a man he'd be a Tarheel. With a jumble of frat-party paraphernalia littering the walls, low-lit Brother Jimmy's brings hickory-smoked Carolina barbecue to New York City. No baby back ribs here, only thick 'n' meaty St. Louis–style ribs, served in hefty dinners that also include cornbread and a choice of country sides—if your kids aren't into collard greens (yeah, right) you can satisfy them with creamed corn or french fries or macaroni and cheese. Two kids 11 and under eat free for each adult meal, which is a bargain you can't refuse: Kids' meals include burgers, hot dogs, grilled cheese, or chicken fingers. The southern road-house atmosphere is laid-back, to say the least, as is the service, for better or worse. It may be best to get here early, before the frat party gets in high gear.

Brother Jimmy's Bait Shack

1644 Third Ave. (at 92nd St.). ☎ **212/426-2020.** Kids' menu, high chairs, boosters. Reservations accepted only for parties of 8 or more. Main courses $9.95–$15.95; salads and sandwiches $3.95–$9.95. AE, CB, DC, DISC, MC, V. Sat–Sun noon–3pm; daily 5pm–midnight. Subway: 6 to 96th St. BARBECUE/AMERICAN SOUTHERN.

The rowdy roadhouse charm of this Brother Jimmy's branch is scarcely dimmed by its emphasis on seafood, which means simply that an oyster bar, blackened catfish, and peel 'n' eat shrimp are featured on a menu otherwise heavy on barbecued chicken, ribs, and pork. The kitchen doesn't stint on the spices, and beer flows plentifully. But kids are welcomed warmly, with a kids-eat-free policy that can't be beat anywhere else in town. (Two kids per parent, and they have to be under 12, but it's still a great deal.) A variety of nightly "events" like All-U-Can-Eat Sundays and White Trash Wednesdays make every evening a party here.

Comfort Diner

142 E. 86th St. (at Lexington Ave.). ☎ **212/426-8600.** Kids' menu, high chairs, boosters. Reservations not accepted. Main courses $5.95–$11.95; kids' menu $3.95. AE, DC, MC, V. Mon–Fri 7:30am–11pm, Sat–Sun 9am–11pm. Subway: 4/5/6 to 86th St. AMERICAN DINER.

This new branch of the kid-friendly Midtown diner (below) is in a prime Upper East Side family location. Diner standards like meatloaf and honey-dipped fried chicken are mixed with a few more 1990s dishes, like wild mushroom potato pancakes, a spinach portobello wrap, or a chicken pot pie with southwestern accents such as black beans and jalapeños thrown in. Crayons for coloring at the booth and prizes for young customers make kids happy.

EJ's Luncheonette

1271 Third Ave. (at 73rd St.). ☎ **212/472-0600.** Kids' menu, high chairs, boosters. Reservations not accepted. Breakfast dishes $5–$6.50; main courses $6–$8.50 at lunch, $8–$14.75 at dinner. No credit cards. Mon–Thurs 8am–11pm, Fri–Sat 8am–11:30pm, Sun 8am–10:30pm. Subway: 6 to 77th St. AMERICAN DINER.

Breakfast is an especially good time to check out this re-creation of an old-style lunch-counter diner (see also Upper West Side and Greenwich Village), but the classic repertoire of burgers, salads, and sandwiches—plus daily specials like skinless fried chicken and turkey meatloaf—makes it a good bet for lunch or dinner too, so long as you can get in. The tile floor and high ceiling usually ring with noise.

Flight 1668

1668 Lexington Ave. (between 93rd and 94th sts.). ☎ **212/426-1416.** Boosters. Reservations not accepted. Main courses $5.95–$12.95; lunch special $4.95. AE, MC, V. Daily 11am–4am. Subway: 6 to 96th St. AMERICAN.

The aviation-themed decor is the chief draw for my second son, who couldn't take his eyes off the model biplane suspended from the high ceiling. Though the place has that dimly bit bar look, neighborhood families do come here in the early evening for the straightforward comfort food—pastas, meatloaf, roast chicken, burgers, crab cakes, and fish and chips; curly fries topped with cheese are a house specialty. Hot dogs and chicken fingers are standard kid choices on the menu. Though it can get noisy as the evening wears on, it certainly feels like a grown-up place, a plus for older kids. There's a sister spot in Chelsea, Flight 151 (below), also named after the numbers in its address.

Googie's Luncheonette

1491 Second Ave. (at 78th St.). ☎ **212/717-1122.** Boosters, sassy seats. Reservations not accepted. Sandwiches $5.95–$8.95; main courses $7.95–$16.95. AE, DC, MC, V. Sun–Wed 9am–midnight, Thurs 9am–1am, Fri 9am–1:30am, Sat 9am–2am. Subway: 6 to 77th St. AMERICAN DINER.

This upscale coffee shop's bright, clean, pastel-toned decor lacks the sassy retro atmosphere of EJ's or the Barking Dog (above), but the food is perfectly fine, especially if your kids, like mine, are pasta omnivores. It's usually bustling, and though the service can be slipshod, no one will hurry you out the door. The menu features a fair number of Italian dishes along with typical diner fare—burgers, club sandwiches, omelets, or even a fairly decent sirloin steak, to be accompanied if at all possible with the excellent shoestring fries. The pasta sauces are a little less spicy than I like, but my kids seem to prefer 'em that way. Googie's is a useful option for a late breakfast, with Italian frittatas in addition to standard waffles, pancakes, and French toast.

✪ Luke's Bar & Grill

1394 Third Ave. (between 79th and 80th sts.). ☎ **212/249-7070.** Boosters, sassy seats. Reservations accepted only for parties of 6 or more. Main courses $5.95–$15.95. No credit cards. Mon–Fri 11:30am–2am, Sat–Sun 10am–2am. Subway: 6 to 77th St. AMERICAN/BURGERS.

It's hard for me to analyze why I like Luke's—it just seems to me like a very civilized place where children are included as a matter of course. Lots of brick and wood give it a warm, clubby look that's also somehow young and casual; there's definitely an active bar scene here, but it never overwhelms the pleasant, relaxing restaurant. Things never get too loud or rowdy, but it's not reverently hushed either. Luke's burgers are really wonderful, firm and yet juicy, with an ever-so-slightly charred outside, and the salads are big, fresh, and well conceived. My younger ones don't like burgers, so they go for the grilled cheese sandwich or one of the pasta dishes. There's no attitude on the part of the waiters: They seem genuinely happy to serve youngsters, even babies. If only more restaurants were like this.

Pig Heaven

1540 Second Ave. (between 80th and 81st sts.). ☎ **212/744-4333.** Reservations recommended. Main courses $10.95–$16.95. AE, DC, DISC, MC, V. Sun–Thurs 11:30am–11:15pm, Fri–Sat 11:30am–12:15pm. Subway: 6 to 77th St. CHINESE.

Rundowns of Manhattan's top restaurants for kids invariably include this East Side designer Chinese spot, so my family and I had to give it a go. To say that I've eaten better Chinese food would be an understatement: Just about everything we ordered had a vinegary edge that was downright distasteful. I'm told, however, that we chose all the wrong dishes—that if you stick with the barbecue and pork specials you'll be happy. So be it. Our sons loved Pig Heaven, though, principally because of the decor, with all sorts of decorative pigs on the pink walls; the general effect is tasteful rather than kitschy, but there's certainly enough of a motif to be entertaining. The staff treated our children well, if not effusively, and the boys filled up on boiled white rice to their hearts' content. Which just left me and my husband yearning for something to take away the taste of those acrid sesame noodles and glutinous baby shrimp with chili sauce. Next time we'll try the suckling pig—if there *is* a next time.

✪ Serendipity

225 E. 60th St. (between Second and Third aves.). ☎ **212/838-3531.** Boosters. Reservations accepted for full meals only. Main courses $6.95–$17.50. AE, CB, DC, DISC, MC, V. Daily 11:30am–midnight. Subway: 4/5/6 to 59th St. AMERICAN DINER/ICE CREAM.

This cheery, bright restaurant with its snugly deep booths and Tiffany-style lamps has a classic coffee shop menu, with especially good burgers. But it's best known in the under-12 population as a source for huge, wickedly rich desserts, fountain sodas, and ice-cream sundaes. The Outrageous Banana Split is priced at $12 and worth every penny.

Tony Di Napoli

1606 Second Ave. (between 83rd and 84th sts.). ☎ **212/861-8686.** High chairs, boosters. Reservations recommended. Main courses (serve 2–3 people) $11–$36; kids' pasta portions $5. AE, CB, DC, DISC, MC, V. Mon–Fri 5–midnight, Sat 2pm–midnight, Sun 2pm–11pm. Subway: 4/5/6 to 86th St. ITALIAN.

Hearty southern Italian food is served family-style at this genial Upper East Side neighborhood spot, which opens a big sidewalk cafe in fair weather. Polaroids of satisfied customers in the front window and black-and-white head shots of race-car drivers on the yellowed plaster walls give it the look of a vintage family-owned red-sauce joint, though in fact it's part of the Dallas BBQ restaurant empire. Sunday lunch is the most popular time for families (Tony's doesn't serve lunch on weekdays), but you'll find kids sprinkled around the boisterous dining room on weeknights too. The family-style menu is strong on pasta dishes, with several chicken and veal offerings as well, plus a two-person steak for dedicated carnivores. If your family can't agree on dishes, half-portions can be ordered for individuals, as well as kid-sized portions of pasta (there's no separate kids' menu). Though I prefer the similar food at Carmine's (on the Upper West Side, above, and in Midtown, below), the scene here is less trendy and the prices are certainly reasonable, considering you can get away at $20 a head, including wine for adults. Note that there isn't room to park strollers beside tables.

INEXPENSIVE

Breadsoul Toy Cafe

1169 Second Ave. (between 61st and 62nd sts.). ☎ **212/759-7228.** Kids' menu. Reservations not accepted. Sandwiches and salads $4.50–$6; kids' menu $2–$4. AE, DISC, MC, V. Daily 8am–8pm (closed Sun in summer). Subway: 4/5/6 to 59th St., N/R to Lexington Ave. BAKERY.

This little storefront near the 59th Street Bridge has an interesting concept: a child-friendly cafe located in a toy shop. The toy selection is actually pretty good, and there are a number of items kids are allowed to play with while they eat; the problem is, there's a consequent pressure from the children to buy something before you leave. The space is small too, with only three tables for eating, though one of them is a child-sized table. Don't expect a hearty meal, since the menu is limited to muffins, health-foody sandwiches, salads, and soups. For kids, there's mostly sandwiches cut in cutesy shapes, which my children didn't find all that fascinating (but maybe that's because they were so distracted by the toys). I wouldn't make a special trip here again, but if you're in the neighborhood and need a place to rest and fuel up, definitely check it out, especially for the muffins and baked goods.

California Pizza Kitchen

201 E. 60th St. at Third Ave. ☎ **212/755-7773.** Kids' menu, high chairs, boosters. Reservations not accepted. Main courses $6.25–$11; kids' menu $3.95. AE, CB, DC, MC, V. Sun–Thurs 11:30am–10:30pm, Fri–Sat 11:30am–11pm. Subway: 4/5/6 to 59th St.; E, F to Lexington Ave. PIZZA/CALIFORNIAN.

Frankly, I think the idea of a pizza topped with barbecued chicken or shrimp is an abomination, but this cheery chain restaurant surmounts that objection for me because it's so darned kid-friendly. The menu does include other items, like salads and soups and pasta dishes, and you can order more traditional pizzas, which come out of a brick oven on the ground floor. My younger son pronounced the pepperoni pizza the best he'd ever had (but remember, he was under the influence of being given crayons and an activity sheet and a take-home plastic cup). Service is decently prompt, and the kids' menu is smartly focused on pizza and pasta, including perfectly plain (no sauce) spaghetti and penne. I found the food tasted rather bland, light on the salt and fat but heavy on scallions and vinegar. (Like in California, dude.) The black-and-yellow decor is clean and modern, neither beachy nor bar-like, and the noise level was just right—we could hear one another talk but didn't feel self-conscious when the kids became exuberant. It's a middle-of-the-road option that comes in real handy.

China Fun

1239 Second Ave. (at 65th St.). ☎ **212/752-0810.** High chairs, boosters. Reservations accepted only for parties of 6 or more. Main courses $6.95–$13.95; noodles and rice $4.95–$7.95; dim sum 95¢–$4.95. MC, V. Sun–Thurs 11am–midnight, Fri–Sat 11am–1am. Subway: 6 to 68th St. CHINESE.

Named after the Mandarin word for "noodle," China Fun lives up to the English sense of the word as well, being a bright and lively informal spot with an immense menu of Chinese standards. Crispy duck, noodle soups, and grilled sea bass are some of the standouts in the kitchen; service is efficient and pleasant, and there's enough clatter and bustle to absorb child ruckus. Like its West Side sibling (above), it's run by Shanghai-born, Taiwan-raised Dorothea Wu, a grandniece of Chiang Kai-shek, and it's even kosher—go figure.

Jackson Hole

1270 Madison Ave. (at 91st St.). ☎ **212/427-2820.** Booster seats. Reservations not accepted. Burgers and sandwiches $4.10–$10.90. AE. Mon–Thurs 6:30am–11pm, Fri–Sat 7am–4am, Sun 8am–10pm. Subway: 4/5/6 to 86th St.; 6 to 96th St. AMERICAN/BURGER.

The largest and sleekest of this chain's handful of Manhattan restaurants, the wood-trimmed Carnegie Hill branch of Jackson Hole deserves special mention because it's perpetually mobbed after 3pm with kids from the clutch of private schools nearby—Spence, Nightingale, Sacred Heart, St. David's, St. Bernard's, Lycée Française, and so on. The main thing here is the burgers, which are fat and luscious (prepare to wipe your child's chin), or is it the substantial french fries? The long list of grilled chicken sandwiches are pretty good, topped with whatever cheese or bacon or chili or salad items you want. No one rushes you and kids feel totally welcome.

John's Pizza

408 E. 64th St. (between First and York aves.). ☎ **212/935-2895.** Reservations accepted only for parties of 5 or more. Pizzas $9.50–$47. AE. Daily 11:30am–11:30pm. Subway: 4/5/6 to 59th St. PIZZA.

The great Village pizzeria (below) has also opened this East Side branch for thin-crust, brick-oven pies, substantial green salads, and a few well-executed pasta dishes. The menu's limited enough so that every dish on it is delectable.

✪ Lexington Candy Shop

1226 Lexington Ave. (at 83rd St.). ☎ **212/288-0057.** Boosters, sassy seats. Reservations not accepted. Main courses $3.95–$10.50. No credit cards. Mon–Sat 7am–7pm, Sun 9am–6pm. Subway: 4/5/6 to 86th St. AMERICAN DINER.

Walking through the door of the Lexington Candy Shop is like passing through a time warp: Inside is a perfectly preserved old luncheonette that makes EJ's (above) look like Planet Hollywood. It's been around since 1925 and looks it. There's a counter with chrome-rimmed stools and a handful of wooden booths, where you can down creamy milkshakes and malteds, fresh lemonade, buttery grilled cheese sandwiches, super BLTs, outstanding cheeseburgers, and crinkle fries. And best of all, the staff seems to positively perk up when they see kids coming. The candy shop component doesn't consist of much more than a rack of Milky Ways and Hershey Bars just inside the door; the front window is also crammed full of stuffed animals for sale, which guarantees that my children never pass by without stopping. And I don't mind, because it's the sort of place that warms the cockles of my heart.

Mary Ann's

1503 Second Ave. (between 78th and 79th sts.). ☎ **212/249-6165.** Kids' menu, high chairs, boosters. Reservations accepted only weeknights for parties of 8 or more. Main courses $5.25–$18.95. DC, MC, V. Mon–Thurs noon–3pm and 5pm–midnight; Fri–Sat noon–4pm and 5pm–midnight; Sun noon–4pm and 5–10:30pm. Subway: 6 to 77th St. MEXICAN.

Mary Ann's on the East Side is fairly family-oriented, serving fresh, authentic food in an atmosphere that's casual and down-to-earth.

Mimi's

1248 Lexington Ave. (at 84th St.). ☎ **212/861-3363.** No reservations. Pizza $1.65 (slice)–$12 (pie); main courses $5–$9. AE, DC, MC, V (over $20 only). Mon–Sat 11am–11pm, Sun noon–10pm. Subway: 4/5/6 to 86th St. PIZZA.

This friendly, popular neighborhood pizzeria may not be able to compete with Patsy's and John's for classic thin-crust perfection, but the sturdy pies are perfectly serviceable, with runny cheese and savory tomato sauce—it's a good option for a quick meal after the museum or before the movies. Sit on a stool at the counter or in chairs at a table; you can order by the slice or by the pie or get heroes, calzones, pastas, and salads, to stay or to go. The homemade bread is a nice treat.

Another location: 1288 Madison Ave., at 91st Street (☎ **212/369-1800**), which has only a counter with stools and no waiter service.

Patsy's Pizzeria

1312 Second Ave. (at 69th St.). ☎ **212/639-1000.** High chairs, boosters. Reservations not accepted. Pizzas $10.95–$12.95; pasta $7–$16. No credit cards. Sun–Thurs noon–11pm, Fri–Sat noon–midnight. Subway: 6 to 68th St. PIZZA.

Superb thin-crust pizza and wonderful filling pastas make this casual pizzeria a worthwhile destination for families. Though there's no kids' menu per se, smaller-size pizzas and small portions of pasta make good kid options, so everybody can be satisfied with different choices from the menu.

ICE CREAM & SWEETS

Ciao Bella Café

27 E. 92nd St. (at Madison Ave.). ☎ **212/831-5555.** No credit cards. Daily 8:30am–midnight. Subway: 6 to 96th St. ICE CREAM.

A favorite hangout for various private schools in the neighborhood, this simple pink-walled little spot has served hand-mixed cones to nearly every member of each school's student body. Gelato is the star, straight from Ciao Bella's SoHo factory. Fruit smoothies and a few food items are also available.

Peppermint Park

1225 First Ave. (at 66th St.). ☎ **212/288-5054.** DISC, MC, V. Sun–Thurs 10am–midnight, Fri 10am–1am, Sat 10am–2am. Subway: 6 to 68th St. ICE CREAM.

The tiled floor and wrought-iron cafe tables give this place a sweetly old-fashioned air; the glass case full of luscious pastries is well-nigh irresistible to anyone with a sweet tooth. It's popular for birthday parties in the grade-school set.

THE CHAIN GANG

Besides the famous Carnegie Hill branch (above), there are two other **Jackson Hole** locations: 234 E. 64th St., between Second and Third avenues (☎ **212/371-7187**), and 1611 Second Ave., at 84th Street (☎ **212/737-8788**). There's also a good-sized **Pizzeria Uno** at 220 E. 86th St., between Second and Third avenues (☎ **212/ 472-5656**), a **Dallas BBQ** at 1265 Third Ave., at 73rd Street (☎ **212/772-9393**), and a **Chirping Chicken** at 1260 Lexington Ave., at 85th Street (☎ **212/517-9888**).

5 Midtown

EXPENSIVE

American Festival Cafe

20 W. 50th St. (at Rockefeller Center). ☎ **212/332-7620.** High chairs, boosters. Reservations recommended. Main courses $12.95–$25.95 at lunch, $13.95–$27.95 at dinner. AE, CB, DC, DISC, MC, V. Mon–Fri 7:30am–11pm, Sat–Sun 9am–11pm. Subway: B/D/F/Q to 47th–50th sts./Rockefeller Center. AMERICAN.

If it weren't at Ground Zero in Midtown, this restaurant might have cause to be snooty about children, because the food is really pretty good renditions of classic American fare (Angus steaks, prime rib, crab cakes, grilled poultry). But as they say in the real estate biz, location is everything and this location couldn't be more of a tourist magnet: Set right on the lower plaza of Rockefeller Plaza, where you can watch the ice skaters in winter and sit out under *Prometheus* in summer. (And if that isn't enough of a thrill, you can ride a tiny glass-enclosed elevator down from sidewalk level to the restaurant.) Where tourists flock, there are bound to be children, and the American Festival Cafe seems to have shrewdly decided to make the most of them—when there are special kid-oriented events at nearby Radio City Music Hall, kids' dishes (macaroni and cheese, hot dogs) are added to the menu.

Benihana West

47 W. 56th St. (between Fifth and Sixth aves.). ☎ **212/581-0930.** Booster seats. Reservations recommended. Lunch $7.50–$14; dinner main courses $14–$40. AE, CB, DC, DISC, MC, V. Sun–Thurs noon–11pm, Fri–Sat noon–midnight. Subway: B/Q to 57th St.; E/F to Fifth Ave. JAPANESE.

Watching the Benihana chefs at work with their flying knives, slicing and dicing the meat, seafood, and vegetables they'll grill on the teppanyaki right at your table, is always quite a show. As far as Japanese food goes, this doesn't require as adventurous a palate as, say, sushi does, so it's a good choice for kids—not to mention the awesome thrill of watching these kitchen samurai at work. For adults, the grilled food is a decent nongreasy option; the portions looked a little small to me, but I felt perfectly full afterward. What with the minimalist decor and the low tables, kids may feel they're getting an exotic Eastern experience, though this operation is slickly tourist-oriented and, truth to tell, the chefs look pretty bored with their work. You wouldn't want to come here every night, but it's an interesting one-night stand.

Another location: 120 E. 56th St., between Park and Lexington avenues (☎ **212/593-1627**).

Cafe Botanica

In the Essex House Hotel, 160 Central Park South (between Sixth and Seventh aves.). ☎ **212/ 484-5120.** Kids' menu, high chairs, boosters. Reservations recommended. Main courses $13–$23 at lunch, $21–$26 at dinner; kids' menu $12; brunch $48 adults, $24 children. AE, CB, DC, DISC, MC, V. Mon–Sat noon–2:30pm and 5:30–10:30pm, Sun 11:30am–2:30pm and 5:30pm–10:30pm. Subway: N/R or B/Q to 57th St. AMERICAN/CONTINENTAL.

I consider this upscale hotel restaurant a real find for family celebrations: Despite the hushed calm, the tinkling fountain, and the tables laid with china and crystal, it's totally kid-friendly, even for busy toddlers like my daughter. Children are given crayons and a coloring book—a thick coloring book, not just a placemat—and offered an excellent menu choice: The Spiderman (burger with or without cheese), the Mickey Mouse (fried chicken and mashed potato), or the Sleeping Beauty (fish of the day). The adult menu is gourmet indeed, with beautiful presentation; I had a roast salmon with lentils that was quite good, and I enjoyed it all the more because no one blinked an eye at my daughter playing peekaboo under the tablecloth. Sunday brunch, a lavish buffet spread served 11:30am to 2:30pm, is the star event for families, so reserve in advance, especially for Mother's Day and other holidays.

MODERATE

Cafe SFA

In Saks Fifth Avenue, 611 Fifth Ave. (between 50th and 51st sts.), 8th floor. ☎ **212/940-4080.** Kids' menu, high chairs, boosters. Reservations accepted only for parties of 5 or more. Main courses $8–$15; afternoon tea $18.50; kids' menu $5.25–$8. AE, DC, DISC, MC, V. Tues–Sat 11am–5pm (to 7pm Thurs), Sun noon–5pm. Subway: E/F to Fifth Ave., B/D to Rockefeller Center. ECLECTIC.

Many things recommend this department store cafe for lunch or afternoon tea: Its high-floor views over Rockefeller Center and St. Patrick's (insist on a window table), the harpist playing weekdays 3 to 5pm, and the smart kids' menu—soup and sandwich, mini-burgers, a hot dog, or a peanut-butter-and-jelly sandwich, with a choice of drinks that includes chocolate milk. Grown-ups will feel very ladies-who-lunch-ish with selections like grilled salmon, turkey club, Cobb salad, a portobello foccacia sandwich, and an asparagus-and-mushroom risotto. The decor is thick-carpeted and pleasant, with golden hues and mahogany-stained wood trim. Just one bit of advice: If you've got older boys, steer to the right when you step off the elevator, because you'll be walking through the ladies' lingerie department— better for them to see the negligees than the bras and garter belts.

Carmine's

200 W. 44th St. (between Seventh and Eighth aves.). ☎ **212/221-3800.** High chair, boosters. Reservations accepted only for parties of 6 or more only after 6pm. Family-style main courses (serve 2–3 people) $14.50–$46. AE, MC, V. Sun–Mon 11:30am–11pm, Tues–Sat 11:30am– midnight. Subway: 1/2/3/9/S/N/R to Times Square. NORTHERN ITALIAN.

Northern Italian, and lots of it. Family-style dinners make this a natural if you're eating out with kids, especially if yours are the kind that suck up spaghetti with gusto. The noisy, casual atmosphere absorbs a lot of tantrums, and service is prompt (if you can't move customers in and out quickly in the Theater District, you're done for). The original branch is on the Upper West Side (above).

Carnegie Deli

854 Seventh Ave. (between 54th and 55th sts.). ☎ **212/757-2245.** High chairs, boosters. Reservations recommended. Breakfast dishes $2.95–11.95; sandwiches and main courses $6.45–$19.95. No credit cards. Daily 6:30am–4am. Subway: 1/9 to 50th St. DELI.

A classic delicatessen restaurant, straight out of Woody Allen's *Broadway Danny Rose,* the Carnegie Deli may borrow its name from nearby Carnegie Hall, but the atmosphere is anything but refined and stuffy. Every table has a little bowl of crisp dill pickles on it, and the sandwiches are piled so high you can hardly get your mouth around one—corned beef, pastrami, brisket, chopped liver, the works, with

Midtown Dining

America 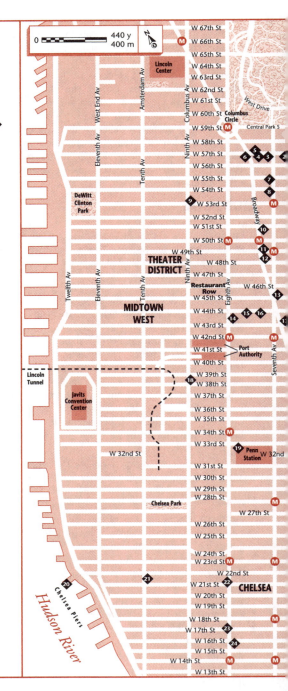 63
American Festival Café 39
Bendix Diner 22
Benihana 34
Benihana West 31
Brooklyn Diner U.S.A. 4
Burger Heaven
    54th St. & Madison Ave. 33
    53rd St. & Fifth Ave. 36
    49th St. between Fifth Ave.
    & Madison Ave. 41
    41st St. & Madison Ave. 48
Café Botanica 1
Café SFA 40
Carmine's 15
Carnegie Deli 7
Chat 'n' Chew 64
Chirping Chicken 57
Ciao Bella Café 3
Comedy Nation 11
Comfort Diner 44
The Crab House 20
Cupcake Café 18
Duke's 61
Ellens Stardust Diner 10
Empire Diner 21
Ess-a-Bagel
    Third Ave. & 51st St. 42
    First Ave. & 21st St. 58
Fashion Café 37
Flight 151 23
Friend of a Farmer 60
Great American Health Bar
    57th St. between
    Fifth Ave. & Sixth Ave. 29
    Third Ave. between
    50th St. & 51st St. 43
Hamburger Harry's 46
Hard Rock Café 5

NA-0368

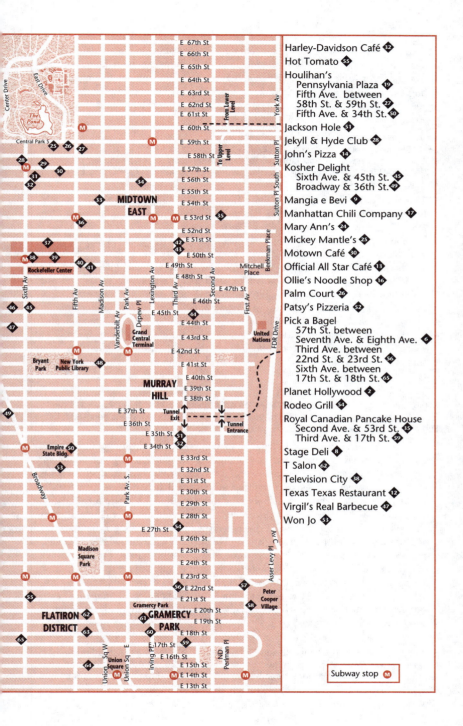

Harley-Davidson Café 42
Hot Tomato 55
Houlihan's
  Pennsylvania Plaza 19
  Fifth Ave. between
  58th St. & 59th St. 27
  Fifth Ave. & 34th St. 50
Jackson Hole 51
Jekyll & Hyde Club 28
John's Pizza 14
Kosher Delight
  Sixth Ave. & 45th St. 45
  Broadway & 36th St. 49
Mangia e Bevi 9
Manhattan Chili Company 17
Mary Ann's 24
Mickey Mantle's 25
Motown Café 30
Official All Star Café 13
Ollie's Noodle Shop 16
Palm Court 26
Patsy's Pizzeria 52
Pick a Bagel
  57th St. between
  Seventh Ave. & Eighth Ave. 6
  Third Ave. between
  22nd St. & 23rd St. 56
  Sixth Ave. between
  17th St. & 18th St. 65
Planet Hollywood 2
Rodeo Grill 54
Royal Canadian Pancake House
  Second Ave. & 53rd St. 35
  Third Ave. & 17th St. 59
Stage Deli 8
T Salon 62
Television City 38
Texas Texas Restaurant 12
Virgil's Real Barbecue 47
Won Jo 53

Subway stop M

199

Russian dressing the condiment of choice. You can also get kosher dairy dishes like blintzes and pirogen and matzoh brei, or Eastern European home-cooking like chicken paprikash, Hungarian goulash, and stuffed cabbage. The menu is as huge as the servings. Ya wanna know what New York was like in the 1940s and 1950s? Come here, order an egg cream, borscht, or gefilte fish, and schmooze away.

✪ Ellen's Stardust Diner

1650 Broadway (at 51st St.). ☎ **212/956-5151.** High chairs, boosters. Main courses $6.95–$11.95; sandwiches and tapas $8.25; breakfast specials $3.95–$6.95. AE, DC, DISC, MC, V. Sun–Thurs 7:30am–midnight, Fri–Sat 7:30am–1am. Subway: 1/9 to 50th St. ECLECTIC/ AMERICAN DINER.

This *Happy Days*–style diner is a block from my husband's office and it's our kids' hands-down favorite place to eat when we visit Dad at work. Enter through what looks like a vintage red subway car and you're in a nostalgic time warp—streamlined chrome trim, turquoise vinyl and Formica, vintage movie posters and ads, and a wall full of subway posters introducing a bevy of Miss Subways (owner Ellen Hart was herself voted Miss Subways in 1959). But what my kids like best are the model train zipping around on an elevated track above our heads and the TV monitors showing old Ed Sullivan segments. The food—your basic grab bag of burgers and fries/salads/omelets/tacos/sandwiches—tastes decent and comes in good-sized portions; Nick at Niters may get a kick out of the cutesy names for menu items, like Fred Mertz-arella Sticks or the Cesar Romero Salad. The waitstaff is super-congenial, and Wednesday through Saturday nights they even sing, as part of a slightly goofy dinner-hour floor show my sons haven't stopped talking about since.

Mangia e Bevi

800 Ninth Ave. (at 53rd St.). ☎ **212/956-3976.** Booster seats, high chairs. Reservations only for 4 or more. Main courses $8.95–$16.95. AE, DC, DISC, MC, V. Mon–Sat noon–midnight, Sun noon–11pm. Subway: C/E to 50th St. ITALIAN.

Graffiti-ish murals outside do their best to stop traffic on Ninth Avenue, drawing customers to this hearty Italian restaurant on the western edge of Midtown. *Boisterous* is the word to describe what goes on inside, with the small tables crammed together and speakers pouring out standard Italian music (we actually heard *O Sole Mio*). The decor is pointedly rustic, with rough white plaster, wood trim, and red-checkered tablecloths, though no true Adriatic taverna would cover the tablecloth with paper and give diners Crayolas to color with. But the southern Italian food is up to the most sophisticated Manhattan standards—truly marvelous gourmet pastas, grilled seafood, and some of the best bruschetta I've ever tasted. The pizza the kids ordered had a divinely thin, crispy crust and big splatters of fresh mozzarella, plenty big enough for two. Our waiter was a tad sullen but totally efficient, and everybody in the restaurant seemed delighted to have the kids there, even our 20- and 30-something fellow diners, who thought our dimply baby daughter was cute (if they only knew . . .).

Mickey Mantle's

42 Central Park South (between Fifth and Sixth aves.). ☎ **212/688-7777.** Kids' menu, high chairs, boosters. Reservations recommended. Main courses $10.95–$24; kids' menu $8.95. AE, CB, DC, DISC, MC, V. Mon–Sat noon–midnight, Sun noon–11pm. Subway: N/R to Fifth Ave. AMERICAN.

Young fanatics hungering for a brush with athletic celebrity may not get the point of this sleek blond-wood sports shrine owned by the late great baseball star Mickey

Pizza Etiquette

Pizza by the slice is a ubiquitous New York food that's a real life-saver when you're out and about with kids. Most kids, even picky eaters, like pizza, and between the tomato sauce and the cheese it actually makes a fairly well-balanced meal. Sometimes it seems there's a narrow little neighborhood pizzeria on every corner here, though of course when you really need one you may not find one for blocks.

Several pizza dynasties have contended for superiority for nearly a century now; the oldest, **Lombardi's** (see Little Italy), declared its coal-oven pizzas the best, but the brick-oven pies at **John's Pizza** in Greenwich Village and **Patsy's Pizzeria** up in East Harlem drew an equal number of supporters. The mid-1990s saw a sudden expansion of both John's and Patsy's, with branches being opened all over town (see Greenwich Village, the Upper West Side, the Upper East Side, and Midtown); surprisingly enough, they've maintained a high level of quality and are well worth a visit. But these are real pizza restaurants, where you sit down and order a whole pie; the sort of storefront spot that sells pizza by the slice is another thing altogether.

The overwhelming majority of pizza places in New York have the name Ray somewhere in the title: Famous Ray's, World Famous Ray's, Famous Original Ray's, Original Ray's, Ray's Famous, Ray's House of Pizza, Ray's Real Pizza. Most of these are trying to cash in on the enormous success of **Famous Ray's Pizza of Greenwich Village** (see Greenwich Village), where you'll often have to stand in line just to buy a slice to go. In most neighborhood pizzerias, a single slice of plain cheese pizza will cost between $1.50 and $2.50, with higher prices for additional toppings.

Most New Yorkers eat pizza without utensils, which can be pretty hard if the crust is nice and thin and the tomato sauce suitably runny. The New York solution: Fold the triangular slice in half lengthwise, hold it by the thick end, and eat it like a sandwich from the narrow end up. Younger kids may need to have their pizza cut up, which is tricky when you're sawing away on a thin paper plate with a plastic knife. Try slicing it into long triangular strips.

Mantle: Among the many autographed jerseys displayed on the walls are those of Ted Williams, Hank Aaron, Stan Musial, Yogi Berra, and Joe DiMaggio, guys I recognize from my brother's baseball cards back in the days when they gave you bubble gum with your cards. Oh, yeah, there's a Shaquille O'Neal autographed basketball, but who's this Johnny Unitas whose name is scrawled on the football next to it?

If all your junior leaguer is interested in is big-name memorabilia, go to the Official All Star Cafe (see Midtown Theme Restaurants, below); if, however, your family is looking for a smart, friendly, casual restaurant that serves more-than-decent food, come here. A couple of upscale dishes like grilled swordfish or herb roasted chicken grace the menu, but most of it's studiedly down-home; Mick's own picks include chicken fried steak, Texas barbecue ribs, and grilled sirloin chili with blue-corn tortillas. The Little League menu has the usual range of chicken fingers, grilled cheese, spaghetti, and burgers. Dig the Scooter Pie sundae. TV monitors everywhere are usually tuned to some sports event, and oil paintings of baseball players festoon the walls of the quieter, carpeted back room.

Tennessee Mountain at Times Square

121 W. 45th St. (between Sixth and Seventh aves.). ☎ **212/869-4545.** Kids' menu, sassy seats, boosters. Reservations recommended. Main courses $6.50–$16.95; kids' menu $3.95–$6.95. AE, CB, DC, MC, V. Mon–Sat 11:30am–11:30pm, Sun 11:30am–10pm. Subway: 1/2/3/9/N/R to Times Sq.; B/D/F/Q to 42nd St. BARBECUE.

Going head-to-head with Virgil's (below) a block away, Tennessee Mountain brings its Southern-style cooking all the way up north from SoHo to the newly family-friendly precincts of Times Square. The barbecued ribs and chicken don't match Virgil's for authentic flavor, but Tennessee Mountain has the edge in catering to families, with a sizable kids' menu offering lots of non-BBQ items; the adult menu ranges as far afield as quiche and salads. The laid-back informality of the SoHo original may be compromised somewhat in the pretheater rush, but it's still an easygoing place where families comfortably chow down in Midtown.

Texas Texas Restaurant and Saloon

1600 Broadway (at 48th St.). ☎ **212/956-7427.** Kids' menu, high chairs, boosters. Reservations recommended. Main courses $10–$25. AE, CB, DC, MC, V. Sun–Thurs 11:30am–midnight, Fri–Sat 11:30am–1am. Subway: 1/9 to 50th St. AMERICAN/BARBECUE.

The fare at this handy Times Square spot—predominantly ribs and chicken, with some burgers and salads and sandwiches thrown in for good measure—is better than you'd expect, with good fresh bread and crisp coleslaw (never mind the unnaturally yellow corn on the cob). The barbecue sauce may not be authentic but it's neither sugary nor too thick, and there are plenty of nonbarbecue choices as well. The choices on the kids' menu are predictable (burgers, chicken fingers) but taste more than decent, with very good ungreasy french fries. Big, well-lit, and clean, the place has friendly, helpful waiters and a Western-themed decor that's not too hokey, plus large picture windows to take in the Broadway razzle-dazzle.

✪ Virgil's Real Barbecue

152 W. 44th St. (between Broadway and Sixth Ave.). ☎ **212/921-9494.** Kids' menu, high chairs, boosters. Reservations recommended. Main courses $10.95–$17.95; kids' menu $4.95. AE, DC, MC, V. Mon 11:30am–11pm, Tues–Sat 11:30am–midnight, Sun 11:30am–10pm. Subway: 1/2/3/7/9/N/R/S to Times Sq. BARBECUE/AMERICAN.

Your cutlery is laid out wrapped up in a maroon hand-towel atop the plastic tablecloth, which tells you all you need to know about Virgil's—this is barbecue and you're expected to get messy eating it. Along with the wood-smoked barbecue specialties, you get sides of down-home stuff like turnip greens, a slaw made with mustard greens, and buttery cornbread, as well as more mainstream choices like french fries and coleslaw for folks whose home isn't below the Mason-Dixon line. Kids who can't handle ribs are offered some safer choices like grilled cheese and hot dogs. The decor is roadhouse chic, with polished wood paneling, ceiling fans, and a clutter of vintage livestock photos. Casual and friendly as it is, Virgil's has a postmodern self-consciousness—come on, that woodpile inside the front door is *not* there just to stoke the barbecue. But you might as well play along with the game when the food is this good, this hearty, this authentic.

Won Jo

23 W. 32nd St. (between Broadway and Fifth Ave.). ☎ **212/695-5815.** High chairs. Reservations recommended. Main courses $9.95–$19.95. AE, MC, V. Daily 24 hours. Subway: B/D/F/N/Q/R to 34 St. KOREAN.

Skip the Japanese sushi bar downstairs and head straight upstairs for do-it-yourself barbecue Korean style. Each of the wooden tables has a small built-in grill and you choose what you want to grill on it—beef, pork, chicken, or mushrooms. The result is food that can be as simple as you want it and an experience that's fun for kids (the same kids who'd be bored to death watching you cook at home). Just make sure they're old enough to refrain from burning themselves on the grill. Other Korean specialties are kimchee (pickled vegetables), a variety of buckwheat noodle dishes, and broiled fish. There are a lot of authentic Korean restaurants in the immediate vicinity, but this one's a standout.

INEXPENSIVE

Comfort Diner

214 E. 45th St. (between Second and Third aves.). ☎ **212/867-4555.** Kids' menu, high chairs, boosters. Reservations not accepted. Main courses $5.95–$11.95; kids' menu $3.95. AE, DC, MC, V. Mon–Fri 7:30am–11pm, Sat–Sun 9am–11pm. Subway: 4/5/6/7/S to Grand Central. AMERICAN DINER.

This is a great place to know about if you're visiting the U.N. or if you're suburbanites on your way in or out of Grand Central. The Comfort Diner certainly lives up to its name, with generous portions of satisfying diner classics—macaroni and cheese, meatloaf, Waldorf salad, tuna melt, BLT, and burgers, as well as a substantial breakfast menu served all day. The clean, cheery look is classic too, with booths and banquettes and a long chrome-trimmed counter with stools; you almost expect the waitress to call you "honey." Service is quick and kids are welcomed, with a joke-laden menu they can color and good-bye prizes "for good eaters." The kids' menu is wonderfully sensible, with PB&J, a pancake, buttered noodles ("with no green stuff"), and a tuna fish sandwich along with the usual burger/grilled cheese/macaroni-and-cheese stuff. Somebody running this place must have young children. Brunch, served weekends 9am to 4pm, is popular with families.

Cupcake Cafe

522 Ninth Ave. (at 39th St.). ☎ **212/465-1530.** Reservations not accepted. Breakfast and lunch dishes under $5.75. No credit cards. Mon–Fri 7am–7pm, Sat 8am–7pm, Sun 9am–5pm. Subway: A/C/E to 42nd St. BAKERY.

The menu here is extremely limited: a couple of soups, slices of quiche, and waffles on weekends, plus a selection of bakery items like muffins, bagels, doughnuts, and tray after tray of beautiful, mouth-watering cupcakes. The setting is so grungy it's hip, with worn wood floors, a pressed-tin ceiling, and about half a dozen small bare tables for customers to sit at; signs on the glass pastry cases are handwritten on paper plates. The clientele is very cutting edge ("Daddy, why is that man's hair green? And why does he have an earring in his tongue?") and yet perfectly friendly and laid-back. When my stubborn toddler planted herself right in front of the front door, not one person in the steady stream of customers coming in or out failed to smile as they stepped around her. A good offbeat choice for a quick, cheap breakfast or lunch, especially if you've got older kids who're dying to be cool.

Hamburger Harry's

145 W. 45th St. (between Broadway and Sixth Ave.). ☎ **212/840-0566.** Booster seats. Reservations accepted only for parties of 6 or more. Main courses $6.95–$11.95. AE, DC, DISC, MC, V. Mon–Thurs 11:30am–11pm, Fri–Sat 11:30am–11:30pm, closed Sun. Subway: 1/2/3/7/9/N/R/S to Times Sq. BURGERS.

This handy Midtown restaurant is more upscale than your typical burger joint, with dark-blue walls and light-wood floors, tables, and chairs. Its hearty 7-ounce hamburgers are mesquite-grilled, which is no longer the newest foodie craze but still tastes awfully good; the menu veers into other territory as well, with burritos, barbecued ribs, and even Cajun catfish, and non–meat eaters may find some refreshing options, like melted cheese and sprouts in pita bread, grilled cheese with tomatoes, a tuna melt on an English muffin, or a Caesar salad. The burgers come with curly fries, which somehow taste very exotic to young palates. Coloring the place mat helps keep youngsters occupied, and the bustling, casual atmosphere feels very comfortable.

✪ John's Pizza

260 W. 44th St. (between Broadway and Eighth Ave.). ☎ **212/391-7560.** High chairs, boosters. Reservations not accepted. Pizzas $10–$14.50; pastas $6.50–$7.25. AE. Daily 11:30am–11:30pm. Subway: 1/2/3/9/N/R to Times Square; A/C/E to 42nd St. PIZZA.

As good as all the John's branches are, this one deserves special mention because it fills such a need in the Theater District for a quick, unpretentious, fabulous meal. The simple white-walled space is stunning too, a two-story dining room converted from a church, with a stained-glass dome in its upper reaches. Pizzas slide out of the brick ovens with incredibly thin, crisp crusts; the satisfying green salads are huge enough for two to split, and the stuffed homemade rolls are a special treat. Okay, so they don't take reservations, but even in the height of the pretheater crush, you might wait 20 minutes at most for a table, and service is prompt enough to get you out again before your curtain. It's too good to be true.

✪ Manhattan Chili Company

500 Broadway (at 43rd St.). ☎ **212/730-8666.** Kids' menu, high chairs, boosters. Reservations recommended. Main courses $8.95–$14.95; salads and sandwiches $4.95–$10; kids' menu $5.50. AE, DISC, MC, V. Daily 11:30am–midnight. Subway: 1/2/3/7/9/N/R/S to Times Square. TEX-MEX/AMERICAN.

This bright and busy little Times Square restaurant welcomes kids with open arms, which is smart as can be considering it's right around the corner from the New Victory Theater and the Warner Bros. Studio Store. The day we went, it was crowded with lunching office workers, yet my 5-year-old still felt totally at home, thanks to the friendly, attentive staff. There are two colorful cartoon murals of the city on the side walls, one of which is reproduced in the paper placemat they give kids to color—my son thought that was really cool. Kids who aren't chili eaters still have plenty of choices; I like the kids' menu because it includes grilled veggies as well as the standards. My chili was spicy and slightly bitter (heavy on the cumin), which I liked a lot as soon as my palate got accustomed to it, but besides the 10 chili varieties there are lots of fajitas, quesadillas, nachos, and even a few burgers for those who don't like Mexican. Noisy, festive, and clean as a whistle, this is definitely one of your better choices around Times Square.

Ollie's Noodle Shop

200B W. 44th St. (between Seventh and Eighth aves.). ☎ **212/921-5988.** High chairs, boosters. Reservations accepted only for parties of 6 or more. Main courses $6.95–$9.95. AE, MC, V. Mon–Thurs 11:30am–midnight, Fri–Sat 11:30am–1am, Sun 11:30am–11:30pm. Subway: A/C/E to 42nd St. CHINESE.

The Midtown branch of this popular Upper West Side noodle shop does a brisk business in the Chinese standards Americans are most comfortable with—egg rolls, barbecued spare ribs, wonton soup, sweet-and-sour pork—with a 1990s nod to newer favorites like Mandarin noodle soups, a sizzling tofu platter, and a grilled tuna kebab with teriyaki sauce. At these prices, who could complain? Fast, noisy, casual, and dependably edible, it may work better for families if you can avoid the pretheater madhouse. See also the Upper West Side branches above.

Patsy's Pizzeria

509 Third Ave. (between 34th and 35th sts.). ☎ **212/689-7500.** High chairs, boosters. Reservations not accepted. Pizzas $10.95–$12.95; pasta $7–$16. No credit cards. Sun–Thurs noon–11pm, Fri–Sat noon–midnight. Subway: 6 to 68th St. PIZZA.

Not far from the Empire State Building and the Morgan Library, this branch of the great pizzeria makes a good choice for families—the kids can feast on a small-size pizza while parents go for memorable, if not too fancy, pastas and salads.

Stage Deli

834 Seventh Ave. (between 53rd and 54th sts.). ☎ **212/245-7850.** Kids' menu, high chairs. Reservations not accepted. Sandwiches $7.95–$14.95. AE, DISC, MC, V. Daily 6am–1:30am. Subway: B/D to Seventh Ave. DELI.

Doggedly trying to compete with the Carnegie Deli up the street (above), the Stage Deli promotes more of a theatrical connection; besides the requisite black-and-white glossies of stars plastered all over the place, near the door there's a large display case of Polaroids taken of more recent stars (I use the term loosely, for folks like Pauly Shore and David Faustino, along with reliables like Dom DeLuise—who, judging from the numbers of pictures posted in restaurants around town, must've eaten *everywhere*). On many factors—the overstuffed sandwiches, dill pickles on every table—the Stage Deli competes head-to-head with its rival, and there are some who even claim its corned beef is better; the cheesecake here is smooth as satin and of heroic proportions. The menu is more limited, sticking mostly to sandwiches. On the whole, the Stage Deli is a little less chummy and a whole lot less authentic feeling than the Carnegie, if ambience is what you're after. Lunch and pretheater hours are crazed, which may mean impatient service, something you don't need when you're with kids.

MIDTOWN THEME RESTAURANTS

The first was the Hard Rock Cafe, then came Planet Hollywood; then suddenly, in the mid-1990s, theme restaurants began sprouting up like weeds along West 57th Street, along with the general mall-ification of Fifth Avenue. Each of these joints has a gift shop attached, so you can buy a T-shirt to proclaim to the world you stood in line to eat here. Not much of a distinction, when everyone else has stood in line and eaten here too.

Brooklyn Diner U.S.A.

212 W. 57th St. (between Broadway and Seventh Ave.). ☎ **212/581-8900.** No reservations. Main courses $9.95–$19.95; breakfast dishes $5–$10. AE, DC, DISC, MC, V. Mon–Thurs 8am–midnight, Fri–Sat 8am–1am, Sun 8am–11pm. Subway: N/R to 57th St.; B/D/E to Seventh Ave. AMERICAN/ECLECTIC/INTERNATIONAL.

The only restaurant on West 57th Street that doesn't have major merchandising action going on is this nostalgic throwback to the days when the Dodgers still played in Brooklyn. Breakfast is especially good, with some local favorites like matzoh brei and corned beef hash joining the usual eggs and pancakes; lunch and dinner throw in some colorful ethnic items such as egg foo yong, blintzes, Hungarian goulash, and baked ziti. With the neon and the shiny chrome trappings, it's snazzy enough to charm your kids, and the sunny waiters call everybody "honey." But is there enough theme here to lure kids away from Planet Hollywood? Probably not—but then you may not have to wait in line, either.

Comedy Nation

1626 Broadway (at 49th St.). ☎ **212/265-5555.** Kids' menu, high chairs, boosters. Reservations recommended. Sandwiches and burgers $8.95–$12.95; main courses $7.95–$19.95; kids' menu $4.95–$9.95. AE, CB, DC, MC, V. Sun–Thurs 11am–midnight, Fri–Sat 11am–1am. Subway: 1 to 50th St.; N/R to 49th St. ECLECTIC.

Of all the theme restaurants, this one works best for 7- to 12-year-olds. Magicians, puppeteers, and stand-up comedians roam around the room performing at peak hours (on weekends, there's a kids' matinee downstairs at Caroline's Comedy Club);

you can push sound buttons to deliver wisecracks and rude sound effects right to your booth; paper napkins are printed with a sassy command to "Wipe that smile off your face." One area of the dining room pays kitschy homage to 1950s TV, while the other emphasizes political satire. Kids especially love to sit on the oversized purple couch in the 1950s area, if you can wangle it. The menu features comfort food like meat loaf, spaghetti and meatballs, maple-glazed pork chops, and baked lasagne, not to mention the popular five-cheese macaroni-and-cheese and a fried chicken recipe that supposedly came from comedian Chris Rock's mother. The atmosphere is busy, fun, and anything but reverential—just like children themselves.

Fashion Cafe
51 Rockefeller Plaza (between Fifth and Sixth aves.). ☎ **212/765-3131.** Reservations accepted only for parties of 20 or more. Main courses $6.95–$18.95. AE, DC, DISC, MC, V. Daily 11:30am–midnight. Subway: B/D/F/Q to 47th–50th sts./Rockefeller Center. AMERICAN/ INTERNATIONAL.

As if they needed more money, supermodels Naomi Campbell, Elle Macpherson, and Claudia Schiffer co-own this themer a few blocks off 57th Street, right on Rockefeller Plaza. Glass display cases feature items of clothing worn by these runway goddesses and other celebrities, videos play a constant fashion shoot, and of course there's a store attached selling Fashion Cafe merchandise. The menu, which goes for well-executed standards rather than creative inventions, features a signature dish chosen by each of the Names: Elle's is barbecued shrimp, Claudia's steak, Naomi's fish and chips. The desserts are rich enough to permanently put an end to your own hopes of being a fashion mannequin. As with most theme restaurants, it's only worth eating here (and waiting in line to do so) if the celebrities attached give you or your kids a particular thrill.

Hard Rock Cafe
221 W. 57th St. (between Broadway and Seventh Ave.). ☎ **212/489-6565.** Reservations accepted only for parties of 20 or more. Main courses $7.95–$13.50. AE, DC, DISC, MC, V. Sun–Thurs 11:30am–midnight, Fri–Sat 11am–2am. Subway: N/R to 57th St.; B/D/E to Seventh Ave. AMERICAN/BURGERS.

Looking like it was rear-ended by a Cadillac, this brassy burger joint promotes its rock 'n' roll theme with such memorabilia as a pair of John Lennon's wire-rims with a cracked lens, a broken guitar used in Nirvana's "Smells Like Teen Spirit" video, and a rhinestone-studded jumpsuit actually worn by Elvis. Various trippy 1960s slogans pepper the place, scripted in neon or proclaimed on posters, but the target audience isn't Baby Boomers nostalgic for Woodstock: it's teenagers, who regard the place as a museum of their parents' goofy past. Despite its lowbrow Disneyland-ish cachet, the Hard Rock is really not an awful restaurant; the burgers and milk shakes are perfectly fine, the prices aren't out of sight, and there's something infectious about the blaring rock soundtrack. And if you've got teenagers in tow, the fact that the place is packed with callow teenagers might even be a plus. (Unless, of course, your teenager is too sophisticated for the place already.)

Harley-Davidson Cafe
1370 Sixth Ave. (at 56th St.). ☎ **212/245-6000.** Reservations recommended Mon–Fri, not accepted Sat–Sun. Main courses $7.50–$19.95. AE, DC, DISC, MC, V. Sun–Thurs 11:30am–1am, Fri–Sat 11:30am–2am. Subway: B/Q/N/R to 57th St. AMERICAN.

It's not just any motorcycle but a Harley-Davidson, mounted on a rotating pedestal above the entrance like some cherished religious icon. And judging from the number of celebrity Harley riders who have donated such memorabilia as autographed seats and gas tanks, this is the hog of choice. To me, the only really impressive article on exhibit in this rowdy two-level cafe is the Captain American bike Peter Fonda rode in *Easy Rider,* but then you don't really come for the displays. You don't really come for the food, either—roadhouse food like sloppy Joes and chili are featured, but the menu covers all bases by including more nouvelle fare as well. The over-the-top desserts, like the Reese's chocolate peanut-butter pie, could really strain the zippers on your black leather jacket.

Jekyll & Hyde Club

1409 Sixth Ave. (near 57th St.). ☎ **212/541-9505.** No reservations. Main courses $7.95–$17.95. AE, DC, DISC, MC, V. Daily 11:30am–2am (opens at 11am Wed, Sat, Sun). Subway: B/Q to 57th St. AMERICAN.

My young kids are terrified of this place—I can barely get them to walk past the entrance, where ghoulish skull heads dangle and there are always throngs of older kids lined up dying to get in. The other theme restaurants have staid display cases full of memorabilia; Jekyll & Hyde delivers a thrill-ride experience, from the crashing ceiling in the vestibule to the creepy artwork that stares back at you from the walls. The waiters all look decked out for Halloween, and there's a continual floor show of ghastly figures telling even ghastlier jokes. The food is somewhat beside the point, but for the record I'll tell you that they serve popcorn shrimp, pizzas, vegetarian sandwiches, gargantuan Hyde burgers, Monster Chicken, Dr. Jekyll's fish and chips, and more; the kitchen's general strategy seems to be to smother things with cheese if at all possible and to grill anything that's grillable.

Motown Cafe

104 W. 57th St. (between Sixth and Seventh aves.). ☎ **212/581-8030.** Reservations accepted Sun–Thurs only. Main courses $7.95–$18.95. AE, MC, V. Sun–Thurs 11:30am–midnight, Fri–Sat 11:30am–1am. Subway: B/Q to 57th St. AMERICAN SOUTHERN.

Originally a Horn & Hardart Automat from the deco 1930s, this bilevel space on Theme Restaurant Row pays tribute to the funky soul sounds of Motown Records, with slick early 1960s decor and big screens projecting vintage clips of Motown artists, not to mention live performances from not-yet-famous newcomers recycling those old hits. A radio-tower light beacon glares over the entrance, and the world's largest 45-rpm record—30 feet across—hangs from the ceiling inside; kids' eyes may pop when they see the Temptations' gold suits inside a display case. The fried chicken and chicken fingers have crispy crusts kids seem to love and the sweet-potato fries are real winners; other dishes include ribs and macaroni and cheese.

Official All Star Cafe

1540 Broadway (at 45th St.), 2nd floor. ☎ **212/840-8326.** Reservations accepted only for parties of 30 or more. Main courses $10.95–$19.95. Daily 11am–2am. AE, DC, DISC, MC, V. Subway: 1/2/3/7/9/N/Q/R/S to Times Sq. AMERICAN DINER.

It's owned by Joe Montana, Ken Griffey Jr., Wayne Gretzky, Andre Agassi, Monica Seles, Tiger Woods, and Shaquille O'Neal, and if you have to ask who these people are then this isn't the place for you. Projection screens play videos of these athletes' days of glory, while big TVs play current sports events; diners sit in booths that resemble giant baseball mitts; à la Planet Hollywood (same designer, same part-owner), the stars' personal memorabilia are on display, including Agassi's chopped-off ponytail and the first backboard Shaq ever shattered. Each owner has chosen a favorite dish for the menu—Gretzky's is steak, Agassi's red-sauce spaghetti—and there are 51 kinds of burgers and 5 kinds of hot dogs (each from a different ball park). Big portions and lotsa distractions make this an overwhelming place to treat a young sports fan.

Planet Hollywood

140 W. 57th St. (between Sixth and Seventh aves.). ☎ **212/333-7827.** No reservations. Main courses $7.50–$18.95. AE, CB, DC, DISC, MC, V, DISC. Daily 11am–2am. Subway: N/R/B/Q to 57th St. CALIFORNIAN.

As a tribute to movies—make that late 20th–century movies—this blockbuster theme restaurant scores more on noise and razzle-dazzle than it does on substance. The walls are covered with props and costume items donated by movie-star pals of the owners (Schwarzenegger, Stallone, and Willis are the marquee names attached), though the vaguely wacked-out decor looks more like outer space than it does like Tinseltown. Beware: Skittish youngsters may find it hard to eat with a stuffed Chewbacca from *Star Wars,* Freddy Krueger's sweater and claw, and the Terminator's ripped-open bionic head looming nearby.

There's a movie trivia quiz on the placemats to entertain you while you wait for service, after you've waited on the sidewalk and then in the bar area to get in. The menu has a California bias, but this being a theme restaurant it's big on burgers; other popular choices are the Hollywood club sandwich, Cajun chicken breast, Mexican shrimp salad, and huge Hollywood Bowl salad. The dessert menu includes apple strudel made from Ma Schwarzenegger's own recipe, and there's a long list of no-alcohol cocktails with cutesy names like Total Recall, Home Alone, and Ace Ventura. You can't deny that this place has a buzz about it.

Television City

74 W. 50th St. (at Sixth Ave.). ☎ **212/333-3388.** Kids' menu, high chairs, boosters. Reservations not accepted during Radio City shows or Christmas season. Main courses $8.95–$17.95 at lunch, $9.95–$14.95 at dinner; kids' menu $7.95. AE, CB, DC, DISC, MC, V. Daily 11:30am–midnight. Subway: B/D/Q to Rockefeller Center. AMERICAN.

With the NBC Studios around the corner and CBS headquarters a couple blocks up Sixth Avenue, Television City is a natural theme choice for this corner restaurant—however, note that it plans to close in mid-1999. Celebrity owners include Jill Eikenberry, Michael Tucker, Regis Philbin, Susan Lucci, and Joan Rivers, none of these names kids will care about, but young tube-a-holics may be fascinated by the 130 TV screens and the live TV studio equipment, which films diners either delivering a mock newscast or projected via blue-screen matting on various filmed backgrounds. (Beware: Your antics will be broadcast all over the restaurant on those 130 screens, and a videotape of your appearance will be sold to you for $20.) The food includes American standards like clam chowder, burgers, Cobb salad, spinach salad, quesadillas, steak, and a wonderful roasted chicken; the kids menu is standard too, with burgers, chicken fingers, and macaroni and cheese. I'm reassured by the fact that the active partners are the Liederman brothers, David (of David's Cookies), and William (who owns Mickey Mantle's, above). The gift shop and waiting-in-line factors aren't significant here, either, which is a refreshing change.

AFTERNOON TEA

Palm Court

In the Plaza Hotel, 768 Fifth Ave. (between 58th and 59th sts.). ☎ **212/546-5350.** High chairs. Reservations recommended for brunch. High tea $27; dinner main courses $19–$30; breakfast $30. Daily 6:30am–2:45pm, 3:45pm–midnight (high tea Mon–Sat 3:45–6pm, Sun 4–6pm). AE, CB, DC, DISC, MC, V. Subway: N/R to Fifth Ave. CONTINENTAL.

The classic choice for a special-occasion outing with grandparents or godparents, the Plaza Hotel's elegant lobby cafe is at its best in the afternoon, with the discreet clink of china teacups and the rustle of shopping bags mingling with soft classical music. The desserts are as ornate as the 19th-century decor, all curlicued gilt and creamy marble. Kids should be on their best behavior; I even saw, honestly, a 5-year-old boy dressed in a sailor suit (let's hope he was European), which tells you what you need to know about the target clientele.

ICE CREAM & SWEETS

Ciao Bella Café

200 W. 57th St. (facing Seventh Ave.). ☎ **212/831-5555.** No credit cards. Daily 8:30am–midnight. Subway: B/Q/N/R to 57th St. ICE CREAM.

A branch of the Upper East Side ice-cream shop (above) offers younger kids a welcome break from the relentless theme-restaurant glitz of 57th Street: It sells gelati (that's Italian for ice cream), regular ice-cream cones, and fruit smoothies, as well as sundaes and shakes.

THE CHAIN GANG

Among **Houlihan's** many branches, the three best locations for families are 767 Fifth Ave., between 58th and 59th streets (☎ **212/339-8850**), in the sunken plaza of the GM Building right next to FAO Schwarz; 2 Pennsylvania Plaza by Penn Station (☎ **212/630-0349**); and 350 Fifth Ave., at 34th Street (☎ **212/630-0339**), on the ground floor of the Empire State Building.

Also near the Empire State Building is a **Jackson Hole** at 521 Third Ave., at 35th Street (☎ **212/679-3264**). There are **Burger Heavens** sprinkled all around Midtown: 20 E. 49th St., between Fifth and Madison avenues (☎ **212/755-2166**); 54th Street and Madison Avenue; 53rd Street and Fifth Avenue; and 41st Street and Madison Avenue. It's breakfast all day long at the **Royal Canadian Pancake House,** 1004 Second Ave., at 53rd Street (☎ **212/980-4131**).

FOOD COURTS

On the top floor of the **Manhattan Mall,** an oddly suburban vertical shopping center at Sixth Avenue and 33rd Street, nearly a dozen food vendors offer a pretty varied smorgasbord of food choices: at last visit, Japanese, Chinese, Indian, Cajun, vegetarian, fish and chips, and good old American hamburgers and cheesesteaks and hot dogs. The marble-clad mall is a bit noisy and the food court's tables are tiny; there are big bathrooms handy, though my husband and sons reported that the men's room was messy and populated by rummies (the women's room was fine—draw your own conclusions). At any rate, you'll ride up in glass-enclosed elevators, which should thrill your little daredevils.

The angle-topped **Citicorp Building,** a stunning white skyscraper between Lexington and Third avenues and 53rd and 54th streets, has a food court in its sunken atrium plaza, with a range of take-out choices: pizza, bagels, frozen yogurt, and so on. There are also several restaurants around the atrium to choose from.

6 Chelsea

MODERATE

The Crab House

At the Chelsea Piers, 23rd St. and Twelfth Ave. ☎ **212/366-4111.** Kids' menu, high chairs, boosters. Main courses $6.95–$10.95 at lunch, $10.95–$39.95 at dinner; kids' menu $4. AE, CB, DC, DISC, MC, V. Sun–Thurs noon–11pm, Fri–Sat noon–midnight. Subway: C/E to 23rd St. SEAFOOD.

On a summer evening when the sun sets in a blaze over the Hudson, you could do far worse than to come to the Crab House, the Chelsea Piers' sit-down family restaurant. The big windows look out over the water toward New Jersey, and the high-ceilinged atmosphere is casual and pleasantly rowdy. Besides the usual kids' menu standbys, the Crab House capitalizes on its seafood specialty by offering children fish and chips, fried shrimp, and a Captain's Combo that includes both of the above along with some chicken fingers; french fries and fruit are included. If you order crabs, you get to smash them open with wooden mallets, which children seem to find endlessly amusing. Adults may find that the seafood's not outstanding—sometimes slightly overcooked or overbuttered—but it's perfectly adequate, and the views and family-friendly ambience help mightily to compensate.

Empire Diner

210 Tenth Ave. (at 22nd St.). ☎ **212/243-2736.** Booster. Reservations not accepted. Main courses $9.95–$16.95. AE, DC, DISC, MC, V. Daily 24 hours. Subway: C/E to 23rd St. AMERICAN DINER.

The enduring popularity of this deco-ish chrome diner, stretching like a waiting limo along Chelsea's far west Tenth Avenue, is no doubt because it stays open to all hours of the morning—the club-happy crew that tramps through here at 5am is a sight to behold. There's only one booster seat in the whole joint, which tells you how little they value family business. But if your kids are older and have developed some restaurant manners, this is a dependable choice in a neighborhood that doesn't offer many places to eat. The menu's big on omelets, burgers, meat loaf, and the like, which won't threaten a youngster's palate. One thing you can be sure of, you'll feel like you're in Manhattan.

Flight 151

151 Eighth Ave. (between 17th and 18th sts.). ☎ **212/229-1868.** Boosters. Reservations not necessary. Main courses $3.95–$7.95 at lunch, $5.95–$13.95 at dinner. AE, MC, V. Sun–Thurs 11am–1am, Fri–Sat 11am–2am. Subway: A/C/E to 14th St. AMERICAN.

Like its sibling Flight 1668 on the Upper East Side (above), this relaxed neighborhood hangout is a welcome spot for families at lunch and dinner, before the drinking crowd settles in for the night. Vintage plane memorabilia decorates the space, an added plus for aircraft-loving kids. The food is middle-of-the-road standards—burgers, pastas, meatloaf, roast chicken—with appetizers like chicken fingers and crab cakes that may make a whole meal for a youngster. Service is friendly and blessedly tolerant.

Hot Tomato

676 Sixth Ave. (at 21st St.). ☎ **212/691-3535.** High chairs, boosters. Reservations recommended. Main courses $9.95–$17.95. AE, DISC, MC, V. Sun–Thurs 11am–1am, Fri–Sat 11am–2am. Subway: F to 23rd St. AMERICAN.

Here's a find: a casual restaurant with some interesting, inventive food for adults that also totally welcomes kids. Since there's no separate kids' menu, you'll have to take a chance your children will like something on the regular menu, but ours were pleased with the macaroni and cheese and the meatloaf; meanwhile, I got to have a beet-and-watercress salad with hazelnuts and goat cheese on top. (We had to fish out the escarole from the chicken noodle soup, though, before my older son would eat it.) Weekend brunch is a good bet (what kid doesn't like pancakes and French toast?), especially if you combine it with the children's events at the Barnes & Noble bookstore across the street.

INEXPENSIVE

Bendix Diner

219 Eighth Ave. (at 21st St.). ☎ **212/366-0560.** High chairs, boosters. No reservations. Main courses $3.25–$7.95. AE, DISC, MC, V. Tues–Sat 8am–2am, Sun–Mon 8am–11pm. Subway: C/E to 23rd St. AMERICAN DINER/THAI.

Garish cartoony murals on the walls give a hip jolt to this friendly Chelsea diner, which proclaims as its happy motto "Get Fat!" The menu mixes American diner specialties—your typical burgers, Greek salads, BLTs, and tuna melts—with some pretty passable Thai food. If you've never tried Thai, at least order the chicken satay appetizers: skewered grilled chicken with peanut sauce even toddlers may find delectable. The more adventurous should undertake pad thai noodles, soft noodles that come stir-fried with chicken, shrimp, bean sprouts, turnips, and tofu; the garlicky fried tofu with broccoli is another good choice. The meeting of East and West works well, and any place that lets me eat pad see eew noodles while my kids share a stack of silver-dollar pancakes is A-OK.

THE CHAIN GANG

The original location of **Mary Ann's,** at 116 Eighth Ave., at 16th Street (☎ **212/ 633-0877**), is less kid-oriented than its Uptown counterparts, but the Mexican food is dandy.

7 The Flatiron District & Gramercy Park

MODERATE

✪ America

9 E. 18th St. (between Fifth Ave. and Broadway). ☎ **212/505-2110.** High chairs, boosters. Reservations recommended. Main courses $10.95–$17.95; salads and sandwiches $3.95–$14.95. AE, DC, DISC, MC, V. Sun–Thurs 11:30am–midnight, Fri–Sat 11:30am–1am. Subway: L/N/R/4/5/6 to Union Sq. AMERICAN/ECLECTIC.

A giant American flag hangs over the entrance and a Statue of Liberty presides over one end of the raised bar area, while figures of Washington and Lincoln hold a confab at the other end. From Albuquerque nachos to Yazoo City fried okra, this USA-themed restaurant assigns every item on the menu a hometown, some of which seem far-fetched—why should alphabet noodle soup belong to Kalamazoo, Michigan, a tuna melt to Minnesota, or the Reuben sandwich to Nebraska? But why quibble with such a big, fun menu, especially when so many selections are kid-pleasers, even for kids too young to get the geography gimmick. Even picky eaters should find something they like, whether it's a Georgia peach pancake, a Fluffernutter sandwich, macaroni and cheese, or a trio of tiny Velveeta-topped "slider" hamburgers; meanwhile, parents can sample exotic items like Puget Sound wild-mushroom ragout, Creole jambalaya, or air-dried duck salad. And surprisingly, the kitchen does a pretty good job with nearly everything. The big dining room's cool minimalist decor will flatter older kids into thinking this is a grown-up restaurant, but never fear—America attracts lots of younger diners and is well used to dealing with them.

Friend of a Farmer

77 Irving Place (between 18th and 19th sts.). ☎ **212/477-2188.** Kids' menu, high chairs, boosters. Main courses $7–$9 at lunch, $12.95–$21.95 at dinner; kids' menu $5.50. AE, DC, DISC, MC, V. Mon–Thurs 8am–10pm, Fri 8am–11pm, Sat 9:30am–11pm, Sun 9:30am–10pm. Subway: L/N/R/4/5/6 to Union Sq. AMERICAN.

Like a little piece of upstate New York plunked down just south of Gramercy Park, rustic low-ceilinged Friend of a Farmer does the country cafe thing right— fresh-baked breads and muffins, hearty soups, filling casseroles, and pot pies on a menu that also offers steaks, roast chicken, pastas, and salads. Young farmhands can choose from macaroni and cheese, chicken with pasta, grilled cheese, or PBJ. Casual and low-key it may be, but the wooden tables are small and set close, service can dawdle a bit, and the lunching neighborhood folks may look askance if rowdy juveniles shatter the usual calm. All the same, I keep coming here to get the kind of home-cooking I never have time to do at home; so long as I have only one kid in tow at a time, it can be a wonderfully relaxing experience.

INEXPENSIVE

✪ Chat 'n' Chew

10 E. 16th St. (between Fifth Ave. and Union Square West). ☎ **212/243-1616.** Kids' menu, high chairs, boosters. Reservations recommended for parties of 5 or more. Main courses $7.25–$12.75; salads and sandwiches $6–$9.95; kids' menu $2.95 at brunch, $3.95 at lunch/dinner. AE, MC, V. Mon–Thurs 11:30am–11pm, Fri 11:30am–11:30pm, Sat 10am–11:30pm, Sun 10am–11pm. Subway: L/N/R/4/5/6 to Union Sq. AMERICAN.

Are they serious about that name? Of course not, and neither should you be. Something about this cozy Flatiron place just makes me smile as soon as I walk in the door. Maybe it's the (nudge, nudge) "down-home" decor—red-painted floors, dark-stained wood, farm implements and road signs on the walls—or maybe it's the casual, friendly way they treat you. The menu's fun to read, with names like the Cesar Romero Salad, Uncle Red's Addiction (honey-dipped fried chicken), 110% Veggie Chili, and the Holy Cow (a 9-oz hamburger); the fried catfish po' boy is especially moist and delicious, and the meatloaf comes with "skin-on" smashed potatoes. Kids get offered a fairly standard menu of favorites, but the names alone will intrigue them: Monster Burger, Flying Saucer Pancakes, Mars Fried Chicken (two pieces of mutant chicken with alien fries). Tongue-in-cheek it may be, but it's not too hip to welcome families, unlike the Coffee Shop and the Union Square Cafe and all those other trendies down the street.

Duke's

99 E. 19th St. (between Park Ave. South and Irving Place). ☎ **212/260-2922.** Kids' menu, high chairs, boosters. Reservations required for parties of 6 or more. Main courses $6.95–$13.95; kids' menu $6.95. AE, DC, DISC, MC, V. Daily noon–1am. Subway: 4/5/6/N/R to Union Sq. AMERICAN SOUTHERN/BARBECUE.

Yet another haven for transplanted Southerners, this roadhouse-style hangout believes in huge portions, a steady noise level, and being friendly to kids. Expect a rock 'n' roll soundtrack, vintage clutter on the weathered-looking walls, and Tennessee-style barbecue (ribs, chicken, fish) that's not terribly authentic. The kids' menu is your usual burger, chicken fingers, and the like, but it includes a drink and a hot fudge sundae, which makes it a decent deal. It doesn't have quite the kitschy sense of fun as Chat 'n' Chew (above), but we thought the food was a half-notch above Rodeo Grill (below), with a similar down-home atmosphere.

Rodeo Grill

373 Third Ave. (at 27th St.). ☎ **212/683-6500.** Kids' menu, high chairs, boosters. Reservations accepted only for parties of 5 or more. Main courses $5.95–$14.95; kids' menu $3.50. AE, CB, DC, DISC, MC, V. Daily 11am–2am. Subway: 6 to 28th St. BARBECUE/TEX-MEX.

Someone had a lot of fun decorating this bilevel space, with the feed-grain silo on the upper landing and the huge stuffed bison on a ledge above the bar. The weathered-wood walls are hung with old highway signs and lots of animal horns; Western music twangs and a basket of taco chips arrives on your table in a flash. Children are a welcome part of the mix: kids' drinks are served in plastic cups, and on Wednesday nights children even eat free. The menu is heavy on burgers, steaks, BBQ, fajitas, and burritos, but there are a fair number of vegetarian items and a short list of salads as well. Children are offered (once again) burgers, chicken fingers, and grilled cheese, with mounds of fries. I found the salsa and hot sauce pretty acrid, but our family enjoyed our meal nevertheless, which just goes to prove that dining out with kids isn't about eating good food.

AFTERNOON TEA

The T Salon

11 E. 20th St. (between Fifth Ave. and Broadway). ☎ **212/358-0506.** Boosters. Main courses $8–$17. AE, MC, V. Sun–Wed 10:30am–8pm, Thurs–Sat 10:30am–10pm. 11:30am–10pm, Fri–Sat 11:30am–midnight, Sun 11:30am–9:30pm. Subway: N/R to 23rd St. ECLECTIC.

This cozy spot is full of artistic types brooding over cups of fragrant brew (herbal as well as caff and no-caff) chosen from a list as long as the wine list at most restaurants. Low ceilings, soft lighting, and settees and armchairs covered in William Morris-y dark brocades complete the look of boho British gentility. Besides tea, the bill of fare has a refreshingly low pastry component, leaning more toward soups, salads, sandwiches, and delicate crepes. Twelve-year-old girls who love Jane Austen movies should eat this place up.

THE CHAIN GANG

There's another **Royal Canadian Pancake House** at 180 Third Ave., at 17th Street (☎ **212/777-9288**); and a handy **Chirping Chicken** at 377 First Ave., between 22nd and 23rd streets (☎ **212/529-4211**).

8 Greenwich Village

EXPENSIVE

Asti

13 E. 12th St. (near Fifth Ave.). ☎ **212/741-9105.** Booster seats. Reservations recommended. Main courses $18–$32. AE, CB, DC, DISC, MC, V. Tues–Thurs and Sun 5:30pm–12:30am, Fri–Sat 5:30pm–1am. Subway: L/N/R/4/5/6 to Union Sq. ITALIAN.

Singing waiters! Hokey it may sound, but since 1925 music's been flowing down here along with traditional red-sauce Italian food, and it's still infectiously fun. Even if your kids are more into rock than opera, they're likely to get caught up in the genial, goofy sing-along show. With all that vocalizing, however, the service staff isn't always able to hustle diners in and out promptly, so don't expect to get out in a hurry.

MODERATE

Arturo's Restaurant-Pizzeria

106 W. Houston St. (at Thompson St.). ☎ **212/677-3820.** Booster seats. No reservations on weekends. Pizzas $10 and up; main courses $8–$22. AE, DC, MC, V. Mon–Thurs 4pm–1am, Fri–Sat 4pm–2am, Sun 3pm–midnight. Subway: 1/9 to Houston St. ITALIAN/PIZZA.

Crowded, dimly lit, and busy, this vintage hangout right on the border between the Village and SoHo—near the Italian part of the West Village, around Father Demo Square—serves some very good thin-crust pizzas; they're slung on your table fresh from a coal-fired oven, so hot the mozzarella could burn the roof of your mouth. You can get various pasta dishes too (go for the baked stuff like ziti and lasagne) or even surf 'n' turf, though that seems a bit beside the point here: Pizzas are the thing to order. Several notches above storefront by-the-slice pizzerias, it's still a casual sort of place where drinks come in plastic tumblers and side salads come in plastic fake-wood bowls, which bodes well if you've got kids in tow. You may have to wait in line, though, and at particularly frantic meal times it can be hard to get your waiter's attention. There's live jazz every night, which may make waiting easier.

Downtown Dining

Angelo's of Mulberry Street ㊾

Anglers & Writers ⑭

Arturo's Restaurant-Pizzeria ⑯

Asti ㉑

Bayamo ㊲

Bendix Diner ㉗

Benny's Burritos
  Greenwich Ave. ②
  Avenue A ㉟

Bleecker Street Pastry Shop ⑫

Bodega ⑲

Bubby's ⑱

Caffè Roma ㊼

Cloister Café ㉜

Corner Bistro ①

Cowgirl Hall of Fame ⑧

Dallas BBQ
  Second Ave. ㉛
  University Place ㉝

De Robertis Pasticceria ㉙

EJ's Luncheonette ⑤

Elephant & Castle ③

Ellen's Café & Bake Shop ㊻

El Teddy's ㊼

Famous Ray's Pizza ④

Fanelli's Café ㊸

Ferrara's ㊽

Fraunces Tavern ㉒

Houlihan's
  Broadway ㊻
  Broad St. ㊾
  Hanover Square ⑥⓪
  Water St. ⑥①

HSF ㊱

Internet Café ㊴

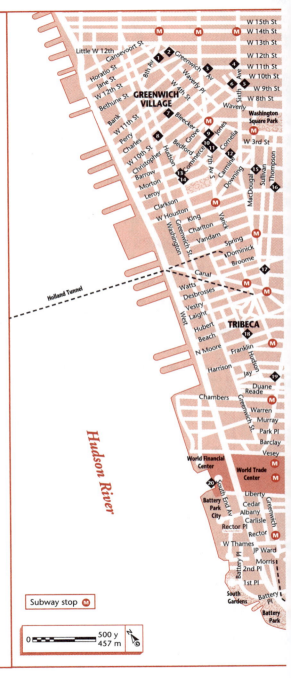

NA-0369

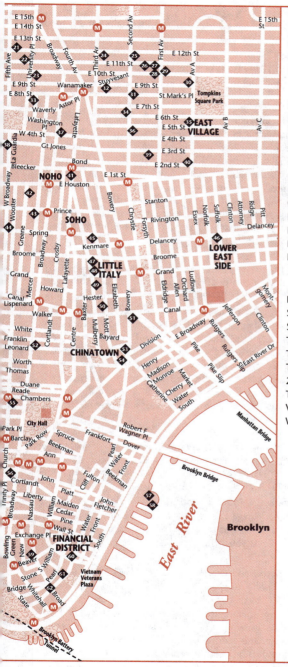

Jekyll & Hyde Pub 9
John's Pizzeria 11
Kelley & Ping 42
Kiev 34
Lemongrass Grill
  Barrow St. 10
  University Pl. 22
Lombardi's Pizza 45
Mary Ann's 36
Moondance Diner 17
Moondog
  Bleecker St. 7
  Avenue A 30
New York Noodletown 53
NoHo Star 41
Patsy's Pizzeria 23
Pier 17 food court 58
Pipeline 20
Pizza Box 15
Pizzeria Uno
  Sixth Ave. 6
  Third Ave. 24
  South Street Seaport 57
Ratner's 46
Sassy's Sliders 28
Second Avenue Deli 25
Tennessee Mountain 44
The Treehouse 13
Tsunami 38
20 Mott Street 54
Two Boots 40
Veniero's 26
Wong Kee 50

215

Arturo's is certainly as authentic as any place officially in Little Italy—and a good deal less touristy.

⭐ Bayamo

704 Broadway (near 4th St.). ☎ **212/475-5151.** High chairs, boosters. Reservations recommended on weekends. Main courses $3.95–$16.95. AE, CB, DC, MC, V. Sun–Thurs noon–midnight, Fri–Sat noon–1am. Subway: N/R to 8th St.; 6 to Astor Place; B/D/F/Q to Broadway/Lafayette. CUBAN-CHINESE.

Students from nearby New York University subsist on Bayamo's hearty Cubano rice and beans. Caribbean spices perk up a number of stews, soups, and stir-fries, but there are plenty of more standard items like pizza and burgers for little ones who aren't into trying new tastes. The noise level in this high-ceilinged space guarantees your children won't disturb your fellow diners, and the festive decor—especially the immense paper dragon that snakes over the room—lends a spirit of Carnival; things get kinda raucous on weekend nights and on Tuesdays and Thursdays when there's live music on tap. The friendly, accommodating staff always seem ready to make allowances for youngsters, but you're better off dining early, before the college crowd crowds in.

Cowgirl Hall of Fame

519 Hudson St. (at 10th St.). ☎ **212/633-1133.** Kids' menu, high chairs, boosters. Reservations recommended on weekends. Main courses $7.95–$16.95; kids' menu $3.50–$4.50. AE, MC, V. Daily noon–11pm. Subway: 1/9 to Christopher St. TEX-MEX.

Think the Old West motif of this West Village theme spot is corny? You're darn tootin' it's corny, and that's why kids get into it. Cowboy hats, boots, and lassos adorn the walls; steer horns poke from the mirrors and antlers from the chandeliers; younger customers are handed crayons to color a paper Indian headdress. Passable barbecue, hearty chili, and a mess of fried catfish are included in the menu round-up; kids' options feature some offbeat items such as corn dogs and cheese enchiladas along with the obligatory chicken fingers. The operation's a little too perky and slick for my tastes (this is part of a small national chain), but kids are easily taken in by all the kitsch.

EJ's Luncheonette

432 Sixth Ave. (between 9th and 10th sts.). ☎ **212/473-5555.** Kids' menu, high chairs, boosters. Reservations not accepted. Breakfast specials $5–$6.50; lunch specials $6–$8.50; dinner specials $8–$14.75. AE. Mon–Thurs 8am–11pm, Fri 8am–midnight, Sat 9am–midnight, Sun 9am–10:30pm. Subway: A/B/C/D/E/F/Q to West 4th St. AMERICAN DINER.

Yet another in this trio of popularissimo retro-1950s diners (see Upper West Side and Upper East Side, above), the Village EJ's follows the same drill: From French toast and flapjacks to meat loaf and mashed potatoes, it's the kind of comfort food your mom used to make (or the kind you wished she had).

Jekyll & Hyde Pub

91 Seventh Ave. South (between Barrow and Grove sts.). ☎ **212/989-7701.** Boosters. No reservations. Sandwiches $7.95–$10.95; main courses $8.95–$16.95. AE, DC, DISC, V. Sun–Thurs noon–2am, Fri–Sat noon–4am. Subway: 1/9 to Christopher St. ECLECTIC.

The original outpost of this horror-themed restaurant, the Village's Jekyll & Hyde is slightly more casual than the Midtown spot (above), in a dining room that opens right onto Seventh Avenue South, and waiting in line is less of a factor here. The menu is slightly different but still features a fairly standard range of burgers, salads, pizza, pasta, and steaks, gussied up with hokey names. And there's a whole new repertoire of spooky special effects, with an ongoing floor show that definitely goes for corny punch lines. Boasting an extensive range of international beers, plus exotic drinking vessels to quaff your brew from, Jekyll & Hyde shoots for an adult crowd, which is all the more reason why teenagers and adolescents think it's cool. This place falls somewhere between Disney World and Madame Tussaud's on the entertainment spectrum; if that's up your kid's alley, you could all have a ball—so long as you don't expect the food to be any good.

✪ NoHo Star

330 Lafayette St. (at Bleecker St.). ☎ **212/925-0070.** Boosters. Reservations not accepted. Main courses $7–$18. AE, DC, DISC, MC, V. Mon–Fri 8am–midnight, Sat–Sun 10:30am–midnight. Subway: 6 to Bleecker St. AMERICAN/CHINESE.

Just a block above Houston Street, this airy loftlike space has a very SoHo-ish feel, with brightly painted columns and an arty tile mural of a newspaper (the fictional *NoHo Star*). Burgers, pastas, and very good omelets are winners for lunch and brunch; the dinner menu goes upscale with items like steak au poivre, lamb chop, a top-drawer Caesar salad, and a range of superb, zestfully spiced Chinese dishes. The best time to come, though, is at breakfast, when it's quiet and never crowded—kids can dive into a stack of pancakes while parents nurse a cup of good coffee. The atmosphere is always relaxed and relaxing, and the waiters are totally friendly to kids.

The Treehouse

436 Hudson St. (between St. Luke's Place and Morton St.). ☎ **212/989-1471.** High chairs, boosters. Reservations recommended. Main courses $8–$16.95 at lunch, $9–$22 at dinner; brunch $9.50. AE, MC, V. Mon–Thurs noon–3pm and 5:30–11pm, Fri noon–3pm and 5:30–11:30pm, Sat 11am–4pm and 5:30–11:30pm, Sun 10am–4pm and 5:30–10pm. Subway: 1/9 to Christopher St. or Houston St. AMERICAN/CONTINENTAL/ECLECTIC.

With tree branches growing in through the windows, this country-charming restaurant in the far West Village seems miles away from Manhattan, and its kid-friendly attitude is decidedly un-urban too. Though there's no specific kids' menu, the kitchen is happy to improvise to suit a child's tastes—buttered pasta, perhaps, or a small portion of fish; the thick homemade fries could be a meal in themselves. At weekend brunches, children join in a cookie baking session and happily run around while their parents enjoy the prix-fixe menu. The menu ranges widely, with several French dishes among the American favorites: burgers, steaks, seafood, soups, and salads.

Tsunami

70 W. 3rd St. (between La Guardia and Thompson sts.). ☎ **212/475-7770.** Boosters. Reservations not accepted. Main courses $1.50 (piece of sushi)–$15 (entree). AE, CB, DC, MC, V. Daily 11:30am–11:30pm. Subway: A/B/C/D/E/F to W. 4th St. JAPANESE.

The name means "tidal wave," the reference presumably being to the fact that this serene sushi restaurant has an actual water canal encircling the central sushi bar. The sushi chefs set little dishes of sushi on the small boats, which drift around the oval; if you see something you like, just lift the plate off the boat. On leaving, your bill is totaled according to the colors of the various plates you've taken. It's a charming gimmick that always fascinates my kids, even though they'd rather watch than dare to eat sushi. Luckily, the menu also offers other Japanese standards like steak teriyaki, grilled chicken, soba noodles, a hearty ramen soup, and a particularly fluffy and golden shrimp tempura, and you can order these even if you're sitting canalside at the sushi counter. The staff tends to be very sweet with youngsters, though the zen-like mood doesn't really suit a rambunctious toddler.

INEXPENSIVE

Benny's Burritos

113 Greenwich Ave. (at Jane St.). ☎ **212/727-0584.** Boosters. Reservations not accepted. Main courses $5–$9.75. No credit cards. Sun–Thurs 11:30am–midnight, Fri–Sat 11:30am–1am. Subway: 1/2/3/9 to 14th St. MEXICAN.

Casual, cheap, and often crowded, Benny's is the kind of little Village joint everyone drifts into sooner or later. (If you can't get a table, hit the take-out shop across the street at 112 Greenwich.) Though there's no kids' menu per se, you can order several items on the regular menu in smaller portions—which is a relief, when you see how gargantuan the burritos here can be.

The Corner Bistro

331 W. 4th St. (at Jane St. and Eighth Ave.). ☎ **212/242-9502.** Reservations not accepted. Main courses $4–$5.25. No credit cards. Daily 11:30am–4am. Subway: A/C/E/1/2/3/9 to 14th St. BURGERS.

Here are your choices: hamburger, cheeseburger, bacon cheeseburger, or chicken sandwich. No doubt about it, this place is a bar, and a dark and smoky one at that, the kind where people huddle in wooden booths and initials have been carved into the tabletops. Which is precisely why some kids will think it's totally cool to come here; others will simply dig into the thick, juicy burgers and piles of fine fries. And if that weren't enough, there's a pretty darn good jukebox. Though the Corner Bistro can get full of drinkers later in the night, at midday or in the early evening it's wonderfully mellow and kids aren't out of place.

Elephant and Castle

68 Greenwich Ave. (at 11th St.). ☎ **212/243-1400.** Booster seats. Reservations not accepted. Main courses $6–$10.75. AE, DC, MC, V. Mon–Fri 8:30am–midnight, Sat–Sun 10am–midnight. Subway: 1/2/3/9 to 14th St. AMERICAN.

Like a holdover from the 1970s, this mellow-eats parlor continues to churn out good burgers and crêpes and fluffy omelets and other stuff kids will generally accept. A cheery, well-lit space, it's best for leisurely brunches; bring a few toys for your offspring and a copy of the Sunday *Times* for you to browse through. Though it isn't inherently child-oriented, E & C is informal and friendly enough that families blend right in.

Famous Ray's Pizza of Greenwich Village

465 Sixth Ave. (at 11th St.). ☎ **212/243-2253.** Reservations not accepted. Pizzas 1.75 (slice)–$13.50 (pie). AE, DC, DISC, MC, V. Daily 11am–3am. Subway: F to 14th St.; A/B/C/D/E/F/Q to W. 4th St. PIZZA.

Definitely the most renowned corner pizzeria in town is Famous Ray's—the Ray's that all those other ersatz Ray's Pizzas around town are hoping you'll confuse them with. Set right in the midst of the Village's prettiest town-house streets, Ray's is easy to spot by the lines snaking out onto the sidewalk, with all sorts of people hungry for a slice to go. A wait is nearly inevitable, but the line moves quickly. Many pizza lovers rave about the extra-cheese pizza here; I find it a bit excessive, but I do like the plain pizza's chewy crust and tangy sauce.

✪ John's Pizza

278 Bleecker St. (near Jones St.). ☎ **212/243-1680.** Reservations recommended for parties of 10 or more. Pizzas $8–$17. No credit cards. Sun–Thurs 11:30am–11:30pm, Fri–Sat noon–12:30am. Subway: 1/9 to Christopher St. PIZZA.

This is the kind of place that's often described as having no ambience, when in fact it has plenty: classic no-frills pizzeria ambience with harsh lighting and bare-topped tables and an open view of the brick ovens where the pizzas are baked. Folks in the Village are always lamenting that John's doesn't sell pizza by the slice, but families should have no problem polishing off a whole pie. The crust is crunchy thin, with savory tomato sauce, bubbly melted mozzarella, and a host of fresh toppings to pick from (nothing too trendy, though). After eating at John's, you can say you've truly sampled New York pizza at its best.

Patsy's Pizzeria

67 University Pl. (between 10th and 11th sts.). ☎ **212/533-3500.** High chairs, boosters. Reservations not accepted. Pizzas $10.95–$12.95; pasta $7–$16. No credit cards. Sun–Thurs noon–11pm, Fri–Sat noon–midnight. Subway: N/R to 8th St.; 4/5/6/L/N/R to Union Sq. PIZZA.

On this restaurant strip just north of the New York University campus, this branch of the Patsy's chain finally gives Village pizza lovers a good alternative if their legs are too tired to walk west to the original John's Pizza on Bleecker Street (above). Classic pizzeria look and an informal atmosphere that works great with kids.

Pizza Box

176 Bleecker St. (between MacDougal and Sullivan sts.). ☎ **212/979-0823.** Reservations not accepted. Pizza $1.50 (slice)–$15 (pie). No credit cards. Daily 11am–midnight. Subway: A/B/C/D/E/F/Q to W. 4th St. PIZZA.

The hippie-like scruffiness of this stretch of Bleecker Street reminds you that you're close to a major university campus (NYU), but among the cheap ethnic hole-in-the-walls lies this pleasant and unpretentious pizza spot, worth noting for its restful back garden, open in fair weather. The pizza is perfectly fine, though connoisseurs may want to head west to John's (above). Pizza Box's advantage is that you don't have to buy a whole pie, as you do at John's, and it has waiter service at tables, unlike Famous Ray's (above). If you've O.D.'ed on pizza but your child is clamoring for it, you can indulge him here while you go for pasta or a hero and enjoy the garden.

AFTERNOON TEA

Anglers and Writers

420 Hudson St. (at St. Luke's Place). ☎ **212/675-0810.** Reservations recommended for parties of 5 or more. Main courses $7–$13.50. No credit cards. Mon–Thurs 9am–11pm, Fri–Sat 9am–midnight, Sun 10am–10pm. Subway: 1/9 to Houston St. AMERICAN.

In a large, airy corner storefront, this relaxed and civilized restaurant seems like a Merchant-Ivory cast-off, with shelves of worn books for browsing, fishing gear hung on the walls, and mismatched china—just like my Aunt Hazel's Adirondack cottage. The problem is, all that West Village serenity is geared to literary adult tastes and the long lines for brunches virtually rule it out for families. Weekdays at tea time is the time to go, perhaps as a treat for a 7-year-old daughter; the pastries, while pricey, are wonderfully flaky.

ICE CREAM & SWEETS

Bleecker Street Pastry Shop

235 Bleecker St. (between Carmine and Cornelia sts.). ☎ **212/242-4959.** Sun–Thurs 7:30am–10pm, Fri–Sat 7:30am–midnight. Subway: A/B/C/D/E/F/Q to W. 4th St. BAKERY.

The West Village has a number of charming small bakeries, authentic French, Italian, and bohemian—whatever. This one's the sweetest when it comes to serving kids. Located on a stretch of Bleecker between Sixth and Seventh avenues that's loaded with Italian food shops, from Faicco's Pork to Rocco's Pastries, the Bleecker Street Pastry Shop has no pretensions to authentic atmosphere, just simple wooden booths and small tables where neighborhood people take a load off for half an hour. On your way in you'll pass glass display cases bursting with cookies and cakes and luscious layered pastries; pick what you'd like and it'll be brought to your table, along with your drink of choice. In winter, kids will really appreciate the wonderfully sweet hot chocolate.

Moondog Ice Cream

378 Bleecker St. (between Perry and Charles sts.). ☎ **212/675-4540.** No credit cards. Daily noon–midnight. Subway: 1/9 to Christopher St. ICE CREAM.

With all the casual charm of a college-town ice-cream parlor, Moondog fits nicely into this quieter part of the Village west of Sheridan Square. The handmade ice-cream is rich and smooth, the array of baked goods tempting. Stop in here after a visit to Tootsie's Children's Books (see chapter 6), then stroll up to the Bleecker Street Playground (see chapter 5) to lick your cones and pore over your new picture books.

THE CHAIN GANG

There are two **Lemongrass Grills** in the Village, one at 37 Barrow St., at Seventh Avenue South (☎ **212/242-0606**), and another at 80 University Place, at 11th Street (☎ **212/604-9870**). The **Dallas BBQ** down the street at 21 University Place, at 8th Street (☎ **212/674-4450**), caters largely to a budget-conscious NYU student crowd. The first **Pizzeria Uno** branch in the city was the bustling one at 391 Sixth Ave., at 8th Street (☎ **212/242-5230**).

9 The East Village

MODERATE

The Cloister Cafe

238 E. 9th St. (between Second and Third aves.) ☎ **212/777-9128.** Reservations accepted only for parties of 6 or more. Main courses $3.95–$12.95. No credit cards. Daily 11am–2am. Subway: 6 to Astor Place. CONTINENTAL.

The main reason to come here (the only reason, really) is for the courtyard garden, with umbrella-shaded tables set out on crooked paving stones and a tiny fountain trying its best to gurgle. The menu's rather predictable fare runs a tired range from salads (the avocado salad isn't bad) to pastas (lasagne, cheese ravioli, linguine with clam sauce) to veal, chicken, and seafood dishes (grilled red snapper, shrimp scampi). The lemonade is refreshingly sour; kids may want to add their own sugar. Service can be slapdash at times, but the garden is a treat, day or night, and things are plenty casual enough to come here with kids.

Second Avenue Deli

156 Second Ave. (at 10th St.). ☎ **212/677-0606.** Main courses $10.95–$16.95. AE, DC, DISC, MC, V. Sun–Thurs 7am–midnight, Fri–Sat 7am–3am. Subway: 6 to Astor Place. DELI/KOSHER.

Once upon a time, Second Avenue was the Yiddish equivalent of Broadway (look for the brass stars embedded in the sidewalk outside the restaurant, commemorating great stars of the Yiddish theater). Though the old theaters down the street have been taken over by hip Off Off Broadway productions, this great kosher deli survives. It may look like just an ordinary coffee shop, but the food is flavorful and authentic, served in generous portions—you haven't tasted chopped liver till you've tried it here, and the chicken soup with matzoh balls can cure more than the common cold. There's plenty on the menu to satisfy plain-eatin' kids, including bagels and omelets and sandwiches stuffed fat with cold cuts. The waiters are famously grumpy; don't worry that your kids are annoying them—they treat everybody that way. Go figure.

INEXPENSIVE

Bendix Diner

167 First Ave. (between 10th and 11th sts.). ☎ **212/260-4220.** High chairs, boosters. Reservations recommended. Main courses $6.95–$12.95. AE, MC, V. Sun–Thurs 8am–11pm, Fri–Sat 8am–midnight. Subway: 6 to Astor Place; L to First Ave. AMERICAN DINER/THAI.

An East Village branch of the popular Chelsea hangout (above), Bendix combines diner classics like burgers and tuna melts with some delicious Thai dishes and yet never seems schizophrenic. Breakfast is served all day, which suits my kids just fine. Weekends can be busy; service is fast but sometimes sloppy.

Benny's Burritos

93 Avenue A (at E. 6th St.). ☎ **212/254-2054.** Booster seats. Reservations not accepted. Main courses $5–$9.50. No credit cards. Sun–Thurs 11am–midnight, Fri–Sat 11am–1am. Subway: 6 to Astor Place. MEXICAN.

Monster-sized burritos and other hearty, healthy Mexican fare are dished up at this East Village branch of the West Village Benny's (above).

✪ Internet Cafe

82 E. 3rd St. (between First and Second aves.). ☎ **212/614-0747.** Reservations not accepted. Sandwiches and salads $5–$8. MC, V. Daily 11am–2am. Subway: 6 to Bleecker St.; F to Second Ave. AMERICAN.

This long, narrow, zenlike space decorated in deep, bold colors invites computer users to linger over the PCs, sustaining themselves with casual low-priced food, designer coffees, and microbrews. The front of the restaurant doubles as an art gallery, with changing shows. Though the software on hand isn't heavy on kids' titles, they do have a few games available, and the place is surprisingly child-friendly, welcoming everyone from infants snoozing in Perego strollers to teenage Net surfers. (When I asked if they had booster seats, the laughing reply was, "No, but we've got the world's largest collection of phone books."). And a big plus: There's a back courtyard open in good weather.

Kiev

117 Second Ave. (at 7th St.). ☎ **212/674-4040.** High chairs. Sandwiches $2.25–$5.95; main courses $3.95–$11.50. No credit cards. Daily 24 hours. Subway: 6 to Astor Place. AMERICAN DINER/UKRAINIAN.

Prowl around the East village and you'll find, beneath the hipster surface, a neighborhood that's still the heart of New York's Ukrainian immigrant community (particularly along 7th Street between Second and Third avenues). Of the handful of restaurants hereabouts catering to that clientele, Kiev is the most accessible and family-friendly. It carries off a balancing act between the old and new East Villages, serving omelets as well as perogies (dumplings filled with potatoes or cheese), burgers as well as feather-light blintzes and robust borscht, in a modern coffee-shop-like setting. Kiev's Eastern European specialties certainly taste wonderful, and it's an added pleasure to be able to sample them at a place where my kids can have omelets and fries too.

Kosher Restaurants

Even if you don't maintain a kosher diet, New York offers the best kosher dining for families outside of Israel. The important thing to remember is that a kosher restaurant will either be meat, dairy, or parve (parve means the food doesn't contain either meat or dairy products)—you won't find a cheeseburger or chicken parmigiana on any menu unless either the meat or the cheese is really an imitated product. This may sound restricting, but restaurants have learned to make do and become extremely creative in the process.

Joseph's Cafe, 50 W. 72nd St., between Central Park West and Columbus Avenue (☎ **212/595-5004;** dairy), for example, has created such delicacies as imitation pepperoni to top the pizzas and other fake meat products for the Mexican and Italian dishes. The menu is eclectic, ranging from salads to veggie burgers, pizzas, and pastas. If you don't need to go the parve route, **China Shalom,** 686 Columbus Ave., between 93rd and 94th streets (☎ **212/662-9676;** meat), offers pretty usual Chinese fare at pretty steep prices, but the service staff is accommodating to families—there's even a kids' menu, with egg rolls, spare ribs, fried chicken nuggets, and french fries.

A trip to **Ratner's,** 138 Delancey St., between Norfolk and Suffolk streets (☎ **212/677-5588;** dairy), is like visiting a Catskills resort in the 1950s: Plastic-covered booths and hideous wallpaper may be an eyesore to some, but many make the trip to the Lower East Side just for Ratner's ambience. The menu is pretty straightforward, but the potato pancakes and blintzes are specialties; in a pinch, kids can't go wrong with the spaghetti in tomato sauce.

In Midtown, **Kosher Delight,** 1365 Broadway, at 36th Street (☎ **212/ 563-3366;** meat), and 1156 Sixth Ave., at 45th Street (☎ **212/869-6699;** meat),

Sassy's Sliders

163 First Ave. (at 10th St.). ☎ **212/228-2900.** Reservations not accepted. Sandwiches 89¢–$1.89. No credit cards. Sun–Thurs 11am–11pm, Fri–Sat 11am–1am. Subway: 6 to Astor Place. BURGERS.

The decor is very 1950s—wall tiles, Formica tables, and linoleum, all in Fiestaware colors—and so is the fast-food concept: 2-inch hamburgers steamed with onions, so small and moist they slide whole down your throat, hence the name "sliders." I've personally been addicted to them ever since I was a kid going to White Castle, and I've turned my older son into a fan as well. But Sassy's Sliders are much better than White Castle's, and with other choices like grilled chicken, ground turkey, or veggie burgers as well (not to mention a small Philly cheese steak), this nifty little spot should satisfy everyone in the family. The slider is a perfect-sized burger for a kid anyway, and at these incredibly low prices, you may be able to feed the whole gang for $20. Most of its business is takeout and delivery, but there are a few tables inside; or pick up a sack of sliders and stroll over to Tompkins Square Park to eat them alfresco.

✪ Two Boots

37 Avenue A (at 2nd St.). ☎ **212/505-2276.** Kids' menu, high chairs, boosters. Reservations accepted only for parties of 6 or more. Main courses $6.95–$9.95; pizzas $5.50–$20.95; kids' menu $3.95–$5.50. AE, DISC, MC, V. Mon–Fri 5pm–midnight, Sat–Sun noon–midnight. Subway: F to Second Ave. CAJUN/ITALIAN/PIZZA.

is the kosher answer to McDonald's and Burger King. Grilled burgers and chicken sandwiches are standard, but you can also chose from a small Chinese menu and Middle Eastern specialties like falafel. Kosher Delight also has free delivery to any location in Manhattan (it's not guaranteed your food will arrive hot or within a reasonable amount of time). **The Great American Health Bar,** 821 Third Ave., between 50th and 51st streets (☎ **212/758-0883;** dairy), and 35 W. 57th St., between Fifth and Sixth avenues (☎ **212/355-5177;** dairy), proves that healthy food doesn't have to be boring and tasteless, offering a varied menu from salads to vegetarian chili to pastas. There are wonderful fresh fruit health shakes blended with milk and yogurt, and kids may get a kick out of the pita pizza—tomato sauce, melted cheese, and vegetables baked on top of pita bread. Unlike most of these restaurants, the Health Bar also serves breakfast, opening at 8am; it's also the only one of these restaurants that doesn't close Friday night and Saturday for the Sabbath.

Finally, the West Side's popular **Dougie's BBQ and Grill,** 222 W. 72nd St., between Broadway and West End Avenue (☎ **212/724-2222;** meat), offers crayons on all tables to keep kids occupied while they're waiting for their food. The service is fast paced and friendly. Burgers and hot dogs are popular items, but the ribs and pasta dishes shouldn't be passed up.

Note: Because of the Sabbath, most kosher restaurants vary their hours on Friday and Saturday, depending on when sundown is on Friday night and when the Sabbath ends on Saturday night. (Some simply close all day Friday.) Call ahead to be sure when they'll be open if you plan to dine on Friday or Saturday.

—by Jennifer Lebin

This dandy East Village restaurant couldn't be better for kids. To start, you've got this witty junk-shop decor (strings of Christmas lights shaped like red chiles, old movie posters, a pair of cowboys boots hanging on pink walls); then when you're seated, the kids get whole coloring books to scribble in, though you don't get to take them with you. You know these people are used to dealing with kids when you see that the milk is served in plastic cups; grown-ups get their drinks in glass mugs shaped like boots, which our boys find hilarious. The service can be pretty casual, but the waitresses relate to kids instantly, which always seems to make my children behave better. The kids' menu has a little originality: mini-raviolis, spaghetti, chicken fingers, fish sticks, or a Pizza Face, a kid-size individual pizza with vegetables arranged to form eyes, nose, and grin. My boys, who normally refuse any toppings at all, adore Pizza Faces. Bigger pizzas are served on cake stands, which is also kind of a kick. I opt for a spicy Cajun sandwich on good chewy bread—the kind of food I can't normally get in the kinds of restaurants my kids like. We all walk out with smiles on our faces. Two Boots is expecting to open a branch in Midtown, on the lower level of Grand Central Station, in late 1998.

Take-out locations: 36 Avenue A, at 2nd Street (☎ **212/505-5450**); 74 Bleecker St., between Broadway and Crosby Street (☎ **212/777-1033**); 75 Greenwich Ave., between Seventh Avenue and 11th Street (☎ **212/633-9096**).

ICE CREAM & SWEETS

DeRobertis Pasticceria

176 First Ave. (between 10th and 11th sts.). ☎ **212/674-7137.** AE, MC, V. Tues–Thurs 9–11pm, Fri–Sun 9am–midnight. Subway: 6 to Astor Place; 4/5/6/L/N/R to Union Sq. BAKERY.

Smaller and not as commercially successful as Veniero's (below), DeRobertis, run by four generations of the DeRobertis family since 1904, still gives its around-the-corner neighbor a run for its money in the realm of Italian pastries: creamy cannolis, anise cookies, fruit tarts, cheesecake. A more relaxed local crowd drifts in here to skip the line at Veniero's. The back room, with its pressed-tin ceiling and small marble tables, feels as authentic as any place in Little Italy.

Moondog Ice Cream

147 Avenue A (between 9th and 10th sts.). ☎ **212/328-0167.** No credit cards. Daily noon–midnight. Subway: 6 to Astor Place. ICE CREAM.

Laid-back Moondog has none of the typical East Village grunge or attitude: The stencilled walls, painted wood, and ceiling fans are a welcome break from Avenue A. The ice cream is creamy and homemade, with free sprinkles on a $1.50 kids' cone; luscious fruit pies, muffins, shakes, and smoothies are also available. A great place to stop in after Two Boots (above) or after a frolic in Tompkins Square playgrounds across the street.

Veniero's

342 E. 11th St. (between Second and First aves.). ☎ **212/674-7264.** AE, DISC, MC, V. Daily 8am–midnight. Subway: 6 to Astor Place; 4/5/6/L/N/R to Union Sq. BAKERY.

This spiffed-up dessert cafe often has a line waiting outside in the evenings, full of people craving after-dinner delights from cakes to cookies to cannolis, plus cappuccino and espresso that put Starbucks to shame. I know many New Yorkers who judge this city's best Italian pastry shop, in or out of Little Italy. With kids, though, your best bet is to come in the afternoon, when you'll have no trouble getting a table.

THE CHAIN GANG

Beatniks must be turning in their graves to see St. Mark's Place, that bastion of bohemian hipness, invaded by **Dallas BBQ** at 132 Second Ave. (☎ **212/777-5574**). Next thing you know, **Pizzeria Uno** will be moving in around the corner . . . oops, it already has, at 55 Third Ave., between 10th and 11th streets (☎ **212/995-9668**). There's also a suitably laid-back **Mary Ann's,** 86 Second Ave., at 5th Street (☎ **212/475-5939**), serving authentic Mexican food and many margaritas to latter-day beatniks.

10 SoHo

MODERATE

Kelley & Ping

127 Greene St. (between Houston and Prince sts.). ☎ **212/228-1212.** High chairs. Reservations not accepted. Main courses $3.95–$7.50 at lunch, $5.25–$16.95 at dinner. AE, MC, V. Daily 11:30am–5pm and 6pm–11pm. Subway: N/R to Prince St. JAPANESE/PAN-ASIAN.

With its pressed-tin ceiling and wooden factory floor, Kelley & Ping looks very SoHo, but its friendliness to kids is unusual in this hyper-urban-chic neighborhood. It started out as an Asian grocery store but soon added an open kitchen in the center of the room; there are still stocks of bottled sauces and woks for sale along the walls. The noodles, stir fries, and grilled meats (Vietnamese pork chops, chicken satay) go down well with children, though some dishes can be super-spicy—ask for your waiter's guidance. Unlike many Asian restaurants, this one does have milk for kids to drink; for dessert, try the fried bananas or the red-bean ice cream.

Tennessee Mountain

143 Spring St. (at Wooster St.). ☎ **212/431-3993.** Kids' menu, sassy seats, boosters. Reservations recommended. Main courses $7–$18.50; kids' menu $3.95–$4.95. AE, CB, DC, DISC, MC, V. Mon–Wed 11:30am–11pm, Thurs–Sat 11:30am–midnight, Sun 11:30am–10pm (later on holiday weekends). Subway: N/R to Prince St.; C to Spring St. AMERICAN/BARBECUE.

The setting is a farmhouse dating from 1807 (back when this part of town was country, long before all the cast-iron architecture went up), which from the outside looks very historic and sedate. Inside, though, the exposed brick walls and simple wooden tables host casual crowds looking for Southern barbecue, served with sides of yams, fries, coleslaw, and whatever. Rib purists, who can be a very critical crowd, tell me this isn't the world's best barbecue, but it seemed plenty tasty to me—what do I know? If barbecue isn't your thing, there's also chili and plenty of blander choices like quiches, salads, and seafood. The kids' menu covers a good range with BLTs and tuna salad sandwiches as well as the usual burgers, chicken fingers, and ribs; they do give kids crayons and a white paper chef's hat, which helps buy parents time to chow down.

INEXPENSIVE

Fanelli's

94 Prince St. (at Mercer St.). ☎ **212/226-9412.** Reservations not accepted. Main courses $7–$12. AE, MC, V. Mon–Thurs 10am–2am, Fri–Sat 10am–4am, Sun 11am–2am. Subway: N/R to Prince St. AMERICAN.

This 19th-century saloon claims to be the second-oldest drinking spot in the city, being descended from a grocery store that opened on this site in 1847 and soon had a good side-business as a "porter shop" (saloon); it became a speakeasy after Michael Fanelli bought it in 1922. Atmospheric Fanelli's still has the requisite carved mahogany bar, pressed-tin ceilings, beery smell, and filtered light, but the fare is refreshingly simple pub grub—burgers, omelets, quiches, pastas, fried chicken, shepherd's pie. Families gravitate to the back room, which is a little sunnier and quieter, for casual lunches and early dinner; later on it may be hard to compete with the drinking scene. The service is friendly and laissez-faire. If the trendy SoHo scene gets you down, retreat here.

Moondance

80 Sixth Ave. (at Grand St.). ☎ **212/226-1191.** Booster seats. Reservations not accepted. Salads and sandwiches $3–$10.95; main courses $6.95–$13.95. AE, DC, MC, V. Mon–Wed 8:30am–midnight, Thurs 8:30am–Sun midnight. Subway: C/E to Spring St. AMERICAN DINER.

Stranded on the western edge of SoHo, where Holland Tunnel traffic tends to back up, this nifty little diner—shiny with aluminum panels inside and out—is a hoot for kids who want to feel plugged into the Downtown buzz. Like the SoHo art world, the menu's a tad schizophrenic, offering burgers and chili dogs as well as health-foody grilled vegetables and whole-wheat fusilli pasta and pesto scrambled eggs; those 1990s comfort-food standbys, meatloaf and mashed potatoes, are thrown in for good measure. The wide range of pancakes, waffles, and French toast served at all times makes my kids happy. Stick to the simpler stuff if you know what's good for you. There's only a handful of tables, plus a few stools at the counter, but you'll rarely have to wait to be seated in daytime or early evening; the real scene happens late at night. Even at breakfast and lunch you'll still spot plenty of rumpled arty types dressed in black.

11 Little Italy

MODERATE

Angelo's of Mulberry Street

146 Mulberry St. (between Grand and Hester sts.). ☎ **212/966-1277.** High chairs. Reservations recommended. Main courses $12–$17. AE, CB, DC, MC, V. Tues–Thurs and Sun noon–11:30pm, Fri noon–12:30am, Sat noon–1am. Subway: 6/N/R to Canal St. ITALIAN.

This crowded, crowd-pleasing Little Italy favorite, which has been around since 1902, turns out an incredibly long list of southern Italian pasta dishes with zestful flavor, all at around $12.50. Make a reservation so you won't get stuck in the line of tourists waiting to get in, but don't be dissuaded by the place's low-brow popularity—this is Little Italy, after all, where tourists flock to eat, and no restaurant here that's any good would be without a line. Order anything with garlic, anything with tomato sauce. If your kids like their pasta plain, as mine do, even they'll benefit from the fresh homemade quality of the food.

INEXPENSIVE

Lombardi's Pizza

32 Spring St. (between Mott and Mulberry sts.). ☎ **212/941-7994.** Boosters. Reservations accepted only for parties of 6 or more. Pizzas $10.50–$20 (feed 2 or more). No credit cards. Mon–Thurs 11:30am–11pm, Fri–Sat 11:30am–midnight, Sun 11:30am–10pm. Subway: 6 to Spring St. PIZZA.

Claiming to be a resurrection of New York's first pizza restaurant, which opened at 53 Spring St. in 1905—and where all the other pizza maestros learned their trade—the new Lombardi's is owned by a grandson of the original Gennaro Lombardi, and it does have an authentic coal oven, taken over from an old bakery. It's a bit far north from the main Little Italy strip along Mulberry Street, in an area that many think of as SoHo these days, and the decor is still too sprucely new to look atmospheric, despite the obligatory red-checkered tablecloths, brick walls, and white tiled floor. Nevertheless, this brash newcomer has won over the skeptics with its wonderful pizzas, with lightly charred thin crusts and totally fresh ingredients. The clam pie is so good that it actually justifies the weird idea of putting seafood on a pizza. Don't expect to just pick up a slice: Sit your family down in a booth and apply yourselves to consuming a whole pie. Eat, already.

ICE CREAM & SWEETS

Caffè Roma

385 Broome St. (at Mulberry St.). ☎ **212/226-8413.** No credit cards. Daily 8am–midnight. Subway: 6 to Spring St.; B/D/Q to Grand St. BAKERY.

This old-fashioned corner pastry shop with hexagonal-tile floors and tiny wrought-iron cafe tables is a great place to duck into for cannoli, those ricotta-filled roll-ups of sweet crisp pastry. Kids can drink frothy hot chocolate or chilled lemonade while parents indulge in cappuccino or espresso, made the classic way (no half-caffè mocha double latte here).

Ferrara

195 Grand St. (between Mulberry and Mott sts.). ☎ **212/226-6150.** AE, DC, DISC, MC, V. Daily 8am–midnight. Subway: B/D/Q to Grand St. BAKERY.

Larger, cleaner, and brighter than Caffè Roma (above), Ferrara has display cases crowded with mouth-watering pastries to go or to stay. There's almost always a crowd, day or night. If your kids want to sample Italian gelato (ice cream), this is a good place for that too.

12 Chinatown

MODERATE

20 Mott Street

20 Mott St. (between Chatham Sq. and Pell St.). ☎ **212/964-0380.** Booster seats. Reservations recommended. Main courses $9–$35. AE, DISC, MC, V. Daily 9am–11pm. Subway: 6/N/R to Canal St. CHINESE.

Large, smart, and clean, this upscale Chinatown winner occupies several levels, and just about everything on the menu is done to authentic perfection. We prefer the downstairs room, where there's a huge fish tank to be mesmerized by (speculate on whether or not those are the fish that show up later on the seafood menu), but when it's crowded you may not have a choice. Come at lunchtime if you don't want to wait, and if you want the waiters (whose English isn't always good) to have time to help you make your choices.

INEXPENSIVE

HSF

46 Bowery (near Canal St.). ☎ **212/374-1319.** Boosters. Reservations recommended. Main courses $8.50–$11. AE, DC, DISC, MC, V. Daily 8am–midnight (dim sum 11:30am–5pm). Subway: 6/N/R to Canal St. CHINESE.

Dim sum is the reason to come here: The waiters wheel around carts of all kinds of delectable dumplings and skewers and rolls, while customers accept tiny dishes of whatever looks good to them. At the end of the meal, they count up your dishes and tell you how much you owe. You don't have to read a menu or communicate with the staff to choose yourself a meal full of wonderful surprises; in fact, you may never learn the name of certain mouth-watering dishes. Eating dim sum is a novel experience that can be loads of fun for older kids who are willing to blindly sample new foods, though no item is really that far from standard Chinese dishes. The only problem may be discovering how high a bill you've run up, taste-testing all those tempting morsels.

New York Noodletown

28½ Bowery (at Bayard St.). ☎ **212/349-0923.** Main courses $3.25–$14.95. No credit cards. Daily 9am–4am. Subway: 6/N/R to Canal St. CHINESE.

Noodles are one Chinese food that even picky-eater kids can often be persuaded to try, and the noodles in this bright, bustling Chinatown spot are delectable, simmered in broth or coated with various savory sauces; a wide range of menu choices mix 'n' match the noodles with grilled or roasted meats and stir-fried veggies. Be prepared to elbow your way in and endure hurried service; smaller kids may have to sit in your lap, as there are no boosters or high chairs.

Wong Kee

113 Mott St. (between Canal and Hester sts.). ☎ **212/966-1160.** Boosters. Reservations accepted only for parties of 5 or more. Main courses $5.95–$15.75. No credit cards. Daily 11am–9:45pm. Subway: 6/N/R to Canal St. CHINESE.

A consistently reliable choice, Wong Kee is contemporary looking (some might say sterile), but the Cantonese food is deeply authentic, the sauces sweet and pungent and the seafood ultra-fresh. The roast pork and noodle dishes are excellent, as are their steak specialties and Hong Shiu chicken, crisp-fried chicken slathered with Chinese vegetables. The waiters have a reputation for speed, which means they may rush you a bit, but at least you won't have to worry about your children getting restless because it's taking so long for their order to get to the table.

13 TriBeCa & Lower Manhattan

EXPENSIVE

Fraunces Tavern

54 Pearl St. (at Broad St.). ☎ **212/269-0144.** Reservations recommended. Main courses $8.95–$22.95. AE, CB, DC, DISC, MC, V. Mon–Fri 7am–9:30pm. Subway: 4/5 to Bowling Green. CONTINENTAL/AMERICAN.

Trading heavily on its historic value (an inn on this site was General Washington's residence in the final days of the Revolution, where he bade farewell to his troops), this redbrick Federal-style reconstruction combines a few upstairs rooms containing historic exhibits with an oak-paneled downstairs dining room, striving for antiquity with a fireplace and Colonial-style pewter plates. It serves largely a tourist trade, with unimaginative renderings of American classics: steaks, chops, and seafood. Still, considering the choices in this area—power-lunch hangouts, fast-food take-outs, and precious little in between (unless you like to drink your lunch)—Fraunces Tavern isn't a bad choice if you've got kids old enough to be awed by the idea that George Washington ate here, or at least hereabouts. The adjoining Tap Room is more clubby and casual, but also more of a bar scene, if that bothers you.

MODERATE

El Teddy's

219 Broadway (at Franklin St.). ☎ **212/941-7070.** Reservations recommended. Main courses $6–$19. AE, DC, MC, V. Mon–Fri noon–3pm and 6–11:30pm, Sat–Sun 6–11:30pm. Subway: 1/9 to Franklin St. MEXICAN.

The main draw here for kids is the campy Statue of Liberty crown projecting over the front entrance and the nutty mosaics over the walls inside; the atmosphere is decidedly Downtown and adult, with a spirited bar scene on weekend nights, so it's probably best for older kids. The Mexican food is perfectly fine, well executed if not adventurous. With TriBeCa getting more and more family-friendly, this may not be your first stop, but it could be a memorable meal for preteens.

Pipeline

2 World Financial Center, 225 Liberty St. (at South End Ave.). ☎ **212/945-2755.** High chairs, boosters. Reservations accepted for parties of 6 or more. Salads and sandwiches $8.25–$15.95; main courses $9.95–$17. AE, CB, DC, DISC, MC, V. Mon–Fri 11am–11pm, Sat–Sun 11am–10pm. Subway: A/C/E/N/R to World Trade Center. AMERICAN/ECLECTIC.

Whimsically designed to look like an oil refinery, with brightly painted ceiling pipes and galvanized steel chairs, Pipeline is a great option if you're down in Battery Park City, with outdoor seating right on the North Cove plaza facing the yacht basin— a great people- and sunset-watching spot. The food is casual and eclectic, borrowing tastes from all over America; the Mexican dishes are more successful than the Italian pastas, but there are also many dependable items like burgers and grilled chicken, and the French fries are superb. The T-shirted waiters have a breezy, friendly manner that sets everyone at ease.

INEXPENSIVE

Bodega

136 West Broadway (between Thomas and Duane sts.). ☎ **212/285-1155.** Kids' menu, high chairs, boosters. Reservations recommended. Main courses $5.50–$15; kids' menu $2.50–$4. AE, MC, V. Mon–Thurs 11am–midnight, Fri 11am–12:30am, Sat 9am–12:30am, Sun 9am– midnight. Subway: 1/9 to Franklin St.; A/C/1/2/3/9 to Chambers St. ECLECTIC.

The basic look is retro diner, with Latin-American overtones; the menu started out as American/Mexican but now samples many other Hispanic cuisines as well. The burgers, burritos, and quesadillas are good, as are more upscale items like grilled skirt steak and Cuban-style roast chicken. Informal and totally kid-friendly, Bodega allows parents to feel TriBeCa hip while their children loll happily on the Naugahyde banquettes. Weekend mornings are especially popular, with a breakfast menu served 9am to noon.

Bubby's

120 Hudson St. (at N. Moore St.). ☎ **212/219-0666.** Kids' menu, high chairs, boosters. Reservations recommended. Main courses $8–$10 at lunch, $10–$12 at dinner; kids' menu $3. AE, CB, DC, DISC, MC, V. Mon–Thurs 8am–11pm, Fri–Sat 8am–midnight, Sun 8am–10pm. Subway: 1/9 to Franklin St.; A/C/E to Canal St. AMERICAN.

Homey is the word for this comforting TriBeCa restaurant, with its wooden chairs, soft recorded jazz, and kitschy clutter. The food is comforting as well, with sandwiches, burgers, and pastas, not to mention breakfast food (served to 4pm—good to know if you've got kid who like scrambled eggs and French toast for lunch), with a few more upscale salads and chicken and fish dishes to please adults. It's the sort of place that understands that kids may like their spaghetti with butter and parmesan instead of tomato sauce and that cooked carrots go down better if you drizzle maple dressing on top. Service may dawdle a bit, but the laid-back ambience somehow makes children willing to linger. The Saturday and Sunday brunch tends to be very popular, but weekdays are generally uncrowded; it's a good halfway stop between the Fire Museum in SoHo and the World Trade Center.

Ellen's Cafe & Bake Shop

270 Broadway (at Chambers St.). ☎ **212/962-1257.** Sassy seats, boosters. Reservations recommended. Main courses $9–$12. AE, DC, DISC, MC, V. Mon–Fri 6am–7pm, Sat 8am–5pm. Subway: 4/5/6/N/R to City Hall, 2/3 to Park Place; A/C to Chambers St. AMERICAN DINER.

Catering to the Wall Street lunch crowd (note the limited hours), this Downtown branch of Ellen Hart's diner empire is a handy alternative to the fast-food outlets around here. The look is more saloonish than Ellen's Stardust Diner (above), but the atmosphere is 100% kid-friendly. The wide-ranging menu includes omelets, salads, burgers, and sandwiches, not to mention a brimming display case of yummy baked goods by the front door.

THE CHAIN GANG

Houlihan's crops up in three locations: 196 Broadway, at John Street (☎ **212/240-1280**); 50 Broad St., near Beaver Street (☎ **212/483-8310**); and 7 Hanover Sq., at the intersection of Wooster and Pearl streets (☎ **212/483-8314**). If you're at South Street Seaport and your kids hate fish, head for that old standby **Pizzeria Uno,** 89 South Street Seaport (☎ **212/791-7999**).

FAST FOOD

If you're into hoisting a huge burrito, the sparkling-clean **California Burrito Co.,** 16 Maiden Lane, between Broadway and Nassau Street (☎ **212/227-7978**), and in the Courtyard at 4 World Financial Center, 250 Vesey St. (☎ **212/233-6800**), dishes out a mess of burritos named after various California towns—the Big Sur has hickory-smoked barbecued chicken, the Palm Springs a more subdued grilled chicken, and so on. Not particularly authentic Mexican, but tasty and filling nonetheless.

FOOD COURTS

On the top floor of the **Pier 17** pavilion at South Street Seaport, a sparkling big food court enjoys the kind of picture-window river views normally reserved for the toniest restaurants. The various food vendors whose booths surround the public seating include several ethnic varieties; there's often live music as well.

Family-Friendly Accommodations

9

The one big problem families have with New York hotels is that the overwhelming majority are in Midtown, between 30th and 59th streets—not the best part of town for parents to be in with their children. The traffic, the noise, the absence of greenery, and the lack of a resident population at night all make Midtown less than desirable. On top of that, Midtown's tourist attractions—the Theater District, Fifth Avenue and Madison Avenue shopping, gourmet restaurants—are less relevant when you've got kids in tow. Of course, Midtown does boast superb hotels whose facilities and service level more than compensate for the location; there are also decent moderately priced hotels that cater well to families. But the list of hotels I recommend also includes nearly every choice in other neighborhoods. If you can, why not stay near Central Park or the American Museum of Natural History or the Metropolitan Museum of Art? Even Lower Manhattan hotels at least are close to South Street Seaport, the Statue of Liberty/Ellis Island ferry, and Hudson River Park.

The other big problem is the cost. Manhattan hotels sit on some very expensive real estate, pay staff wages in a top urban job market, and (often serving as flagships of various lodging chains) definitely tilt toward the high end of the luxury spectrum. Consequently, the city has the highest average room rate in the country, reaching $200 a night in some months. Occupancy rates are high too, often topping 85%, which means hotels don't have to discount to fill their beds. And many hotels market themselves to business travelers and conventioneers, whose expense accounts presumably cover those hotel bills—so why court penny-pinching families? (That line of thinking, of course, ignores the fact that more and more business travelers and conventioneers are trying to bring their families with them, turning a business trip into a family vacation as well.)

If a swimming pool is important to you and your kids, I warn you now: Few Manhattan hotels have had the room to include them and some that do have had to maximize their investment by turning their pool/health club into a profit center, selling memberships to adult New Yorkers who may not care to have the pool taken over by a bunch of kids doing cannonballs in the deep end. I've listed nearly every hotel that does have a pool but tried to give you an idea of how welcoming those pools really are for families.

One thing my family has always made use of when traveling is a kitchenette—if you can throw together breakfasts and lunches in your room, you could easily save $100 a day, not to mention keep your children's stress levels lower by not requiring them to use their restaurant manners three times a day. Suite hotels in general get my vote whenever they include some kind of kitchen facilities; they're also great with younger kids, because you can put toddlers to bed at 8pm and repair to the other room for a room-service dinner, a movie on cable TV, whatever. Seems a shame to spend your evening this way when you're in Manhattan, but for one or two evenings of a 1-week stay it can be a restful relief.

On this built-up island, there just isn't the range of properties you'd find even in other expensive markets, like London and Paris. You've got fleabags, you've got palaces—and not a whole lot in between. But face it: In between is where most families need to be. I've concentrated on ferreting out mid-range hotels that are at least decent if not always charming and atmospheric. When I do include some of the high-priced four-stars, it's because they offer something families especially value—not necessarily stunning decor, hushed privacy, and meticulous valet service (three things that don't mix well with small children anyway), but a pool, a kids' program, or a family-friendly location.

WHEN IS HIGH SEASON?   Funny thing about Manhattan hotels: There are two definite patterns of activity. Some report that their slow time is January to early March; others say that July and August are their slow times. I gave up trying to predict which would be which—it seems to have nothing to do with location, price range, or whether they depend more on business travelers or on leisure travelers. Just about all hotels, however, are booked way in advance from Thanksgiving to mid-December. When a big convention hits town, it can be impossible to find a room for love or money, as I discovered when I started doing hotel visits during the big PC Expo in June. Moral of the story: Call for reservations as soon as you know you're coming to New York, to make sure you won't get shut out. But the other side of the coin is also true—call at the last minute and you may get lucky even at one of the most popular properties.

Because New York attracts lots of business visitors as well as tourists, it's also hard to predict whether a given hotel is more likely to have a room free on weekends or on weekdays. A few hotels do offer weekend packages to bolster occupancy rates when corporate types have gone home at the end of a working week, so it's always wise to check.

RESERVATION SERVICES   Central Reservations (☎ **800/356-1123**) will book you into any of 35 hotels, including all the Manhattan East suite hotels, the Plaza, the Radisson Empire, the Doubletree Guest Suites, the Crowne Plaza, Le Parker Meridien, and chains like the Dorals; there's no charge and they can often get you discounts of 25% to 40%. The nationwide **Central Reservation Service** (☎ **800/873-4683**) also offers a discount, quoted as 10% to 40%, when they help you book rooms in New York; mostly they handle chain hotels. The **Hotel Reservations Network** (☎ **800/96-HOTEL;** www.180096hotel.com.com) offers discount hotel booking, at savings of up to 65%, in several large cities across the country, including New York.

A NOTE ABOUT HOTEL SERVICES   Certain services are so standard in Manhattan hotels I haven't noted them in individual reviews. Because tall buildings here interfere badly with TV reception, every hotel that offers in-room TVs—and that's virtually all of them—offers **cable TV,** which means you'll have a range of channels to surf. Most hotels also have Spectravision or Pay Per View or some other

in-room movie service feeding into the TVs. In the more expensive hotels, **dry cleaning** and **laundry services** are usual. No hotels provide their own **baby-sitters,** but just about every concierge or front desk has a list of sitters they've used before, usually provided by one of the city's many child-care agencies. Rates can be steep— around $12 per hour, with additional fees for more children, plus cab fare to get home afterward ($5 to $7). What you'll get will be professional baby-sitters, many of them from Europe, Asia, or South America as well as North America. They'll come to your hotel room and take care of your children there.

Parking at just about all these Manhattan hotels, whether the hotel has its own garage or merely gives you a discount at nearby garages (the latter being more usual), is based on a per-night rate that assumes you won't be taking your car in or out during the day. Once you start moving the car, you'll have to pay more. Just another reason for not using your car while you're visiting Manhattan.

A NOTE ABOUT PRICES   I've categorized hotels according to a fairly basic rate for a family of four. In some hotels, that'll be the price for a double room with two double beds. In others, it may require a connecting pair of double rooms (though hardly any hotels will guarantee you'll get two rooms that connect—they're covering themselves in case the folks next door don't check out as expected—but, in general, if you request connectors you'll get them). In some hotels I've had to base things on the assumption that a small suite will be the best family deal. At any rate, I call a hotel **Inexpensive** if that fictional family of four can stay for less than $200 a night; **Moderate** if their bill will run $200 to $275; **Expensive,** $275 to $350; and **Very Expensive,** over $350. (Those terms are, of course, relative to the Manhattan lodging price structure in general.) Quoted rates *don't* include the 13.25% New York City hotel tax or the occupancy tax, which is $2 per room per night.

These are based on "rack rates," the hotel's standard rates for peak times: Corporate discounts and package deals can bring them in at as much as $100 lower a night, so I've also noted which hotels regularly offer good discounts. Some hotels regularly offer summer packages, while others are likely to activate package deals at the last minute, when occupancy rates appear to be falling short of projected levels. (Yield management is the name of the game, with hotels as well as with airlines.) Even if you've already secured a room at rack rates at a lower-priced hotel, just before you arrive you might call a couple of pricier places to see if any special deals have kicked in. You could get a premium room for less, if you're lucky.

1 Best Bets

- **Most Family Friendly:** The **Doubletree Guest Suites,** 1568 Broadway (☎ **212/719-1600**), provides not only standard two-room accommodations sleeping four or six but also kitchenettes, baby equipment, child-proofed rooms, and a super toddler playroom. The hotel is busy developing an activities program as well, and you can just tell when you walk in that the staff is happy to see children. The **Loews New York,** 569 Lexington Ave. (☎ **212/752-7000**), and **Le Parker Meridien,** 118 E. 57th St. (☎ **212/245-5000**), are two more friendly Midtown hotels, both with essential child equipment on hand and welcoming packets for young guests.
- **Best Suite Deals:** Any of the Manhattan East Suite hotels—the **Surrey Hotel,** 20 E. 76th St. (☎ **212/320-8027**); the **Lyden Gardens Suite Hotel,** 215 E. 64th St. (☎ **212/355-1230**); the **Beekman Tower,** 3 Mitchell Place, First Avenue at 49th Street (☎ **212/355-7300**); and six other Midtown properties

listed in the Beekman Tower's write-up below—deliver a tidy little apartment with a full kitchen for a reasonable amount of cash. The Upper East Side's charming **Hotel Wales,** 1295 Madison Ave. (☎ **212/876-6000**), has some well-priced small suites that are wonderful for a smaller family. In Midtown, the **Roger Smith,** 501 Lexington Ave. (☎ **212/755-1400**), has some homey country-decor suites with lots of room for a fair price.

- **Most Peace & Quiet:** It's all relative in New York, of course, but the **Beekman Tower,** 3 Mitchell Place, First Avenue at 49th Street (☎ **212/355-7300**), is in a quiet nook of the East 50s, and the **Stanhope,** 995 Fifth Ave. (☎ **212/288-5800**), sits right on the cultured serenity of Museum Mile. The **Gracie Inn,** 502 E. 81st St. (☎ **212/628-1700**), is tucked away on an Upper East Side street near the East River, and the **Larchmont,** 27 W. 11th St. (☎ **212/989-9333**), lies on a calm Greenwich Village block of town houses.

- **Best Views:** While several hotels boast Central Park views on higher floors, you'll often pay a good deal for them, with the notable exception of the pleasantly down-to-earth **Mayflower Hotel,** 15 Central Park West (☎ **212/265-0060**). Go instead for river views, which are rarities in Manhattan: The **Regal U.N. Plaza Hotel,** 44th Street and First Avenue (☎ **212/758-1234**), dazzles with its high-rise East River vistas (other rooms have equally dazzling skyline views), while the **New York Marriott Financial Center,** 85 West St. (☎ **212/385-4900**), features panoramas of Battery Park, the Hudson River, and New York Harbor from most of its rooms.

- **When Price Is No Object:** My vote goes to the **Carlyle,** 35 E. 76th St. (☎ **212/744-1600**), for its dignified East Side calm, its well-nigh perfect service, and the spaciousness of its designer-decorated rooms, which really deserve to be called apartments. And since money is no object, make sure you get a suite with a Central Park view and a grand piano.

- **When Price Is Your Main Object:** You can't go wrong with the **Travel Inn,** 515 W. 42nd St. (☎ **212/695-7171**), which delivers roomy, clean, fairly quiet motel rooms, plus a huge pool and free parking, for only $119 a night. Unfortunately, despite its unprepossessing location far to the west of the Theater District, it's booked up way in advance—the desk clerk laughingly told me people should call a year ahead to make sure of a reservation.

- **Best Lobby:** You've gotta love the classic art deco lobby of the **Waldorf-Astoria,** 301 Park Ave. (☎ **212/355-3000**), with its marble-faced pillars, deep red-patterned carpeting, ornamental plasterwork touched with gilt and silver accents, and parade of neoclassical figures on the cornice frieze. Guests ensconce themselves in the plush armchairs, and Peacock Alley and Sir Harry's Bar open off to the sides; budding Eloises will be tempted to wander around all sorts of corridors trailing off to elevator lobbies, ballrooms and banquet halls, and classy shops with venerable names like Sulka, H. Stern, and Cellini. For hushed elegance and big-city buzz, it can't be beat. The **Plaza,** 768 Fifth Ave. (☎ **212/759-3000**), rivals it in architectural detail, but the Plaza's lobby has one fatal flaw: There's absolutely no place to sit and drink it all in, unless you want to pay through the nose for a table at the Palm Court cafe.

- **Best Pool:** The pool at the **Regal U.N. Plaza Hotel,** 44th Street and First Avenue (☎ **212/758-1234**), has it all: views, cleanliness, handsome tilework, and not much of a crowd.

- **Best Fitness Center:** The three largest and best-equipped, without a doubt, are the health clubs at **Le Parker Meridien,** 118 W. 57th St. (☎ **212/245-5000**);

the **Crowne Plaza,** 1605 Broadway (☎ **212/977-4000**); and the **Marriott World Trade Center,** 3 World Trade Center (☎ **212/938-9100**). However, all three also sell memberships to nonguests, so people staying in the hotel don't have exclusive use of the facilities. Kids may feel hesitant to try out exercise equipment geared for adults, anyway.

- **Best Bathrooms:** The **Four Seasons,** 57 E. 57th St. (☎ **212/758-5700**), has absolutely stunning huge bathrooms with the finest fixtures, and the water pressure's so good the bathtubs reputedly fill in 60 seconds. The **Mark,** 25 E. 77th St., at Madison Avenue (☎ **212/744-4300**), has large, beautifully out-fitted marble baths too, with soaking tubs and bidets and separate shower stalls, depending on various layouts.

- **Best Room Service:** The **Surrey Hotel,** 20 E. 76th St. (☎ **212/320-8027**), has room service provided by Café Boulud, headed by master chef Daniel Boulud—many foodies claim his Restaurant Daniel, now moved nearby to 65th and Park Avenue, is the best restaurant in Manhattan these days.

- **Best Coffee Shop:** I'm kind of partial to Raffles, the bright and cheery coffee shop attached to the **Hotel Lexington,** 511 Lexington Ave. (☎ **212/755-4400**), but the **Crowne Plaza Manhattan,** 1605 Broadway (☎ **212/977-4000**), comes in a close second with its skylit Balcony Cafe, offering a hearty breakfast and lunch buffet.

- **Best Hotel Restaurant for Kids:** At the **Marriott World Trade Center,** 3 World Trade Center (☎ **212/938-9100**), the Greenhouse Cafe has a kids' menu and a placemat to color.

- **Tops for Toddlers:** When all is said and done, the **Hotel Wales,** 1295 Madison Ave. (☎ **212/876-6000**), wins for its Carnegie Hill location, friendly staff, residential calm, and Puss-in-Boots theme. The complimentary continental breakfast buffet is another big plus when you've got a fidgety youngster. The **Doubletree Guest Suites,** 1568 Broadway (☎ **212/719-1600**), scores big here too, for its suite convenience and toddler playroom.

- **Tops for Teens:** Budding Bohemians may want to be in Greenwich Village at the **Washington Square Hotel,** 101–105 Waverly Place (☎ **212/777-9515**), while the athletically minded are likely to appreciate the fitness options at **Le Parker Meridien,** 118 W. 57th St. (☎ **212/245-5000**), which also puts you spot in the middle of Theme Restaurant Row. Trendsetters will gravitate to the way-cool decor and hipster cachet of the **Paramount,** 235 W. 46th St. (☎ **212/764-5500**), and the **Franklin Hotel,** 164 E. 87th St. (☎ **212/369-1000**).

2 The Upper West Side

EXPENSIVE

Radisson Empire

44 W. 63rd St. (at Broadway), New York, NY 10023. ☎ **800/333-3333** or 212/265-7400. Fax 212/315-0349. 376 units. A/C MINIBAR TV TEL. $270–$330 double; $350–$700 suite. Children 13 and under stay free in parents' room. Rollaway or crib $20. Corporate packages available. AE, CB, DC, DISC, MC, V. Parking $25. Subway: 1/9 to 66th St.

For visitors focused on Lincoln Center, the Empire, across from the center's plaza, is the logical place to stay—petite dioramas of Metropolitan Opera stage sets are displayed on the handsome lobby's paneled walls, along with a couple of full-length canvases of great opera stars of the past, and CD players in every room bespeak a clientele that includes many performers as well as classical music fans. For families,

Uptown Accommodations

 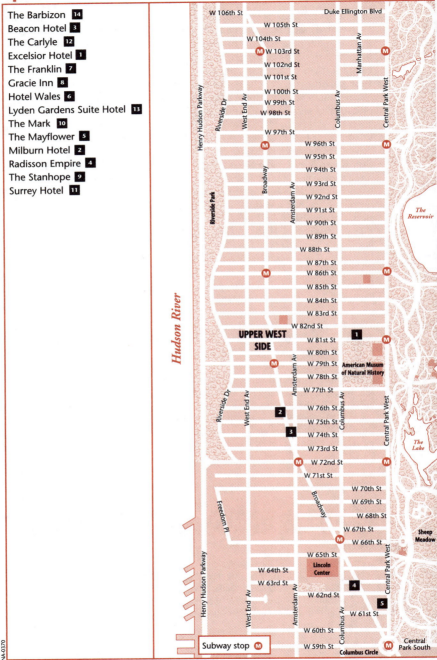

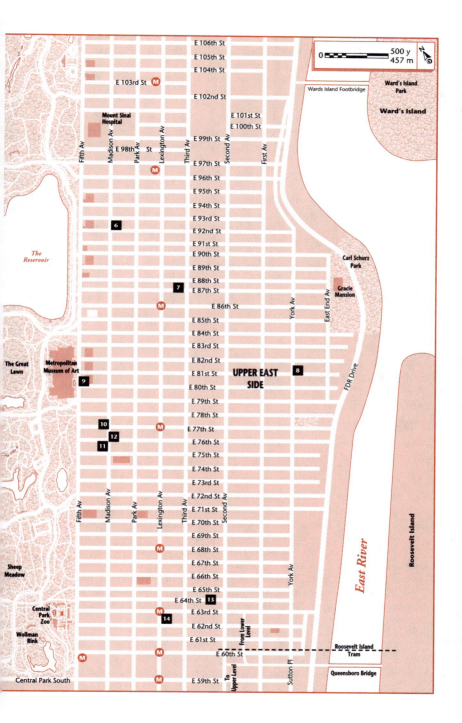

however, the rooms, with their bland, upscale traditional decor, can be a bit cramped. Don't try to economize by going for a standard room and bringing in an extra bed; upgrade to one of the front-facing rooms with two double beds—those will actually work better than the smaller suites, which have only one bed in the bedroom and a foldout couch in the sitting room.

More than a century old, the Empire became a Radisson in 1990, and the gradual renovation has been glossy if somewhat superficial: The baths are fitted out with hair dryers and makeup mirrors and a profusion of little amenities, but the molding in the rooms still looks lumpy from years of painting and repainting, and new phone lines have been strung along the molding rather than buried in the walls. There are VCRs in every room and 24-hour video rental is available, but the closets are unbelievably tiny. The long halls are painted one of the most lurid shades of pink I've ever seen.

Bright, clean, and perfectly respectable, the Empire feels like what it is—a big midprice chain hotel—but at least it's outside of Midtown. The location isn't as restful as that of most other Upper West Side hotels, however, since this stretch of Broadway is lined with hulking modern buildings and the Empire is at the bottom of a frantic intersection where Broadway cuts diagonally across lower Columbus Avenue. But Central Park is only a block away.

Dining: The rather stodgy West 63rd Street Steakhouse is on the premises. Another, hipper restaurant, Iridium, is in the same building but not affiliated; kids might like to pop in here just to see the slightly surreal decor. The neighborhood is loaded with restaurants, and every one of them is full at dinnertime before Lincoln Center's 8pm curtains.

Amenities: Concierge, 24-hour room service, laundry/valet, VCRs and video rentals, CD players and CD rentals, complimentary access to New York Sports Club health club.

MODERATE

✪ The Mayflower

15 Central Park West (at 61st St.), New York, NY 10023. ☎ **800/223-4164** or 212/265-0060. Fax 212/265-5098. 377 units. A/C TV TEL. $180–$220 double; $215–$600 suite. Rollaway or crib $20. AE, CB, DC, DISC, MC, V. Valet parking $28. Subway: 1/9/A/B/C/D to Columbus Circle.

The Mayflower seems like a perfect name for this dowdy old-line dowager overlooking Central Park. From the flowered hall carpets to the clean but worn bath fixtures to the door frames thick with layers of paint, this genteel hotel keeps up appearances but can't be bothered to keep up with the times—and that's the beauty of it. These rooms are truly spacious (a crib or rollaway will fit easily into one of the doubles) and the large windows (which you can actually open) let in loads of light, especially if you've paid the extra $25 or so for a breathtaking park view. The traditional decor opts for sensible plain colors and dark woods, except for the reed-patterned wallpaper that looks straight out of the 1950s. The closets are huge and plentiful, and nearly every room has a simple, functional pantry alcove with a refrigerator and sink but no cooking facilities.

To get a family-friendly room configuration, ask about the several connecting doubles, though a suite is probably a better deal—with two double beds in the bedroom and a queen-size sleeper sofa in the sitting room, they comfortably sleep six. There's a $15 charge for an extra person in a double, though they hardly ever charge it for kids under 12—except over Thanksgiving weekend, when the park-view rooms are one of the city's prime places to watch the Macy's parade pass by.

The small, pleasant Conservatory restaurant serves all meals, with room service to 11pm. A small second-floor exercise room caters to fitness addicts, but kids will more likely want to hit the park across the street. Lincoln Center is conveniently nearby; Midtown is only a couple of blocks away, close enough to walk to. The staff's easygoing, unpretentious manner adds to the sense that the Manhattan hustle just doesn't apply to the Mayflower.

INEXPENSIVE

✪ Beacon Hotel

2130 Broadway (at 75th St.), New York, NY 10023. ☎ **800/572-4969** or 212/787-1100. Fax 212/724-0839. 183 units. A/C TV TEL. $155–$170 double; $225–$450 suite. Children 16 and under stay free in parents' room. Rollaway $15; crib free. AE, DC, DISC, MC, V. Parking $20. Subway: 1/2/3/9 to 72nd St.

Converted from an apartment building in the early 1990s (some residents still live in the building), the Beacon offers just what we need more of in this city: clean, respectably furnished rooms with all the important amenities and none of the glitzy frills, in a neighborhood great for kids. Riverside Park is 2 blocks west and Central Park 3 blocks east; the American Museum of Natural History and the Children's Museum of Manhattan are just a few blocks up the street, and Lincoln Center isn't far down Broadway. You'll find a quiet marble-clad lobby; wide, well-lit corridors; and good-size rooms freshly done up in a traditional decor (glossy dark Queen Anne–style furniture, muted rose and tan color schemes, framed botanical prints on the walls). There's a full kitchenette in every room; the baths aren't large but look sparkling clean and have proper drinking glasses and tidy little amenities baskets.

Even the doubles are big enough for a family, since they have two double beds and enough space for a crib or rollaway. Suites add on a sitting room with a foldout couch; if you've got more than four people staying in a suite, there's a $15 charge per extra person. There's no room service, but a coffee shop is right on the corner. Though this is a busy stretch of Broadway, the rooms are pretty well soundproofed; since the 25-story hotel is one of the tallest buildings in the neighborhood, the upper-floor rooms facing west have nice views over Riverside Park and the Hudson. As you'd expect, the Beacon gets a steady stream of business, so reserve as far in advance as possible, especially in June and October; weekdays tend to be less busy than weekends, so plan accordingly.

✪ Excelsior Hotel

45 W. 81st. St. (between Central Park West and Columbus Ave.), New York, NY 10024. ☎ **800/368-4575** or 212/362-9200. Fax 212/721-2994. 146 units. A/C TV TEL. $149–$189 double; $179–$389 suite. Children under 14 stay free in parents' room. Rollaway $10; crib free. AE, DC, DISC, MC, V. Parking garages nearby. Subway: B/C to 81st St.

Perhaps feeling the competition from the nearby Beacon (above), the old neighborhood standby Excelsior underwent a top-to-toe renovation in 1997, exchanging its shabby shag carpeting and wicker headboards for a French provincial motif in soothing greens and soft browns. The bathroom fixtures are sparkling new and up-to-date, with nice country-French tile accents. The rooms are good-size—a family of four could fit comfortably into one of the double-doubles (double room with two double beds), though a one-bedroom suite, with its pullout couch in the smallish sitting room, would give even more privacy (some one-bedroom suites have two doubles in the bedroom, so request this if your family needs to sleep more than four). Unfortunately, the renovations did away with all the kitchenettes; the rooms don't even have minibars, though you can request a small fridge for an extra $10 a night. The charming old-fashioned coffee shop off the lobby is being

Cool Pools

The largest pool has to be the blue Olympic-size one at the **Travel Inn,** which has a very pleasant patio area around it for lounging but is surrounded by wings of the hotel—no views. The small rooftop pool at the **Days Hotel Midtown** has decent views of surrounding skyscrapers, though it's only 15 stories up; the **Holiday Inn Midtown 57th Street** has a small outdoor rooftop pool, but again it's not on top of a very tall building and the surrounding buildings are undistinguished. Neither of these latter two pools permits diving, which might be a drag for rambunctious kids.

You'll get better views—and get them year-round—at the glass-enclosed atrium pool at **Le Parker Meridien,** which is up 42 stories with panoramas of Central Park and the Midtown skyline. The enclosed pool at the **Regal U.N. Plaza Hotel** may be only 27 stories up but it's right on the East River, which means not only river views but also unobstructed skyline views south (you can even see the World Trade Center). What's more, the U.N. Plaza's pool is especially lovely, with handsome tilework and an exotic spangled canopy overhead. Also in Midtown, the **Crowne Plaza Manhattan** and the **Sheraton Manhattan** have 50-foot indoor lap pools; the Crowne Plaza's has windows with a nice view, if that matters to you.

Downtown, the busy 50-foot pool at the **Marriott World Trade Center** is on the 22nd floor and has boffo harbor views. The **Millenium Hilton**'s 40-foot fifth-floor pool looks right out on the spire of St. Paul's Church; the **New York Marriott Financial Center**'s 50-foot pool has no views but is sparkling clean and quiet.

eliminated as well, with a "fine dining" restaurant promised in its place; a breakfast room will be added, where guests can have complimentary continental breakfast. The wood-paneled lobby, with its ornate plasterwork ceiling, should be refurbished by early 1999 and a small fitness room installed.

You can't deny the location is superb—facing the wooded side yard of the American Museum of Natural History, on a clean and relatively quiet West Side block of luxury apartment buildings. You're half a block from Central Park, and there are loads of good restaurants and stores around the corner on Columbus Avenue. Now that's it's been brought up to snuff, the Excelsior is busier than ever, particularly with weekend business—reserve a couple of months ahead, if you can.

Milburn Hotel

242 W. 76th St. (between Broadway and West End Ave.), New York, NY 10023. ☎ **800/ 833-9622** or 212/362-1006. Fax 212/721-5476. 167 units. A/C TV TEL. $119–$145 double; $159–$185 suite. Rollaway or crib $10. AE, CB, DC, MC, V. Parking $16. Subway: 1/9 to 79th St.; 1/2/3/9 to 72nd St.

I'd rank the Milburn a couple of notches below the Beacon and the Excelsior (above): It has the smallest rooms of the three, but the simple modern furnishings are attractive and everything is crisply maintained (the day I visited, the smell of carpet glue in the narrow corridors bespoke recent decoration). Adding a crib or rollaway would make one of the doubles seriously cramped; a family should probably go for a suite, which adds a sitting room with foldout couch. Kitchenettes have been smartly crammed into room corners: an up-to-date microwave, unstocked minifridge, coffeemaker, two-burner range, and tiny sink.

The Milburn's entrance is just around the corner from Broadway, making it convenient for shopping and restaurants—a plus, since it has no restaurant or room service (they do offer some dining discounts at good local restaurants). Considering you'll have a kitchenette, it's good to know that food shopping is especially great in this neighborhood, with the Fairway market and Citarella's fish market a couple blocks south and H&H Bagels and Zabar's gourmet emporium a few blocks north. Riverside Park is only 2 blocks away too. Though the Milburn has no health club, guests can use the nearby Equinox Health Club, one of the city's best, for $11 a day. If the Beacon's booked up, try here next.

3 The Upper East Side

VERY EXPENSIVE

✪ The Carlyle

35 E. 76th St. (at Madison Ave.), New York, NY 10021. ☎ **800/227-5737** or 212/744-1600. Fax 212/717-4682. 192 units. A/C MINIBAR TV TEL. $375–$650 double; $600–$2,500 suite. AE, DC, MC, V. Parking $39. Subway: 6 to 77th St.

In my opinion, this is the best hotel in Manhattan—and lots of people seem to agree with me. The roster of celebrity guests includes everyone from Jack Nicholson to JFK, from Brooke Astor to David Bowie, from Jessica Lange and Sam Shepard to Goldie Hawn and Kurt Russell. Many of the staff, from the bellmen to the concierges, make working at the Carlyle a lifetime career, delivering white-glove service that's rare indeed. Surprisingly enough, all this makes the Carlyle a great family hotel, if the prices aren't beyond your budget. The neighborhood is wonderfully quiet and well behaved and the rooms are huge—even a double is big enough for a smaller family, with a crib or rollaway brought in.

All the rooms are done in beautiful traditional style, with gorgeous chintzes and drapes and thick carpets; from its first decorator in the 1930s, Dorothy Draper, to its current one, Mark Hampton, the Carlyle has been furnished by Manhattan society's top residential designers. *Residential* is the key word—if a room has shelves, they'll be stocked with books; vases and china dishes and ormolu clocks are set out on the occasional tables; every sitting room and bedroom has its own entertainment center with a VCR and CD player. More than a dozen rooms have grand pianos, some of them Steinways, others Baldwins like the one Bobby Short plays downstairs in the Cafe Carlyle. The suites have sleek modern kitchens, while even the double rooms at least have an alcove with a sink and well-stocked minibar. The baths are big and gleaming, with Givenchy toiletries, thick towels and terrycloth robes, hair dryers, and makeup mirrors; most tubs have Jacuzzis in them.

The hotel is 35 stories tall, so if you're lucky enough to snag a room overlooking Central Park, you'll have a view you could gaze at for hours, day or night. Carlyle guests are near enough to the park to scamper right over and play, as well as being close to the Fifth Avenue museums and to the glorious children's shops of upper Madison Avenue.

Dining/Diversions: The dark, romantically ornate Carlyle Restaurant serves breakfast, lunch, and dinner, with a lavish luncheon buffet every day except Sunday. Bistro-style suppers and Sunday brunches are served in the Cafe Carlyle, best known as the cabaret ($50 cover charge) where pianist/singer Bobby Short has performed for three decades; in the months he's not there, Eartha Kitt, Dixie Carter, or Barbara Cook may fill in, and on Monday evenings Woody Allen plays the clarinet with the Eddy Davis New Orleans Jazz Band. Bemelmans Bar is an atmospheric cocktail lounge even children will want to visit, to see the murals painted by Austrian artist

Ludwig Bemelmans, creator of the Madeline books ("In an old house in Paris, covered in vines, lived twelve little girls in two straight lines. . . ."). Jazz vocalist Barbara Carroll performs at night in the bar ($10 cover). Breakfast coffee, afternoon tea, cocktails, and posttheater snacks are served in the Turkish-style red-velvet Gallery, a lobby area with a few small tables.

Amenities: Concierge, 24-hour room service, twice-daily maid service, secretarial services, VCRs and CD players; small health club with sauna, steam room, exercise machines.

The Mark

25 E. 77th St. (at Madison Ave.), New York, NY 10021. ☎ **800/843-6275** or 212/744-4300. Fax 212/744-2749. 180 units. A/C MINIBAR TV TEL. $375–$420 double; $550–$2,500 suite. Children under 17 stay free in parents' room. Rollaway $30; crib free. Corporate, weekend, and summer packages (including breakfast) available. AE, CB, DC, DISC, MC, V. Parking $35. Subway: 6 to 77th St.

Compared to its near neighbor the Carlyle (above), the Mark looks hipper and more corporate, though it's still one of the city's finest hotels. (Don't worry, they've fixed up the room Johnny Depp so famously trashed.) Many of its guests are visiting New York on business, and 40% of the clientele is European—not surprising, since the hotel is part-owned by a Monaco-based hotel company, the Rafael Group. But families still fit into the mix pretty well, especially since summers and weekends—prime times for family travel—are less busy here.

One thing the Mark offers that few other Uptown hotels do: connecting doubles that can be closed off with their own private doorway and vestibule. Double rooms have either twin beds or a king-size bed, and rooms are plenty large enough for a crib to be brought in. The so-called executive suite is another good option for families, with a queen-size bed in one room and foldout couch in the other. The decor is neoclassical English-Italian, with lots of warm browns, overstuffed chairs, and eye-catching draperies. The baths are bigger than average, with stunning black-and-white tiles and fixtures, including deep tubs, separate shower stalls, and heated towel bars (my kids always find these a kick for some reason—well, it is pretty nice to swathe yourself in a warm towel when you step out of a bath). The neighborhood is restful, with a sort of monied calm, and Central Park is only a block away. At 16 stories, the Mark offers views over many neighboring rooftops. The small but state-of-the-art second-floor health club is hardly ever used, so no one may mind if kids pop in to goof around on the treadmills, Exercycles, and Stairmasters.

Dining: Mark's, consistently rated one of the city's top restaurants, serves breakfast, lunch, dinner, Sunday brunch, afternoon tea, and posttheater drinks and desserts. It's a handsome clublike dining room with velvet banquettes, brass railings, mahogany armchairs, and tables spaced well apart. Mark's Bar is a snug, dark-walled lounge serving cocktails (with some light food) and late supper.

Amenities: 24-hour room service, limousines, business services, laundry/valet, VCRs, in-room fax capability; twice-daily shuttle to Wall Street, weekend shuttle to the Theater District; small health club with sauna, steam room, exercise machines. The Mark's highly regarded concierge, Argentinian Giorgio Finocchiaro, is a member of Clefs d'Or, the worldwide organization of concierges.

The Stanhope

995 Fifth Ave. (at 81st St.), New York, NY 10028. ☎ **800/828-1123** or 212/288-5800. Fax 212/517-0088. 180 units. A/C MINIBAR TV TEL. $375–$450 double; $500–$1,400 suite. Rollaway or crib $35. Weekend packages (including continental breakfast). AE, CB, DC, DISC, MC, V. Parking $40. Subway: 4/5/6 to 86th St.; 6 to 77th St.

With its small gold-leaf-trimmed lobby and large plush rooms, the Stanhope is definitely one of the Upper East Side's handful of true luxury hotels, and you can't beat that location right across from the Metropolitan Museum of Art. Few rooms have park views, since the museum is in the way, but museumgoers find it awfully handy to be just steps from the Metropolitan and right on Museum Mile, in one of Manhattan's calmest, safest, and most elegant neighborhoods (Jackie O used to live 4 blocks up the street).

The rooms, with floral fabrics and pastel wall coverings and ornate furniture (the decorator clearly was into chinoiserie), are easily big enough for a crib or rollaway, but if you have more than one kid, go for a one-bedroom suite, which on weekends costs only a little more than a double does on weekdays. The suites have excellent pullout sleeper sofas, a second bath, and two TVs; request one with a kitchenette and you'll be set. Only guests have key access to the elevator, which means security isn't a worry here (and, hey, this neighborhood is hardly Times Square). Though it may seem a trifle too sedate for families, the Stanhope certainly welcomes kids, provided they don't pry the inlaid wood out of the armoires.

Dining: The hotel's restaurant, Nica's, is run by noted chef Matthew Kenny and serves Mediterranean cuisine; it's super for ladies who lunch but perhaps a bit too refined if you've got vocal kids in tow. The Terrace, the popular small sidewalk cafe on Fifth Avenue, may be your better bet for drinks or a light meal. If your kids are really into etiquette, dress them up in their cotillion clothes and treat them to afternoon tea served in the library, with scones and finger sandwiches and the works.

Services: Concierge, 24-hour room service, VCR, in-room fax capability, kitchenettes in deluxe doubles and suites, fitness center with sauna, complimentary limo to Midtown.

EXPENSIVE

The Franklin

164 E. 87th St. (between Lexington and Third aves.), New York, NY 10128. ☎ **800/600-8787** or 212/369-1000. Fax 212/369-8000. 51 units. A/C TV TEL. $219 double. Rates include continental breakfast. Rollaway or crib free. AE, MC, V. Free parking. Subway: 4/5/6 to 86th St.

Less homey than its sibling the Wales (below), the Franklin has the tone of a groovy Downtown hotel, with its minimalist decor of neutral grays, spotlighting, and brushed steel. There's a hip touch of style in the beds, which feature asymmetrical padded headboards and canopylike gauzy white cloth. The halls look a tad grim, though, with industrial-looking gray steel doors, a reminder of the hotel's prerenovation past, and the rooms are indisputably small—add a crib or rollaway and you'd have to squeeze to get to the snug (but spick and span) bath. Room size is what bumps this reasonably priced property up into a higher price range, since you'll need to book two rooms—and there aren't even any connecting doubles available. I'd recommend this hotel mostly for families with teenagers who can handle being in separate rooms from their parents; teens would be most likely to appreciate the postmodern hipness, anyway (I've been told that a lot of models stay here). Every room has a VCR, and there's a video library in the reading room just off the lobby, though its choices run more toward *Pulp Fiction* than *Pinocchio*.

The free breakfast—granola, muffins, cappuccino—is served in a smart but corporate-looking lounge; families might prefer to take theirs up to their room. There's no restaurant and no room service, but the area is lousy with good restaurants that deliver. The general manager insists that the doorman will even run out and pick up something for you. Now that's service!

✪ Hotel Wales

1295 Madison Ave. (at 92nd St.), New York, NY 10128. ☎ **212/876-6000.** Fax 212/860-7000. 86 units. A/C TV TEL. $249 double; $329–$399 suite. Rates include continental breakfast. Rollaway or crib free; extra person $25. AE, MC, V. Valet parking $28. Subway: 6 to 96th St.

There's more than a touch of Edwardian Kensington to this charming hotel in Carnegie Hill, a historic Upper East Side neighborhood full of top-notch private schools and well-off families. Only a block from Central Park and Museum Mile, the hotel is smack in the middle of upper Madison's strip of upscale children's shops. The lobby looks like the entry hall in a private mansion, with its marble staircase, carved wood banisters, dark wainscoting, and striped wallpaper, and the room decor is tastefully traditional—beautiful woodwork, original cabinets, and cedar-lined closets. Absolutely the only drawback to staying in this hotel is that the rooms are so small you can barely fit in a crib—but at these rates, a suite isn't a bad idea; suites consist of a fair-size bedroom and an adjoining sitting area with a pullout sofa. (There are no connecting doubles.) The baths are tiny yet outfitted with top-quality fixtures. No rooms have kitchenettes, but you can have a minirefrigerator on request. Every room has a VCR; the Wales's growing popularity with families has resulted in the addition of many more kids' movies to its VCR library.

Kids might get a kick out of the hotel's Puss-in-Boots theme, discreetly carried out with framed prints on the walls and designs on the bath toiletries. The Pied Piper Room, where guests can help themselves to a granola-and-muffins breakfast and a late-night dessert buffet, is a big comfy space with potted palms and Victorian settees where chamber music is played at teatime and on Sunday evening. Popular Sarabeth's Restaurant, though separately owned, is right downstairs and provides room service 7am to 11pm.

✪ Surrey Hotel

20 E. 76th St. (at Madison Ave.), New York, NY 10021. ☎ **800/ME-SUITE** or 212/320-8027. Fax 212/465-3697. 130 units. A/C TV TEL. $290–$330 studio suite; $345–$385 one-bedroom suite; $635–$655 two-bedroom suite. Rollaway $20; crib free. Weekly and monthly discount rates available. AE, CB, DC, DISC, MC, V. Parking garages nearby. Subway: 6 to 77th St.

If you haven't got the dough to stay nearby at the Carlyle or the Mark (above), you can still enjoy this ace East Side neighborhood with a much more affordable suite at the Surrey. Its clean, well-maintained rooms are positively huge—you could easily fit a crib or rollaway into the so-called studio suites. The one-bedroom suites could sleep six, with two double beds in the bedroom and a foldout sofa in the sitting room. The decor is tasteful, if not fussy, with Chippendale-ish reproductions. The baths are sparkling clean, though the fixtures aren't necessarily luxurious. Every unit has a kitchen or kitchenette, with a full-size refrigerator, sink, stove, cutlery, and plates, and guests here really do seem to use their kitchens—the staff will even do your food shopping for only $5 (plus the cost of the groceries, of course). If cooking's not your idea of a vacation, there are scads of restaurants within a short walk and the room service is provided (7am to 10pm) by the kitchen of one of Manhattan's most stellar chefs, Daniel Boulud, whose Café Boulud is downstairs.

The ample reception area, with marble columns, a chandelier, and a genteelly faded Oriental rug, resembles many Upper East Side apartment building lobbies—indeed, staying here is one way to discover what it's like to live in New York as a family, as you troll the Madison Avenue children's shops and hang out at the East 76th Street Playground in Central Park. The Surrey's residential air is enhanced by the fact that many guests are on long stays—corporate relocations, local families holing up during apartment renovations (laundry facilities in the basement make life easier for those folks, as do VCRs and a small exercise room). Nevertheless, the Surrey welcomes short-stay guests, especially on weekdays and in the July/August slow period, so don't hesitate to check if there's a room, even on short notice.

MODERATE

The Barbizon

140 E. 63rd St. (at Lexington Ave.), New York, NY 10021. ☎ **800/223-1020** or 212/838-5700. Fax 212/888-4271. 300 units. A/C MINIBAR TV TEL. $250 double; from $475 suite. Children under 13 stay free in parents' room. Rollaway $20; crib free. AE, DC, DISC, MC, V. Parking $29 nearby. Subway: Q/N/R to Lexington Ave.; 4/5/6 to 59th St.

In its days as a ladies' residence hotel, the Barbizon Hotel for Women—a tawny Spanish-Gothic brick tower close to Bloomingdale's—was home to such future luminaries as Grace Kelly, Ali McGraw, and Candice Bergen, as well as legions of other young women starting their careers in Manhattan. The tiny studios of those days were revamped in 1997 to create bigger rooms for the transient market, making it a very viable option for families, considering the clean East Side location. Superior and deluxe doubles hold either a king- or a queen-size bed or a pair of double beds and are roomy enough for a crib or rollaway as well. Junior suites have a queen-size bed in the bedroom and a pullout sofa in the sitting room. Some rooms have terraces, though the views aren't anything special.

The hotel's renovation has spiffed up all the rooms with a cool and restful decor of blond woods, soft green colors, white louvered shutters, and wrought-iron bedsteads; the pristine white baths are smallish but well fitted. Though the breakfast room is open only 6:30 to 11am, there's 24-hour room service, and the neighborhood is swimming in restaurants. And speaking of swimming, guests can use the on-site Equinox health club with an indoor pool.

Gracie Inn

502 E. 81st St. (between York and East End aves.), New York, NY 10028. ☎ **212/628-1700.** Fax 212/628-6420. 12 units. A/C TV TEL. $169–$199 studio suite; $199 one-bedroom suite; $599 two-bedroom suite. Rates include continental breakfast. Rollaway or crib $25. Discounts offered for weekly and monthly stays. AE, DC, DISC, MC, V. Parking garages nearby. Subway: 6 to 77th St.

If only New York had more places like the Gracie Inn! First off, there's the neighborhood—Upper East Side, on a side street near the East River, not far from Carl Schurz Park. This is the part of the East Side where middle-class families live and shop and go to school. Then there's the thoughtful service and quiet unhotel-like atmosphere, which make this a welcome retreat from Manhattan bustle—the sort of bed-and-breakfast boutique hotel you can find all over Europe but rarely in the States.

Once you get past the unprepossessing exterior and minuscule lobby, the five-story town house (with elevator) has individually decorated suites. Antiques, stenciled wallpapers, rag rugs, hardwood floors, and lace curtains go for a country inn look that's never too frilly or precious; fresh flowers are set out in the rooms and plump snowy duvets are on the beds. Every suite has a tidy little kitchen with all utensils, and a continental breakfast is brought to your room each morning. Cribs or rollaways could fit handily even in the studios, though a one- or two-bedroom suite would be better for a family, especially the penthouse duplex (kids will have a blast running up and down the snug wooden staircase). With skylights, a greenhouse wall, and weathered wood terraces, the penthouse suites get loads of sun, but even rooms on the lower floors are fairly light. Don't expect to walk to the subway—York Avenue is a long way east from the subway line—but buses and taxis are easy to find and the neighborhood has plenty of good, reasonably priced restaurants.

Lyden Gardens Suite Hotel

215 E. 64th St. (between Second and Third aves.), New York, NY 10021. ☎ **800/ME-SUITE** or 212/355-1230. Fax 212/758-7858. 130 units. A/C TV TEL. $259–$539 suite. Rollaway $20; crib free. AE, DC, DISC, MC, V. Children under 13 stay free in parents' room. Parking $20 at nearby garage. Subway: 4/5/6 to 59th St., or 6 to 68th St.; B/Q to Lexington Ave.

Manhattan East Suites hotels offer great deals for extended-stay visitors or families: reasonably priced suites with fully equipped kitchens (the staff will even do your grocery shopping—for a modest fee), along with essential hotel services. (There's no room service, but some nearby restaurants will deliver and there are loads of family-friendly restaurants nearby.) The Lyden Gardens attracts a lot of business from the cluster of hospitals around 68th Street and York Avenue, but this relatively residential neighborhood also makes sense for families on a short stay. From the stylish small lobby on, the decor is clean, simple, and contemporary—good innocuous surroundings to crash in after a long day. Request a junior suite with a pullout couch as well as two double beds or go for the one- or two-bedroom suites, which have separate bedrooms and sitting rooms, with sleeper sofas. There's also an on-premises Laundromat and a health club with weight training equipment and a Stairmaster. In general, the staff seems helpful and friendly, accommodating whatever requests guests have.

4 Midtown West

VERY EXPENSIVE

The Plaza

768 Fifth Ave. (between 58th and 59th sts.), New York, NY 10019. ☎ **800/759-3000** or 212/759-3000. Fax 212/546-5234. 815 units. A/C MINIBAR TV TEL. $260–$550 double; $650–$15,000 suite. Rollaway or crib free; extra person $35 (after first 3 in room). Summer and weekend packages available. AE, CB, DC, DISC, MC, V. Valet parking $35. Subway: N/R to Fifth Ave.

The only New York hotel designated a National Historic Landmark, the Plaza is truly lovely—even if you're not staying here, you should stroll up the red-carpeted steps to have a walk through the turn-of-the-century baroque lobby: From the neoclassical mosaic floors to the dazzling crystal chandeliers to the gilded cornices with inset heirloom tapestries, it's a sight to behold. (Don't miss a peek into the Edwardian Room and Oak Room to see their inimitable carved Gothic rafters and burnished wood paneling.) It's surprising, then, especially considering the steep rates, that the clientele looks so unsophisticated—an uncanny number of folks in shorts and polo shirts assiduously snapping photos of themselves "in the Plaza." The gracious concierge desk busily books guests into stodgy expensive restaurants, while the theater ticket window seems to do a brisk business in *Beauty and the Beast* tickets. The moral: Don't be intimidated by the Plaza—if you opt to stay here, you'll certainly feel you're someplace special but won't have to worry about being outclassed.

Lots of families stay here (did everybody see *Home Alone 2?* has every child dreamed of living here like Eloise?), and management has very intelligently responded by setting up the Young Plaza Ambassadors, a VIP program for kids 6 to 19. For a $150 annual fee (discounts for additional siblings), young guests get turn-down cookies and milk; in-room movies; coupons and special perks at restaurants, shops, and museums around the city; and discounts on various kid-oriented events around the hotel. Certain floors will be designated as kid-friendly, there's a special kids menu with an emphasis on indulgent desserts (including the Home Alone Sundae), and a lounge has been set up on the 17th floor, with videos, a bulletin board, games, and space for kids to meet other kids.

Families should steer away from the standard double rooms, which have only a double bed and not enough room for a crib or rollaway. For that, you'd have to get what they call a Classic room; better yet, get a Deluxe room that has two double beds. By that time you're up to at least $450 a night (unless you've snagged one of the weekend packages, which not only reduce the room rate but throw in free parking or breakfast). Of course, if you'd like to go all out, the Astor Suite costs a mere $4,000 a night: You'll get a huge living room, a formal dining room, a full kitchen, and three bedrooms, all fitted out in Versailles-style gilt and brocade—not to mention a master bath with Central Park views from the Jacuzzi. (The gold swan-shaped faucets are an Ivana Trump touch—she supervised the refurbishment of the hotel when she and the Donald ran the place.)

All the guest rooms betray a taste for the palatial—but, then, what else would go with 14-foot-high ceilings, ornamental plaster moldings, and original crystal chandeliers? Here's a tip: If you're paying the extra $200 or so a night for a room facing Central Park, insist on floors five to eight—you'll be up high enough to see, and, by virtue of the exterior's Parisian wedding-cake design, the windows are much larger there than on the higher floors. Or save dough by opting for a Fifth Avenue view, where you can look down on Grand Army Plaza's gilded statue and fountain, not to mention FAO Schwarz across the street.

Dining: Breakfast, lunch, and dinner are served in the Palm Court (see chapter 8) and the Edwardian Room (for fine dining; closed Monday night). The Oak Room (for grilled American food; closed Saturday lunch and Sunday dinner) and the Oyster Bar (for seafood) serve lunch and dinner. All are very pricey.

Amenities: Concierge desk (four Clefs d'Or on staff), 24-hour room service, VCRs, in-room fax capability; fitness room with exercise machines; access to Atrium Health Club and Cardio-Fitness Center nearby; business center; shopping arcade; first-run movie theater on the lower level; courtesy car to the theater if you dine in the hotel.

EXPENSIVE

✪ Le Parker Meridien

118 W. 57th St. (between Sixth and Seventh aves.), New York, NY 10019. ☎ **800/543-4300** or 212/245-5000. Fax 212/307-1776. 700 units. A/C MINIBAR TV TEL. $325–$365 double; $395–$2,500 suite. Rollaway or crib free. Weekend packages available. AE, CB, DC, DISC, MC, V. Valet parking $32. Subway: N/R/B/Q to 57th St.

With its splendid glass-enclosed atrium pool, sundeck, eighth-of-a-mile roof jogging track, and top-notch health club, this French-owned hotel is a super choice for any athletic family. The 57th Street location is in the middle of all the theme restaurants and not far from FAO Schwarz, the Warner Bros. Store, and the Disney Store; several rooms on the 42-story hotel's upper floors—say, from 20 on up—offer Central Park views. The property looks snooty enough, with a pink-columned baroque lobby and neoclassic guest-room decor—the gold-and-white-striped wallpaper has a black-and-gold border that looks copied from a Grecian urn—but Le Parker Meridien does a good job of making families feel welcome.

On arrival, kids are given a packet containing stuff like crayons and coupons for kid-appealing activities. Items like high chairs, night lights, bottle warmers, and safety plugs are available on request. The suites have full kitchenettes (pots and

Midtown Accommodations

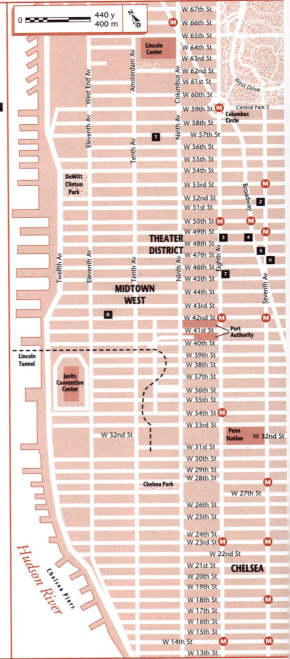

NA-0371

E 67th St
E 66th St
E 65th St
E 64th St
E 63rd St
E 62nd St
E 61st St
From Lower Level
York Av
E 60th St
Roosevelt Island Tram
Queensboro Bridge
E 59th St
To Upper Level
E 58th St
Queens
E 57th St
Sutton Pl
E 56th St
Sutton Pl South
E 55th St
E 54th St
MIDTOWN EAST
E 53rd St
E 52nd St
E 51st St
E 50th St
Beekman Place
Rockefeller Center
E 49th St
Mitchell Place
E 48th St
E 47th St
E 46th St
E 45th St
Second Av
First Av
E 44th St
E 43rd St
United Nations
Grand Central Terminal
E 42nd St
E 41st St
Bryant Park
New York Public Library
Queens–Midtown Tunnel
MURRAY HILL
E 40th St
E 39th St
E 38th St
FDR Drive
E 37th St
Tunnel Exit
E 36th St
Tunnel Entrance
E 35th St
E 34th St
Empire State Bldg.
E 33rd St
E 32nd St
East River
Broadway
E 31st St
E 30th St
Park Av. S.
E 29th St
E 28th St
E 27th St
E 26th St
Madison Square Park
E 25th St
E 24th St
E 23rd St
Asser Levy Pl
E 22nd St
Gramercy Park
E 21st St
Peter Cooper Village
E 20th St
FLATIRON DISTRICT
GRAMERCY PARK
E 19th St
E 18th St
E 17th St
Stuyvesant Town
Union Sq W
Union Square
Union Sq E
Irving Pl
E 16th St
ND Perlman Pl
E 15th St
E 14th St
E 13th St

Sixth Av
Fifth Av
Madison Av
Park Av
Vanderbilt Av
Depew Pl
Lexington Av
Third Av
Center Drive
East Drive
The Pond
Central Park S

plates and condiments can be requested), and all rooms have CD players and VCRs. The rooms are of good size by Manhattan standards—a double with two double beds could accommodate a family for a short stay—though the Tower Suites aren't a bad deal, with a king-size bed in one room, a pullout couch in the other, a bath, a kitchenette, and an awesome skyline view on upper floors.

Dining/Diversions: Bar Montparnasse offers a breakfast buffet, light fare for lunch and dinner, and entertainment in the evening.

Amenities: Concierge, 24-hour room service, business center, indoor pool, extensive health club with squash and racquetball courts, sauna, sundeck, jogging track.

The Paramount

235 W. 46th St. (between Broadway and Eighth Ave.), New York, NY 10036. ☎ **800/225-7474** or 212/764-5500. Fax 212/354-5237. 610 units. A/C MINIBAR TV TEL. $260–$350 double; $425 one-bedroom suite; $600 two-bedroom suite. Rollaway $20; crib free. AE, DC, DISC, MC, V. Parking $18. Subway: A/C/E to 42nd St.; C/E to 50th St.; 1/2/3/7/9/N/R/S to Times Sq.

Not many families stay here, despite the relatively low rates and the fact that it has one of the city's few in-hotel playrooms for little kids. Maybe parents feel intimidated by the aggressively hip decor by ultratrendy Philippe Starck: Stepping into the minimalist gray lobby with its asymmetrical rug, cartoonishly shaped armchairs, and free-standing stairway of brushed stainless steel can be unnerving. The rooms have severe-looking white linen bedcovers, black-and-white checkerboard carpets, and oversize gilt frames for headboards; the baths have an inverted cone of brushed steel for a sink.

Truth to tell, though, it's stunning, and kids might really get into its futuristic weirdness. The playroom may be tiny and not have many toys, but it's a gas: Three armchairs are made of stuffed animals sewn together (one is all Tweety Birds; another, Sylvester the Cats; another, Pink Panthers), a small TV monitor is encrusted with small plastic figures, and three fish tanks gurgle in one wall. If the guest-room decor's not a problem, the size may be—some double rooms do have two double beds, but that doesn't leave a whole lot of space. The west-of-Times-Square location is less of a turnoff than it used to be, as Eighth Avenue is quickly sprucing up (a tickle-down effect from 42nd Street's remarkable transformation). The Paramount is close to Broadway theaters, so there are always lots of people around, and Eighth Avenue still boasts some cheap ethnic restaurants and coffee shops that may be fun for families. All in all, I think this is a super place for a few nights' stay, provided your kids are sophisticated enough to appreciate the hypercoolness.

Dining: The Mezzanine Restaurant—its tiny tables lit by jewel-toned lamps, set on a narrow mezzanine overlooking the lobby—serves breakfast, lunch, and dinner, as does the Library Lounge. Coco Pazzo Teatro is also available for lunch and dinner. A smart Dean & Deluca espresso bar is off the lobby, and the Whiskey Bar is a happening place for after-work singles.

Amenities: Concierge, 24-hour room service, VCRs and video rentals, fitness room with exercise machines, children's playroom, business center.

MODERATE

✪ Crowne Plaza Manhattan

1605 Broadway (between 48th and 49th sts.), New York, NY 10019. ☎ **800/2-CROWNE** or 212/977-4000. Fax 212/333-7393. 770 units. A/C MINIBAR TV TEL. $200–$400 double; $450–$1,050 suite. Children 19 and under stay free in parents' room. Rollaway $20; crib free. AE, CB, DC, DISC, MC, V. Valet parking $34. Subway: 1/9 to 50th St.; N/R to 49th St.

With the ongoing turnaround of Times Square, the Crowne Plaza is nicely positioned to grab a big chunk of the Midtown market. With a reception area one floor up from Broadway (security is thorough but not oppressive) and tight sound-proofing, you can feel removed from the tumult but not bunkered in—many windows overlook the razzmatazz, including some around the pool and at the end of every corridor. The guest floors begin on the 16th story (several floors of offices are in between the lobby and the guest rooms), so many rooms have great skyline or river views. Yet this contemporary 46-story building sticks firmly to the middle of the road, in style as well as rates. Its lobby has some marble and brass and plush touches, but it's not overbearing; the room decor is traditional and corporate, with greens and browns and lots of table lamps.

Families have several layout options: a double room with two double beds; connecting doubles; a smallish sitting room with your choice of one or two bedrooms connecting; or a large sitting room (complete with a wet bar/serving area and dining table) with your choice of one or two bedrooms connecting. Along with pullout sofas, the Crowne Plaza has some pull-down Murphy beds, which kids might enjoy. Some extra amenities (terry bathrobes, a jar of hard candies) are offered on Crowne Plaza Club floors, for which you'll pay $30 to $50 more, but it might be worth it if only because you can get continental breakfast free in the lounge, a huge windowed parlor with dynamite views; once the corporate travelers have cleared out at 9am or so, the room is virtually empty. The health club is an obvious attraction for families, though there are some caveats: The fitness center is run by the New York Sports Club, whose members get priority over hotel guests weekdays at lunchtime and after work. The 50-foot lap pool, however, is open to guests at all times; if you want to make sure there's room, call ahead to reserve a lane.

Dining: Samplings, a contemporary-looking continental restaurant off the lobby, serves dinner along with some stunning second-floor Times Square views. The Broadway Grill serves more casual fare—pizza, pasta, burgers—for lunch and dinner. The Balcony Cafe does breakfast and lunch, with a big buffet at both meals, as well as à la carte service. Another morning option is to pick up a light breakfast to go from the Lobby Bar—coffee, juice, muffins, bagels—just enough to satisfy kids before you dash off for sightseeing.

Amenities: Concierge, 24-hour room service (with kids' menu), theater desk, tour desk, newspaper delivery, 50-foot indoor pool, 29,000-square-foot health club (with exercise machines, aerobics classes, sauna, massage), business center, shopping arcade.

✪ Doubletree Guest Suites

1568 Broadway (at 47th St. and Seventh Ave.), New York, NY 10036. ☎ **800/222-8733** or 212/719-1600. Fax 212/921-5112. 460 units. A/C MINIBAR TV TEL. $229–$329 suite. Children 17 and under stay free in parents' room. Rollaway or crib free. AE, CB, DC, DISC, MC, V. Valet parking $30. Subway: 1/9 to 50th St.; N/R to 49th St.; B/D/F/Q to 47th–50th sts./Rockefeller Center.

Quite possibly the most family-oriented hotel in Manhattan, the Doubletree more than makes up for what might be an off-putting location, smack dab on Times Square. There are two entire floors fitted out for families with younger children—plastic drinking cups, childproofed power outlets, padded bump guards on furniture edges, spout covers in the tubs. Older children might prefer (or insist, if they're like my nieces) to stay on the two floors designated as Green Suites, which are cleaned with environmentally sound cleansers and offer recycling and optional fewer linen changes. The suite concept is a natural for families anyway, since you automatically get sleeping space for four or six, depending on whether you request a king-size bed or two doubles in the bedroom (there's a foldout sofa in the sitting room). Both rooms lead into the bath, and though these suites don't have full kitchenettes, there's a microwave, a coffeemaker, a sink, a marble counter, and an empty minirefrigerator, as well as a stocked minibar. The low-key contemporary decor features calm grays and subdued geometric designs that don't show spills. Both rooms have TVs, and you can request VCRs.

Now let's get to the really unusual ways the Doubletree provides for families: There's no charge for cribs, playpens and strollers, and you can request that the cable movie service be shut off if you're worried your kids will go wild with the remote. Next to the restaurant and health club is a delightful large playroom with a stunning Statue of Liberty design on the carpet; it's equipped with well-chosen picture books, big stuffed animals, colorful large foam blocks, and a clever wall-mounted city maze around which kids can steer small taxis. Security is good, though not as forbidding as at the big Marriott across the way: There's a ground-floor foyer with monitored elevators leading up to the guest lobby, and a separate bank of elevators going up to guest-room floors. After 11pm guests have to show their key card to be admitted into the guest-room elevators. At 43 stories, the Doubletree does have some high-floor rooms with Midtown views, but what's more important about the height is that it means there are lots of rooms, so more families can take advantage of this great deal.

Dining: The Center Stage Cafe has whimsical wall murals carrying out its Broadway theater theme—face one way and you'll feel like an audience watching the stage, face the other and you'll feel like performers looking up at the audience in the painted balcony. The restaurant serves a breakfast buffet, lunch, and dinner and has a kids' menu.

Amenities: Room service (to 4am), newspaper delivery, kitchenettes, VCRs and video rentals, small fitness room with exercise machines, children's playroom, children's activities programs, business center, Laundromat.

Renaissance New York

714 Seventh Ave. (between 47th and 48th sts.), New York, NY 10036. ☎ **800/682-5222** or 800/HOTELS-1, or 212/765-7676. Fax 212/765-1962. 305 rms. A/C MINIBAR TV TEL. $210–$390 double; $425–$475 suite. Children 15 and under stay free in parents' room. Rollaway or crib free. AE, DC, DISC, MC, V. Valet parking $29. Subway: N/R to 49th St.; B/D/F/Q to 47th–50th sts./Rockefeller Center; 1/9 to 50th St.

Sleek and corporate-looking as it is, the Renaissance isn't the kind of hotel families automatically gravitate to, but those who do wind up here might be very pleasantly surprised. First, you're right in the thick of the exciting Times Square action, but in a good way—the famous neon Coca-Cola sign hangs on the hotel's south wall, the TKTS half-price ticket booth is a few steps away, many rooms look out onto one or another of the fabled supersigns, and the hotel's Foley's Fish House restaurant offers the best panoramic view of the Times Square intersection. (You couldn't ask for a better ringside seat on New Year's Eve.) Yet the riffraff gets screened out by the ground-floor security lobby (the guest lobby is up on the third floor), and double-paned windows do an amazing job of keeping out traffic noise.

Inside, everything is mahogany and brass and marble and truly handsome. Families can fit nicely into the doubles, which are roomier than most Midtown doubles—go with a king-size-bedded room with a rollaway or a room that has two queen-size beds. Suites consist of a king-size-bedded sleeping room and a sitting room with a pullout couch. Minibars are set under a marble countertop with a coffeemaker, which makes a handy place for fixing snacks or lunches, and TVs (tucked into a cabinet with a videoplayer) have 25-inch screens.

Dining: On the third floor off the guest lobby, Foley's Fish House—which has dark glass windows on three sides offering a thrilling view of the Great White

Way—serves lunch and dinner. Its specialty is seafood. Breakfast is served in The Dining Room nearby. A cocktail lounge, also on the third floor, has windows overlooking Broadway too, though facing away from Times Square. A pianist plays here about 5:30 to 8pm.

Amenities: Concierge, 24-hour room service, newspaper delivery, videoplayers, small gym with fitness machines.

Sheraton Manhattan

790 Seventh Ave. (between 51st and 52nd sts.), New York, NY 10019. ☎ **800/325-3535** or 212/581-3300. Fax 212/315-4265. 658 units. A/C MINIBAR TV TEL. $209–$289 double; from $575 suite. Rates include continental breakfast. Rollaway or crib $20. AE, DC, DISC, MC, V. Parking $22. Subway: 1/9 to 50th St.; N/R to 49th St.; B/D/F/Q to 47th–50th sts./ Rockefeller Center.

This business-oriented upscale chain hotel has one giant plus for traveling families: an indoor pool on the fifth floor, with an outdoor sundeck. Though guests from the Sheraton New York across the street are also allowed to use the pool, during the day it's usually not crowded if your kids want to splash around. Compared to the larger Sheraton, a megahotel with vast public areas, this 22-story hotel feels downright intimate, with a small, slick marble lobby, and the entire property is run like the concierge level in many hotels, with a lounge on the fifth floor serving free breakfast mornings and free hors d'oeuvres (5 to 7pm). The doubles have two double beds, which makes them do-able for many families; there's not a lot of extra room, but it's sufficient—and if you've chosen to stay here, just off Times Square, chances are you don't intend to lounge around your room much anyhow. The decor is unspectacular and traditional.

Dining: Russo's Steak and Pasta, off the lobby, serves lunch and dinner (no lunch on weekends).

Amenities: Concierge, 24-hour room service, newspaper delivery, in-room fax/copier, indoor pool, complimentary access to the health club at the Sheraton New York.

INEXPENSIVE

Days Hotel Midtown

790 Eighth Ave. (at 48th St.), New York, NY 10019. ☎ **800/572-6232** or 800/325-2525, or 212/581-7000. Fax 212/974-0291. 367 units. A/C TV TEL. $155–$219 double; $250–$305 one-bedroom suite; $290–$400 two-bedroom suite. Third person $20; children 18 and under stay free in parents' room. Rollaway $20; crib free. AE, CB, DC, DISC, MC, V. Parking $11. Subway: C/E to 50th St.

The Days Hotel is the kind of place New Yorkers love to sneer at, because it's a mass-market chain popular with low-end tour groups (high school class trips, foreigners on package trips), but there's really nothing seriously wrong with the place. So long as you're careful about heading south when you leave the front door, this location actually isn't all that bad—just to the north on Eighth Avenue you'll find the Big Apple Tour buses, the Worldwide Plaza office complex (which has a great multiplex cinema), and several casual trendy restaurants. To the south, however, there are still a few peep shows and scuzzy bars and homeless hangouts, remnants of the old 42nd Street sleaze.

The Days Hotel may be as bland as a suburban mall but it's respectably clean, with a marble-and-brass lobby and neat, fresh, motel-like traditional furnishings in the rooms. Considering how small many Manhattan hotel rooms are, these are relatively large, with space for a crib or rollaway even if you opt for a room with two double beds. At these prices, though, larger families may be able to afford two connecting doubles, of which there are lots. The rooftop pool, one of the Days Hotel's bigger drawing points, is a bit of a disappointment—it's not big enough for lap swimming, and you aren't allowed to dive in. The small sundeck surrounding the pool is crammed with cheap lounge chairs; there's also a poolside snack bar. Just off the lobby, the bright but bare Metro Deli serves casual food 6am to midnight and provides room service (an unexpected perk in this price range) while it's open.

Holiday Inn Midtown 57th Street

440 W. 57th St. (between Ninth and Tenth aves.), New York, NY 10019. ☎ **800/HOLIDAY** or 212/581-8100. Fax 212/581-7739. 599 units. A/C TV TEL. $159–$259 double; $350–$700 suite. Rollaway $15; crib free. AE, DC, DISC, MC, V. Parking $13.50. Subway: 1/9/A/B/C/D to Columbus Circle.

This characterless motor inn suits its characterless surroundings on Midtown's far west fringe. If you're driving into Manhattan, the low parking rate from the attached garage may appeal to you, especially since this property is close to the West Side Highway. And if you think your kids can't survive a vacation without a pool handy, the outdoor rooftop pool (open in summer only) may be a draw. But otherwise this hotel has few virtues to overcome its out-of-the-way location (it's a long walk even to the Hard Rock Cafe) and its typical chain-motel layout, with large modern windows looking out at nothing particularly scenic.

The double rooms are of decent size by Manhattan standards—out-of-towners may think they're cramped, but they do fit two double beds comfortably, which means a whole family may be able to fit in. There are a number of connecting doubles, if your family wants more space to spread out. Rooms have neutral-toned contemporary-style furnishings; those who are interested in swimming might try to snag one in the south tower, where the pool is. The Gotham Café serves breakfast, and the Via Strada restaurant serves Italian food for lunch and dinner; room service operates 6:30am to 10:30pm, and there's a small exercise room.

Travel Inn

515 W. 42nd St. (between Tenth and Eleventh aves.), New York, NY 10036. ☎ **800/869-4630** or 212/695-7171. Fax 212/967-5025. 160 units. A/C TV TEL. $150–$165 double. Rollaway or crib $15. AE, DC, DISC, MC, V. Free parking. Subway: A/C/E to 42nd St./Port Authority. Bus: M42.

One of New York's very best deals is this bright, clean, sprucely decorated motor inn way at the end of 42nd Street—beyond the sleaze, beyond Theater Row, in an area of warehouses and parking lots and not much else. One reason to stay here is you get free parking; of course, what you save in parking you could easily spend in taxi fare, since the only attractions within walking distance are the Circle Line boat tours and the *Intrepid* Sea-Air-Space Museum (see chapter 4). Still, the Travel Inn remains very busy—there are many times when it's sold out months and months in advance—partly because it's so handy for conventioneers attending meetings at the nearby Javits Convention Center.

If you don't mind the grungy surroundings (the hotel certainly seems secure enough), you could save a whole lot by staying here: A family could fit comfortably in these rooms, which have two double beds, a desk, a dresser, and upholstered chairs. The decor is modern, and everything is well kept up; the baths are spotless. And as befits a true motor inn, there's a pool—not only that, an Olympic-size pool, set in a spacious tiled area with lots of lounge chairs and room to stroll around. A number of rooms overlook the pool area from balconied walkways—request one of these, as opposed to the ones overlooking the street. There's no room service (what do you expect at this price?), but the attached Riverwest Cafe and Deli will deliver up to your room 6am to 8pm.

5 Midtown East

VERY EXPENSIVE

The Four Seasons

57 E. 57th St. (between Madison and Park aves.), New York, NY 10022. ☎ **800/332-3442** or 212/758-5700. Fax 212/758-5711. 370 units. A/C MINIBAR TV TEL. $545–$900 double; $975–$9,000 suite. Extra person in room $50. Rollaway or crib free. AE, DC, MC, V. Parking $33. Subway: 4/5/6 to 59th St.

This stunning 57th Street hotel designed by I. M. Pei has set new standards in New York for service, upscale chic, and high prices. The tortoise-shell onyx skylight and soaring octagonal limestone columns in the cathedral-like foyer instill a sense of awe, and everything from there on is hushed and decorous and knowingly subtle. Smartly dressed guests wander through the lobby toting the right designer shopping bags; the attentiveness of the staff is wonderful, without a trace of fawning or condescension. The guest rooms are furnished with sleek built-in cabinetry of blond English sycamore, beautifully streamlined stuff Frank Lloyd Wright would approve of. The marble baths are huge and superbly appointed, with roomy adjacent dressing areas.

The room layouts aren't particularly handy for families: A maximum of one extra bed is allowed per room (crib or rollaway) and there are only a few adjoining doubles that could be set off by shutting a common door to the corridor. Larger families will have to go for a suite, which knocks you up into the $1,000-plus range. All the suites are on the higher floors, 31 and above (the hotel is 52 stories tall), which gives many of them stunning Central Park views. But the Four Seasons does value its young guests enough to have welcoming cookies and milk, as well as a gift pack.

Dining: The Fifty Seven Fifty Seven restaurant serves contemporary American food, and the Lobby Lounge serves light American/continental fare for breakfast, lunch, tea, and dinner.

Amenities: Concierge, 24-hour room service; health club with exercise machines, whirlpool, sauna, spa services; business center.

Regal U.N. Plaza Hotel

One United Nations Plaza (44th St. and First Ave.), New York, NY 10017. ☎ **800/222-8888** or 212/758-1234. Fax 212/702-5051. 427 units. A/C MINIBAR TV TEL. $350 double; $450–$1,500 suite. Rollaway $25; crib free. Weekend packages available. AE, CB, DC, DISC, MC, V. Valet parking $27. Subway: 4/5/6/7/S to Grand Central.

The Regal U.N. Plaza's neighborhood hardly qualifies as Midtown—across from the United Nations, it's deliciously quiet, safe, and residential. When you combine that with the peerless views (all rooms are on the 28th floor or above, overlooking the East River or the skyline, uptown or down), the premium prices start to make sense. The clientele is heavily international, with foreign businesspeople as well as some United Nations visitors, and one signature note of the hotel's decor is the many international textiles hanging framed in the halls, echoed in the rooms by interesting textures in the upholstery, drapes, and bedspreads. Although it's a sleek corporate-style hotel, families may well be attracted not only by the neighborhood but by the fact that it has a great pool—what may well be the prettiest pool in town, with a haremlike canopy hanging overhead and those dynamite views from windows on two sides.

There are two towers to choose from, connected by a disconcertingly slick lobby: the original East Tower, built in 1976, and the newer West Tower, built in 1980. While the East Tower is on the same elevator bank as the pool and has better river views, the West Tower makes up for it with floor-to-ceiling windows that really let you drink in the panorama. (Each room that ends in 31 is a lush two-bedroom suite, with a wedge-shaped living room that enjoys both river and skyline views, perfectly heavenly day or night.) The rooms feel slightly like ocean-liner cabins to me, with their richly hued wood trims, streamlined modern decor, and tidy built-in cabinets and desks and dressers. They're on the small side, which can be a problem for families. The double rooms have only a king-size bed or two twins—there are no doubles with two double beds—and fire laws permit only one extra bed. Larger families will have to go for a suite (with kitchenette) or hope they can get connecting doubles (not guaranteed but almost always possible).

Dining: The Ambassador Grill serves American grill fare, with an open kitchen showing off the wood-fired rotisserie spits. Breakfast, lunch, and dinner are available, with brunch replacing the lunch menu on weekends.

Amenities: Concierge, 24-hour room service, newspaper delivery, in-room fax capability; health club with pool, exercise machines, weights, saunas; indoor tennis court on the 39th floor; business center; complimentary limo to Wall Street and Park Avenue weekdays, transportation to the Theater.

W New York

541 Lexington Ave. (at 49th St.), New York, NY 10017. ☎ **800/22-DORAL** or 212/755-1200. 717 units. A/C MINIBAR TV TEL. $239–$325 double; $450–$1,500 suite. Rollaway or crib free. AE, DC, DISC, MC, V. Valet parking $34. Subway: 6 to 51st St.

In its latest incarnation, this large 1929-vintage property on Lexington's Midtown hotel row has improbably positioned itself as a boutique hotel for hip business travelers—and surprisingly, it works. The interior design, by the acclaimed David Rockwell, is distinctive, featuring bleached wood furniture, stunning metallic headboards, and beds piled high with pillows and duvets. Despite the central location a couple of blocks north of Grand Central, the mood is restful and surprisingly serene, down to the soothing messages printed on the sheets. It isn't ideal for a tourist family with young active kids, but for parents bringing an older child along on a business trip, it's great. Make that parent, singular: The rooms are on the small side, with a double holding only a queen-size bed or two twins—a rollaway would be a tight fit. There aren't many connecting doubles, and even a one-bedroom suite would require a rollaway, since none of the sitting-room sofas folds out. No rooms have kitchenettes, either. But if you don't have a big family along and can squeeze into a double, the room rates are quite reasonable. The 10,000-square-foot health spa is another definite plus, with its range of spa services.

Dining: Celebrity restaurateur Drew Nieporent runs the hotels' Heartbeat restaurant, which specializes in natural organic cuisine. Lighter fare is available at the Lobby Juice Bar; the hotel's bar is called, simply enough, Bar.

Amenities: Concierge, 24-hour room service, newspaper delivery, VCRs, CD players, health club, business center.

EXPENSIVE

The Drake Swissôtel

440 Park Ave. (at 56th St.), New York, NY 10022. ☎ **800/DRAKE-NY** or 212/421-0900. Fax 212/371-4190. 496 units. A/C TV TEL. $285–$425 double; $450–$1,000 suite. Rollaway or crib $30. AE, CB, DC, DISC, MC, V. Valet parking $36. Subway: 4/5/6 to 59th St.

The Drake is owned by Swiss Air, which may or may not have any connection to the fact that the wood-paneled lobby has an intricate big clock in a glass cube, its gears exposed and different faces showing the time in different time zones. This is a business-oriented property, with a top-notch business center and a corporate-looking room decor. Still, it has some definite virtues for families. Like the W New York (above), the Drake has been around since the 1920s under one ownership or another, but it has the virtue of really good-sized rooms—a double with two double beds doesn't feel too cramped. Be aware that if you bring in a crib or rollaway you'll be charged an extra $30, which is pretty steep compared to what other hotels charge. The minirefrigerator comes unstocked—you won't have to worry about your 6-year-old innocently wolfing down a $5 candy bar or your 12-year-old sneaking out little bottles of liquor (there's a vending area down the hall where you can buy snacks and drinks at reasonable prices). And the Park Avenue location is relatively safe and serene, handy to both Midtown attractions and Upper East Side museums and shopping.

Dining: The Drake Bar, at one end of the lobby, is a popular place, well set up for buffet breakfast and buffet lunch, as well as drinks (it really hops at happy hour). The American menu has some Swiss specialties.

Amenities: Concierge, 24-hour room service, newspaper delivery, weekday morning limo to Wall Street, in-room fax capabilities; health club with sauna, spa facilities; excellent business center with private computer work stations to rent, secretarial support, color laser printers and color copiers, four private conference rooms, and cell phones, pagers, and laptops to rent.

✪ The Roger Smith

501 Lexington Ave. (at 47th St.), New York, NY 10017. ☎ **800/445-0277** or 212/755-1400. Fax 212/758-4061. 133 units. A/C TV TEL. $255 double; $310–$415 suite. Rates include continental breakfast. Extra person $20. Rollaway or crib free. Weekend and seasonal packages available. AE, CB, DC, DISC, MC, V. Valet parking $23. Subway: 4/5/6/7/S to Grand Central.

The Roger Smith is decidedly quirky, which may be why so many musicians and artists and Europeans choose to stay here. The small oval lobby is a minigallery in itself, with paintings and sculptures and polished wainscoting inset with bronze sculptural forms. Upstairs, however, the look is more like a country inn, with individually decorated rooms featuring such items as canopy beds, stocked bookshelves, and chintz upholstery and bedspreads. Lots of hotels boast of a homey feeling, but the rooms here really do qualify. There's a variety of room layouts, including some connecting rooms and a junior suite that has a double bed and a foldout couch in the same room. For the price of a double at the Waldorf or the Plaza, here you can get a suite that includes not only a pullout couch in the sitting room and a double bed in the bedroom but also a second cozy bedroom with a twin bed.

Though none of the rooms has a full kitchen, many have pantries with a refrigerator, microwave, and coffeemaker. And as if that weren't enough, continental breakfast is included (rare enough in New York hotels), served every morning in Lily's, a spunky little bistro with gaudy murals; Lily's also serves an interesting continental menu for lunch and dinner (closed weekends). For $10 a day, Roger Smith guests can get a day pass to the Excelsior Club, an excellent health with a pool, only 10 blocks away. This lively, fun hotel does a pretty brisk business, but its slowest months are July and August—peak family travel time—so cross your fingers and call ahead if you're visiting New York in summer.

✪ Waldorf-Astoria

301 Park Ave. (between 49th and 50th sts.), New York, NY 10022. ☎ **800/WALDORF** or 800/HILTONS, or 212/355-3000. Fax 212/872-7272. 1,568 units. A/C MINIBAR TV TEL. $295–$390 double; $335–$1,075 suite. Children stay free in parents' room. Rollaway or crib free. Weekend packages available. AE, CB, DC, DISC, MC, V. Parking $37. Subway: 6 to 51st St.

This is my sentimental favorite among Manhattan's grand hotels, because I stayed here at age 13 when my dad came to New York for a convention. That was long before the Waldorf became a Hilton, but the chain seems to have kept up this flag-ship property very well, devoting a lot of taste and money to maintaining its char-acter. The wide stately corridors, the vintage deco door fixtures, the white-gloved bellmen, the luxe shopping arcade, and that knockout lobby all trumpet Grand Hotel, and there's a certain electric thrill about being here, even among the well-heeled guests. Enter from the Park Avenue side and you'll cross a stunning round mosaic under an immense crystal chandelier; in the main lobby, the four-sided free-standing Waldorf clock, covered with bronze relief figures, should fascinate your children as much as it did me all those years ago.

Upstairs, the silent plush-carpeted corridors seem to run on forever. The room decor is pleasant if unremarkable—a sort of traditional English country-house-style look. The standard double rooms are larger than those at the Plaza (above)—the Waldorf was, after all, built 24 years later; request a room with two double beds if you've got more than one kid. A minisuite, combining one king-size-bedded room with a sitting room, might work better, though not all have foldout couches; some suites have kitchenettes, so ask for one if that's important. There's also a number of connecting doubles you can request. The staff seems unfailingly gracious, though in such a large hotel you won't get the personal service you might at a smaller place. There are 195 rooms in the Waldorf Towers, with a separate entrance; the duke and duchess of Windsor and John F. Kennedy are among the guests who've resided here. Staying in the pricier Towers, which have more distinctive antique-laden decor, snags you some extra amenities, like complimentary continental breakfast and hors d'oeuvres in a lounge on the 26th floor.

Dining: The Waldorf has four restaurants: Both the casual cafe Oscar's and the ornate French restaurant Peacock Alley serve breakfast, lunch, and dinner; you can also get lunch or dinner in the Japanese Inagiku or the clubby steak-and-seafood the Bull and Bear. Sir Harry's Bar, fitted out like an African safari, serves drinks.

Amenities: Concierge, 24-hour room service, health club with steam rooms and exercise machines ($30 charge to guests), business center, shopping arcade.

MODERATE

✪ Beekman Tower

3 Mitchell Place (First Ave. at 49th St.), New York, NY 10017. ☎ **800/ME-SUITE** or 212/355-7300. Fax 212/753-9366. 174 units. A/C TV TEL. $279 studio suite; $319-$359 one-bedroom suite; $575 two-bedroom suite. Rollaway $20; crib free. AE, DISC, MC, V. Valet parking $23. Subway: E/F to Lexington/Third aves.

In many respects, the Beekman Tower offers the best of all worlds. You're convenient to Midtown but in the posh residential East 50s, where peace and safety reign. You have all the roominess of a small apartment but with lots of hotel services. You get some super views but don't have to pay through the nose for them.

This orange-brick deco tower rising on a slope just north of the United Nations is known to New Yorkers for the Top of the Tower, a pleasant and unpretentious restaurant and lounge with a wonderful view of the skyline and East River. What New Yorkers don't seem to know is what a great deal this all-suite hotel is. Its smallest suite, the studio, will work only for a small family—it has a queen- or full-sized bed and a small sofa (not all of them fold out), but there's plenty of room for a crib or rollaway, and it has a kitchenette. The one-bedroom suites are perfectly fine, with a foldout couch in the spacious living room and a separate bedroom with a king- or queen-size bed.

And they have full kitchens—a four-burner stove, a full refrigerator, a big sink, a microwave, a coffeemaker, pots and pans, and, incredibly enough, a dishwasher.

With clean, up-to-date appliances and a grocery-shopping service ($5 charge), these are kitchens people really can use. Ask for a "C-line suite" and you'll also get a dynamite East River view. The traditional room decor is easy to live with. Other hotel perks include a Laundromat, a small fitness room (free to guests), a concierge, and room service until 1am; deluxe suites also have VCRs, in-room fax machines, and, on top floors, balconies. The Top of the Tower serves lunch and dinner, and the Zephyr Grill serves upscale American food for breakfast, lunch, and dinner. On top of it all, the staff is very accommodating. July and August are particularly good times to snag a room; you may be able to negotiate on rates then.

The Beekman Towers is part of Manhattan East Suites hotels, as are the Surrey and Lyden Gardens (above). Other Manhattan East Suites hotels in Midtown are the **Dumont Plaza,** 150 E. 34th St., between Third and Lexington avenues (☎ **212/481-7600**); **Eastgate Tower,** 222 E. 39th St., between Second and Third avenues (☎ **212/687-8000**); the **Lyden House Suite Hotel,** 320 E. 53rd St., between First and Second avenues (☎ **212/888-6070**); the **Plaza Fifty Suite Hotel,** 155 E. 50th St., at Third Avenue (☎ **212/751-5710**); the **Shelburne Murray Hill Suites,** 303 Lexington Ave. at 37th Street (☎ **212/689-5200**); and the **Southgate Tower,** 371 Seventh Ave. at 31st Street (☎ **212/563-1800**). All are in roughly the same price category, and reservations at any of them can be made by calling ☎ **800/ME-SUITE.**

Hotel Lexington

511 Lexington Ave. (at 48th St.), New York, NY 10017. ☎ **800/448-4471** or 212/755-4400. Fax 212/751-4091. 714 units. A/C TV TEL. $205–$265 double, $275 VIP room, $325 junior suite, $375 one-bedroom suite. Rollaway $15; crib free. AE, DC, DISC, MC, V. Parking nearby $25–$35. Subway: 6 to 51st St.; 4/5/6/7/S to Grand Central.

One of the best family values along Lexington's Midtown hotel strip is this handsome place owned by Taj International Hotels of India. From the spiffy brass porte-cochère above the 48th Street entrance to the quietly sedate mahogany-paneled lobby with its big crystal chandelier, the Lexington looks like an upscale boutique hotel, but at 27 stories and 700-plus rooms it's much larger than it feels. Look and listen and you'll notice it has a sophisticated international clientele (not surprising in a foreign-owned hotel, especially one in the U.N. vicinity). Though it's an older property, it has been neatly kept up, with few signs of age; the baths have been tidily modernized with gray marble floors and modern white fixtures, except for one stunning suite bath I saw with vintage maroon-and-yellow tilework and fixtures.

The guest-room decor shows quiet verve, with tasteful framed prints on the walls and furniture of light cherry wood styled in neoclassical forms—neither too corporate nor too chintzy. The one-bedroom suites are positively rambling, with a huge bedroom and sitting room and a neat kitchenette (no cooking facilities, but enough to make sandwiches); some of the one-bedroom suites even have little terraces where you can step outside and study the skyscrapers all around. Junior suites have somewhat smaller rooms but still two baths; all suite sitting rooms have foldout couches. What the hotel calls its VIP rooms are perhaps the best buy for small families: These are basically large double rooms that have a double bed, a single bed, and two baths, as well as plenty of space for a crib or rollaway, all for only $275. VIP rooms also have microwaves and coffeemakers and fridges. There are also lots of connecting pairs of doubles, and this is the only hotel I visited that says it'll guarantee you the connecting rooms when you make reservations. The whole place seems well run, with thoughtful, friendly service; it's dignified enough to be restful, but not at all stuffy.

Dining: Breakfast, lunch, and dinner are served in Raffles, a cheery dinerlike corner coffee shop, and all three meals are also served in Vuli, an Italian bistro just off the lobby. The hotel's upscale restaurant is J. Sung Dynasty, a lovely gourmet Chinese restaurant that does a brisk lunch and dinner business with nonguests as well as guests. Guests get complimentary admission to the country-and-western nightclub Denim and Diamonds, also on the premises.

Amenities: Concierge, room service (7am to 10:30pm), small fitness room with exercise machines.

✪ The Kimberly

145 E. 50th St. (between Lexington and Third aves.), New York, NY 10022. ☎ **800/683-0400** or 212/755-0400. Fax 212/486-6915. 184 units. A/C MINIBAR TV TEL. $245–$325 double; $265–$435 one-bedroom suite; $409–$675 two-bedroom suite. Rates include continental breakfast. Children under 18 stay free in parents' room. Rollaway or crib free. Weekend rates and summer packages available. AE, CB, DC, DISC, MC, V. Valet parking $23. Subway: 6 to 51st St.; E/F to Lexington/Third aves.

More people ought to know about this plush smaller hotel on a spruce Midtown East block heading toward the town houses of Turtle Bay. The glitzy small lobby, full of pale shiny marble and gilt rococo furnishings, has pizzazz but not a high snobbery quotient, thanks to a friendly, unpretentious veteran staff. Since the 30-story building was designed in the mid-1980s as an apartment building (though it was turned into a hotel immediately), the rooms are all big—even the standard doubles don't feel crowded when they have two double beds in them (a great set-up for families on a short visit). The closets are sizable, as are the nicely appointed baths. The one-bedroom suites could sleep six, with two double beds in the bedroom and a pullout couch in the sitting room. The decor is traditional, with quality furniture in dark woods; vases and framed prints and other accents give each room a bit of a residential flair. All suites have kitchenettes, galley kitchens with cooking burners, pots and pans, and full-size refrigerators stocked with complimentary sodas and juices (no rip-off minibars here). And now here's the kicker: Almost every room has a balcony where you can sit and have breakfast or cocktails while watching the Manhattan ad execs, lawyers, and publishing types scurry to or from their offices far below.

Dining/Diversions: Breakfast, lunch, and dinner are served in Tam-Tam, serving an eclectic American menu. The hotel's other restaurant, Tatou, which serves lunch and dinner, has one of the more interesting restaurant interiors in New York, looking like a rather louche little Parisian theater; there's a late-evening cabaret show here nightly, and the cover charge is waived for guests Monday to Thursday.

Amenities: Concierge, 24-hour room service, newspaper delivery; free hors d'oeuvres 5 to 7pm in Tatou; complimentary access to all branches of the New York Health & Racquet Club (same owner), with Saturday-morning swim session for kids; limo service to nearby NYHRC branch; complimentary sailing on NYHRC party yacht from South Street Seaport; Laundromat in basement.

Loews New York

569 Lexington Ave. (at 51st St.), New York, NY 10022. ☎ **800/836-6471** or 212/752-7000. Fax 212/752-3817 for reservations, 212/758-6311 for guest use. 722 units. A/C MINIBAR TV TEL. $199–$265 double; $229–$270 junior suite; $345–$470 one-bedroom suite; $720–$899 deluxe suite. Extra person $10; children 12 and under stay free in parents' room. Rollaway $10; crib free. AE, DC, DISC, MC, V. Parking $24. Subway: 6 to 51st St.; E/F to Lexington/Third aves.

Surprisingly smart and sophisticated for its price range, the Loews has a spirited air that begins in the streamlined lobby with its mahogany-and-chrome neo-deco look.

All the rooms sport a contemporary decor that carries on the vaguely Japanese/art deco/Frank Lloyd Wright feel. A double with two double beds is probably the way to go—the reasonably priced junior suite isn't really two rooms but a large room divided by a built-in cabinet into sleeping and sitting areas (the sitting area does have a pullout couch, but still . . .). Some suites have kitchenettes (no cooking facilities).

A refreshingly unstuffy sort of place, the Loews enjoys a decent location in the cleaner part of Midtown, handily above a subway station—and many of the guests who stay here look like people who aren't above using the subway. A few pluses: high chairs, strollers, nonskid tub mats, and child-proofing kits are available on request; they have a stock of board games and Nintendo for kids on request; and both the restaurant and room service have kids' menus. The staff has put together a handout for families, recommending restaurants, stores, and museums (but since you already have this book, it'll contain nothing you don't already know).

Dining: The sleek but reasonably priced Lexington Avenue Grill serves American fare for breakfast, lunch, and dinner. The grill and its bar are open to the lobby, which makes for good people-watching.

Amenities: Clefs d'Or concierge, room service (to midnight), health club (no one under 16 allowed), business center, shopping arcade. Business-class rooms have newspaper delivery, coffeemakers, in-room fax machines, and complimentary breakfast.

INEXPENSIVE

Vanderbilt YMCA

224 E. 47th St. (between Second and Third aves.), New York, NY 10017. ☎ **212/756-9600.** Fax 212/752-0210. 415 units, 7 with bathroom. A/C TV. $71 double without bathroom, $110 double with bathroom; $120 quad (two bunk beds) without bathroom. AE, MC, V. Parking $20–$25 nearby. Subway: E/F to Lexington/Third aves.; 6 to 51st St.; 4/5/6/7 to Grand Central.

You can't reserve the quad rooms in advance at this clean, big, friendly Midtown East Y, but if your kids are old enough that you'd be willing to stay here even in two separate doubles, it's a great money-saving option. The rooms are pleasant if dormlike, but they do have curtains and mirrors and a TV on a stand in the corner, and the down-the-hall baths are quite clean; many rooms have washbasins, which means you don't have to trot down the hall every time you want to wash your face or brush your teeth. The seven en-suite rooms have an adjoining bathroom (shower only) and private phones. There's even a Laundromat and a tour desk on premises. And the location can't be beat, on a clean, safe block not far from the United Nations. The on-premises International Cafe serves decent, cheap deli fare, but there are so many good restaurants nearby you probably won't use it much. Best of all, the Y has extensive up-to-date sports facilities, including an indoor jogging track, loads of classes for kids, and two stellar indoor pools, which guests can use for free during their stay.

6 Gramercy Park

INEXPENSIVE

Gramercy Park Hotel

2 Lexington Ave. (between Gramercy Sq. and 22nd St.), New York, NY 10010. ☎ **800/ 221-4083** or 212/475-4320. Fax 212/505-0535. 359 units. A/C TV TEL. $160 double; $190–$230 suite. Rollaway $10; crib free. AE, CB, DC, DISC, MC, V. Parking $25 nearby. Subway: 6 to 23rd St.

Not only does this hotel have views of leafy green Gramercy Park—a delightful London-style enclosed private square—but guests can even get a key to go inside the iron fence and stroll around on the gravel paths, a privilege many New Yorkers would envy. To me, this isn't enough incentive to stay here, but the Gramercy Park doesn't seem to be hurting for business. The clientele is an odd mix of bedraggled hipsters (rock musicians, alternative journalists, fashion world hangers-on) and bewildered Middle American tourists, whose travel agents must've picked the hotel out of some directory. The rooms are certainly large enough to spread out in, but the furniture is battered and mismatched; the closets are huge, but the baths have worn old fixtures and don't look all that clean. If you're staying here to save money, request one of the double rooms that have two double beds, as opposed to the ones with a king-size bed. Suites have a king-size bed in one room and a foldout couch in the other, so you won't be getting more bed for the money, only more awkward space.

The hotel is 18 stories high, but only floors 12 and above have real views and only rooms in the 02, 03, 04, and 05 lines have park views (they hardly compete with the Central Park views at the Mayflower or Carlyle, above). Some suites have kitchenettes; all other rooms have, instead of a minibar stocked with little liquor bottles and expensive snacks, an empty minirefrigerator that can be handy for keeping children's essentials like milk, apple juice, and peanut butter. Right off the knotty-pine-paneled lobby is a stodgy dining room, serving a continental menu straight out of the 1960s, and a dimly lit shabby cocktail lounge. At the far end of a corridor is a tiny beauty salon that looks lost in a time warp. Room service (7:30am to 10:30pm) is reasonably priced compared to what some hotels charge, and there's a discount rate arranged with a nearby health club.

7 Greenwich Village

INEXPENSIVE

The Larchmont

27 W. 11th St. (between Fifth and Sixth aves.), New York, NY 10011. ☎ **212/989-9333.** Fax 212/989-9496. 55 units, none with bathroom. A/C TV TEL. $60–$70 single, $85–$99 double. Rates include continental breakfast. Rollaway $15. AE, CB, DC, DISC, MC, V. Parking at nearby garages. Subway: F to 14th St.; A/B/C/D/E/F/Q to W. 4th St. (the north end of the platform is at 8th St.).

On what I think is Greenwich Village's most beautiful town-house block, the Larchmont offers pleasant no-frills lodging, best for people who don't plan to spend much of their visit in their rooms. It's also best for families with older kids, since there are no suites and the doubles are too small to add a third person without making things awfully cramped (the hotel doesn't have any cribs but does have rollaways). No rooms are connecting, but if you think your offspring could handle staying in a separate room down the hall, you could go for two doubles or a double and single, depending on how many kids you have. Security seems reassuringly good, with a locked front door and locked corridor access. Another drawback for some families: There are no private baths. The rooms do have washbasins, but the toilet and shower (modern and very clean) are down the hall in the European manner.

The reception room and breakfast room are handsome, with cream-colored walls, potted plants, and tapestry-print upholstery; at first it's disconcerting to enter the narrow, rather grim-looking guest-room halls, but the rooms themselves are neat and soothing, with peach and pastel colors, rattan furniture, drapes, and framed artwork. A few full-time residents from before the building's 1995 conversion still live here, so there are small kitchenettes off the halls for their use;

Downtown Accommodations

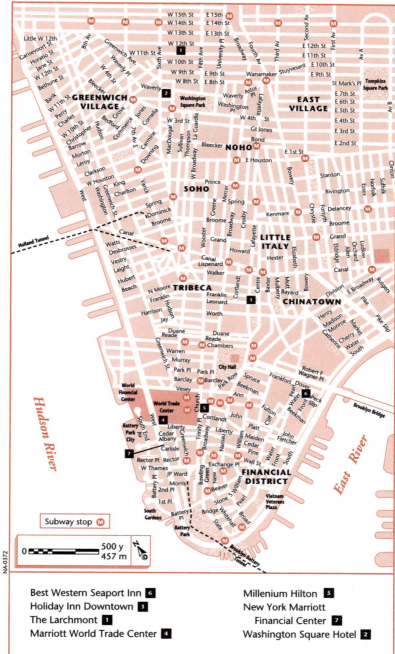

Subway stop Ⓜ

0   500 y
457 m

NA-0372

Best Western Seaport Inn **6**
Holiday Inn Downtown **3**
The Larchmont **1**
Marriott World Trade Center **4**

Millenium Hilton **5**
New York Marriott
   Financial Center **7**
Washington Square Hotel **2**

guests might be able to store perishable food in the refrigerator, though there are no community utensils for cooking. All told, the Larchmont's a pretty fair choice for that dead-low price—if the configuration works for your family.

✪ Washington Square Hotel

103 Waverly Place (between Sixth Ave. and MacDougal St.), New York, NY 10011. ☎ **800/ 222-0418** or 212/777-9515. Fax 212/979-8373. 170 units. A/C TV TEL. $129–$170 double. Rates include continental breakfast. Rollaway $20; crib free. AE, MC, V. Parking at nearby garages. Subway: A/B/C/D/E/F/Q to W. 4th St.

With its fantastic location at the corner of Washington Square Park, the focal point of Greenwich Village—Bob Dylan and Joan Baez lived here, when it was the Hotel Earle in the folkie 1960s—the Washington Square Hotel would probably do well even if it weren't so nice. The good news is that this small hotel is a winner on its own account: clean, cheery, and tastefully furnished—and very low priced. Absolutely book a room here as soon as you know you're coming to New York, because lots of people have found out about this gem and it's nearly always full.

The rooms are just big enough to comfortably accommodate a crib or rollaway, but at these prices a family might as well spring for a quad room, which has two double beds; request no. 902, the largest, which is in front with a super view of leafy Washington Square Park. (Any front room on the fifth through ninth floors has good park views.) If you want to spring for connecting doubles—and at these prices, why not?—request Rooms 219 and 220, which share a bath. All other rooms have their own small but spruce white tiled baths; the bedrooms are simply furnished in restful tones, with bleached wood and padded headboards creating a contemporary look that seems more Californian than New York. There are plenty of generous-size mirrors and reading lamps, operating on the novel assumption that guests might actually like to read in bed.

After the Parisian-looking little lobby, with its wrought-iron gate and marble staircase, the Holiday Inn–ish decor of the rooms might disappoint some, but only those who haven't seen what else is available in this price range in Manhattan. There's even a small exercise room, with all the essential machines, right off the lobby. Besides getting continental breakfast free in the CIII restaurant downstairs, guests get a 10% discount on other meals they might take in the restaurant (including afternoon tea), which serves an eclectic menu that draws locals on its own merits. There's no room service, but this part of the Village is crawling with restaurants in all price ranges that stay open all hours, and walking around here is a pleasure at night. True, street musicians may be performing into the wee hours in the park across the street, but compared to the bustle of Midtown that's a minor annoyance.

8 Lower Manhattan

EXPENSIVE

Millenium Hilton

55 Church St. (between Fulton and Dey sts.), New York, NY 10007. ☎ **800/HILTONS** or 212/693-2001. Fax 212/571-2316. 560 units. A/C MINIBAR TV TEL. $300–$360 double; $450–$1,500 suite. Children stay free in parents' room. AE, CB, DC, DISC, MC, V. Parking $35. Subway: 1/9 to Cortlandt St.; C/E to World Trade Center.

This slim black-glass high-rise plinth faces the World Trade Center across Church Street and soot-blackened historic St. Paul's church across Fulton Street. The place positively screams V.I.P., with a beautiful but spare lobby and sleek, subtle room decor. Streamlined golden maple cabinets and built-ins pack a lot into the space, while large windows let in floods of light; floors 31 to 55—the high-rise rooms, on a separate elevator bank—have astounding daytime views of neighboring skyscrapers, as well as snatches of the Hudson and the harbor and the East River. The baths are quite upscale, with black marble counters and all the chi-chi amenities.

Families will probably do best with the double-doubles (double rooms with a pair of double beds); the suites are tailored to high-level execs who need to do some entertaining, so they have only minimal kitchen facilities and don't necessarily have pullout couches. Why should a family stay here? One reason is that there's a lovely 40-foot pool that seems empty most of the time, overlooking the landmark church next door. The views can be great, and the location is handy, though Lower Manhattan does get deserted at night. Children are welcomed with a gift at check-in, and toys and games are available on loan during their stay.

Dining: American food is served in the upscale Taliesin restaurant (named after Frank Lloyd Wright's home, presumably because Wright influenced the hotel's sleek decor). The Grille is a more casual alternative. Both restaurants serve breakfast, lunch, and dinner.

Amenities: Concierge, 24-hour room service, newspaper delivery, indoor pool, fitness center with exercise machines, in-room fax capability, business center.

MODERATE

Holiday Inn Downtown

138 Lafayette St. (between Canal and Howard sts.), New York, NY 10013. ☎ **800/HOLIDAY** or 212/966-8898. Fax 212/966-3933. 223 units. A/C TV TEL. $175–$209 double; from $229 suite. Rollaway $15; crib free. AE, CB, DC, DISC, MC, V. Valet parking $25. Subway: 6/N/R to Canal St.

At the nexus of Chinatown, Little Italy, and SoHo, this modern midrange hotel occupies a converted factory/warehouse a block north of Canal Street. Take your basic contemporary Holiday Inn decor and add Asian accents—a stylized floral still life here, a subtle woven wallpaper there—and you've got an idea of what this place looks like: sparkling clean and only a bit impersonal-looking (the staff, many of whom are Asian, seem very helpful).

The lobby is one floor up from the busy, grubby commercial street; the rooms haven't been well soundproofed and the windows are a bit high, which makes things feel institutional. The rooms aren't large (high ceilings make them look smaller), so only a limited number of doubles contain two double beds; larger families may want to get connecting doubles, which might have a king-size or a queen-size bed, or two twin beds. The Pacifica restaurant serves all meals, including a big breakfast buffet, with a menu that straddles both Western and Chinese cuisine. Room service runs to 11pm. About 40% of the clientele is foreign, which may simply mean that travel agents in other countries can spot a good deal when they see one.

Marriott World Trade Center

3 World Trade Center, New York, NY 10048. ☎ **800/228-9290** or 212/938-9100. Fax 212/444-3444. 831 units. A/C MINIBAR TV TEL. $155–$339 double; $425–$1,750 suite. Rollaway or crib free. Weekend and summer packages available. AE, CB, DC, DISC, MC, V. Valet parking $25 (unlimited in/out). Subway: C/E to World Trade Center; 1/9 to Cortlandt St.

As the Vista Hotel, this gleaming 22-story property went through a multimillion-dollar renovation after "the incident," as people at the World Trade Center refer to the 1993 terrorist bombing. Marriott took over in late 1995 and hasn't had to do much since, except watch business climb back up. What's special about this hotel is its in-the-thick-of-it location—walk out the back doors and you're on the World Trade Center's sprawling plaza, with its huge fountain, pushcart cafes, and occasional free outdoor entertainment; you're right next door to the WTC observation deck, so you can beat the lines first thing in the morning. Just about all the rooms have excellent views, especially those overlooking Battery Park City and the Hudson to the west (it's worth having room-service dinner just to watch the sunsets).

There's also a super rooftop health club—open to nonguest members, however, which means it can get overly busy at peak lunch and after-work hours. The 50-foot indoor pool has panoramic windows on both sides, but exercise machines have been set up around it, which is quite disconcerting. The rooms here are of a decent size, with upscale traditional decor. If you get a double with two double beds, there's still room for a crib or rollaway, but not much left over. Basically, this is a big, rather soulless hotel with a can't-be-beat location; it's full of corporate types on weekdays, but book on a weekend and you may save as much as a $100 off weekday rates.

Dining: The Greenhouse Cafe is a cheery, casual atrium restaurant serving American food for breakfast, lunch, and dinner, with a standard kids' menu (and placemats to color) at all meals. The Tall Ships Bar & Grill is a clubby spot for lunch or dinner.

Amenities: Concierge, 24-hour room service, indoor pool, full-service health club (jogging track, saunas, exercise machines, massages), business center.

✪ New York Marriott Financial Center

85 West St. (at Albany St.), New York, NY 10006. ☎ **800/228-9290** or 212/385-4900. Fax 212/227-8136. 517 units. A/C MINIBAR TV TEL. $145–$339 double; $450–$1,600 suite. Rollaway or crib free. Weekend packages available. AE, CB, DC, DISC, MC, V. Valet parking $25. Subway: C/E to World Trade Center; 1/9/N/R to Rector St.

From Lower Manhattan's top three choices—the Marriott World Trade Center (above), the Millenium Hilton (above), and the New York Marriott—this one's my choice for families. The smallest of the three, it's also the least snooty. It has the same wonderful skyline and harbor views as the Marriott World Trade Center (and even better views than lower floors at the Millenium Hilton) and has its own 50-foot pool, bigger than the one at the Millenium Hilton and more private than the one at the Marriott WTC. So what if the pool has no views? When they're splashing in the water, kids don't care if there are glorious vistas at hand. The small lobby is less of a knock-out than those other two, with a more traditional marble-and-mahogany look, but it's less intimidating too.

The double rooms with two double beds are roomy enough to take a crib or rollaway, there are plenty of connecting doubles, and the executive suite is a decent option for families, with a pullout couch in the sitting room. Some rooms have a traditional neoclassical decor, while others tend toward Japanese contemporary. The baths are good-sized, and the staff is very accommodating. If you're going to be in Manhattan for the weekend, ask if weekend packages are in effect—they could save you nearly $100 a night over the weekday rates, plus throwing in a complimentary breakfast. You'll be right across from Battery Park City, within walking distance of the Statue of Liberty/Ellis Island ferry, and not far from South Street Seaport—and have a very comfy hotel room to boot.

Dining: JW's serves a casual, eclectic/American menu for breakfast, lunch, and dinner. The Battery Park Tavern serves lunch and dinner; Pugsley's Pub is an on-site microbrew pub.

Amenities: Concierge (limited hours), room service (to midnight), indoor pool, fitness room with exercise machines, business center.

INEXPENSIVE

Best Western Seaport Inn

33 Peck Slip (between Front and Water sts.), New York, NY 10038. ☎ **800/HOTEL-NY** or 212/766-6600. Fax 212/766-6615. 72 units. A/C TV TEL. $134–$174 double. Children 17 and under stay free in parents' room. Rollaway $25; crib free. AE, DC, DISC, MC, V. Parking $20 nearby. Subway: 4/5/6 to City Hall.

This spunky little hotel in a converted 19th-century redbrick building has an offbeat location—on a cobbled street just north of the Fulton Fish Market, a couple of blocks up from South Street Seaport, in the lee of the Brooklyn Bridge's Manhattan entrance ramps (a delightful trompe-l'oeil mural on a brick building just east of the hotel shows you what the view through the bridge's arches would look like if the building weren't in the way). Walk through the front door to find a spruce Federal-style decor, a cheerful staff, and goofy laser-disk flames blazing away in a mock fireplace; upstairs are quiet, bright corridors and quite decent guest rooms. Some have two double beds, while others have a queen-size bed plus a foldout couch. The baths are up-to-date and dazzlingly clean—so what if they have wrapped plastic drinking tumblers? (This is a Best Western.) While you don't get kitchenettes, there's an unstocked minirefrigerator in every room, as well as a VCR (pick up a tape at the lobby's self-service rental machine). Some upper-floor rooms have Astroturfed terraces with lawn furniture and partial views of the East River and Seaport; others may have Jacuzzis.

The immediate area's a bit deserted and some nearby buildings look derelict, but you'll be fine walking around here during the day (Pace University is a block away) and there's no trouble getting cabs at night if you walk the block to Pearl Street. Though the inn has no restaurant and no room service, local restaurants will deliver, and there are some fun casual spots quite near, including the Bridge Cafe a block north; Chinatown is quite close, too. For what you save on frills, you can easily afford to spend a little money on cabs by staying here.

10

Side Trips from New York City

by Mercer Warriner

Though New York City has enough attractions to keep even the most active child busy and interested, sometimes it's tempting (at least for parents) to get away from all the bustle, honking horns, and crowded streets—if only for a little while. When the weather's nice, a day trip from Manhattan can be just the ticket.

The following places are all within an hour of the city, and in some cases are close enough to each other to combine in a day—the Hudson Valley Children's Museum and Philipsburg Manor, for example, are just across the Tappan Zee Bridge from each other.

With the exception of the Liberty Science Center, a delightful and quick ferry ride from Lower Manhattan, a car would be the most convenient way to reach these places. But if you have the time and want to make getting there part of the experience, a train or boat ride to Philipsburg Manor would be fun (though the boat excursion is an awfully long sightseeing trip for kids under 12). Buses, run by Metro North or NY Waterway, meet the trains and excursion boats in Tarrytown and bring visitors to the manor.

If you're interested in exploring farther afield, you might want to check out *Frommer's Wonderful Weekends from New York City.*

1 Hudson Valley Children's Museum

Approximately 45 minutes from Manhattan.

GETTING THERE

BY CAR   Take the Henry Hudson Parkway north to the George Washington Bridge; exit after the bridge onto the Palisades Parkway going north. Take Exit 9 to get onto the New York State Thruway (I-87), heading east toward the Tappan Zee Bridge. At Exit 11, take N.Y. 59 going east, which becomes Main Street. Turn right on Broadway to the first left on Burd Street and go 1½ blocks to 21 Burd St. (there's free parking adjacent to the museum).

SEEING THE MUSEUM

Kids 2 to 12 will love the friendly **Hudson Valley Children's Museum,** 21 Burd St., Nyack, N.Y. (☎ **914/358-2191**), where learning through hands-on exploration is actively encouraged. My sons were immediately drawn to the **Gadget Garage,** where they were greeted by a 1966 Deux Chevaux Citröen; the hood of the car has been replaced by glass, so kids can see what happens inside the engine when they push the pedals. Also in the Gadget Garage is a workbench where children of all ages have fun experimenting with gears, pulleys, and tools.

In keeping with the theme of learning through doing, there's also the **Roller-coaster Exhibit,** featuring a zany roller-coaster type of structure made out of tubes and clamps that kids create themselves. Once the course is set, a child cranks a fluorescent golf ball up to the starting point and watches, fascinated, while the ball hurtles down the track. In the back of the museum, the **Royal Bubble Factory** includes all sorts of bubble-making devices. Kids seem especially delighted by the bubble hoop—as they hoist this hoop, a giant bubble immediately grows up around them.

There's also an enormous globe of the world with steps leading up to it, a workshop area built of imaginatively recycled materials, and a sound and music area featuring all sorts of instruments, including a drum that roars like a lion. In the **Young People's Theater,** an "open mike" session every Saturday afternoon lets young would-be entertainers from the audience take the stage. A continual lineup of art workshops draw kids into various hands-on projects.

The **Early Childhood Area** makes a safe haven for kids 5 and under, though these younger kids will definitely want to explore the rest of the museum too. Parents will appreciate the gorgeous views of the Hudson River outside.

Admission: $4 (when it's crowded, time tickets are sold). **Open:** Tuesday to Saturday 10am to 5pm, Sunday noon to 5pm. Also open on most Monday school holidays.

WHERE TO EAT

Bring sandwiches and eat at tables in **Memorial Park,** a wonderfully scenic park on the banks of the Hudson River. As you leave the museum, head left out the door and then take your first left onto Piermont Avenue. The park, which also includes a nice playground, is 2 blocks down Piermont on the left.

2 Philipsburg Manor

Approximately 45 minutes from Manhattan

GETTING THERE

BY CAR   Take the Henry Hudson Parkway north to the Saw Mill River Parkway, which you follow to Exit 20, turning west onto the New York State Thruway (I-87/287) toward the Tappan Zee Bridge and Albany. Get off I-87 at Exit 9, Tarrytown, the last exit before the Tappan Zee Bridge. Go left on N.Y. 119, then take a quick right onto U.S. 9 north. Philipsburg Manor is 2 miles north on the left. The small parking lot next to the entrance can get crowded; for overflow parking, turn right out of the driveway, take another immediate right, and then turn right again into a gravel lot that says KYKUIT (another manor owned by Historic Hudson Valley). Follow the path toward the visitor center.

BY TRAIN   Metro North (☎ **800/METRO-INFO** or 212/532-4900) offers train service from Grand Central Terminal to Tarrytown (a 40-minute trip on express trains, 50 minutes otherwise). One-way adult fares are $5.50 to $7.50, depending on whether you travel at peak or off-peak times; children's fares are 50¢ (age 5 to 11 with an adult). From the station catch a cab, which should cost about $5. Call for details.

BY BOAT   NY Waterway (☎ **800/53-FERRY** for reservations) runs a Sleepy Hollow Cruise once a day, on weekends and holidays, from the West 38th Street pier. A shuttle bus meets the ferry in Tarrytown. The fare (including boat, bus, and Philipsburg Manor admission) is $35 adults and $17.50 children 4 to 11 (kids 3 and under free). The ferry departs at 10:30am and returns at 6:00pm. Estimated time on the ferry is 1½ hours, but the full-day round-trip takes 7 hours and also includes sightseeing at Sunnyside, Washington Irving's manor in Tarrytown, which would interest adults and teenagers but not necessarily younger kids.

TOURING THE MANOR

Philipsburg Manor, U.S. 9, Tarrytown, N.Y. (☎ **914/631-8200**), is an 18th-century colonial farm with a working gristmill, a yard full of animals, a farmhouse, and a tenant house. It's a great excursion for children 6 to 17. Alongside the mill pond is a narrow stream—kids may be awed to learn that 300 years ago it was wide enough to accommodate ships for loading and unloading cargo. A long wooden bridge crosses the mill pond, connecting the gift shop area with the farmhouse, mill, and barn; kids love running across it, not only because it's long and close to the water but also because it gives the feeling of sweeping you straight into the 18th century once you reach the other side.

The guides, decked out in 18th-century dress, demonstrate various farm activities of that era: milling, sheep shearing, plowing, and dairying. Every half hour a guide gives a tour of the farmhouse, where the wealthy Philipse family once lived. (It was African slaves who actually worked the property for the Philipse family, however, laboriously threshing their wheat and grinding it into flour—there's a history lesson here that should stick with your kids.) The stone manor house, built between 1682 and 1720, includes interesting details of colonial life, including a night box to guard candles from rat attacks and a big white mound in the kitchen you later learn is sugar (the guide allows kids several guesses on that one).

Older children (8 and up) would most likely enjoy the tours and historic information, but there's less here to occupy younger children. While they'll certainly get a kick out of the sheep, chickens, cows, and cats wandering about the barnyard, they're not allowed to pat the animals and will quickly tire of the lectures on 18th-century life. But if you're trying to accommodate several ages and interests, don't despair: Your older child can learn about history while your younger child explores the spacious grounds outside. Just be aware that with the pond and the stream so close, parental supervision is necessary at all times.

Admission: $4 kids 6 to 17, $8 adults, $7 seniors; 5 and under free. **Open:** May through December Wednesday to Monday 10am to 4pm.

WHERE TO EAT

To the left of the gift shop is a small **cafe** where you can buy decent gourmet-type sandwiches or salads (under $5). There's not much here to entice children, though, so it might be easier to bring a picnic lunch and eat at the tables by the mill stream.

3 Playland

Approximately 50 minutes from Manhattan

GETTING THERE

BY CAR   Take the Henry Hudson Parkway north to I-95, the Cross Bronx Expressway. Take I-95 to Exit 19 in Rye (Playland Parkway) and then follow the signs to Playland. Parking costs $3 Tuesday to Friday, $5 Saturday and Sunday, and $6 holidays.

BY TRAIN   **Metro North** trains (☎ **800/METRO-INFO** or 212/532-4900) take about 45 minutes from Grand Central Terminal to the Rye station. Adult one-way fares are $6.75 peak and $5 off-peak; children travel for half fare. From the Rye station, take bus no. 76 to Playland. Metro North also organizes seasonal Playland packages, including train and bus fare and a book of tickets; call for details.

ENJOYING THE PARK

In 1923, the Westchester County Park Commission announced it would create an "unequaled seaside public park to provide clean, wholesome recreation for the people of Westchester County." So **Playland,** Playland Parkway, Rye, N.Y. (☎ **914/967-2040**), opened in 1928 and since then has lived up to its lofty declaration—except it doesn't get too self-righteously hung up on the wholesome part, thank goodness. Situated right on Long Island Sound, Playland is the sort of place kids 2 and over overwhelmingly tend to love; it features so many rides, food stalls, game booths, and other amusements it would be impossible to list them all here. Plan on staying for several hours—your kids will insist on nothing less.

No mere rinky-dink midway, Playland is actually listed on the National Register of Historic Places. You'll be happy to know this is not only the cleanest amusement park I've ever seen but that it has also retained its fun retro look: striped awnings, painted wooden fences enclosing the rides, and festive-looking ticket booths. In fact, it's a lovely spot, with wide water views, meticulous landscaping, and art deco buildings (this was the first of several famous deco projects designed by the award-winning architectural firm of Walker and Gillette).

Kids 5 and under should be steered straight to **Kiddyland,** which has rides tailored to their size: The Kiddy Whip, Kiddyland Bumper Cars, the turtle aviators, and the swings are especially popular. For older kids, the park is their oyster. Some of the most thrilling rides are the **Go-Carts** (for 12 and up only), the **Hurricane Coaster,** the **Whip,** the **Ferris Wheel,** and the **Dragon Coaster.**

In addition to the rides, Playland has a **beach,** a **pool,** an **indoor skating rink,** and a **lake** for boating. These are open seasonally.

Admission: Free, but you must buy tickets for rides—$7.50 for a book of 12, $14 for a book of 24, $18 for a book of 36 (rides cost three to five tickets). **Open:** April through October Tuesday to Thursday 10am to 4pm, Friday to Saturday noon to midnight, Sunday noon to 11pm. Skating rink open year-round.

WHERE TO EAT

Playland offers many types of food in **concession stands**—and just the kind of junky food kids go crazy for. There are also attractive picnic areas.

4 Long Island Children's Museum

Approximately 50 minutes from Manhattan

GETTING THERE

BY CAR   Take the Midtown Tunnel to the Long Island Expressway, then exit heading east on the Grand Central Parkway, which becomes the Northern State Parkway. Turn south on the Meadowbrook Parkway, which you follow south to Exit M3 west. At the first light, go right onto Stewart Avenue and continue 1½ miles to the free parking lot on your right, directly across from 550 Stewart Ave.

BY TRAIN   Take the **Long Island Rail Road** (☎ **718/217-5477**) from Penn Station to the Garden City station. One-way adult fares are $4.25 to $6.25, depending on time of travel; children's fares (ages 5 to 11) are 50¢ to $3.25. A cab ride from the station to the museum costs about $5.

EXPLORING THE MUSEUM

The **Long Island Children's Museum,** 550 Stewart Ave., Garden City, N.Y. (☎ **516/222-0207**), occupies a block-shaped white building owned by the Long Island Lighting Co. But don't be put off by the stark entryway: The moment you step into the museum itself, you and your child will be richly rewarded by the staff's abundant creativity. Though the space is small (5,000 square feet), the hands-on exhibits go a long way toward stretching the imaginations of kids 2 to 12.

In the **Communication Station** there are no limits—the entire world is there for a kid via the Internet (parents will be reassured to know there are checks and balances on this system to make sure whatever's accessed is appropriate). Also in this corner is a mock TV station that was a big hit during my visit—children see themselves projected on a giant TV screen as big-time news broadcasters (needless to say, they're instantly captivated). Nearby is a phone exhibit where kids can play with telephones from all different eras. Next to the Communication Station is **Working on the Railroad,** with everything a train-obsessed kid might want: a virtual train for children to drive, train crew clothes to dress up in, an explanation of signal lights, Long Island Rail Road maps, and a ticket punch game, among other things.

Hands On is a fun exhibit about . . . well, hands—kids have their fingerprints taken, look at their hand bones on an X-ray machine, study various animal hands, and look at all kinds of gloves. Children 6 and up enjoy an exhibit called **What If You Couldn't . . . ,** aiming to sensitize kids to certain disabilities. Though it may sound too p.c., in reality kids really get enthralled here: There are wheelchairs and crutches to experiment with, braille to touch, lenses showing what the world looks like to people with diminished sight, a phone that plays only muted conversation, and writing as it might appear to a dyslexic child. And then there's the **bubble room,** where you can make bubbles of all sizes to your heart's content.

The museum also offers special events and workshops on Saturday and Sunday—call ahead for details.

Admission: $4; kids under 2 free. In inclement weather, call ahead for time ticket schedule. **Open:** Tuesday to Friday 10am to 4pm, Saturday to Sunday 10am to 5pm (in summer, opens at noon on Sundays).

WHERE TO EAT

There's no on-site food service or any place to picnic within walking distance (the museum's on a busy road). However, there are a number of **fast-food restaurants** along Stewart Avenue between the museum and the entrance to the Meadowbrook Parkway. Nearby **Roosevelt Field Mall** has some good kid restaurants upstairs; to reach the mall, turn left from the museum parking lot onto Stewart Avenue, then take your first left at the light.

5 Liberty Science Center

Approximately a 20-minute drive or a 5-minute ferry ride from Manhattan

GETTING THERE

BY CAR   Take the Lincoln Tunnel, the Holland Tunnel, or the George Washington Bridge to the New Jersey Turnpike heading south; go to Exit 14B and follow the signs to the Science Center. Parking is $4.

BY FERRY   NY Waterway (☎ **800/533-3779**) operates ferries from the World Financial Center to the Colgate Center in New Jersey; there's a free shuttle bus to the center once you've landed. Ferries depart every 15 minutes weekdays and every half-hour weekends. The ferry costs $2 and takes about 5 minutes.

BY TRAIN   Take the **PATH train** from its various Manhattan stations (along Sixth Avenue at 33rd Street, 23rd Street, 14th Street, or 9th Street; or Christopher Street; or the World Trade Center) to Grove Street station in New Jersey, where a free shuttle bus to the Science Center meets visitors every half hour.

CHECKING OUT THE MUSEUM

The enormous four-story ✪ **Liberty Science Center,** 251 Philip St., Jersey City, N.J. (☎ **201/200-1000**), seems to vibrate with energy the moment you enter. On the main floor you're instantly greeted by the sight of a 700-pound steel expandable **geodesic globe,** continually opening and closing. Just up the escalator are interactive exhibits on **health,** including holograms showing how fatty deposits work on arteries, a fitness center where kids can test their balance and endurance, and a fully equipped ambulance to explore. The second floor's highlight is indubitably the **Touch Tunnel,** a pitch-black 100-foot-long tunnel that takes about 5 minutes to crawl through, with only your sense of touch to guide you. Forget it if you're the least bit claustrophobic—kids 6 and under aren't even allowed.

The top floor's theme is **the environment,** and here you're treated to a number of fascinating displays of live insects, including some giant cockroaches from South America that'll make your skin crawl. But kids of all ages love this floor, which includes exhibits of estuaries with live fish and the **MicroZoo** featuring tarantulas and scorpions from around the world (there's also the "Touch-a-Bug" table). And you can't miss the 20-foot "lighthouse," with a solar telescope inside. On the bottom floor, the focus is **invention.** Here, among other things, you'll find a model of an Indy 500 racecar, a "resonance tube" that shows you through your own voice how fast sound travels, and some fun do-it-yourself laser optics.

If you decide to visit during school hours, be advised that it's fairly crowded with school groups. In general, kids 5 and under might feel overwhelmed by the noise and activity. Since the exhibits are fairly sophisticated, school-age children and their parents would be most apt to enjoy this excursion.

Special exhibits at certain times are worth inquiring about; the day we visited, I learned that an exhibit on bats was opening the next week, which my son would really have loved to have seen. In addition to the exhibits, there's the **Kodak OMNI theater,** the nation's largest domed IMAX theater, with a six-story screen showing 3-D films like *Everest, The Magic of Flight,* and *The Living Sea.* The 3-D laser light shows *Brain Trek* and *The Web of Life* are especial draws.

Admission: Museum only, $6.50 kids 2 to 12, $9.50 adults, $8.50 students/seniors; museum plus IMAX, $9.50 kids 2 to 12, $13.50 adults, $11.50 students/seniors; *Brain Trek* and *The Web of Life* can be viewed without museum admission, $2 per person. **Open:** Daily 9:30am to 5:30pm.

WHERE TO EAT

The **Laser Lights Cafe** on the center's main floor has decent inexpensive food that'll appeal to a range of tastes. A cheese pizza is $1.50, while the most expensive item on the menu the day I was there was the special, a chicken burrito with salad for $4.95.

6 Maritime Aquarium at Norwalk

Approximately 1 hour from Manhattan

GETTING THERE

BY CAR   Take I-95 heading east/north to the South Norwalk exit (Exit 14) off I-95 and follow the signs to the Maritime Center; it's about a 6-minute drive from the highway. Or take the Hutchinson River Parkway north, which becomes the Merritt Parkway in Connecticut. From the Merritt Parkway, take Exit 39A and follow the signs on U.S. 7 to the Maritime Center. There's parking at the center, which costs up to $3.

BY TRAIN   Metro North trains (☎ **800/METRO-INFO** or 212/532-4900) run frequently to South Norwalk; the one-way adult fare is $8 to $10.75 (children travel for half price) and travel time is about 60 minutes. Call for details. From the South Norwalk station, take a short taxi ride or walk—it's only about 3 blocks. When you get off the train, turn left and go down the stairs at the end of the platform; turn right at the bottom of the stairs, walk under the bridge, and go 1½ blocks to the first traffic light, at the intersection of Main and Monroe streets. Turn left onto Main Street and go to the next traffic light, then turn right onto Washington Street. Go under another bridge and continue past shops and restaurants to the next traffic light, at the corner of Washington and Water streets. You'll see the large redbrick Maritime Aquarium on your left.

SEEING THE AQUARIUM

The **Maritime Aquarium at Norwalk,** North Water Street, Norwalk, Conn. (☎ **203/852-0700**), gives families a fascinating hands-on look at the ecology of Long Island Sound. Go up freestanding stairs in the lobby and across a midair bridge to the second-floor entrance, where carpeted walkways lead through a softly lit series of 20 marine environments, progressing from salt marsh to the ocean depths. You'll see a thousand or so marine creatures of more than 125 species; my kids' favorites were the sleek speckled harbor seals that flop around an indoor/outdoor pool in the lobby (seal feedings at 11:45am and 1:45 and 3:45pm are extremely popular), but the bright-eyed otters in the woodland shoreline habitat run a close second. The sand tiger sharks circling and glaring at you through the glass in the enormous ocean tanks are also mesmerizing (12:45pm feeding time), as is the Jellyfish Encounter at the ocean end of the long walkway. Kids who want to get really close to some less creepy sea creatures—sea stars, horseshoe crabs, whelks—can linger at the Touch Tank, or, if they're bold enough, pet a live ray at the Ray Touch Pool.

Beside the series of environments, the two-story **Maritime Hall** has loads of interactive educational displays on fish, but my younger son and my brother-in-law were just as interested in the displays on navigation and the boat shop for building wooden boats. The aquarium also boasts Connecticut's ony IMAX theater, showing a rotation of several megascreen natural-history films. An excellent gift shop lies in wait to cash in on all the parental goodwill created by the center's various delights. It's just as pleasant a place to view marine life as the New York Aquarium in Coney Island (see chapter 4), and if you've got a car it's perhaps easier to get here; it's certainly easier to get here from Manhattan than it is to visit the Mystic Aquarium at the other end of Connecticut.

Admission: Museum only, $6.50 kids 2 to 12, $7 seniors, $7.75 adults; museum plus IMAX, $9.50 kids 2 to 12, $10.50 seniors, $12 adults; IMAX only, $4.75 kids 2 to 12, $5.50 seniors, $6.50 adults. **Open:** Daily 10am to 5pm (to 6pm July to Labor Day); IMAX open for evening shows Friday–Saturday.

WHERE TO EAT

The **Oyster Bar,** at the end of Maritime Hall, offers some fairly good seafood, not all of it fried, at reasonable prices. It's open Saturday and Sunday 11:30am to 3pm, and operates daily July to Labor Day; at other times you can grab a hot dog or other simple fare at the more pedestrian **snack bar** nearby. There's table seating provided.

Appendix:
For Foreign Visitors

New York is the largest city in the United States, and even other Americans can be intimidated by this fast-moving metropolis with its seemingly impenetrable code of arcane rules and regulations (many of them unwritten). With a family tagging along, you don't want to take chances, which is why I've prepared this information to help you navigate New York successfully.

Rule No. 1: Always ask for advice from a passerby, your hotel concierge, a restaurant waiter, a museum staffer, a bus driver—anyone who can clear up any confusion you may have about the best route to take or the proper way to accomplish something. Despite their bustling demeanor, New Yorkers are generally willing and eager to help visitors.

Rule No. 2: Take it easy—don't jump on that bus if you're not sure it's the right one, even though the locals may be dashing madly for the door. It won't be the last bus of the day.

1 Preparing for Your Trip

ENTRY REQUIREMENTS

DOCUMENT REGULATIONS   Canadian nationals need only proof of Canadian residence to visit the United States. Citizens of the United Kingdom and Japan need only a current passport. Citizens of other countries, including Australia and New Zealand, usually need two documents: a valid **passport** with an expiration date at least 6 months later than the scheduled end of their visit to the United States and a **tourist visa** available at no charge from a U.S. embassy or consulate.

To get a tourist or business visa to enter the United States, contact the nearest American embassy or consulate in your country; if there is none, you'll have to apply in person in a country where there is a U.S. embassy or consulate. Present your passport, a passport-size photo of yourself, and a completed application, available through the embassy or consulate. You may be asked to provide information about how you plan to finance your trip or show a letter of invitation from a friend with whom you plan to stay. Those applying for a business visa may be asked to show evidence that they won't receive a salary in the United States. Be sure to check how long your visa permits you to stay; usually it's 6 months. If you want to stay longer, you may file for an extension with the Immigration and Naturalization Service once you're in the country. If permission to stay is granted, a new visa isn't required unless you leave the United States and want to reenter.

MEDICAL REQUIREMENTS   No inoculations are needed to enter the United States unless you're coming from, or have stopped over in, areas known to be suffering from epidemics, particularly cholera or yellow fever.

If you have a disease requiring treatment with medications containing narcotics or with drugs requiring a syringe, carry a valid signed prescription from your physician to allay any suspicions that you're smuggling drugs. Your doctor should provide a generic prescription, since brands you're accustomed to buying in your country may not be available in the United States.

CUSTOMS REQUIREMENTS   Every visitor age 21 or over may bring in, free of duty: 1 liter of wine or hard liquor; 200 cigarettes or 100 cigars (but no cigars from Cuba) or 3 pounds of smoking tobacco; and $100 worth of gifts. These exemptions are offered to travelers who spend at least 72 hours in the United States and who haven't claimed them within the preceding 6 months. It's altogether forbidden to bring foodstuffs (particularly cheese, fruit, cooked meats, canned goods) and plants (vegetables, seeds, tropical plants) into the country. Foreign tourists may bring in or take out up to $10,000 in U.S. or foreign currency with no formalities; larger sums must be declared to Customs on entering or leaving. For more information call **U.S. Customs** at ☎ **800/697-3662.**

INSURANCE   Unlike many other countries, the United States doesn't have a national health-care system. Because the cost of medical care is extremely high, we strongly advise all travelers to secure health coverage before setting out on their trip.

You may want to take out a comprehensive travel policy that covers (for a relatively low premium) sickness or injury costs (medical, surgical, hospital); loss or theft of your baggage; trip-cancellation costs; guarantee of bail in case you're arrested; and costs of accident, repatriation, or death. Such packages (for example, Europ Assistance in Europe) are sold by automobile clubs at attractive rates, as well as by insurance companies and travel agencies and at some airports.

MONEY   The U.S. monetary system has a decimal base: One American **dollar** ($1) = 100 **cents** (100¢). **Bills** commonly come in $1 (a "single" or "buck"), $5, $10, $20, $50, and $100 denominations (the last two aren't welcome when paying for small purchases and are usually not accepted in taxis or at subway token booths). There are six **coin** denominations: 1¢ (one cent or a "penny"); 5¢ (five cents or a "nickel"); 10¢ (ten cents or a "dime"); 25¢ (twenty-five cents or a "quarter"); 50¢ (fifty cents or a "half dollar"); and the $1 pieces (both the older, large silver dollar and the newer, small Susan B. Anthony coin).

Credit cards are the most convenient and widely used method of payment at hotels, motels, restaurants, and retail stores. Commonly accepted cards in descending order are Visa (BarclayCard in Britain), MasterCard (EuroCard in Europe, Access in Britain, Diamond in Japan), American Express, Discover, Diners Club, enRoute, JCB, and Carte Blanche.

Credit cards are necessary to secure a deposit when renting a car and are useful for cash advances and withdrawals. Check with your bank before leaving home to confirm that your card is accepted by ATMs found throughout New York City and the country. Also find out if your bank charges a service fee on cash advances or money withdrawals and if there are limits on the frequency and amount of money you can access. If you plan to travel for several weeks or more in the United States, you may want to deposit enough money into your credit-card account to cover anticipated expenses and avoid finance charges in your absence.

Traveler's checks in U.S. dollars are accepted at most hotels, motels, restaurants, and large stores. Sometimes picture ID is required. American Express, Thomas Cook, and Barclay's Bank traveler's checks are readily accepted in the United States.

You can **wire money** or have it wired to you very quickly using Western Union at ☎ **800/325-6000** or American Express's MoneyGram at ☎ **800/926-9400.**

SAFETY   Although tourist areas are generally safe, crime is a national problem, and U.S. urban areas tend to be less safe than those in Europe or Japan. The crime rate in New York has been falling in recent years (it's by no means America's most dangerous city, despite a gritty image from movies and TV), but you should always stay alert, use common sense, and trust your instincts. If you feel you're in an unsafe area or situation, you probably are and should leave as quickly as possible. Keep valuables at home, don't wear flashy jewelry or clothing, be discreet when reading maps, and always keep your hotel room door locked. For specific information about personal safety in Manhattan, see "Safety" under "Fast Facts: New York City" in chapter 3.

DRIVING   Safety while driving is particularly important. Question your rental agency about personal safety and ask for a brochure of traveler safety tips when you pick up your car. Obtain from the agency written directions or a map with the route marked in red showing how to get to your destination. And, if possible, arrive and depart during daylight hours.

Always keep your car doors locked, whether the vehicle is attended or unattended. Never leave any packages or valuables in sight because thieves will break car windows. If someone attempts to rob you or steal your car, don't resist. Report the incident to the police department immediately.

Having said all this, I'll stress one more time: Don't drive in New York if you don't have to. Between the confusing one-way street patterns, the crush of traffic, and the expensive parking, you'd be much better off using public transportation—buses, subways, or taxis—which will get you anywhere you want to go, swiftly and safely.

Note that in all U.S. states, children under 40 pounds and 4 years of age are required to ride in secure car seats. Seat belts are also generally required to be used by all passengers.

2   Getting to the United States

Travelers from overseas can take advantage of the **APEX (advance-purchase excursion) fares** offered by all major U.S. and European carriers. Aside from these, attractive values are offered by **Virgin Atlantic** (☎ **01293/747-747** in the U.K.; www.flyvirgin.com) from London's Heathrow to New York.

In addition to the domestic airlines listed in chapter 2, many international carriers serve John F. Kennedy International Airport. **British Airways** (☎ **0345/222-111** in the U.K.; www.british-airways.com) has daily service from London as well as direct flights from Manchester and Glasgow. Canadian readers might book flights on **Air Canada** (☎ **800/776-3000;** www.aircanada.com), which offers direct service from Toronto, Montréal, Calgary, and other cities, or on **Canadian Airlines** (☎ **800/426-7000;** www.cdair.ca).

Continental (☎ **01293/776-464** in the U.K.; www.flycontinental.com) flies to Newark from London (Gatwick), Manchester, Madrid, Paris, and Frankfurt.

Aer Lingus flies from Dublin and Shannon to New York (☎ **01/844-4747** in Dublin, 061/415-556 in Shannon). **TWA** (www2.twa.com) has nonstop service to New York from Barcelona, Madrid, Milan, Paris, and Rome. **United** (☎ **0181/ 990-9900** in the U.K.; www.ual.com) serves those cities and London, Amsterdam, Brussels, and Zurich. **American** (☎ **0181/572-5555** in the U.K.; www. americanair.com) flies nonstop from London, Manchester, Paris, Brussels, and Zurich. **Delta** (☎ **0800/414-764** in the U.K.; www.delta-air.com flies to New York from most major European cities. **Qantas** (☎ **13-12-11** in the Australia; www.qantas.com.au) and **Air New Zealand** (☎ **13-2476** in the New Zealand; www.airnewzealand.com.nz) fly to the West Coast and will book you straight through to New York City on a partner airline.

If you're arriving by air, no matter what the port of entry, cultivate patience and resignation before setting foot on U.S. soil. Getting through Immigration control may take as long as 2 hours on some days, especially summer weekends, so read this guidebook while you wait and continue planning your stay in New York City. When you book your flight, allow 2 to 3 hours to clear Customs and Immigration between international and domestic flights.

In contrast, for the Canadian traveler arriving by car or by rail from Canada, the border-crossing formalities have been streamlined to the vanishing point. And for the traveler by air from Canada, Bermuda, and some places in the Caribbean, you can sometimes go through Customs and Immigration at the point of departure, which is much quicker.

3 Getting Around the United States

The United States is a huge country and, unlike in Europe, travel by rail, bus, or even car isn't the most convenient way to undertake a whirlwind cross-country tour. The fastest way to cover large distances is by airplane.

In conjunction with their transatlantic or transpacific flights, some large U.S. airlines offer special discount tickets for any of their U.S. destinations (American Airlines' **Visit USA** program and Delta's **Discover America** program, for example). These cut-rate tickets or coupons are not available in the United States and must be purchased before you leave home. This system is the best, easiest, and fastest way to see the United States at low cost. You should obtain information well in advance from your travel agent or the office of the airline concerned, because the conditions attached to these discount tickets can change without advance notice.

International visitors can buy a **USA Railpass,** good for 15 or 30 days of unlimited travel on Amtrak. The pass is available through many foreign travel agents. Prices in 1998 for a 15-day pass were $260 off-peak (September 1 to May 31) and $375 peak; a 30-day pass cost $350 off-peak and $480 peak. Children 2 to 15 travel for half fare, and children under 2 ride free. With a foreign passport, you can also buy passes at some Amtrak offices in the United States, including locations in New York, Boston, Chicago, Los Angeles, Miami, San Francisco, and Washington, D.C. Reservations are generally required and should be made for each part of your trip as early as possible by calling ☎ **800/USA-RAIL.**

Train travel is relatively quick, inexpensive, and convenient along the Northeast corridor between Boston, New York, and Washington, D.C. You zip from city center to city center, without having to travel to and from far-flung airports. However, keep in mind the limitations of long-distance rail travel in the United States. For example, it can take up to 20 hours between New York and Chicago. In addition, service is rarely up to European standards: Delays are common, routes limited and often infrequently served, and fares rarely significantly lower than discount air travel. Thus, approach a long cross-country train trip in America with these caveats in mind.

Though bus travel between cities has traditionally been the most economical form of public transit, at this writing bus passes are priced slightly higher than similar train passes. Greyhound, the sole nationwide bus operator, offers an **Ameripass** for unlimited travel for 7 days for $199, 15 days for $299, 30 days for $409, and 60 days for $599; children 2 to 11 travel for half price, and children under 2 travel free if sitting in an adult's lap. Bus travel can be both slow (New York to Chicago can take 19 hours) and uncomfortable, so this option isn't for everyone. In addition, bus stations are often located in undesirable neighborhoods. For more information, contact Greyhound Bus Lines at ☎ **800/231-2222.**

FAST FACTS: For the Foreign Traveler

Automobile Organizations   Auto clubs are an excellent source of travel information, including maps, suggested itineraries, guidebooks, accident and bail-bond insurance, and emergency road service. The American Automobile Association (AAA), or Triple A, is the United States' largest auto club, with offices nationwide. Some foreign auto clubs have reciprocal agreements with the AAA; inquire with your auto club before leaving home if you can benefit from the AAA's services. Otherwise, some car-rental agencies provide maps, itineraries, and other services, so inquire when reserving.

Automobile Rental   To rent a car in the United States you'll need a valid driver's license, a passport, and a major credit or charge card. The minimum age is usually 25, but some companies will rent to younger people and add a surcharge. It's a good idea to buy the maximum insurance coverage unless you're positive your own auto insurance is sufficient. Car-rental companies often charge extra for one-way dropoffs, refueling, child seats (required for kids 4 and under), additional drivers, and returning the car early. All major car-rental agencies have branches in Manhattan; check the Yellow Pages directory under "Automobile Renting" for the location nearest your hotel. Rates can vary, so it pays to call around. Stick to the major companies (Avis, Alamo, Budget, Dollar, Enterprise, Hertz, National) because what you might save with smaller companies might not be worth the headache if you have mechanical troubles on the road.

Business Hours   In general, **retail stores** are open Monday to Saturday 10am to 6pm and Sunday noon to 5pm (see chapter 6 for precise information). **Banks** tend to be open Monday to Friday 9am to 3pm (some stay open later on Friday) and sometimes Saturday morning. **Post offices** are open Monday to Friday 10am to 5 or 6pm and Saturday 9am to noon; New York's Main Post Office, on Eighth Avenue between 31st and 33rd streets, is open 24 hours. **Business offices** are generally open Monday to Friday 9am to 5pm.

Currency   See "Money" under "Preparing for Your Trip," earlier in this appendix.

Currency Exchange   Foreign exchange bureaus, common in Europe, are rare in America. You'll find some in major international airports and major tourist cities, but not in smaller cities and towns. So it's a good idea to bring traveler's checks—*denominated in U.S. dollars only* (traveler's checks denominated in foreign currencies will probably not be accepted)—and rely on credit or charge cards for paying hotel, restaurant, and other large bills.

In New York City the best exchange rates are usually available at the expanding **Avis Currency Exchange,** formerly Harold Reuter & Co. (☎ **212/661-0826**). You can check the daily exchange rates on the Internet at **www.avisnet.com**. There are five locations: Room 332 East in 200 Park Ave., at 45th Street; the sixth floor in Stern's department store, 899 Sixth Ave., at 33rd Street; the main concourse of Grand Central Terminal, 42nd Street between Vanderbilt and Lexington avenues; the lobby of One World Trade Center; and Times Square at 1451 Broadway, between 41st and 42nd streets.

Other reliable, though often slightly more costly, choices: **American Express** (☎ **800/AXP-TRIP**), which has many offices throughout the city, including JFK Airport; 1185 Sixth Ave., at 47th Street; 374 Park Ave., at 53rd Street; Seaport Plaza at 199 Water St.; Macy's department store at Herald Square, 34th Street and Broadway; and Bloomingdale's department store, 1000 Third Ave., at 59th Street; and **Thomas Cook Currency Services** (☎ **212/753-0132**), which has locations at JFK Airport; 1590 Broadway, at 48th Street; and 511 Madison Ave., at 53rd Street.

Drinking Laws　The laws governing alcoholic beverages are different in every state, but in general the minimum age is 21. In New York, the minimum legal age to purchase and consume alcoholic beverages is 21. Liquor stores, the only outlets for wine as well as hard liquor in New York, are closed on Sundays, holidays, and election days while the polls are open. Beer can be purchased in groceries and delis Monday to Saturday until 4am and Sunday from noon to 4am.

Electricity　Electricity in the United States is 110 volts, 60 cycles A.C., versus the 220 volts, 50 cycles A.C. used in most of Europe. If you're bringing electrical appliances, like a hair dryer or shaver, that aren't dual voltage, you'll need a voltage transformer and a plug adapter with two flat parallel pins.

Embassies/Consulates　All embassies are in Washington, D.C. Some countries have consulates located in major U.S. cities, and most have a mission to the United Nations in New York City.

Australia: Embassy, 1601 Massachusetts Ave. NW, Washington, DC 20036 (☎ **202/797-3000**); consulate general, 630 Fifth Ave., New York, NY 10111 (☎ **212/408-8400**).

Canada: Embassy, 501 Pennsylvania Ave. NW, Washington, DC 20001 (☎ **202/682-1740**); consulate general, 1251 Ave. of the Americas, New York, NY 10020 (☎ **212/596-1600**).

Ireland: Embassy, 2234 Massachusetts Ave. NW, Washington, DC 20008 (☎ **202/462-3939**); consulate general, 345 Park Ave., New York, NY 10154-0037 (☎ **212/319-2555**).

New Zealand: Embassy, 37 Observatory Circle NW, Washington, DC 20008 (☎ **202/328-4000**). There's no New Zealand consulate in New York.

United Kingdom: Embassy, 3100 Massachusetts Ave. NW, Washington, DC 20008 (☎ **202/462-1340**); consulate general, 845 Third Ave., New York, NY 10022 (☎ **212/745-0200**).

Emergencies　Dial ☎ **911** for **fire, police,** and **ambulance** in an emergency. If you have a medical emergency that doesn't require an ambulance, hospitals have 24-hour emergency rooms with separate entrances. For a list of hospitals, see "Fast Facts: New York City" in chapter 3. The Poison Control Center is ☎ **212/764-7667** or 212/340-4494. The Crime Victims Hotline is ☎ **212/577-7777**

and the Sex Crimes Report Line is ☎ **212/267-7273.** For a list of 24-hour pharmacies see "Fast Facts: New York City" in chapter 3.

Gasoline (Petrol)   One U.S. gallon equals 3.79 liters and .83 British imperial gallon. Most rental cars run on unleaded gas that costs about $1.30 a gallon if you fill your own tank (self-serve) and about 10¢ more per gallon if the station attendant does it (full service).

Holidays   On the following national legal holidays, banks, government offices, post offices, and many stores, restaurants, and museums are closed: January 1 (New Year's Day), third Monday in January (Martin Luther King, Jr., Day), third Monday in February (Presidents' Day), last Monday in May (Memorial Day), July 4 (Independence Day), first Monday in September (Labor Day), second Monday in October (Columbus Day), November 11 (Veterans Day/Armistice Day), last Thursday in November (Thanksgiving Day), and December 25 (Christmas Day). The Tuesday following the first Monday in November is Election Day, and is a holiday in presidential election years (next in 2000).

Legal Aid   If you're stopped for a minor infraction (like speeding), never attempt to pay the fine directly to a police officer. You may be arrested on the much more serious charge of attempted bribery. Pay fines by mail or directly to the clerk of the court. If you're arrested, it's best to stay calm and say nothing to the police before consulting a lawyer. Under U.S. law, an arrested person has the right to have an attorney present during any questioning and is allowed one phone call to a party of his or her choice. Call your embassy or consulate.

Mail   The Main Post Office in New York City, Eighth Avenue between 31st and 33rd streets, is open 24 hours daily. You may receive mail in care of general delivery at the main post office of the city or region you're visiting with prior arrangement. To receive general-delivery mail in New York City, call ☎ **212/330-3099.** The addressee must pick it up in person and show proof of identity.

Mailboxes on street corners are blue with a red-and-white logo and carry the inscription U.S. MAIL. Within the United States, it costs 32¢ to send a first-class letter weighing up to 1 ounce and 20¢ for a standard 4.25- by 6-inch postcard. To Canada, it costs 46¢ for a letter up to one-half ounce and 40¢ for a postcard. Air mail to Europe, Australia, New Zealand, and elsewhere costs 60¢ for a letter up to one-half ounce, 50¢ for an aerogram stationery letter (which can be purchased at post offices), and 50¢ for a postcard.

Newspapers/Magazines   The city's best-known newspaper is the *New York Times,* a morning daily that's read and respected all across the country. It has become almost more a national paper than a local one, with extensive coverage of international events (much appreciated by the city's many resident foreigners) as well as thoughtful reporting on local news and culture. The Friday "Weekend" section and Sunday's "Arts & Leisure" section are your best bets for comprehensive listings of special events, gallery and museum exhibitions, theater, film, and music concerts. Look for the "Family Fare" column in Friday's "Weekend" section for up-to-date highlights of kid-oriented activities; the "Arts & Leisure" section has a run-down of current films suitable for children. The highly regarded *New York Times Book Review,* also included in the massive Sunday paper, has a special section on children's books as well.

New York's two other major dailies, the *Daily News* (a morning paper) and the *New York Post* (an evening paper) are tabloid-sized and more oriented to metro happenings—though in New York, national political scandals are always considered fair game. Their eye-catching, sensational headlines usually generate a buzz on the streets, targeting a middle- and working-class audience, with reporting that can be very aggressive.

New York being the country's financial capital, it makes sense that the *Wall Street Journal,* one of the world's major business dailies, is also published here; New York is also more or less the capital of U.S. magazine publishing, and three national weekly newsmagazines—*Newsweek, Time,* and *U.S. News & World Report*—are headquartered here, though they have bureaus all over the country. Among the many other national magazines emanating from Manhattan, *The New Yorker* in many ways sets itself up as the country's premier cultural magazine—despite its title and excellent entertainment listings, it's less oriented to New York life and local events than in past years. *New York* magazine, another cultural weekly with exhaustive entertainment listings, focuses more on life in the city, yet with a tiresomely scandalmongering slant. For a more alternative twist on the arts, look for the weekly newspapers the *Village Voice* and the *New York Press* (both free in Manhattan).

Many newsstands in New York City carry a selection of international newspapers and magazines. For nearly all major newspapers and magazines from around the world, head to **Hotalings News Agency,** 142 W. 42nd St., between Broadway and Sixth Avenue (☎ **212/840-1868**).

Taxes   In the United States there's no value-added tax (VAT) or other indirect tax at a national level. There's a $10 Customs tax payable on entry to the United States and a $6 departure tax, usually added on to the price of an international airline ticket. Sales tax is often levied on goods and services by state and local governments and varies from state to state and city to city. It's usually not included in the price tags on merchandise but is added at the cash register. These taxes are not refundable. In New York City, the sales tax is 8.25%. The hotel tax is 13.25% plus $2 per room per night. The parking garage tax, added to already high basic fees, is 18.25%.

Telephone/Fax   In New York City there are generally coin-operated pay phones on at least one corner at every other intersection—if you don't see one, walk a block uptown or downtown. Don't be surprised, though, if the phone doesn't work.

Pay phones can also be found in the lobbies of some public buildings and in restaurants, stores, and gas stations. The local telephone company, NYNEX, charges 25¢ for the first 5 minutes, payable in nickels, dimes, or quarters. Pick up the receiver, deposit the coins, and when you hear the dial tone, dial the number. There are four area codes in the city. Manhattan has two: 212 and the new 646 instituted in the fall of 1998; and Brooklyn, the Bronx, Queens, and Staten Island are all 718. For a Manhattan-to-Manhattan call, don't dial the 212 area code, just the seven-digit number. When you're calling the Bronx, Queens, Brooklyn, or Staten Island from Manhattan, dial 1, then the 718 area code, then the seven-digit number. Calls from 212 to 718, or vice versa, still cost only 25¢. The fourth area code, 917, covering all of New York City, is for voice mail, beepers, and cellular phones.

For long-distance calls: To make a direct domestic long-distance call, dial 1, the area code, and the seven-digit local number. To make an operator-assisted long-distance call (collect, credit card, and so on), dial 0, the area code, and the local number; an operator will come on the line and assist you. Phone numbers with an 800 or 888 area code are toll-free calls; those with a 900 area code are billed at an additional rate. In the United States, there are a number of long-distance carriers: AT&T, MCI, and Sprint are the largest and most reliable, and each individual telephone is affiliated with one specific carrier or another. It's not generally a good idea to make long-distance calls from pay phones, which will entail feeding lots of coins into the slot. Credit-card pay phones, which are most often found in hotel lobbies and airport terminals, allow you to make a long-distance call if you have a credit card with one of the long-distance carriers. Be aware that many hotels tack on big surcharges for making long-distance calls directly from your room; ask the hotel operator what these charges are before you make your call. You may be able to avoid these charges by using your own telephone credit card.

For direct international calls: Dial 011, the country code, the city code, and the phone number. To make an operator-assisted call, dial 01, the country code, the city code, and the phone number; an operator will come on the line after the call is dialed. Some country and city codes are as follows: **Australia,** 61 (Melbourne, 3; Sydney, 2); **Ireland,** 353 (Dublin, 1); **New Zealand,** 64 (Auckland, 9; Wellington, 4); **United Kingdom,** 44 (Belfast, 232; Birmingham, 21; Glasgow, 41; London, 171 or 181). **Canada** is included in the U.S. country code. You can request to be connected to an overseas operator by dialing 0 (zero).

Most hotels have **fax** machines available for their guests, usually for a charge in addition to the cost of the call; some hotels will even charge you for receiving a fax. Some stationery stores and copying centers also have public fax machines. Rates can run as high as $5 for the first page.

Telephone Directories The local phone company provides two kinds of phone directories. The most useful one for travelers is the **Yellow Pages,** which lists local businesses and services by industry type. Look here for car-rental agencies, drugstores, places of worship, and all kinds of other information. At the front of the book, the Inside Interest pages are a guide to Manhattan with museums and sites, transportation information, seating plans of some sports stadiums and performance centers, and much more. An address locator follows this section.

The general directory, the **White Pages,** lists personal residences and businesses separately in alphabetical order by name. The first few pages are devoted to community-service numbers and include a guide to long-distance and international calling and a list of area and country codes. At the center of the White Pages, edged in blue, is a guide to local, state, and federal government offices.

For **local directory assistance** (area codes 212, 646, and 718), dial ☎ **411.** This is a free call from NYNEX public pay phones and can also be used to ask for addresses. For numbers in all other area codes, check the carrier, then dial 1, the appropriate area code, and **555-1212.**

Time The United States covers such a large area that it falls across six time zones, an important thing to keep in mind when calling and traveling long distances. From east to west, standard time zones are eastern (EST), central (CST), mountain (MST), Pacific (PST), Alaska (AST), and Hawaii (HST). When it's noon in New York City, it's 11am in Chicago, 10am in Denver, 9am in Los Angeles, 8am in Anchorage, and 7am in Honolulu.

In most of the United States (except Arizona, Hawaii, and part of Indiana) daylight saving time is in effect from the first Sunday in April to the last Saturday in October. In other words, clocks are set ahead 1 hour in spring and turned back 1 hour in fall (mnemonic device: spring ahead, fall back).

For the correct local time in New York City, dial ☎ **212/976-1616.**

Tipping Tips are a very important part of certain people's salaries, so it's necessary to be aware of the appropriate gratuities. Unlike in most of Europe, tips aren't automatically added to restaurant and hotel bills. A tip to the waiter or waitress of 15% to 20% of the total check is customary (in New York City just double the 8.25% tax to figure the appropriate tip).

Other tipping guidelines: 10% to 15% of the tab to bartenders, $1 to $2 per bag to bellhops, 15% to 20% of the fare to taxi drivers, $1 per day to hotel maids, $1 per item to checkroom attendants, $1 to valet parking attendants, and 15% to 20% to hairdressers. It's not the practice to tip theater ushers, gas station attendants, or cafeteria and fast-food restaurant employees.

Traveler's Assistance Travelers Aid is an organization that helps distressed travelers with all kinds of problems, including accident, sickness, and lost or stolen luggage. There are offices throughout the United States. The New York City office is on the second floor at 1451 Broadway, at 41st Street (☎ **212/944-0013**); there are also offices at JFK Airport (☎ **718/656-4870**) in the international arrivals building and at Newark Airport (☎ **201/623-5052**).

Weather New York's weather is generally temperate, although July and August can be sticky and hot, and January and February piercingly cold. Sheltered by skyscrapers, New Yorkers generally don't get hit with the cold as much as the surrounding suburbs do, but there's little escape from the heat except to stay inside air-conditioned buildings or to hang out in the parks. Daily weather forecasts are printed on the front page of the *New York Times;* you can also call ☎ **212/976-1212**, or, if you have access to cable TV, turn on the Weather Channel for detailed information, not just for New York but for localities around the country and around the world.

Index

See also separate Accommodations and Restaurant indexes, below.

Page numbers in italics refer to maps.

ACCOMMODATIONS

RESTAURANTS

FROMMER'S® COMPLETE TRAVEL GUIDES

Alaska
Amsterdam
Arizona
Atlanta
Australia
Austria
Bahamas
Barcelona, Madrid & Seville
Belgium, Holland &
  Luxembourg
Bermuda
Boston
Budapest & the Best of
  Hungary
California
Canada
Cancún, Cozumel &
  the Yucatán
Cape Cod, Nantucket &
  Martha's Vineyard
Caribbean
Caribbean Cruises & Ports
  of Call
Caribbean Ports of Call
Carolinas & Georgia
Chicago
China
Colorado
Costa Rica
Denver, Boulder &
  Colorado Springs
England
Europe
Florida
France

Germany
Greece
Greek Islands
Hawaii
Hong Kong
Honolulu, Waikiki & Oahu
Ireland
Israel
Italy
Jamaica & Barbados
Japan
Las Vegas
London
Los Angeles
Maryland & Delaware
Maui
Mexico
Miami & the Keys
Montana & Wyoming
Montréal & Québec City
Munich & the Bavarian Alps
Nashville & Memphis
Nepal
New England
New Mexico
New Orleans
New York City
New Zealand
Nova Scotia, New Brunswick
  & Prince Edward Island
Oregon
Paris
Philadelphia & the
  Amish Country
Portugal

Prague & the Best of the
  Czech Republic
Provence & the Riviera
Puerto Rico
Rome
San Antonio & Austin
San Diego
San Francisco
Santa Fe, Taos &
  Albuquerque
Scandinavia
Scotland
Seattle & Portland
Singapore & Malaysia
South Pacific
Spain
Switzerland
Thailand
Tokyo
Toronto
Tuscany & Umbria
USA
Utah
Vancouver & Victoria
Vermont, New Hampshire
  & Maine
Vienna & the Danube Valley
Virgin Islands
Virginia
Walt Disney World &
  Orlando
Washington, D.C.
Washington State

FROMMER'S® DOLLAR-A-DAY GUIDES

Australia from $50 a Day
California from $60 a Day
Caribbean from $60 a Day
England from $60 a Day
Europe from $50 a Day
Florida from $60 a Day

Greece from $50 a Day
Hawaii from $60 a Day
Ireland from $50 a Day
Israel from $45 a Day
Italy from $50 a Day
London from $75 a Day

New York from $75 a Day
New Zealand from $50 a Day
Paris from $70 a Day
San Francisco from $60 a Day
Washington, D.C.,
  from $60 a Day

FROMMER'S® PORTABLE GUIDES

Acapulco, Ixtapa &
  Zihuatanejo
Alaska Cruises & Ports of Call
Bahamas
California Wine Country
Charleston & Savannah
Chicago

Dublin
Las Vegas
London
Maine Coast
New Orleans
New York City
Paris

Puerto Vallarta, Manzanillo
  & Guadalajara
San Francisco
Sydney
Tampa & St. Petersburg
Venice
Washington, D.C.

Frommer's® National Park Guides

Family Vacations in the
   National Parks
Grand Canyon

National Parks of the
   American West
Yellowstone & Grand Teton

Yosemite & Sequoia/
   Kings Canyon
Zion & Bryce Canyon

Frommer's® Memorable Walks

Chicago
London

New York
Paris

San Francisco
Washington D.C.

Frommer's® Irreverent Guides

Amsterdam
Boston
Chicago

London
Manhattan

New Orleans
Paris

San Francisco
Walt Disney World
Washington, D.C.

Frommer's® Driving Tours

America
Britain
California

Florida
France
Germany

Ireland
Italy
New England

Scotland
Spain
Western Europe

The Complete Idiot's Travel Guides

Boston
Cruise Vacations
Planning Your Trip to Europe
Hawaii

Las Vegas
London
Mexico's Beach Resorts
New Orleans

New York City
San Francisco
Walt Disney World
Washington D.C.

The Unofficial Guides®

Branson, Missouri
California with Kids
Chicago
Cruises
Disney Companion

Florida with Kids
The Great Smoky &
   Blue Ridge
   Mountains

Las Vegas
Miami & the Keys
Mini-Mickey
New Orleans

New York City
San Francisco
Skiing in the West
Walt Disney World
Washington, D.C.

Special-Interest Titles

Frommer's Britain's Best Bike Rides
The Civil War Trust's Official Guide
   to the Civil War Discovery Trail
Frommer's Caribbean Hideaways
Frommer's Gay & Lesbian Europe
Israel Past & Present
Monks' Guide to California
Monks' Guide to New York City
New York City with Kids
New York Times Weekends
Outside Magazine's Adventure Guide
   to New England
Outside Magazine's Adventure Guide
   to Northern California

Outside Magazine's Adventure Guide
   to Southern California & Baja
Outside Magazine's Adventure Guide
   to the Pacific Northwest
Outside Magazine's Guide
   to Family Vacations
Places Rated Almanac
Retirement Places Rated
Washington, D.C., with Kids
Wonderful Weekends from Boston
Wonderful Weekends from New York City
Wonderful Weekends from San Francisco
Wonderful Weekends from Los Angeles

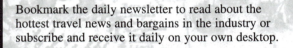